# THE
# BALLET
# GOER'S
# GUIDE

# THE BALLET
# GOER'S GUIDE

*Mary Clarke & Clement Crisp*

Alfred A. Knopf · New York · 1981

*Dedication*  To the artists of the Royal Danish Ballet, to Henning Kronstam and
Kirsten Ralov, in gratitude for the Bournonville Centenary Festival in
November 1979—and with especial thanks to Niels Kehlet.

*The Ballet Goer's Guide* was conceived, edited and designed by
Dorling Kindersley Limited, 9 Henrietta Street, London WC2

THIS IS A BORZOI BOOK
PUBLISHED BY ALFRED A. KNOPF, INC.

Library of Congress Cataloging in Publication Data
Clarke, Mary, 1923–
  The ballet goer's guide.

  Includes index.
  1. Ballet—Addresses, essays, lectures.
I. Crisp, Clement.   II. Title.
GV1787.C563   1981        792.8′4        81-47496
ISBN 0-394-51307-X                       AACR2

Manufactured in the United States of America
First American Edition

# Contents

# Introduction

Any guidebook must inevitably omit more than it includes. Our brief has been to provide an introduction to "ballet," the form of classical academic dance which has evolved in the Western theatre. We have had to ignore those many other forms of dancing—contemporary, social, ethnic—which are quite as important an expression of human movement; we have also had to dispense with the work of many choreographers and with many ballets which are widely admired but which have a specifically national audience. In selecting ballets for description we have chosen those that we hope are representative of the international repertory today. We have therefore provided the basic classical nineteenth-century repertory and the chief surviving relics of the Diaghilev era; thereafter we have been guided by a desire to do justice to the most important and significant creators of our time as represented by the major companies of our time.

In dealing with the classical repertory and with very popular scores—such as Prokofiev's *Romeo and Juliet*—we have listed and given details of alternative stagings or have indicated slight variants in production as presented by different troupes. The dreadful popularity of ballet has brought a mushrooming of companies and of new versions of established works. Thirty years ago *Swan Lake* was *Le Lac des Cygnes*, with a text which no one presumed to alter. Today there seem as many *Swan Lakes* as there are ballet companies. If in this case, as in many others, we have cited only the most radical recensions, it is because space would not permit a full listing of every least change from the accepted Petipa/Ivanov text. Furthermore, changes in production occur far too frequently to permit us to make any definitive listing. In choosing photographs we have sought to provide illustrations of original casts or of especially noteworthy interpretations which have brought new lustre and continuing life to the ballets.

We must express our gratitude to Amy Carroll for her untiring help and efficiency as our London editor, and to Robert Gottlieb in New York, who knows why and how.

# BACKGROUND TO THE BALLET

## History of the Ballet

Pre–
Eighteenth-
Century
Dance

When we consider the extreme richness and diversity of theatrical dancing today we must remember that ballet, which is the matter of this book, represents the development of over five centuries of ways of using dance as an art form. It is not the province of this book to discuss the great variety of dance as an expression of the human spirit from primeval times; rather, we are concerned with the ways in which society adapted dancing, and adopted it as a form of display which eventually led to its emergence as a theatrical entertainment.

It is possible to see the germs of what we accept as ballet today in the court entertainments of the Renaissance. In the activities of those dancing masters who worked in the courts of the Italian city-states we find dance considered as an important aspect of "polite" and aristocratic behaviour.

Early dance manuals of the fifteenth century show a concern with the technique and the presentation of social dancing; the elaborate and extravagant displays that were to be so important a part of princely entertaining and propaganda showed the emergence of an essentially theatrical form that combined declamation, song, dance, and beautiful costuming. This was also the period when the first achievements in devising theatrical spectacle with machines, fireworks, and processional festivities were recorded. All these celebrations were concerned in some way with the persona of the prince. To celebrate a dynastic marriage, a birth, some important alliance, the whole apparatus of display was employed.

Court
Spectacles

There emerged from this a tradition which was to lead to the amazing spectacles staged by such families as the Medici in Florence, and which was then to become essentially linked with the French court. By the middle of the sixteenth century Italian dancing masters were working in France, attracted in part by the presence of Catherine de'Medici as Queen of France, and it is at this time we note the emergence of the *ballet de cour*.

The *ballet de cour* was an art form which served both to entertain and to instruct on political terms the society in which it was performed. *Le Ballet des Polonais* of 1573 is a typical example: it was devised to celebrate the nomination of Henri d'Anjou as King of Poland. When the Polish ambassadors came to the court of the Valois they were entertained to this spectacle: in a hall in the Palace of the Louvre ladies of the Dowager Queen Catherine's retinue appeared placed on a huge silver rock. Repre-

*Costume design by Daniel Rabel for Music in* Le Ballet des Ridicules *of 1625, a role danced by King Louis XIII.*

*In* Le Grand Carrousel, *Philippe, Duc d'Orléans, known as "Monsieur," led one of the five quadrilles of horsemen, the Persian entrée, wearing a typically extravagant costume designed by Henri Gissey.*

senting the provinces of France, they declaimed verses, then descended and trod through the carefully devised patternings set for them by the Italian-born dancing master and violinist Baldassarino de Belgiojoso (known in France as Balthasar de Beaujoyeux).

Eight years later, in 1581, the grandest of these court ballets took place in the Louvre as part of a series of celebrations given over a period of two weeks in September to mark the marriage of the Duc de Joyeuse, a favourite of King Henri III, to the Queen's half-sister, Marie de Lorraine. This was *Le Ballet Comique de la Reine Louise*. (It was preceded by an evening devoted to equestrian display, and an evening of masquerades, and it was followed by other elaborate occasions which stressed the importance attributed to a politically and religiously significant marriage at a time when France was stricken with unease.)

The *Ballet Comique* was considered so important that a handsome book explaining the libretto was published to elucidate the long and complex action and also give a wider awareness of its splendour. This superbly illustrated account indicates the detail and beauty of the five-hour performance.

The *Ballet Comique* was exceptional in that it offered a continuous dramatic narrative—the word *comique* indicating not comedy but a dramatic action. It was concerned with Ulysses' escape from the enchantress Circe, implying the eventual defeat of evil forces and the transfer of political power into the hands of the monarch. With the accession of Henri IV as King of France in 1589, the type of court ballet changed, becoming simpler and less extravagant. Nevertheless the participation of members of the court in danced entertainments continued and was to be an important aspect of court life, culminating in the great days of Louis XIV.

As a youth, Louis appeared in court ballets, always assuming a central role and acquiring his title of Le Roi Soleil from his performance as the Sun in *Le Ballet Royal de la Nuit* of 1653. It was typical of Louis' ambitions that the early years of his majority should be marked by a culminating burst of splendour in such court festivities at Versailles as the three-day *Les Plaisirs de l'Ile Enchantée* in 1664, which involved ballets, plays, firework displays, mock combats, and banquets, and called upon the services of Molière to provide a text for *La Princesse d'Elide*, a comedy ballet, and of the Italian designer Carlo Vigarani.

In 1662 the birth of the dauphin was celebrated by a horse ballet, *Le Grand Carrousel*, for these were a favourite entertainment throughout Europe. Louis XIV's brother, the Duc d'Orléans, led one of the quadrilles of horsemen.

## Académie Royale de Danse

It was symptomatic of Louis XIV's attitude towards the arts that he should have sought to organise and rationalise the teaching and presentation of music and dance through the foundation of academies. It is ironic that the Académie Royale de Danse, which was founded in 1661, with the aim of "re-establishing the art of dance in its perfection," should have proved ineffectual in the larger development of theatrical dancing. It was the Académie Royale de Musique, founded (as the Académie d'Opéra) in 1669, which was to be the seed-bed from which the most significant professional dancing was to emerge.

The Académie Royale de Danse became chiefly concerned with the codification and teaching of social dance; it was the *privilège* (the Royal Warrant) granted to the Académie Royale de Musique, allowing it the exclusive right to present opera, which led to the emergence of the theatrical form of the opera-ballet. This, initiated by Jean-Baptiste Lully (1632–1687), became a theatrical form dominant for over half a century, combining vocal scenes with danced interludes which illustrated the musical action.

At this time Louis XIV had ceased to appear in court ballets; the immediate decline in court interest and the establishing of the Académie led to the crucial transfer of much dance activity to the professional stage and to the consequent need to develop professional dancing. In 1681 the first four professional female dancers took the stage in the opera-ballet *Le Triomphe de l'Amour*.

In 1713 the disorganised manner of preparing dancers for the stage was finally rationalised by a royal edict in January which established a permanent dance school for the Paris Opéra (by which this Académie can now be conveniently known). Thus, with the turn of the eighteenth century, we enter the era of the professional dancer and witness the emergence of a training system and a theatrical form which led on to the ballet we know today.

*Rowlandson's drawing* The Prospect Before Us *shows Didelot dancing with Madame Théodore in* Amphion and Thalia *at the Pantheon Theatre, London, in 1791.*

# Eighteenth-Century Dance

The opera-ballet as an art form was to be perpetuated well into the mid–eighteenth century, reaching its apogee in the superb creations of Jean-Philippe Rameau (notably *Les Indes Galantes* of 1735). But the opera-ballet was an artificial form denying any sort of dramatic verity, and as the century progressed it sunk into unthinking formalism.

There were brilliant dancers like Marie Camargo (1710–1770), an exceptional and dazzling technician, remembered today also for the fact that she shortened her skirts so that the public might see her feet twinkling in the *entrechat quatre* that she had mastered.

*Madame Ronzi Vestris'
costuming gives a fair idea
of the radical change in
costume for the female
dancer which came about in
the pre-Romantic era.*

Her rival, Marie Sallé (1707–1756), offered a complete artistic and technical contrast—in Sallé's art we note early attempts at a more truthful dramatic style of dancing which placed expressive grace above virtuosity. Sallé is an indication of a movement in eighteenth-century ballet which sought the creation of a dramatic style of dancing—the *ballet d'action*, or narrative dance. In Sallé's appearances in London in the ballet *Pygmalion* in 1734, she aimed at a greater simplicity and naturalness of costume in presenting the idea of a classic Greek goddess.

In London, too, the dancing master John Weaver (1673–1760) produced dance works ("pantomimes") which told such narratives as *The Loves of Mars and Venus* through mimetic gesture and dance, while his many writings argued for a more expressive dance form.

The Austrian dancing master Franz Hilferding (1710–1768) worked throughout Europe and was a no less powerful influence in the development of the *ballet d'action*, a cause which was also taken up by his pupil Gasparo Angiolini (1731–1803). These men worked in many capitals of Europe, but it was the ballets and the writings of Jean-Georges Noverre (1727–1810) which typify for us today the eighteenth-century dance's quest for independence and for recognition as an expressive and truthful art form.

In his celebrated *Letters on Dancing and Ballets* of 1760 Noverre provides both an indictment of the sterile attitudes of the opera-ballet and its executants, and also a powerful advocacy of a form of dancing which was eventually to dominate European stages. In the work of his successors—such choreographers as Dauberval, Viganò, and Didelot—we see the triumph of the *ballet d'action* and the preparation for the next development in ballet.

# Nineteenth-Century Dance

This was the emergence of Romanticism on the ballet stage. The great upheavals in Europe which attended the French Revolution and the Napoleonic Wars were to be manifest first in the grandiose neoclassic movement which seemed so acutely a reflection of Napoleon's identity as the new Augustus Caesar.

With the post-Napoleonic era and the beginnings of an industrialised Europe, the current Romanticism was to sweep strongly through all the arts. It was to affect ballet last, for the style of creativity was still dominated by ideals more retrograde than in any other of the arts: the Paris Opéra, under the direction of Pierre Gardel for nearly forty years, was influential in preserving the old heroic style of ballet which seemed by the 1820s to be a curious survival of an ealier age.

## The Romantic Ballet

It is the figure of Marie Taglioni (1804–1884) which signals the arrival of the Romantic era in ballet, and the domination by the ballerina of the stage, which was to persist in Western Europe thereafter.

Daughter of an Italian ballet master, Marie Taglioni was an unlikely figure to be recognised as the supreme ballerina of her time. She was thin, long limbed, rather prim in expression, at a time when the balletic ideal of beauty was something more blatant and sexually obvious. But careful training and a final rigorous polishing by her father Filippo was to produce a style quite airy, demure, and totally easy. This style was brought into complete artistic focus in 1832 when Taglioni was seen as the Sylphide in her father's production of *La Sylphide* at the Paris Opéra.

*Marie Taglioni as the Sylphide in an idealised portrait by Alexandre Lacauchie.*

*Carlotta Grisi is shown leaping into the arms of Lucien Petipa in this engraving of the climactic moment in* La Péri, *a ballet by Coralli staged in Paris and London in 1843.*

Here was "Romanticism applied to the dance," as one of the newspapers of the period observed.

The newly installed gaslight allowed Marie to be seen as a vaporous figure in drifting white muslin forever out of the reach of the mortal whom she has enchanted—one of the central images of the Romantic age.

Its opposite but no less true image came with the appearance of Taglioni's great rival Fanny Elssler (1810–1884), an Austrian dancer of great physical allure and fire whose repertoire offered the exotic "foreign" ideal of the female dancer, typified by her Spanish solo *La Cachucha*. A dramatic artist of exceptional power, Elssler was hailed as a thrilling interpreter of the role of Giselle.

The ballet *Giselle* had been created for yet another divinity of the era, Carlotta Grisi (1819–1899). Grisi was the pupil and mistress of Jules Perrot, and it was he who shaped her career and encouraged the technical brilliance which was so to delight audiences throughout Europe. These three ballerinas and their many colleagues dominated the stages from Italy to Russia (and, in the case of Elssler, the United States). They toured extensively, and the two decades which followed the production of *La Sylphide* mark a high point in ballet history.

This was also the period when pointe work—dancing on the very tips of the toes—became the norm for the ballerina. Its emergence as an adjunct of female dancing had first of all come as a circus feat which was possible only with difficulty because of the lightness and insubstantiality of the ballerina's shoe. It was Taglioni who first showed it as an artistic aspect of dancing—a means of stressing her lightness and her rejection of the ground.

Later ballerinas showed it as both a symbol of virtuosity and a means of revealing character. It was not until the Italian shoemakers produced

blocked shoes offering greater support to the foot later in the century that the kind of sustained pointe work which we would recognise today became possible for most dancers.

The domination of the ballet stage by the ballerina was to be one of the causes of the decline of Romantic ballet by the mid–nineteenth century in Paris, which set the entire artistic tone for Europe. In Copenhagen and Russia, however, we can see how ballet was preserved. The Royal Danish Ballet in Copenhagen experienced a wonderful renaissance under August Bournonville, and it is through Bournonville's work that we see the clear stylistic links of the Romantic dance with the dance of the eighteenth century.

*August Bournonville and Carlo Blasis*

Bournonville was a pupil of Auguste Vestris (1760–1842), who was himself the bastard son of Gaetano Vestris (1729–1808), an Italian dancer who became recognised as the "god of the dance" in Paris. The supreme performer in the noble style, Gaetano shaped his son Auguste's development as a *demi-caractère* dancer of unprecedented brilliance. When his dancing career was over, Auguste became a teacher, and the innovations which he introduced into dance training helped the emergence of the Romantic style. It is significant that two of his most important pupils were Jules Perrot and August Bournonville. The entire structure of Bournonville's teaching method is based upon his loving preservation of Vestris' instruction, which Bournonville received in Paris for over five years.

Another vitally important influence upon the technical development of nineteenth-century ballet must be seen in the work of Carlo Blasis (1795–1878). Working in Milan, he trained generations of brilliant Italian virtuoso dancers who shone in balletic performances throughout Europe in the middle of the nineteenth century. Through his codification of dancing methods—published in his *Elementary Treatise* of 1820 and *The Code of Terpsichore* of 1828—Blasis provided a solid foundation for much of the later technical training of the century.

Because of the comparative isolation of Copenhagen from the main artistic streams of European art and because of Bournonville's own concern with preserving the importance of the male dancer (he was himself an exceptional *danseur*), the repertory in Copenhagen remained lively and was fed by Bournonville's genius until his retirement in 1877.

Further east, in St. Petersburg, too, ballet was maintained as a lively and important theatrical art when it had fallen into disfavour elsewhere in Europe. The history of ballet in Russia during the nineteenth century may be seen as reflected in the work of a series of great French ballet masters who were imported to supervise the Imperial Ballet and provide its repertory.

*Foreign Ballet Masters and the Imperial Ballet*

Charles Louis Didelot (1767–1837) worked in Russia from 1801 until 1834, apart from a brief interruption, creating a strong repertory and company. From 1848 until 1859 Jules Perrot was first ballet master, staging many of his masterpieces there, of which fragments have survived until today. His assistant was Marius Petipa, but when Perrot left Russia it was Arthur Saint-Léon (1821–1870) who was appointed to succeed him until 1869. Saint-Léon, a skilled craftsman, fulfilled the role of ballet master both in Petersburg and at the Paris Opéra for much of this period. He finally returned to Paris in 1869, at which moment he was succeeded as first ballet master in Petersburg by Marius Petipa, who remained as master of the Imperial Ballet until 1903.

The era of Marius Petipa (for details of his work see page 349) marks the apogee of the Imperial Russian Ballet. Various elements contributed to the magnificence of the Russian style of dancing by the end of the nineteenth century. Petipa's own French training was part of the continuing reliance upon the French ballet masters; also, the presence in Russia of Christian Johannsen (1817–1903), had brought the Bournonville School to Russia. The Swede Johannsen had studied with Bournonville. In 1841 he accompanied Marie Taglioni to Russia as her partner and remained in St. Petersburg thereafter, first as *premier danseur* and then as an immensely influential teacher.

The tradition whereby Italian virtuoso ballerinas, many of them products of the Blasis school, were invited to Petersburg and Moscow to appear as stars for the season during the latter years of the century meant that Milanese virtuosity was also to be a contributory influence. This influence was further extended by the arrival in Russia of Enrico Cecchetti (1850–1928), a pupil of Lepri, who was a pupil of Blasis. Cecchetti was an exceptional virtuoso dancer and he remained in Petersburg as a teacher, after which he went to Warsaw and then returned to Russia as a private teacher to Anna Pavlova. In 1909 he became teacher to Diaghilev's troupe and finally settled in London, where he opened a school in 1918. He returned to Italy in 1923 as director of the school at La Scala, Milan. One of the greatest and most significant teachers in ballet history, Cecchetti offered a strict but infinitely variable "school"; codified by a group of devoted pupils in London, it remains a widespread method of dance instruction.

*Ballerinas of Note*

Petipa's great ballets were complex theatrical machines whose motor force was the ballerina. The Italian ballerinas who came to Petersburg were seen as the heroines of such ballets as *Swan Lake*, *Raymonda*, and *Cinderella*—all created for Pierina Legnani, who introduced her trick of thirty-two *fouettés* into Petipa's *Cinderella* and then performed them in his third act of *Swan Lake*. Carlotta Brianza became the first Aurora in *The Sleeping Beauty* (in which ballet Cecchetti was both Blue Bird and Carabosse); Antonietta dell'Era was the first Sugar Plum Fairy in *Nutcracker*. Russian ballerinas were no less important—Petipa's favourite was Yekaterina Vazem, for whom he created eight ballets, notably *La Bayadère*. Her exceptional longevity (from 1848 to 1937) provides a prodigious link between the golden years of Petipa and the Soviet ballet after the Revolution.

One other figure was of rare influence. The "divine" Virginia Zucchi (1847–1930), a pupil of Blasis, staggered Petersburg by the dramatic intensity as well as the technical ease of her dancing. At a time when the ballet public had become apathetic, the fire and passion of Zucchi's performances reawoke the audience's interest in the possibilities of ballet as an art form. It is of no small significance that her performances during the three seasons in which she was seen in Petersburg inspired the young Alexandre Benois with his first passion for dancing.

Benois' passion was communicated to a group of young intellectuals in Petersburg—their members included Bakst and Diaghilev—who were responsible for the artistic movement which surrounded the magazine *The World of Art* (*Mir Iskusstva*) and the enterprises which came from it, not least of which were the Diaghilev Ballets Russes seasons.

## Twentieth-Century Dance

By the beginning of the twentieth century it must be seen, looking back, that the Imperial Ballet in Petersburg was in the doldrums. Certainly there were brilliant dancers, headed by the official *prima ballerina assoluta*, Mathilde Kshessinskaya, and a generation of truly exceptional ballerinas and younger stars followed in her wake. They included Olga Preobrazhenskaya, Lubov Egorova, Vera Trefilova, Julia Sedova (all later to become great teachers in the West), Anna Pavlova, Tamara Karsavina, and male dancers like Mikhail Fokine and the young Vaslav Nijinsky. But the repertoire at the end of Petipa's forty-year reign had become hidebound and predictable.

## Mikhail Fokine and Serge Diaghilev

Mikhail Fokine (1880–1942) was the voice of change. He urged upon the directorate of the Imperial Theatres the need for dramatic truth, for a correspondence between music and design in the service of dance narrative, and for greater stylistic truth in performance. All these appeals fell upon deaf ears, though his ballet *Le Pavillon d'Armide*, designed by Benois, was an early attempt in 1907 to create the "new" ballet.

It was Serge Diaghilev who was to provide the essential showcase for Fokine's work. Diaghilev was born in Perm in 1872. At the age of eighteen he came to St. Petersburg to study law, staying with his relatives, the Filosofov family, through whom he was introduced to the Benois circle. This group of young men provided the provincial Diaghilev with an essential education in the arts. Within a decade Diaghilev was launched upon Petersburg as an arbiter of taste, organizer of exhibitions, and editor of *The World of Art*.

The culmination of these Russian years came in 1905 with the great exhibition of Russian historical portraits in Petersburg. Thereafter Diaghilev seemed determined to show the wealth of Russia's artistic life to the West. The exhibition in 1906 of Treasures of Russian Art in Paris was followed in 1907 by a series of concerts in Paris of Russian music and in 1908 by a summer season at the Paris Opéra of Russian opera with the great basso Chaliapin as star. From this emerged the decision to stage a four-week opera and ballet season in Paris in 1909.

The operatic productions were to repeat the skill and care which had been taken in presenting *Boris Godunov* the previous year. That production had been prepared with exemplary taste. As far as the dancing was concerned, it would have been unthinkable to take to Paris the cumbersome and dated spectacles of the Petipa repertory. Hence Diaghilev's willingness to show the choreographies of Mikhail Fokine. In the event, because of certain matters of patronage, the operatic productions were reduced. (Only one full-scale opera, *Ivan the Terrible*, was shown; acts from *Prince Igor*, *Russlan and Ludmila*, and *Judith* by Serov were included.) Instead, the season stressed the beauty and excellence of the dancing. At the *répétition générale* on May 18, and at the official first night on May 19, Paris was entirely bowled over by the dancers. The programmes included a restaging of Fokine's *Le Pavillon d'Armide*, *Les Sylphides*, *Cléôpatre*, a divertissement called *Le Festin*, and the Polovtsian scene from *Prince Igor*.

It was the barbaric energy of the Polovtsian warriors, headed by Adolph Bolm, which created the most immediate excitement—male dancing was a lost art in Europe—and the genius of Nijinsky was no less acclaimed. The participation of Anna Pavlova and Tamara Karsavina revealed standards of artistry undreamed of in the sterile and foolish productions of the Paris Opéra Ballet.

The season was, in sum, a gigantic artistic and social success. Diaghilev was ever aware of the importance of society's patronage, and it can be truly said that this 1909 visit, by a temporary troupe of artists from the Imperial Theatres in St. Petersburg and Moscow, marked the reawakening of ballet as an art form in Western Europe.

It was obvious that the season must be repeated. The 1909 visit had had to be presented at the Théâtre du Châtelet, a melodrama house on which Diaghilev had lavished money to make it a fitting setting for his troupe. Now Diaghilev was invited to appear at the Paris Opéra. The 1910 season marked the emergence of a more truly Diaghilevian enterprise. Two important works were created which presaged events to come. In one, *Schéhérazade*, a new design identity was given to dancing, thanks to the genius of Leon Bakst, master of the emotive power of colour and of inspired evocation of the past. The other was *The Firebird*, which was Stravinsky's first ballet score (he had helped in the orchestration of *Les Sylphides*). Here was the new music of the twentieth-century theatre, discovered and fostered by Diaghilev.

It is significant that one work in this season was a comparative failure. This was *Giselle*, which had been staged at the insistence of Alexandre Benois, leading member of the committee of artists and consultants who

Left: *Tamara Karsavina as Columbine in* Le Carnaval. *The ravishing costume is by Leon Bakst.*

Right: *Anna Pavlova in* The Dying Swan. *This studio portrait shows Pavlova in her swan costume, although the pose does not come from the dance.*

contributed much in the discussions which surrounded the planning of each of Diaghilev's ventures. Even with Karsavina and Nijinsky in the leading roles, and in a production beautifully designed by Benois, Paris found *Giselle* old-fashioned—the capital of European culture already associated Diaghilev with the exotic and the new.

It was the winter of 1910–11 which was to determine Diaghilev's future. Following an incident involving a costume he wore during a performance of *Giselle* at the Maryinsky Theatre in St. Petersburg, Nijinsky was dismissed from the Imperial Ballet. He had been for some years Diaghilev's lover, and now Diaghilev was placed in the position of having to provide a permanent company to show off Nijinsky's powers. Thus he set about establishing his own company.

He relied, of course, upon Russian dancers. Because of the extended holidays of the Imperial Theatres, most of the principal dancers were available to him for nine months of the year; a permanent corps de ballet was recruited and Maestro Cecchetti engaged as ballet master: Serge Grigoriev, who had already acted as company manager for the first seasons, now became, and remained, Diaghilev's right-hand man and trusted administrator. Karsavina was, in effect, principal ballerina, while Fokine became choreographer to the company. (Although Pavlova continued to give occasional performances for Diaghilev, she was fundamentally unsympathetic to his quest for novelty. She was shortly to form her own troupe, and for twenty years she toured the world, dancing often where no one had danced before. Her art, her genius, inspired a love for

Left: *The French theatrical magazine* Comoedia Illustré *brought out special numbers to mark Diaghilev's early seasons in Paris. In May 1912 its cover was this fantasy by Leon Bakst showing Nijinsky as the Faun in his first ballet*, L'Après-midi d'un Faune.

Right: *Leonide Massine as the Peruvian in his ballet* Gaîté Parisienne, *a performance which is preserved on film as* The Gay Parisian.

ballet throughout the world, and it is to her we must pay tribute as the great apostle of ballet whose name is still synonymous with the art she served. Never adventurous in artistic matters; she nevertheless preserved standards of classical dancing as she understood them.)

## The Ballets Russes

The 1911 season marked the beginning of extensive touring by what was effectively Diaghilev's Ballets Russes. It was also a season marked by two of Fokine's finest works for Diaghilev, *Petrushka* and *Le Spectre de la Rose*. By the end of the following season Fokine had left. Diaghilev, ever in quest of the new—his search for novelty was to be the one constant in the twenty years of his company—had decided to encourage Nijinsky as a choreographer. Thus in 1912 he mounted *L'Après-midi d'un Faune*, and the time spent in preparing the work as well as its scandalous success seemed to put into the shade three less considerable Fokine works created in that year: *Le Dieu Bleu*, *Thamar*, and *Daphnis and Chloe*.

By 1913, Nijinsky had produced two further works: *Jeux* and *Le Sacre du Printemps*. In these as in *Faune* he was concerned with the new dance of the century, but his disastrous marriage to Romola de Pulsky, when the Ballets Russes went to South America in 1913 (without Diaghilev), meant instantaneous dismissal by Diaghilev and the virtual end of his career.

## Leonide Massine

Diaghilev, by now committed entirely to the Ballets Russes, lured back Fokine in 1914 to produce four ballets, none of which was entirely successful. It was, however, the staging of *The Legend of Joseph*, originally intended as a vehicle for Nijinsky, which brought a new young protégé into Diaghilev's life. He saw the beautiful young Leonide Massine in Moscow, dancing a minor role in a performance of *Swan Lake* at the Bolshoi Theatre, and decided that here was the stage presence needed for the boy Joseph.

Thus in the last year of peaceful Europe Diaghilev found his next great creative talent. The declaration of war in 1914 brought a total disruption of the Ballets Russes' existence. The dancers scattered, most of them returning to Russia, and Diaghilev, with a small group of associates and friends, took up residence in Switzerland. Massine remained with him, and within a year Diaghilev had reconstituted a new ensemble and Massine had made his first choreography—*Soleil de Nuit*. The war years were disastrous for Diaghilev: the troupe barely survived but somehow managed to make fitful tours in Europe and North and South America.

For the visits in 1916 and 1917 to North and South America, Nijinsky, at the insistence of an American impresario, returned. He was already showing signs of instability. His *Tyl Eulenspiegel* in New York in 1916 was a shambles, despite brilliant ideas, and his last performances on a tour of South America in 1917 revealed the onset of the mental disease which was to destroy him. Diaghilev, meanwhile, did not lower his artistic sights. Despite all the difficulties resulting from the war and restricted touring, he still planned and still sought the new.

In 1917 he presented a *son et lumière* show of Stravinsky's *Fireworks* in Rome. In Paris in the same year he presented the Cubist ballet *Parade* and Massine's first assured comedy work, *Les Femmes de Bonne Humeur*. The blackest year for the company was 1918, with no ballets staged and the company stranded in Spain. (Lydia Sokolova's memoirs, *Dancing for*

*Diaghilev*, give a vivid and moving account of this time.) The company was rescued by an offer to appear in music hall at the London Coliseum. Thus London rediscovered the "new" Ballets Russes, and, ever faithful to Diaghilev, welcomed back the troupe for a six-month season. During this time the company regained its equilibrium and was able, when it moved to the Alhambra Theatre in 1919, to stage two Massine ballets which had been prepared during the war years. These were *La Boutique Fantasque* and *Le Tricorne*. But the war had irrevocably cut Diaghilev off from Russia, and postwar Europe could not sustain the extensive tours nor provide the private patronage so necessary for the company

## *"The Sleeping Princess"*

Massine was dancer and choreographer until he, too, incurred Diaghilev's displeasure by marrying, and he left the company. His departure impelled Diaghilev into one of his most extraordinary enterprises—the decision to mount the greatest of the Petipa masterpieces, *The Sleeping Beauty*, under the title of *The Sleeping Princess*.

To design it he turned to Leon Bakst, who was by then a sick man. Fortunately Bakst had designed an extravagant staging of this same ballet when Anna Pavlova had mounted it in abbreviated form in a Broadway revue five years earlier. Bakst was able to rework his designs to produce what must surely be among the most beautiful and opulent stagings presented in this century. To ensure something of the modernity which Diaghilev knew his audiences would expect he asked Igor Stravinsky to edit the score and also to provide a panegyric about Tchaikovsky for the programme.

The production was mounted by Nikolay Sergueyev, who had been *régisseur* at the Maryinsky Theatre between 1904 and 1917. When he left Russia at the time of the Revolution he brought with him the detailed notes of every production in Stepanov notation. From these he could revive accurately the old ballets, and it was his presence in the West which meant that subsequently many companies, above all de Valois' Vic-Wells Ballet, were able to present the classics of the nineteenth-century Russian repertory.

To provide a suitable cast, Diaghilev turned to the established ballerinas of the Maryinsky Theatre who had fled Russia, and those members of his company who had been trained there. Additionally, he invited Olga Spessivtseva, one of the most sublime classical dancers of this century, to join his company from Petrograd, where she was ballerina (she had earlier danced for him on the American tour of 1916). Spessivtseva was the first Aurora in this production; subsequently the role was danced by Vera Trefilova, Lubov Egorova, and Lydia Lopokova.

Two extraordinary links with the original production, over thirty years before, were the presence in the cast of Carlotta Brianza, the first Aurora in Petersburg, and Enrico Cecchetti, the first Blue Bird and Carabosse, who marked his golden jubilee as a dancer by making a single appearance on January 5, 1922, as Carabosse. Diaghilev had hoped that the fifty-four-year-old Brianza might dance Aurora again. She asked for six months to prepare herself; this Diaghilev could not afford, and so the first Aurora became, instead, the Carabosse of the production.

*The Sleeping Princess*, alas, failed in its intent. Diaghilev had hoped that, like the musical comedy *Chu Chin Chow*, it would run for a thousand performances, and allow him to acquire some financial stability and plan for the future. This was not to be. With notable exceptions among the more enlightened members of Diaghilev's audience, the London public was not able to comprehend the beauties of this nineteenth-century masterpiece, so unlike the exotic and short-breathed excitements to which Diaghilev had conditioned them. On February 4, 1922, after 105 consecutive performances, *The Sleeping Princess* had to be withdrawn. The company limped off to Paris, where Diaghilev was trying to organise its future. Two positive results emerged from this misadventure. The third act of *The Sleeping Princess*, rechristened *Aurora's Wedding*, became a staple of the Diaghilev repertory until the end, and survived in the Ballet Russe companies of the 1930s and 1940s. Even more important, a choreographer emerged to replace Massine.

*Bronislava Nijinska*

Bronislava Nijinska, an original member of the first Russian seasons, had returned to Russia when her brother left Diaghilev. She came back to the Ballets Russes as a dancer for this Petipa revival and also provided the choreography for some additional items. Her skill encouraged Diaghilev to see her as a future creator, and in 1922 she staged Stravinsky's *Renard* for him. It was sufficiently successful for him to entrust her with *Les Noces* in 1923, and this production confirmed her as a major creative force for the ballet.

It was this same year which provided a solution to one of the most serious problems that affected the Ballets Russes—its lack of a home theatre. In 1923 Diaghilev was invited to take up residence in Monte Carlo for six months of each year, providing both ballet seasons and dancers for the operatic stagings. Since the company had two months' holiday every year, this new arrangement meant that the Diaghilev troupe needed only to tour for four months in every year. It now had a base and a home theatre.

The remaining five years of its existence were marked by this long residence in one of the great centres of high fashion at the time. The repertory inevitably reflected the influence of French taste in design and music. These are the years in which Diaghilev turned to the School of Paris and *Les Six*. Many of the resultant works were markedly lightweight but always chic. Nijinska's *Les Biches*, for example, displayed how genius could transcend the ephemeral.

Nijinska, however, was to leave Diaghilev after a mysterious quarrel; Massine returned intermittently during the next four years, but the important acquisition was a group of dancers, products of the Petrograd Academy and members of the one-time Imperial—now Soviet State—Ballet, who arrived in the West after a summer tour of the Baltic in 1924. They were led by the young choreographer Georgy Balanchivadze and included Alexandra Danilova, Tamara Gevergeva, and Nicholas Efimov.

In Balanchivadze, whom he renamed Balanchine, Diaghilev had found the choreographer who could produce the opera ballets and amusing trifles for Monte Carlo. He had also found a choreographer of genius whose final works for the company in 1928 and 1929 were *Apollo*, *Le Bal*, and *The Prodigal Son*. In these later years, Diaghilev's troupe continued to maintain the traditional repertory and it attracted exceptional young dancers whose careers Diaghilev helped shape—notably Anton Dolin, Serge Lifar, and Alicia Markova.

For two years an Irish girl whose stage name was Ninette de Valois danced with the Diaghilev company, her intention being to learn how a great repertory ballet company worked, for she had already determined that such a company must be established in England. Her chance was to come sooner than she had perhaps anticipated. In 1929 Diaghilev died. His death meant the immediate cessation of the Ballets Russes. No one else had the ability to hold this collection of talents together.

For twenty years Diaghilev had used the greatest musicians and designers in the service of ballet. He had launched major talents and given the world masterpieces which live to this day. He had set an example of taste and constant adventurousness in ballet-making which was to influence the art thereafter. Diaghilev's Ballets Russes remains the greatest single artistic enterprise of the twentieth century.

## Ballet Russe de Monte Carlo

With Diaghilev's death it must have seemed that a balletic dark age had begun. But this, in fact, was not so: the cessation of the Ballets Russes meant the opportunity for national companies in England, France, and the United States eventually to flourish. But the Ballets Russes image did not die. Three years after Diaghilev's death it was reborn from Monte Carlo. There the manager of the Monte Carlo theatre, René Blum, a man of exceptional taste, had initiated a dance troupe which became, in 1932, the Ballet Russe de Monte Carlo, taking up the banner and the repertory, and some of the senior artists, of the Diaghilev troupe.

For a brief time George Balanchine was choreographer, but it was Leonide Massine who soon became the dominant creative figure. At the same time Blum was joined by a Cossack army officer who called himself Colonel W. de Basil. De Basil was an astute businessman and it was soon apparent that he was the decisive figure in this enterprise.

Within a year, the Ballet Russe de Monte Carlo, with its trio of baby ballerinas (Tatiana Riabouchinska, Irina Baronova, and Tamara Toumanova, all in their early teens and all exceptional technical and interpretative artists), had conquered both London and New York. The company was a strong one; in addition to the much publicised (deservedly so) baby ballerinas, it boasted such artists as Alexandra Danilova and a superb male contingent led by Massine, Leon Woizikowski, David Lichine, and Yurek Shabelevsky.

It soon gained additional renown through the presentation of the first of Massine's "symphonic ballets," *Les Présages*, danced to the Fifth Symphony of Tchaikovsky, which was first staged in Monte Carlo in 1933. This was followed by *Choreartium*, to Brahms's Fourth Symphony, in London in October of that year, and both works sparked off a tremendous controversy between music and ballet critics about the sanctity of symphonic music.

Once launched, the Ballet Russe swiftly won the traditional audience who wanted the glamour and excitement associated with the Russian ballet. Ceaseless and very arduous touring for little financial reward took the company through Europe and the United States, but it built a tremendous and devoted audience.

Inevitably, though, there were rifts between the gentle and cultured Blum and the devious de Basil. There ensued a series of splits and realigning of forces and many changes of the names of the holding companies—often connected with the magic words Monte Carlo. Two companies emerged by 1938: the Original Ballet Russe and the Blum Ballet Russe de Monte Carlo. The first presented much of the traditional Diaghilev repertory and was under the directorship of Colonel de Basil.

It was this company which toured Australia and eventually arrived in the United States after harrowing wartime years and then proceeded to Europe in 1947, where it soon expired after the death of de Basil in 1951. The company had returned to Europe in poor shape and its appearance at Covent Garden in 1947 showed that the Ballet Russe image had been superseded by the image of a British national ballet.

The Blum Ballet Russe de Monte Carlo was longer lived, with Leonide Massine as its creative force, although at one time Mikhail Fokine was also involved with it. This company, led at times by such artists as Danilova, Markova, Toumanova, Mia Slavenska, Igor Youskevitch, Frederic Franklin, and André Eglevsky—a prodigious roster—went to the United States in 1939.

Blum remained in Europe and died in Auschwitz in 1942, and the management passed to Serge Denham, a Russian-American banker. The company remained in the U.S. from 1939 onwards, touring incessantly and winning a devoted and wide-ranging audience. The company lasted, with Danilova and Franklin its miraculous leaders, until increasingly hard times and the cost of touring reduced its activities. Danilova retired in 1957; the Denham Ballet Russe gave its last performance in 1962.

The presentation of ballet throughout the U.S. depended for many years upon the impresario Sol Hurok. Inevitably Hurok was concerned with novelty, stars, and the "Russian" image of ballet. Inevitably, too, he patronised one company after another in an endeavour to maintain public interest, and for a short time he presented the newborn Ballet Theatre as "the greatest in Russian Ballet," although this company was determinedly American—the American Ballet Theatre of today.

## American Ballet Theatre

American Ballet Theatre, founded by Richard Pleasant and Lucia Chase in 1939, was intended to rival the Ballet Russe companies while presenting indigenous choreography as well as masterpieces of the traditional repertory. It started off with Russian stars, but there emerged an American dramatic ballerina in Nora Kaye, who won fame in the works created for her by the British choreographer Antony Tudor, notably *Pillar of Fire*. In Jerome Robbins it discovered a choreographer who gave the company a smash-hit success with *Fancy Free*, his first ballet. It is characteristic of the company that it could not retain Robbins as a choreographer—over the years ABT's identity has been that of a conglomeration of stars with an eclectic repertory but one lacking any positive creative identity.

It has, during its more than forty-year existence, acquired stagings from nearly every major choreographer; its list of stars ranges from Markova to Makarova, from Bruhn to Baryshnikov. For many years its leading figures were Kaye, Alicia Alonso, and Youskevitch, and such stars of the American repertory as John Kriza and Sallie Wilson. In 1980 Lucia Chase, who had directed (and often financed) the company since its inception, retired. She was replaced as director by Mikhail Baryshnikov, the former Kirov star who chose to dance in the West from 1974 onwards and had found a home company with ABT, where he had joined the other ex-Kirov star, Makarova.

ABT has always had the glamorous but impermanent image associated with the post-Diaghilev Ballet Russe companies. But the authentic American classical ballet is that established through the activities of Lincoln Kirstein and George Balanchine which culminated in the New York City Ballet.

### George Balanchine and Lincoln Kirstein

George Balanchine had worked throughout Europe in the years immediately following the death of Diaghilev, his activities encompassing the staging of *Schéhérazade* (among other Diaghilevian chestnuts) in Copenhagen for the Royal Danish Ballet, and the creation of ballets for the first season of the Blum company. In 1933 he worked for the extraordinary troupe which centred upon the Viennese dancer Tilly Losch, an ensemble financed by her then husband Edward James, and named Les Ballets 1933. Although short-lived, this company staged ballets of exceptional merit and decorative distinction.

It was during their London season that Lincoln Kirstein, a young American man of the arts, determined that Balanchine was the man who could realise his dream of founding a school and company dedicated to the classical dance in America. Kirstein's vision was of an authentically American ballet. In 1934, a school was opened in Hartford, Connecticut, as preparation for an American ballet company. It was for the students of this school that Balanchine made *Serenade*, and it is this enterprise which during the 1930s, having moved to New York, was the seed-bed for the New York City Ballet.

Left: *Casimir Kokitch, Agnes de Mille, and Frederic Franklin, the original cast of* Rodeo, *created by de Mille in 1942 for the Ballet Russe de Monte Carlo.*

Right: *Hugh Laing and Nora Kaye in* Pillar of Fire.

## New York City Ballet

Above: *Eugene Loring (in striped trousers, centre) as Billy the Kid, and the original cast of* Billy the Kid, *created in 1938 by Loring for Lincoln Kirstein's Ballet Caravan, a precursor of the New York City Ballet.*

In 1946, Kirstein and Balanchine founded Ballet Society in New York to provide subscription performances of lyric theatre works. The seasons were so successful that in 1948 Morton Baum, a lawyer who was chairman of the New York City Center, invited Kirstein and Balanchine to establish their company permanently in his theatre. Once installed, the company's activities developed into the amazing achievement that is today the New York City Ballet.

NYCB's present-day eminence is due to the fact that it is a classical ensemble exactly attuned to the genius of the greatest classical choreographer of this century. Although the listings of the company cite George Balanchine as one of its three ballet masters—along with Jerome Robbins and John Taras—it is Balanchine's guiding presence which has furnished so much of the repertory and provided the essential inspiration behind the associated School of American Ballet.

Lincoln Kirstein, as General Director of the company, never wavered in his belief and labours for the classical dance as refined and made American by Balanchine. It is to Balanchine that we turn for the great body of works which are the bedrock on which City Ballet so grandly stands. Indicative of the company's style and the intensity of Balanchine's musicality was the 1972 Stravinsky Festival, during which no fewer than thirty-one ballets to Stravinsky music were danced, of which twenty-one were brand new.

Among these the Balanchine contribution was of staggering power, ranging from *Duo Concertant* to the great *Symphony in Three Movements* and *Violin Concerto*. (Earlier ballets he had made to Stravinsky music included *Apollo*, *Orpheus*, and *Agon*.)

The success of City Ballet from its first installation into the City Center was such that by 1964, when the Lincoln Center complex was completed, Kirstein and Balanchine could bring their company into the State Theater, which had been largely conceived as a ballet house for City Ballet. Since that time the identity of City Ballet seems to have become clearer and more brilliant, these qualities resulting from the training and the choreography, and from the demands made upon the dancers in number of performances. Part of City Ballet's international reputation inevitably resides in the high musical standards demanded by Balanchine and the intense musical alertness instilled into the dancers, who are unafraid when faced with the most arduous contemporary music but who also respond with entire sympathy to the wide-ranging choice of traditional concert music used by Balanchine, and also his affection for and understanding of popular music.

Although a company determinedly without stars, City Ballet inevitably produces them. Such artists as Suzanne Farrell, Allegra Kent, Merrill Ashley, Karin von Aroldingen, Patricia McBride, Kyra Nichols, and Heather Watts lead the female contingent. In its early years the men in the company were given fewer opportunities, but by the 1970s increasing demands were made upon them and today's roster includes such exceptional performers as Francisco Moncion and Jacques d'Amboise as senior artists, Bart Cook, Sean Lavery, and the very important Danish contingent headed by Peter Martins, Ib Andersen, Adam Lüders, and the Icelandic but Danish-trained Helgi Tomasson.

Parallel with the development of ballet in the U.S. there was the emergence of a British ballet. It was to the efforts of two women—Ninette de Valois and Marie Rambert—during the 1920s that we owe the companies that made ballet a British activity.

## *Ninette de Valois and the Vic-Wells Ballet*

Ninette de Valois began her career as a child dancer, but quickly recognised the need for highly professional training. By 1923 she had determined to join Diaghilev. In his company she knew she would learn the mechanics of operating a repertory ballet company and would also be brought into direct contact with the finest elements in the art she was intent upon fostering in England.

Extraordinarily, de Valois was concerned with the idea of a national repertory ballet. But her efforts would have been unavailing—or at least postponed—had she not entered in 1926 into a "ladies' agreement" with Lilian Baylis. Miss Baylis, one of the most important figures in British theatrical history, was then managing the Old Vic Theatre in South London, but planning to rebuild the Sadler's Wells Theatre as its counterpart in North London. Both these theatres she sought to use as homes for classic drama and opera in English. It seemed logical therefore that ballet in English should also be placed under her protection.

By 1931 Sadler's Wells had reopened. De Valois moved her school into the theatre. The small group of dancers she had used to provide dances in plays and operas, and also in short curtain-raising ballets at the Old Vic, now became the Vic-Wells Ballet. It was in these infant days of British ballet that the Camargo Society presented evenings of ballet in the West End of London which involved all the talent available in Britain at this time (with Spessivtseva as a unique guest artist during a 1932 season).

For this enterprise—masterminded by Philip J. S. Richardson, editor of *The Dancing Times*; Edwin Evans, the music critic and counsellor to Diaghilev; and the enthusiastic young critic Arnold Haskell—several important works were created. Today there survive Ashton's *Façade* and de Valois' *Job* as reminders of its importance. By 1934 the Vic-Wells Ballet was clearly established and it became the inheritor of much of the Camargo Society's remaining assets.

The early years of the Vic-Wells were marked by the presence of Alicia Markova as ballerina, who set standards for both dancers and audience and made possible the staging of the classical repertory which was to be the cornerstone of de Valois' achievement. For Markova, *Giselle* and the full-length *Swan Lake* were mounted by Nikolay Sergueyev. He also produced *Nutcracker* and *Coppélia*—all these works had been mounted within four years of the company's inception. By 1939, the Vic-Wells Ballet had also acquired Sergueyev's production of *The Sleeping Princess*. These classics were an essential frame of reference for both dancers and audiences.

Markova's departure in 1935 to found the Markova-Dolin Ballet in association with her partner Anton Dolin, who had also contributed to the early performances of the Vic-Wells company (he was the first Satan in *Job*), meant that the company had to find a successor from within its ranks. This was the sixteen-year-old Margot Fonteyn. Her emergence as a ballerina was gradual, and it owed much to the teaching of de Valois, and the arrival in 1935 of Frederick Ashton as a resident choreographer to the company. The third vital architect of the national company was its musical director, Constant Lambert, who was with the company from its beginning until his untimely death in 1951. Lambert, as conductor, composer, arranger, and artistic mentor, was of incalculable importance.

The outbreak of war in 1939 might have been thought a mortal blow to a young ballet company. On the contrary, the war years, spent touring for the most part round Britain interspersed with London seasons, took the company to a national audience which remained loyal thereafter. At this time the partnership of Margot Fonteyn and Robert Helpmann gained popular recognition and Helpmann became a figure crucial to the company's life. With Ashton and most of the male dancers called up for military service, he not only sustained the leading roles in most ballets but also provided choreography of vivid theatrical effect, his *Hamlet* being particularly popular.

*The two founding figures of British ballet at work. Left: Dame Ninette de Valois with students of the Royal Ballet School. Right: Dame Marie Rambert coaches Lucette Aldous, at that time a leading dancer of the Ballet Rambert.*

*The Royal Ballet*

In 1946, Ninette de Valois was invited to take her company to Covent Garden to reopen the Royal Opera House. With Margot Fonteyn and Robert Helpmann in *The Sleeping Beauty*, redesigned by Oliver Messel, and with Lambert in the pit, the Sadler's Wells Ballet, as the company now was known, came of age.

The next four decades saw the company acknowledged as a national treasure wherever it played throughout the world. Ashton's choreographies and those of John Cranko and Kenneth MacMillan; the ballerinas led by Fonteyn and the generations who came after her—Pamela May, Moira Shearer, Beryl Grey, Violetta Elvin, Nadia Nerina, Svetlana Beriosova, Antoinette Sibley, Merle Park, and Lynn Seymour—who sustained the classical identity of the company; the male dancers who followed Helpmann—Michael Somes, David Blair, Alexander Grant, Brian Shaw, Anthony Dowell, David Wall, Stephen Jefferies, and Wayne Eagling, and the galvanic presence of Rudolf Nureyev; a corps de ballet which at its best was a superlative instrument: these are the ingredients of the company's success in the post-war years, a success recognised in 1956 with the granting of a Royal Charter and its renaming as The Royal Ballet.

Parallel with the developments at Covent Garden were the activities of a second company, established in 1946 to maintain the traditional link with the Sadler's Wells Theatre. This company, known successively as the Sadler's Wells Theatre Ballet, the Royal Ballet Touring Company, the New Group, and now the Sadler's Wells Royal Ballet, acquired the role of The Royal Ballet's touring section throughout Britain and occasionally on extended foreign visits. It also served as a nursery for talent, both creative and interpretative—many of the stars of the Covent Garden ensemble learned their craft with the "junior" company.

Left: *Alicia Markova as the Betrayed Girl in de Valois'* The Rake's Progress, *the role she created in 1935 for the Vic-Wells Ballet.*

Right: *Robert Helpmann as Dr. Coppélius.*

The necessary sustenance for these companies comes from the Royal Ballet School, which consists of two establishments: the junior school at White Lodge in Richmond Park and the upper school in London.

## Marie Rambert and the Ballet Rambert

Marie Rambert, Polish born, had started a career as a free dancer under the influence of Isadora Duncan. She had subsequently trained with Emile Jaques-Dalcroze in eurhythmics; this training led her to become associated with the work of Nijinsky for Diaghilev. She joined the Ballets Russes for two seasons, but at the outbreak of war in 1914 she came to London and in due time married the English writer Ashley Dukes. By the early 1920s she had opened a school in London, and her creative energy led her into encouraging her students to produce ballets. At a time when there was little other dance creativity (apart from the Diaghilev seasons) Rambert's efforts were vital in preparing the ground for the future.

At the tiny Mercury Theatre in Notting Hill Gate, West London, which her husband owned, Rambert instituted performances through her Ballet Club. Her audience was small but select, a cross-section of the cream of London's social and intellectual *beau monde*, who came to these occasional Sunday performances. They were to see the first choreographies of Ashton, Tudor, Andrée Howard, and Walter Gore; the dancing of Markova, Maude Lloyd, Diana Gould, Harold Turner, and Hugh Laing, among others. For these were the artists and choreographers whom Rambert nursed and goaded and who contributed to the emergence of the Ballet Rambert by the early 1930s.

History's perspective shows us that the function of Marie Rambert and her company was to discover and nourish talent which would then go on to larger things. Thus it proved with Ashton, Tudor, Gore, and Frank Staff, who, with Andrée Howard, were the architects of the admirable repertory which the Ballet Rambert presented during the 1930s and 1940s. But financial problems were to take their toll of the Ballet Rambert, which by the 1950s had to tour extensively and provide a repertory amenable to regional taste.

In 1966, the company was reorganised as a "contemporary" troupe inspired by the success of the adventurous Nederlands Dans Theater. The work of director Norman Morrice and choreographer Glen Tetley has been central to the attitudes of the "new" Ballet Rambert.

## London Festival Ballet

The middle-brow audience was to find pleasure in the emergence of a company in 1950: Festival (now London Festival) Ballet. Initiated by Alicia Markova and Anton Dolin, the company inevitably set out to show those classics of the traditional repertory and of the Ballets Russes with which its two stars were associated. With invitations to such illustrious dancers as Danilova and Franklin, Yvette Chauviré, Toumanova, Riabouchinska and Lichine, Slavenska, and its own stars like John Gilpin, the Danish guests Toni Lander and Flemming Flindt, and the later presence of Galina Samsova and André Prokovsky, Festival Ballet won a devoted audience wherever it played.

For many years the company was sustained by the astute financial manoeuvres of Julian Braunsweg. It was eventually to receive official financial support and to find a London home after years of peripatetic existence. The company still delights audiences with its lavish stagings, which include a *Romeo and Juliet* by Rudolf Nureyev and Peter Schaufuss' British production of *La Sylphide*.

## Regional Ballet Companies in Britain and the United States

The post-war years have brought a necessary expansion of dance activity in both Britain and the United States. In Britain, ballet was brought to Scotland in 1970 when the ten-year-old Western Theatre Ballet (a gallant enterprise originated by Elizabeth West and Peter Darrell as a small regional company, based in Bristol) was transferred to Glasgow and transformed into today's Scottish Ballet. A small ballet company, Northern Ballet Theatre, was established in Manchester in 1969.

In the United States the regional ballet movement has flourished. In addition to innumerable semi-professional companies drawn from schools throughout the country there are also professional companies based in San Francisco, Boston, Salt Lake City, Houston, Cincinnati, and Philadelphia, among others, whose work is invaluable in fostering a ballet audience at a time when it is no longer financially possible for major troupes to tour as once they did.

Two other American companies have done much to extend the range and availability of classical ballet in the United States. Both are associated with the work of their choreographer directors: Robert Joffrey and Eliot Feld. The Joffrey Ballet, of which the principal choreographer is Gerald Arpino, has maintained its identity of youthful energy over the near quarter-century of its existence, and lately has done valuable work in reviving ballets which its director sees as historically important: these range from Bournonville's *Konservatoriet* and Massine's *Parade* to Kurt Jooss' *The Green Table* and *The Big City* and samples of the Ashton repertory.

Eliot Feld began his career as a dancer and choreographer with American Ballet Theatre and left in 1969 to form his own troupe, which has been largely sustained by his choreographies for a decade.

## Ballet in Canada, Australia, and South Africa

Beyond regional expansion there has been an international flowering of dance since the Second World War. The example of the Sadler's Wells Ballet led to the emergence of national companies in those British dominions which still retained artistic, if not political, links with the mother country. In Canada, the Royal Winnipeg Ballet was established in 1939 by the English Gweneth Lloyd with Betty Farrally; but it was the tour by the Sadler's Wells Ballet in 1949 which inspired a desire in Toronto for a company of similar style.

Celia Franca, a former Rambert and Sadler's Wells dancer, came to Canada and laboured mightily to establish the troupe that is now the National Ballet of Canada. The link with Britain was clear in the classically based repertory that the company presented. These links were further strengthened by the arrival of Alexander Grant in 1976 as artistic director, and by the staging of ballets by Ashton and MacMillan. Associated with this company is the excellent school founded in 1959 by Celia Franca and Betty Oliphant. There are additionally the Montreal-based Les Grands Ballets Canadiens, and smaller troupes which offer classical and modern repertory.

In Australia, where ballet has a lengthy history, the impact of the touring Ballet Russe companies during the 1930s led to the formation of a professional company led by Edouard Borovansky in 1944. But it was not until the demise of the Borovansky troupe in 1961 that a truly national company emerged, the Australian Ballet, under the directorship of Peggy van Praagh—like Franca, a graduate of the Rambert and Sadler's Wells companies. The Australian Ballet was also modelled on The Royal Ballet and this link was confirmed when, in 1965, Robert Helpmann joined van Praagh as director.

The repertory is classically based, with a wide range of international borrowings. The company draws its dancers from all over Australia, and has a graduate school in Melbourne. In 1974 van Praagh retired and two years later Helpmann resigned. The company is now directed by Marilyn Jones, a former ballerina of the company. As in Canada, there exist also some smaller troupes concerned with both classical and modern dance.

In Southern Africa it was not until 1963 that professional companies emerged, despite the fact that South Africa and Zimbabwe have admirable teachers and for many years fed The Royal Ballet, in particular, with magnificent dancers: Nadia Nerina, David Poole, Maryon Lane, Patricia Miller, Johaar Mosaval, John Cranko, Merle Park, Desmond Doyle, Monica Mason, Deanne Bergsma, Vergie Derman, Vyvyan Lorrayne, and many more.

Cape Town has been the cradle of ballet in South Africa. There, in association with the University, the distinguished teacher Dulcie Howes began a dancing school in 1934. It took thirty years of work, which produced many exceptional talents, to achieve the full professional status of the CAPAB Ballet, which came into being in 1965.

In 1969 Dulcie Howes retired, to be succeeded by David Poole (one of her many gifted pupils), who had been an exceptional dramatic artist with the Sadler's Wells Theatre Ballet during the years he spent in England. The company offers several classical stagings and has found in Phyllis Spira a true ballerina.

From 1963 government aid has been available in most of the South African provinces to encourage ballet performances, and this has meant that in Johannesburg the PACT Ballet Company has also been able to build a repertory and to tour.

## Post-war Ballet in France

Just as Diaghilev's death and the demise of his company resulted in a more national approach to ballet in Britain and the United States, with all the subsequent offshoots, so too in France was the moribund Paris Opéra to be brought alive by the arrival there of Serge Lifar. Lifar, Diaghilev's last *premier danseur*, was appointed to the Opéra when, in 1929, illness prevented George Balanchine from staging there *The Creatures of Prometheus*. Lifar, engaged as principal dancer in the production, was invited to provide the choreography as well, and, as a result, Jacques Rouché, then director of the Paris Opéra, appointed him ballet master and *premier danseur*.

Lifar's reign at the Opéra lasted for twenty-eight years. During that time he produced a considerable body of choreography in which he not only reasserted the dignity and importance of the *danseur*, but also gave proper attention to the galaxy of ballerinas who led the Opéra company with him. They included Solange Schwarz, Lycette Darsonval, Camille Bos, Yvette Chauviré, and Nina Vyroubova, and such exceptional guests as Olga Spessivtseva, Marina Semyonova, and Tamara Toumanova.

With a brief interruption in the immediate post-war years, Lifar's domination of the French ballet scene was to result in an increased popularity and respect for dance, and the creation of generations of very fine dancers from the Paris Opéra School, which culminate in the roster of artists in the Paris Opéra Ballet today.

But there were inevitable reactions against the Opéra Ballet as an "establishment." Immediately after the Liberation, there came a burst of creativity among the youngest dancers in Paris which centred upon the Opéra-trained Roland Petit. Petit's achievement has been the creation of a varied range of spectacle from ballet to music hall, always allied to his theatrical verve and his taste for brilliant design. In 1972 he was appointed director of the Ballet de Marseille, one of the several regional companies in France which pursue a lively creative existence. Petit's work in Marseille has meant that the company is now recognised as one of the most important in France.

Other national companies are associated with the opera houses in the provinces, and the creative standards of such troupes as the Ballet-Théâtre Français based in Nancy, the Ballet du Rhin based in Strasbourg, and the companies in Lyon and Toulouse exemplify the constant activity throughout the country.

## Post-war Ballet in Germany

In Germany, classical ballet is a post-war manifestation which owed much, initially, to the activities of such ballet masters as Nicholas Beriozoff, Walter Gore, and Alan Carter, who first revealed to the German public the attractions of the academic style. (Germany had during the 1920s and 1930s been the home of a considerable amount of modern-dance activity, typified by the work of Mary Wigman, Kurt Jooss, and Harald Kreutzberg.) But it was the arrival of John Cranko in Stuttgart as ballet master in 1960 which seemed to give exceptional impetus to the German ballet scene.

The example of his Royal Ballet experience taught him the value of a school as well as of a classically based repertory, and his success in association with his muse, Marcia Haydée, who was eventually to become his successor, provided a stimulus for companies in Munich, West Berlin, Frankfurt, Hamburg, and other cities. Unfortunately there seems a constant game of musical chairs among directors and dancers of the many houses in Germany, with their essentially operatic bias. Thus no continuing creativity can be seen in them, save in the case of Hamburg, where, since 1973, John Neumeier has been director, and, of course, Stuttgart.

## Post-war Ballet in the Low Countries

A comparable post-war balletic expansion has also been seen in Holland. The two major companies are the Dutch National Ballet, based in Amsterdam, and the Nederlands Dans Theater, based in The Hague. The pioneer work of Sonia Gaskell gave the Dutch National Ballet a huge international repertory, but it is the influential triumvirate of Hans van Manen, Rudi van Dantzig, and Toer van Schayk which has given it a more adventurous image today.

Van Manen was also an original member of the Nederlands Dans Theater, which was formed as a breakaway troupe from the National

Ballet in 1959. Its policy, then as now, was of exceptional creativity—often ten new ballets being staged each year, Its style was originally a blend of classical and modern attitudes, and the choreographies of Glen Tetley and other American moderns were central to its image. Van Manen made many works for it before moving to the National company, and in 1976 Jiří Kylián became artistic director and has produced ballets contributing to the company's present energetic image.

In neighbouring Belgium the image of ballet is inevitably dominated by the activity of Maurice Béjart in Brussels. With his twenty years as director of the Ballet du XXième Siècle at the Théâtre Royal de la Monnaie, Belgium was given a company which acquired a vast international audience, thanks to the popularity of Béjart's spectacles. There are also two classical companies, the Ballet Royal de Wallonie and the Royal Ballet of Flanders.

*Scandinavian Ballet Companies*

Of the Scandinavian companies, the Royal Swedish Ballet has an honourable tradition dating back for two centuries to 1773, when King Gustav III founded his opera and introduced ballet and a ballet school. In the immediate post-war years the company acquired an eclectic repertory which ranged from historical reconstructions by Mary Skeaping to works specially created or staged by Tudor, Yuri Grigorovich, Tetley, Birgit Cullberg, Ivo Cramér, and today's international classical repertory from Ashton, Balanchine, MacMillan, and Robbins. There are small companies in Gothenburg and Malmö, and a troupe associated with the choreographer Birgit Cullberg. In Norway, a good school, directed by the Englishwoman Joan Harris, feeds the Oslo-based Norwegian National Ballet—another post-war development.

*Royal Danish Ballet*

But it is to Copenhagen that ballet lovers have turned since the extraordinary moment when—it must seem—the Royal Danish Ballet plucked up courage to invite six British critics to see the repertory in Copenhagen. The revelation of the Bournonville repertory, the Bournonville school, and the wonderful tradition of dramatic mime confirmed the view, encouraged by the performances of certain Danish dancers who had appeared outside Denmark, that here was a treasure-house of ballet.

In 1954 the Royal Danish Ballet came to Covent Garden and conquered absolutely, as it was subsequently to do wherever it performed. For twenty years ballet festivals in Copenhagen attracted devoted attendance from dance-lovers, who travelled from England and America to savour the Bournonville repertory in its home theatre, and the continuing excellence of the Danish dancers.

It was Harald Lander who had inaugurated these festivals as director of the ballet company until 1952. After a variety of directorial appointments, Flemming Flindt became director in 1966 and sought to bring about a modernisation of the company's image through his own choreographies. In 1978 he and his wife, the dancer Vivi Flindt, took a leave of absence to stage *Salome*, with its Peter Maxwell Davies score, in the Circus Theatre in Copenhagen. Flindt was succeeded by Henning Kronstam, assisted by Kirsten Ralov. To them and their colleagues goes credit for the immensely successful Bournonville Centenary Festival of 1979, when an entire week was devoted to the extant repertory, and an international audience from Russia, France, Britain, and the United

States converged to pay homage to a great choreographer and a great company.

## Post-war Ballet in the Soviet Union

In the Soviet Union ballet still holds a hallowed place. The Revolution of 1917 brought an essential change to ballet in Russia. Its identity as an art intimately associated with the Tsarist court must have seemed suspect, but thanks, in part, to the work of Anatoly Lunacharsky as People's Commissar for Education, who fought to preserve ballet as an art for the enrichment of the new society, and to the work of A. Y. Vaganova, the great teacher who helped shape the image of ballet for the new society, the classical ballet survived.

There was a parallel achievement of staging new ballets which reflected the aesthetic of the new nation and preserving the traditional repertory. The first wholly successful ballet of the Soviet era was *The Red Poppy*, produced in Moscow in 1927: its revolutionary theme—the liberation of Chinese workers from oppression—was expressed in a firmly academic form.

The subsequent emergence of a tradition of Soviet ballets also meant the emergence of a heroic style of dancing, grander and more exultant in outline, and there resulted a typically Soviet style of ballet much concerned with themes of struggle and liberation. Ballets such as *The Fountain of Bakhchisaray* by Zakharov, *The Flames of Paris* and *Mirandolina* by Vainonen, and *Laurencia* by Chabukiany are examples of the genre. Lavrovsky's *Romeo and Juliet* must inevitably remain a central masterpiece of this "new" style, which has led on to the works of Yuri Grigorovich in *Spartacus* and *Ivan the Terrible*.

Although Moscow was to become the administrative capital of Russia following the Revolution, the historical supremacy of Petersburg/ Petrograd/Leningrad has been a persistent fact in Soviet ballet. It was here that Vaganova spent thirty vitally important years in teaching, devising that method which is the bedrock upon which all teaching in the Soviet Union rests. It was also from here that most of the creative figures of Soviet ballet have sprung.

The traditional difference between Tsar Peter the Great's more cosmopolitan and aristocratic city and the merchant-bourgeois Moscow continues in the contrasted styles of dancing of the Leningrad Kirov and Moscow Bolshoi companies. The former is still supremely elegant; the latter exultantly dramatic. The difference can easily be appreciated in the presentation of the nineteenth-century repertory, which has been carefully edited but no less carefully preserved and honoured in the two cities. It is the difference between the dancing of the senior ballerinas of the two companies: the serene Irina Kolpakova in Leningrad and the dionysiac Maya Plisetskaya in Moscow.

Throughout all the Republics of the Soviet Union opera and ballet companies have been encouraged, and there are now some forty ballet troupes. Their repertory reflects both a national identity and the folk themes and dances of their region.

Following the end of the Second World War, the Soviet domination of Eastern Europe meant the expansion of Soviet ideas in ballet, and the companies in Hungary, Bulgaria, Romania, Poland, Czechoslovakia et al. have benefited from Russian teaching while also acquiring much of the Soviet repertory.

*Ballet in Cuba*

A hemisphere away the ballet in Castro's Cuba is inspired both by the ideals of a Communist society and by the presence of Alicia Alonso. This Cuban ballerina, born in 1921, had an international career with American Ballet Theatre, but following the establishing of the Castro regime in 1959, she has devoted her energies to the school and company in Havana. Under her guidance the Ballet Naçional de Cuba and Cuban dancers have achieved renown throughout the world.

*Among the Soviet dancers who have chosen to leave their country to pursue careers in the West is Natalia Makarova, shown here with Anthony Dowell in The Royal Ballet's production of Swan Lake.*

# Making a Ballet

It is one of the excitements as well as one of the great perils of ballet making and ballet going that no one really knows how a ballet is going to turn out until its first performance on stage before a live audience. It is rather like making a soufflé. One can make sure that all the ingredients are of the best, and that the artistic oven is at the right temperature, but it is only when you bring it out that you know that either it has risen or is cowering hideously in the bottom of the dish.

The reasons for producing a new ballet can be many: the need to maintain public interest in a company; the much greater need to preserve a creative life within a company; the need, equally important, to

*The Bolshoi Ballet in* Raymonda, *with Rimma Karelskaya as the heroine.*

give fresh opportunities to established dancers, or to discover new talent. The artistic director of the company must inevitably take the first decision. Thereafter it is his choice of choreographer which will govern the collaborative process that is going to result in the new work.

## The Role of the Choreographer

The choreographer's initial choice must be whether his new piece will be narrative or plotless. With a plotless work, the prime consideration for the choreographer will be a piece of music to which he wishes to give choreographic expression. For a narrative work there are greater problems in choice of music, since the availability of a score which will suit his dramatic scheme is often rare. There must result from this the need either to commission a brand new score—which entails both a lengthy period, during which the composer's contribution has to be written, and considerable expense—or to have a score carpentered from existing

music by an arranger who understands the needs of ballet. This task is sometimes undertaken by the principal conductor or the musical director of the ballet company. Rare are the occasions on which a score has been provided after a choreographer has set to work. Today it is almost unknown for a choreographer to start work without lengthy study of his score.

It is not until all this necessary preparation has been completed that the decision is usually taken about the nature of the design for the piece. Consultations with the designer about the visual identity of the ballet then ensue, and while the choreographer sets to work with his dancers, the designer will watch the progress of the ballet and absorb ideas about the movement in relation to the way in which the dancers will be clothed and the kind of setting required.

## The Choreographer and His Dancers

The choreographer's choice of dancers is governed by many considerations: his need to use certain artists; his greater desire to feature special dancers whom he admires and whose talents he is exploring; his wish to extend the range of these dancers, and also their suitability to the kind of role he has in mind.

The relationship between a choreographer and his cast is a very delicate one. Many choreographers find it impossible to work with dancers they do not know; if a new choreographer comes to work with a company he will spend considerable time watching the dancers in class, in rehearsal, and in performance, before making his choice. For a choreographer who is working with dancers he knows, the task is more often to extend their capabilities. Inevitably, choreographers have favourite types and preferred dancers. Some celebrated examples of choreographers and their "muses" are Mikhail Fokine and Tamara Karsavina; George Balanchine and Suzanne Farrell; Frederick Ashton and Margot Fonteyn in what is probably the longest such collaboration in ballet history; John Cranko and Marcia Haydée; Kenneth MacMillan and Lynn Seymour; and Roland Petit and Zizi Jeanmaire.

Right: *George Balanchine in rehearsal with the New York City Ballet.*

Opposite: *Sir Frederick Ashton in rehearsal with The Royal Ballet.*

*Rehearsals*  The first rehearsal of a new ballet is notoriously difficult. Very few choreographers go into a rehearsal room with any preconceived ideas about steps. They will have as food for their inspiration their feelings about the score or their understanding of the dramatic outline which has to be fleshed out and the characters to be developed. (For a narrative work, choreographers will have prepared a careful and detailed scenario. Marius Petipa always worked to the most detailed plans in creating his great nineteenth-century spectacles, as did August Bournonville. In our time, Frederick Ashton approached the making of both *La Fille Mal Gardée* and *Ondine* armed with an almost minute-by-minute plan of the action: similarly Kenneth MacMillan turned to the novelist and film writer Gillian Freeman to provide the dramatic structure on which he created both *Mayerling* and *Isadora*.)

At the first rehearsal the movement will often emerge from a collaborative relationship between the choreographer and the dancers, which can initially be no more than a request from the choreographer to a dancer to "move from over there to here" in a particular fashion. A first dynamic sketch emerges. This will be repeated, altered, reversed in direction or position, and suddenly the choreography starts to take shape. The choreography may not be the beginning of the ballet: MacMillan often starts with a pas de deux; Balanchine will use whatever dancers are available for rehearsal. And the logistics of arranging a creative rehearsal in the busy schedule of a large company's rehearsals is often difficult; daily class and maintenance of the rest of the current performance repertory, as well as the rehearsing of dancers in new roles, all have to be slotted into the dancers' working day.

A successful rehearsal will sometimes produce two minutes of choreography for the eventual ballet. If the auguries are right and the choreographer is in an inspired mood, a pas de deux or an important dance can be achieved in a morning's work. Sometimes nothing will result; the eternal problem for choreographers is to feel themselves goaded into creativity by the sheer fact of a large group of dancers sitting around waiting to be used.

The accompaniment to these rehearsals will be a piano reduction of the score or a specially prepared tape of the music. Working to a piano score is difficult for both the choreographer and the dancers, since the orchestral timbre is entirely missing and themes that may seem clear upon a piano can be obscured in the body of the orchestral sound, while the anticipated orchestral effects may not prove to be what the choreographer expected when he hears the first run-through of a new score.

Eventually the choreographic text is complete. Then come the series of costume fittings and the preparations for stage rehearsals, at which time the practicalities of the scenery and the problems of the lighting have to be reconciled as the dancers adjust their performances to the stage area and to the orchestral sound.

They have also to accustom themselves to working in costume. For ballets in which period or complicated dress is used, rehearsals will already have been conducted in which the dancers wear approximations of what the designer intends them to wear on stage. Nevertheless, amounts of fabric can impede the limbs and may also weigh down upon the dancers—it is inadmissible that costuming should obscure the line of the dancers and of the choreography, or that heaviness or excessive decoration in a costume should upset the dancer's equilibrium, physical or spiritual.

At the final stage rehearsals all the ingredients come together. The very last dress rehearsal will be an uninterrupted run-through of the ballet, broken only by occasional cries from the choreographer, who will survey the action either from the dress circle or the orchestra and, armed with a microphone, will be able to vent his despair to the dancers if something looks terribly wrong. There follow disconsolate moments as parts of the ballet are run through again, the dancers "marking" the choreography with walking steps and hand gestures rather than exhausting themselves still further by dancing full out.

But in ballet, as in the theatre, a seemingly disastrous dress rehearsal can often presage a triumphant first night, for it is only at the first night, with an audience out front, that the dancers can pace and start to work on their interpretations. (There is, for example, no way in which a dancer can time or play a comedy role without the reaction of the audience: he cannot tell in advance precisely where the laughter will come and where he will receive that wonderful "feedback" from his public.)

One last hazard to a first performance is the function or malfunction of any sort of stage property or stage effects. Explosions, animals, trapdoors, and transformations are all areas of danger and sometimes disaster. We have seen a dancer prostrate with grief as Albrecht in *Giselle*'s second act made even more prostrate by a glancing blow from a flying Wili; pigeons in *The Two Pigeons* do not always find their proper roost; the behaviour of the pony in *La Fille Mal Gardée* is unpredictable and a small token of its participation in the performance has sometimes been left on the stage.

Opposite: Lieutenant Kije *was created by Alexander Lapauri and Olga Tarasova for the Bolshoi Ballet in 1963. It used a Prokofiev score and designs by Boris Messerer to tell the story of the ink blot brought to life as a lieutenant in the Tsarist army through a clerical error. The enchanting Raissa Struchkova was the wife of the "lieutenant" and is seen, centre, in the marriage ceremony. The groom, understandably, is invisible.*

## Design for Ballet

When the curtain first goes up on a ballet, what the audience sees is not dancing but a stage picture. The visual identity of the work the public is about to see is thus established. Although bad design can seldom keep a good ballet down, good design can sometimes redeem an otherwise indifferent work: *Schéhérazade* today is justified only by the splendour of the Bakst decoration; the revivals of *Parade* are a matter for art historians interested in seeing Picasso's Cubist constructions in their proper surroundings. Ballet design has always attracted notable artists—in this it reflects the art's origins in the court entertainments of the Renaissance, where the talents of Buontalenti and Parigi, the genius of Leonardo, were put to the service of court display. The great traditions of Italian design for the theatre from the sixteenth century onwards were of magnificent and opulent fantasy. Such families as the Bibienas dominated the European stage throughout the eighteenth century, and Italianate design, in the work of Sanquirico, was to prove equally impressive in the early decades of the nineteenth century in Milan. But there was also the perpetuation of received decorative ideas, which meant that by the end of the nineteenth century much ballet design was bad, boring, and painfully literal.

## Diaghilev's Influence

It was the revolution in ballet announced by Diaghilev's first Russian season in Paris in 1909 which brought design for ballet out of these

doldrums. It must be remembered that Diaghilev's previous artistic activities, his exhibition of Russian art and his Paris concerts of Russian music and the 1908 opera season, had reflected his reliance upon a "committee" of advisers, who included the artists Alexandre Benois and Leon Bakst. Diaghilev had further been influenced by the example of Savva Mamontov. A millionaire industrialist in Moscow, Mamontov had been patron to a group of artists who were eager for the revival of a native Russian tradition inspired by the vitality of folk art and the possibilities of indigenous painting. Mamontov encouraged the performance of Russian operas which had been ignored by the officialdom of the Imperial Theatres, and in arranging his private operatic stagings he made use of the painters whom he patronised to decorate the productions. They included such outstanding talents as Vasnetsov, Vrubel, and Korovin. Mamontov's example impressed Benois and the whole Diaghilev group. It was one of their arguments that theatre design must be freed from the domination of the official stage painters who produced such predictable décors for the majority of the ballets staged in Petersburg and Moscow. The presence in the Diaghilev circle of the two contrasting talents of Benois and Bakst meant that the decorative element in all Diaghilev's early ventures was superlative in quality, and the subsequent history of the Ballets Russes can be seen as a gallery of some of the greatest painters of the twentieth century.

*The London Festival Ballet's production of* Schéhérazade.

## The Russian Aesthetic

Above: *Design by Leon Bakst for* Schéhérazade.

In the first five years of the Diaghilev enterprise the designers were predominantly Russian, as was the entire aesthetic of the troupe. These are the years of the great Bakst décors: of *Cléopâtre* of 1909, with Ida Rubinstein's beauty being revealed as veils were removed from her body; of *Schéhérazade*, with its torrid, clamorous colours: of the Greek trilogy of *Narcisse, L'Après-midi d'un Faune*, and *Daphnis and Chloe*; and of the Hindu *Dieu Bleu*. Bakst also produced the felicities of the girl's bedroom in *Le Spectre da la Rose* and the Biedermeier charm of *Le Carnaval*. From Benois, partly French by birth and a confirmed Francophile, came the elegant period evocation of *Le Pavillon d'Armide* and the design for the first (and best) *Les Sylphides*, as well as most sensitive designs for *Giselle*, Benois' sense of history, one of the strongest qualities in his design, is superlatively shown in his evocation of the 1840 Butterweek Fair for *Petrushka*.

Diaghilev's increasing dominance in the Ballets Russes after 1911 meant that he was to lose the close relationship with Benois and Bakst, both of whom he contrived to offend. He nevertheless relied upon Russian artists: Boris Anisfeld with *Sadko*, Nicholas Roerich with both the Polovtsian Dances and *Le Sacre du Printemps*, Mstislav Dobuzhinsky with *Midas*, and Sergei Soudeikin with *La Tragédie de Salomé*, all worked for him. The only non-Russian to provide design in the years before World War I was José-Maria Sert, the Spanish husband of Diaghilev's closest woman friend, Misia Sert.

The constant in all Diaghilev's creativity was his quest for the new,

*Designs by Alexandre Benois.* Top: *The Kingdom of Sweets, Act II of* The Nutcracker. Centre: *The Blackamoor's cell in* Petrushka. Bottom: *The fairground scene in* Petrushka.

and this brought him an early association with two avant-garde painters from Moscow, Mikhail Larionov and Natalia Goncharova. Goncharova was to decorate Diaghilev's 1914 staging of *Le Coq d'Or*, but it was the assistance of this devoted couple during the wartime years which was to be of particular importance.

Larionov and Goncharova remained trusted collaborators for the rest of Diaghilev's life. Larionov was used to guide and help the young Massine in his earliest ballets; Goncharova is still represented by two very contrasting décors in the repertory of today. In *The Firebird*, which she redesigned in 1926 when the original, and superb, decorations by Alexander Golovin had been ruined by damp, we see her ability to produce a colourful Russian fairy-tale world; in Nijinska's *Les Noces*, which she had originally planned to decorate in similarly colourful fashion, she accepted the choreographer's wishes and made it austere and earthy.

## The Use of "European" Design

But with the separation from Russia implicit in Diaghilev's decision to remain in Europe after the outbreak of World War I, and the subsequent severing of relations after the Revolution, there came the turn towards Western European design and Parisian taste. In 1917 in Rome Stravinsky conducted a performance of his *Fireworks* during which constructions by the Italian Futurist Giacomo Balla were illuminated; in the same year the Cubist *Parade* with its Picasso designs was presented in Paris. *Parade* was the brainchild of Jean Cocteau (who had been attracted to the Russian Ballet from its first appearance in Paris and who was to remain a weathercock for fashionable taste, very useful to Diaghilev). These two works indicate the new decorative identity of the Ballets Russes. Henceforth, with notable exceptions—the Bakst *Sleeping Princess* being the most important—Diaghilev became associated with the School of Paris and made every effort to involve painters in maintaining the adventurous image of his company, so necessary to keep his fashionable audience loyal.

*Designs by Natalia Goncharova for* Le Coq d'Or. *Above:* Costume for a Russian woman. *Right:* The Act I backcloth. *The opera-ballet was first staged by Diaghilev at the Paris Opéra in 1914.*

*Opposite: A painting by René Bull showing the first scene of* The Firebird *in its original design by Golovin, which established an extraordinary air of mystery.*

*Overleaf: Pablo Picasso's drop curtain for* Parade.

*Setting by Pedro Pruna for* Les Matelots, *choreographed by Massine for the Diaghilev ballet in 1925.*

The artists employed in the last decade of the Ballets Russes seem a galaxy of the finest painters of the day. Picasso produced *Le Tricorne* and *Pulcinella*; André Derain decorated *La Boutique Fantasque* and *Jack-in-the-Box*; Henri Matisse designed the 1920 *Chant du Rossignol*; Juan Gris decorated *Les Tentations de la Bergère*; Marie Laurencin designed *Les Biches*; Georges Braque decorated *Les Fâcheux* and *Zéphire et Flore*; Pedro Pruna was entrusted with *Les Matelots* and *La Pastorale*; Maurice Utrillo decorated *Barabau*; Pavel Tchelitchev was responsible for the adventurous *Ode*; and Giorgio de Chirico and Georges Rouault both worked for Diaghilev in the last year of the company, respectively on *Le Bal* and *The Prodigal Son*. Fashionable taste was evident in the invitation to Gabo and Pevsner to decorate *La Chatte* and the involvement of Max Ernst and Joan Miró in the Surrealist *Roméo et Juliette*, and in the invitation to the Soviet artist Yuri Yakulov to design the proletarian *Pas d'Acier*. Victorian toy-theatre sheets inspired *The Triumph of Neptune* (at the instigation of the Sitwell brothers); Coco Chanel provided the clothes for *Le Train Bleu*.

This catalogue of great figures is testimony both to Diaghilev's catholicity of taste and to the importance of the Ballets Russes, which could attract the collaboration of such painters. No one since then has been able to repeat Diaghilev's distinction of design. A tradition was established which was to be emulated—though seldom matched—by ballet companies throughout the world thereafter.

## Ida Rubinstein and the Ballets Suédois

*Design by Pierre Bonnard for Debussy's* Jeux *as staged by the Ballets Suédois, with choreography by Jean Börlin, in 1920.*

It is worth recording that two companies which worked at the same time as Diaghilev's Ballets Russes emulated the Diaghilev procedures, but are remembered today only because of their design elements. The less important of these was the company variously assembled across the years by Ida Rubinstein to further her ambitions of being a theatrical star. She employed both Leon Bakst and Alexandre Benois, but her creations made little impact. More considerable in matters of design was the five-year period of the Ballets Suédois (1920–1925) during which the troupe's director, Rolf de Maré, employed some of the most considerable talents of the 1920s to support the choreography of the Swedish dancer Jean Börlin. Rolf de Maré, an immensely rich Francophile Swede, invited Steinlen, Foujita, Léger, de Chirico, Picabia, and Bonnard, among others, to produce designs. It was for the Ballets Suédois that Picabia produced the extraordinary decorations for *Relâche*, that Léger designed *La Création du Monde*, and that Bonnard produced a ravishing *Jeux*.

*Design and the Ballet Russe Companies of the '30s*

The influence of the Ballets Suédois was minimal, but Diaghilev's influence was strongly felt in the Ballet Russe companies of the 1930s, notably in those associated with Leonide Massine. Massine used Miró (*Jeux d'Enfants*), Chagall *(Aleko)*, Dali *(Tristan Fou, Labyrinthe,* and *Bacchanale)*, Matisse *(Rouge et Noir)*, Tchelitchev *(Nobilissima Visione)*, Dufy *(Beach)*, and, in his later years, Balthus *(Le Peintre et son Modèle)*. The Ballet Russe companies of the 1930s, by perpetuating the Diaghilev repertory, also accepted the Diaghilev attitudes of visual distinction in production, and Goncharova was used by de Basil for an exceptional *Cinderella*. In 1932 when René Blum chose the young Christian Bérard to decorate Balanchine's *Cotillon* he had engaged the services of one of the most important designers of the next twenty years. Bérard worked with Balanchine again in the following year when he designed *Mozartiana* for Les Ballets 1933. He also produced exceptional designs for two of Massine's symphonic works: the Berlioz *Symphonie Fantastique* and the Beethoven *Seventh Symphony*.

Of the other designers of the 1930s, Eugene Berman and Pavel Tchelitchev are notable for the distinction of their work in Europe and America. Berman worked for the Ballet Russe de Monte Carlo, for American Ballet Theatre (a beautiful *Romeo and Juliet*), the New York City Ballet (his last work was the ravishing *Pulcinella* in 1972), and for the Sadler's Wells Ballet (*Ballet Imperial*).

*Setting by Natalia Goncharova for* Cinderella *as staged by the de Basil Ballet Russe in London in 1938 with choreography by Fokine.*

Right: *Design by Joan Miró for* Jeux d'Enfants, *choreographed by Leonide Massine for the Ballet Russe de Monte Carlo in 1932.*

Below: *Design by Eugene Berman for Balanchine's production of* Le Bourgeois Gentilhomme *presented by the Ballet Russe de Monte Carlo in New York in 1944.*

*Post-war
French Design*

But it was Bérard who was to provide an important link with post-war ballet. As a patron and godfather to the Ballets des Champs-Elysées at its inception in 1945, he and Boris Kochno (Diaghilev's one-time secretary) encouraged a respect for design in the young Roland Petit. From the first superb designs which Petit showed in the immediate post-war years it was clear that the Champs-Elysées troupe might merit the accolade of being called Diaghilev's successor in matters of design. Bérard launched the company with the potent simplicity of *Les Forains*. The discovery of Antoni Clavé as a designer for *Los Caprichos*, and later for *Carmen*, brought vivid life to the stage. Thereafter, in the various companies which he has directed, Petit has reasserted the pre-eminence of French design in elegance, adventurousness, and the kind of daring taste which is impossible for other countries. His collaborators have included Paul Delvaux, Léonor Fini, Marie Laurencin, Jean Cocteau,

*A sketch by Antoni Clavé for a dancer in Roland Petit's* Carmen *for the Ballets des Champs-Elysées.*

*Setting for* Los Caprichos, *the first work designed by Clavé for the Ballets des Champs-Elysées.*

and Jean Carzou (the spectacular *Le Loup*), and he has not been afraid to turn to the great couturiers Christian Dior, Pierre Balmain, Jacques Fath, and Yves St. Laurent.

The Paris Opéra has, since Lifar's arrival, had a distinguished decorative history. Lifar, like Massine, maintained the Diaghilev aesthetic of beautiful decoration, and Picasso designed a version of Lifar's *Icare*; Chagall decorated his *Daphnis et Chloé*; and Carzou produced an outstanding and idiomatic design for *Giselle*.

One other French company, the Ballet-Théâtre Contemporain, has invited the collaboration of many exceptional artists—Alexander Calder, Sonia Delaunay, and a notable catalogue of younger talents engaged by the company's director, Jean-Albert Cartier, to produce their first works for the theatre.

## Design in British Ballet

The young British ballet of the 1930s made a positive attempt to present fine design. Even on the pocket-handkerchief stage of the Mercury Theatre and with minimal funds, the Ballet Rambert could present a work as elegant as the Sophie Fedorovitch *Les Masques*. Fedorovitch was a life-long friend and collaborator of Frederick Ashton, but her most outstanding design remains the exquisite, muted *La Fête Etrange* for Andrée Howard. Ninette de Valois in her first seasons used Duncan Grant and Vanessa Bell; later Edward Burra, E. McKnight Kauffer, Graham Sutherland, and Rex Whistler contributed to the company repertory—some indication of the distinction as well as the range of style in ballets by Ashton and de Valois. Robert Helpmann in his wartime creations for the Sadler's Wells Ballet also acknowledged the importance of design, and it is to him that we owe the introduction to the theatre of Leslie Hurry, who produced an amazing setting for Helpmann's *Hamlet* ballet in 1942.

Of other wartime productions Burra's decoration for *Miracle in the Gorbals* by Helpmann and Oliver Messel's designs for his *Comus* must be mentioned, as must Graham Sutherland's two backcloths for Ashton's *The Wanderer*. It was Messel who gave the Sadler's Wells Ballet its visual signature in post-war years when he designed *The Sleeping Beauty*, with which the company reopened the Royal Opera House, Covent Garden, in 1946.

The post-war years saw the Sadler's Wells Ballet as the great propagandist for the full-length ballet. Large-scale ballets in opera houses need grand design, and The Royal Ballet, with its classics, and with the subsequent emergence of a native tradition of three-act ballets from Ashton and MacMillan, has commissioned such excellent designs as those by Robin and Christopher Ironside for *Sylvia*, by Lila de Nobili for *Ondine*, by Nicholas Georgiadis for *Romeo and Juliet*, by Barry Kay for *Anastasia*. In the United States the full-length ballets presented by American Ballet Theatre are undistinguished in decoration, save for the exceptional work of PierLuigi Samaritani for Makarova's 1980 staging of the full-length *La Bayadère*.

The big Soviet spectaculars are of no great distinction in design, although we must record that the Leningrad *Giselle* and *Sleeping Beauty* are ideal and unrivalled in their sense of period decoration. That good design does not necessarily lose its power is proved by the Kirov *Bayadère*, whose scenery dates from the beginning of this century, and is superb. This is a message which the Royal Danish Ballet seems to be ignoring; recent replacements of "traditional" decoration for their ballets have not been as happy or as "right" as the earlier décors.

Above: *The final scene of Kenneth MacMillan's* Isadora, *with Barry Kay's sets and costumes.*

Opposite: *Marion Tait and Desmond Kelly with members of the Sadler's Wells Royal Ballet in Kenneth MacMillan's* Elite Syncopations. *The costumes by Ian Spurling are simple unitards which have been decorated with extravagant fantasy.*

Design today has moved away from the Diaghilev example of the easel painter as decorator, and the specialist stage designer is the more usual collaborator. The example of contemporary dance in an austerity of design image is also apparent, but so too is an increased awareness of the possibilities of stage lighting as a design element in its own right. Such pioneers as the German free-dance choreographer Kurt Jooss, as well as the contemporary modern-dance choreographer Alwin Nikolais, gave examples of how light in various colours might enhance the identity of the dancer and create a potent atmosphere.

Parallel with the idea of the "dressed" dancer has been the combination of austerity and frankness about dancers' physiques which can be seen in the practice dress favoured by Balanchine for his New York City Ballet, and in the all-over, "second-skin fit" of the stretch fabric leotard much used today.

## Music for Ballet

If Diaghilev established an image for ballet in matters of design, no less so did his Ballets Russes show the new musical identity of ballet. During the twenty years of his company's existence Diaghilev commissioned scores from no fewer than eighteen composers. If we cite the names of Igor Stravinsky, Claude Debussy, Maurice Ravel, Richard Strauss, Erik Satie, Manuel de Falla, Serge Prokofiev, and Francis Poulenc, it is because each produced major scores which are now part of musical as well as balletic history and have an existence quite separate from their theatrical life. As with design, the attraction of working with Diaghilev, and the cachet of his company, was sufficient inducement for the greatest musicians of the first decades of this century (with the intriguing exception of the Vienna School) to provide scores.

No companies have been able to come anywhere near Diaghilev's creative record in the field of music. The vast increase in dance activity has not in fact meant any great increase in the number of outstanding commissioned scores for ballet. From the Diaghilev era it was Serge Prokofiev who was to make the most considerable contribution thereafter by producing three major scores: *Romeo and Juliet*, *Cinderella*, and *The Stone Flower*. But these were due to the special circumstances of ballet in the Soviet Union, where the art was taken seriously and the continuity in staging long ballets encouraged the composition of major scores from many composers, including Dmitri Shostakovich and Aram Khachaturian.

Stravinsky retained his association with ballet throughout his life, his music proving constantly attractive to choreographers, and the collaboration with Balanchine which began with *Apollo* lasted all his life. He was to produce three scores specially for Balanchine: *Jeu de Cartes*,

*Below: Sketches by Christian Bérard for characters in Roland Petit's* Les Forains *to music of Henri Sauget.*

*Opposite: Stephanie Saland and Robert Weiss in Balanchine's* Divertimento No. 15 *of Mozart. The costumes are by Karinska.*

*Dancers of the New York City Ballet in George Balanchine's* Stravinsky Violin Concerto. *The two couples in the foreground are Peter Martins and Karin von Aroldingen, Bart Cook and Kay Mazzo.*

*Orpheus*, and *Agon*, and one other score, *Scènes de Ballet*, for Markova and Dolin in a Billy Rose revue on Broadway, later choreographed by Ashton for the Sadler's Wells Ballet. The culminating statement about Stravinsky as a composer for dance was to come in 1972 with New York City Ballet's Stravinsky Festival.

Few of today's major composers have been attracted to ballet, and few companies seem concerned with preserving a lively musical tradition or consistently high standards of orchestral playing, with the ever honourable exception of the New York City Ballet. This company, in fact, thanks to Balanchine, has shown a readiness to use the music of composers as diverse as John Philip Sousa and Anton von Webern.

Such practical considerations as time and money—the need to allow a composer a considerable period to prepare a score and to reward him or her adequately for it—govern the commissioning of scores today. We would note the record of British ballet, which has to its credit such full-length scores as Benjamin Britten's *The Prince of the Pagodas*, Hans

Werner Henze's *Ondine*, and Richard Rodney Bennett's *Isadora*, all for
The Royal Ballet, and Thea Musgrave's *Beauty and the Beast* for Scottish
Ballet.

Ballet music is, of course, still commissioned (and the record of the
Paris Opéra in this matter is admirable, as is that of Roland Petit's
various companies) but the generality of ballet scores now tend to be
either existing concert works or arrangements put together by a musical
craftsman. John Lanchbery has provided several scores of this kind,
notably *La Fille Mal Gardée* for Ashton and *Mayerling* for MacMillan.
(The "doctoring" of scores, which produces such vulgarities as the
accompaniment to the Cranko *Carmen* and *Taming of the Shrew* and
the Bolshoi's *Carmen Suite*, is to be deplored as a form of brutalisation of
defenceless music. In certain other cases it must seem that Baron
Frankenstein has been entrusted with musical matters, when scores are
crassly compounded. The Beethoven score for Birgit Cullberg's *Red Wine
in Green Glasses* is a dreadful example.)

It is a cliché that, because words are not involved, ballet is an international art, and all dance is immediately comprehensible and acceptable to audiences throughout the world. This is not so. National taste in every component of a ballet—choreography, music, design, theme, style of dancing—varies as sharply as language itself. The aesthetic and social reasons behind the ballet presented, quite as much as their expression, speak in very nationalistic terms. National pride and chauvinism nourish prejudice.

Nevertheless, great ballets and great dancing are international. Like every other form of art, they transcend boundaries. For dancing is the first and most basic of the arts. Everywhere people react to rhythm and melody. The classical academic dance is the most refined and demand-

*Artists of the New York City Ballet in a television production of* Emeralds, *which is the opening section of George Balanchine's* Jewels. *Sean Lavery and Karin von Aroldingen are the central couple, with Merrill Ashley and Gerard Ebitz on the right.*

Overleaf: *Artists of the Bolshoi Ballet in Chopiniana, which is the original title of Fokine's* Les Sylphides *and is still retained for both the Bolshoi and the Kirov productions.*

ing of physical activities in Western culture and can prove the most rewarding to any watcher who is prepared to accept it on its own terms. The art of great dancers—Pavlova, Ulanova, Danilova, Markova, Fonteyn—was hailed wherever they appeared. So it will ever be. The most important guide to ballet going is simply to go to the performance and, as the American modern choreographer Merce Cunningham has said, "bring your faculties into action." Pleasure in the performance is the best test of ballet going. Great dancing in any form, like great skating or great gymnastics, speaks directly to the eye. If, first of all, the audience keeps the mind as well as the eyes open, appreciation and understanding will follow on from that first enjoyment.

# STORIES OF
# THE BALLET

*Suzanne Farrell and Peter
Martins in the second
movement of Balanchine's*
Symphony in C.

# Afternoon of a Faun

*Ballet in one scene. Music by Claude Debussy. Choreography by Jerome Robbins. Scenery by Jean Rosenthal. Costumes by Irene Sharaff. First performed by the New York City Ballet at the City Center, New York, on May 14, 1953, with Tanaquil Le Clercq and Francisco Moncion.*

Robbins' brilliant commentary on Nijinsky's original, in which the faun and the nymph become young dance students, is a masterpiece in miniature. It catches the sensuality so essentially part of the music and the theme, and updates it.

SYNOPSIS

The scene is a ballet studio. A young male dancer lies curled asleep on the floor. He stretches and begins to flex his muscles in preparation for work. Gazing at himself into the auditorium —for the proscenium arch must be understood as the looking-glass wall of a ballet studio—he practices at the barre. A girl now enters from the back of the studio. We are made to realise that they are only aware of each other as reflections in the glass, and although they dance together their gaze never meets, save in the mirror. Suddenly the boy kisses the girl. The spell of work is broken; she leaves; he lies down again on the floor to sleep.

*Peter Martins and Allegra Kent in* Afternoon of a Faun. *Martins is a product of the Royal Danish Ballet and is one of a number of Danish artists in the New York City Ballet. Allegra Kent, one of the most lyric and poetic talents in the City Ballet, made the role of the girl very much her own.*

# Agon

*Ballet in one act. Music by Igor Stravinsky. Choreography by George Balanchine. First performed by the New York City Ballet at the City Center, New York, on November 27, 1957, with Diana Adams and Arthur Mitchell.*

The names of the music's sections indicate the starting point for Stravinsky's score, which was a seventeenth-century French dance manual. But like the ballet's Greek title (meaning "contest" or "struggle"), these are mere pretexts for dance and music. The score was commissioned from Stravinsky and was only his third work specially created for George Balanchine, the others being *Orpheus* and *Jeu de Cartes*. *Agon*, which reaches its culmination in the magnificent pas de deux of the fourth section, is one of the greatest and most typical pieces of the entire Stravinsky-Balanchine collaboration. It is a plotless exploration of the musical structure created by Stravinsky. In it we see one of the truest images of the classical academic dance in the latter half of our century. The dances are brilliant, witty, self-contained; their function, in a work of the most thrilling functional elegance, is to reveal how music and the classical academic dance work at the command of our century's master composer and choreographer. *Agon* has been danced by other companies but it belongs, essentially, to New York itself and to the company which created it. Significantly, the only other viable staging has been that of Arthur Mitchell's Dance Theatre of Harlem.

**SYNOPSIS**

*Agon* is choreographed for four men and eight women who are seen in three sections, each containing three dances. The first section consists of a male quartet, a female double quartet, and a triple quartet. The second section consists of two trios and a pas de deux: the first trio comprises a Sarabande for a man, a Gaillard for two women, and a coda for all three; the second trio comprises a Bransle simple for two men, a Bransle gay for one woman, and a Bransle de Poitou for all three; then comes the pas de deux. The third section consists of four duets and four trios, followed by a coda that returns to the opening formation.

*Peter Martins and Suzanne Farrell in the pas de deux from* Agon.

# *Anastasia*

*Ballet in three acts. Music: Act I, Pyotr Ilyich Tchaikovsky (Symphony No. 1); Act II, Tchaikovsky (Symphony No. 3); Act III, Bohuslav Martinů (Fantaisies Symphoniques). Choreography by Kenneth MacMillan. Scenery and costumes by Barry Kay. First performed by The Royal Ballet at the Royal Opera House, Covent Garden, on July 22, 1971, with Lynn Seymour as Anastasia, Svetlana Beriosova as the Tsarina, Derek Rencher as the Tsar, Adrian Grater as Rasputin, Antoinette Sibley as Kshessinskaya, Anthony Dowell as her partner, David Adams as Anna's husband.*

Opposite: *Lynn Seymour as the young Anastasia in the picnic scene in Act I.*

Kenneth MacMillan had long been fascinated by the historical figure of Madame Anna Anderson, who for many years proclaimed herself to be the Grand Duchess Anastasia, survivor of the Bolshevik massacre of the Russian Imperial family at Ekaterinburg in 1918. Thus he created a one-act work which studied the feelings and sufferings of the woman who believed herself to be Anastasia. This *Anastasia* was first performed on June 25, 1967, at the Deutsche Oper, Berlin, where MacMillan was ballet director, with Lynn Seymour in the title role.

When in 1970 MacMillan returned to Covent Garden as director of The Royal Ballet, he determined to amplify the work by providing two acts which would explore the historical world of the young Grand Duchess, and these were to become the first two acts of the full-length ballet, with the Berlin *Anastasia* as its final section. Superbly designed by Barry Kay, the three-act *Anastasia* shows MacMillan bringing events of the real world to the full-length ballet. The result is a work which explores the problem of identity which has so concerned the art of our time, and the ballet shows a deep concern for portraying accurately through dance historical figures in the social setting of their time. Like his contemporary, Yuri Grigorovich at the Bolshoi Ballet in Moscow, MacMillan is also concerned with extending the possibilities of the three-act ballet's form, and exploring the potential of dance as an expressive narrative language.

Made to celebrate the exceptional dramatic and dance artistry of The Royal Ballet at the time, *Anastasia*'s central role has been dominated by the superlative quality of Lynn Seymour's impersonation, which has rightly been hailed as a performance of greatness.

## SYNOPSIS

**Act I**
*The Baltic coast, August 1914*

The Russian Imperial family is picnicking. A group of officers from the Imperial yacht are in attendance, as the Tsar and his family relax. The youngest of his four daughters is the tomboyish Anastasia. There is a moment of drama when the Tsarevich falls but the danger from haemophilia is averted by Rasputin's ministrations. At the end of the act the Tsar receives news of the outbreak of war and takes leave of his family.

**Act II**
*Petrograd, March 1917*

There is unrest in the streets but the Tsar has decided to celebrate Anastasia's coming of age with a ball in the Winter Palace. Among the guests are his erstwhile mistress, the *prima ballerina assoluta* Mathilde Kshessinskaya, and her partner, who perform a pas de deux to entertain the guests. Anastasia is puzzled by the undercurrents of emotion she notes among the grownups of her world: the Tsar's reliance upon the Tsarina and the Tsarina's complete obsession with Rasputin as a supposedly holy man. Revolution finally erupts in the streets and the Winter Palace is stormed by the crowd.

*Act III*
*Berlin,*
*early 1920s*

In a hospital the woman who believes herself to be the Grand Duchess Anastasia seeks to assure herself of her own identity and to persuade the world of it. Past events are mingled and confused. She recalls the happiness of her childhood, the horrors of revolution, the massacre of her family, her flight from Russia, the birth of her child, and her loss of the man she married. Despite the rejection of her claim by the survivors of the Imperial family, Anastasia finally acquires the inner strength to survey the world, sure of her identity as a woman.

# Apollo

*Ballet in one act. Music by Igor Stravinsky. Choreography by George Balanchine. Scenery and costumes by André Bauchant. First performed (as* Apollon Musagète*) by Diaghilev's Ballets Russes at the Théâtre Sarah Bernhardt, Paris, on June 12, 1928, with Serge Lifar as Apollo, Alice Nikitina as Terpsichore, Lubov Tchernicheva as Polyhymnia, and Felia Dubrovska as Calliope.*

"*Apollo* I look back on as the turning point of my life. In its discipline and restraint, its sustained oneness of feeling, the score was a revelation. It seemed to tell me that I could dare not to use everything, that I too could eliminate. I began to see how I could clarify, by limiting, by reducing what seemed to be multiple possibilities to the one which is inevitable." Thus George Balanchine wrote in *Stravinsky in the Theatre* (1949).

The importance of this ballet lies in the fact that, confronted by Stravinsky's score, Balanchine was able to reconsider his choreographic identity in the light of the classicism of Marius Petipa, in which he had grown up, and of its subsequent developments in Russia and with Diaghilev's Ballets Russes' choreographers. When he went to the United States in 1933 the implications of *Apollo* were to be realised, and without exaggeration we may see the germs of the greatness of the New York City Ballet today in this crucial work.

The score was commissioned by Elizabeth Sprague Coolidge for performance in the Library of Congress, Washington, D.C., with choreography by Adolph Bolm. It was first seen on April 27, 1928. Two months later, the Diaghilev production was given with the young Lifar radiantly beautiful as Apollo and Alexandra Danilova (the choreographer's first choice) alternating with Alice Nikitina as Terpsichore.

The design by André Bauchant, a "Sunday painter," did not survive the Diaghilev company's production. The Balanchine version of the ballet was first given in America by the American Ballet (a forerunner of the New York City Ballet) in 1937, and in recent years Balanchine has decided upon an absolutely austere decorative manner for the piece. *Apollo* is in the repertories of American Ballet Theatre, The Royal Ballet, and ballet companies around the world.

SYNOPSIS

The theme of this ballet is the birth of Apollo and his identity as leader of the Muses. A prologue is set on the island of Delos where Leto is in labour with a child that she is bearing by Zeus. She is placed high on a rock. Below her, in an alcove, Apollo appears wrapped in swaddling bands. He hops forward and two handmaidens appear and unwind the cloth: before they have completed the task the god spins free of these constraints. The handmaidens present him with a lute and show him how he must hold it. He plucks the strings; he has discovered his calling. Blackout. When the light returns, Apollo plays his lute and summons three Muses. They are Calliope, Muse of Poetry; Polyhymnia, Muse of Mime; and Terpsichore, Muse of Dance. After a general dance in which they greet the god he gives each Muse an attribute of her art: a tablet to Calliope, a mask to Polyhymnia, a lyre to Terpsichore. Now each Muse performs for the god. Calliope dances first, and her variation shows her in bold movements while she mimes writing. At the close of her solo she shows the god what she has written but he is not impressed. Polyhymnia now dances, finger to lips to remind us that mime is a silent art, but she herself forgets this at the end and finishes her variation with a silent "shout." She is aghast and the god dismisses her.

*Mikhail Baryshnikov and Heather Watts of the New York City Ballet in* Apollo.

Finally Terpsichore appears and the perfection of her movement satisfies the god. Apollo now dances and his final pose brings him to the ground, one hand outstretched. Terpsichore enters and in an electric moment she joins her finger to his. There follows a pas de deux, and then the other two Muses enter and join in a quartet whose finale comes when the Muses clap and Apollo rests his head against their outstretched hands. At this moment the orchestra tells us that the voice of Zeus can be heard summoning his son. Apollo stands listening. The Muses recline on the ground, their legs raised, then curve their arms so that the god may raise them. They become a chariot team with Apollo as their driver, and finally he leads them to the ramp (which is the ballet's only set today) that represents the slopes of Mount Olympus. Apollo mounts up to his father and the Muses follow him. Leto makes an appearance, watching her son's ascent, then collapses into the arms of her handmaidens.

*Apollo* as now staged by the NYCB is shorn of its prologue, and of the final ascent to Olympus. The ballet thus acquires a ritualistic concentration, with no loss of power or beauty.

# L'Après-midi d'un Faune

*Ballet in one scene. Music by Claude Debussy. Choreography by Vaslav Nijinsky. Scenery and costumes by Leon Bakst. First performed by Diaghilev's Ballets Russes at the Théâtre du Châtelet, Paris, on May 29, 1912, with Vaslav Nijinsky as the Faun and Lydia Nelidova as the Nymph.*

Vaslav Nijinsky made only four ballets, of which *Faune* was the first. Like the other two works, *Jeux* and *Le Sacre du Printemps*, which he made under the tutelage of Diaghilev (his last ballet, *Tyl Eulenspiegel*, was staged unsupervised and disastrously in New York in 1916) *L'Après-midi d'un Faune* is an innovative and extraordinary creation. Instead of the classical disciplines of turn-out and academically correct dance he opted for a style of movement which sought to re-create the two-dimensional effect of Greek vase paintings and bas reliefs. The dance is based on walking steps on a single plane, the torso twisted to face the audience, the head held in profile. The result was a brief choreographic poem of great stylistic cohesion and originality, but also a ballet which created an appalling scandal at its first performance, since the Faun's final gesture of sinking onto the scarf was thought to be obscene.

Nijinsky's insanity after 1918 meant an end to a career equally thrilling as dancer and choreographer. *Faune* is the only one of his works which has survived (although the scores of his other works have been used by other choreographers). His successor as the Faun, the great Polish character dancer Leon Woizikowski, performed and taught the role extensively during the 1930s, and the choreography remained in the repertory of the Ballet Rambert until the 1970s, although the superb Bakst backdrop was never used.

In 1979 the Joffrey Ballet mounted the work with its original décor for a season with Rudolf Nureyev, and this glorious set was loaned to London Festival Ballet when Nureyev danced with them in London in the summer of the same year.

SYNOPSIS

The scene is a sunny hillside in classical Greece. A faun reclines on a rock. Below him he sees seven nymphs, who are on their way to bathe at a pool. Stirred by desire, the faun descends from the rock and approaches them. Alarmed by his presence, they leave. One returns and dances briefly with the faun. She too is fearful and flees, leaving behind her scarf. The faun takes the scarf and returns to his rock. He consoles himself by embracing it.

*Opposite: Rudolf Nureyev as the Faun and Margot Fonteyn as the leading Nymph in London Festival Ballet's staging of L'Après-midi d'un Faune for the Nureyev Festival at the London Coliseum in 1979.*

# As Time Goes By

*Ballet in one act. Music by Franz Josef Haydn. Choreography by Twyla Tharp. Costumes by Chester Weinberg. First performed by the Joffrey Ballet at the City Center, New York, on October 24, 1973, with Beatriz Rodriguez and Larry Grenier.*

*As Time Goes By* was Twyla Tharp's second commission for the Joffrey Ballet, and it couldn't have been more different from the first. *Deuce Coupe*, created in 1973 and set to the goofy songs of the Beach Boys, was an overnight sensation that eventually went the way of most rock groups. Set to the immortal notes of Haydn, *As Time Goes By* is timeless. Whereas *Deuce Coupe* celebrated youth and its passing, *As Time Goes By* is about itself: music and dance. It penetrates with Tharp's typical wit and complexity of means the structure of her chosen music and the conventions of ballet itself. In this sense, one may call *As Time Goes By* classical in concept, if not in language. The Joffrey dancers prove superbly accommodating to Tharp's distortions of ballet vocabulary and subtle dislocations of ballet rhythms.

Light brown skirts for the women and loose-fitting shorts for the men, created by fashion designer Chester Weinberg, parallel in vernacular terms the simple elegance of the traditional practice costume.

SYNOPSIS

The ballet uses the last two movements of Haydn's Symphony No. 45 (the "Farewell") but is divided into four parts. "After the Fact" is a terse solo done in silence. In "Ten Make Six" the soloist is joined by five others in a demonstration of partnering and other devices of harmonious exchange. Their chamber music becomes symphonic in "The Four Finales," where every mishap of big ensemble dances almost happens. As the music's instrumentation thins out in the final adagio, so does the dance. "Then" begins with a cast of eight and concludes with a lone man moving sensuously—and, it seems, eternally—to Haydn's "farewell" chords.

# At Midnight

*Ballet in one act. Music by Gustav Mahler. Choreography by Eliot Feld. Scenery by Leonard Baskin. Costumes by Stanley Simmons. First performed by American Ballet Theatre at the State Theater, Lincoln Center, on December 1, 1967, with Bruce Marks, Cynthia Gregory, Christine Sarry, and Terry Orr.*

The ballet takes its title from the first of the four Rückert Songs by Mahler which Feld uses as his score. He does not, however, offer dance illustrations of the lyrics of the songs, preferring rather to create four studies which seem announced thematically in the first song he uses—"At Midnight"—an agonised study suggesting all the sorrow and disillusion of a man at odds with love. The succeeding songs provide a commentary on the joyful passion of young lovers and on the isolation felt by an observer who sees an ecstatic happiness he once knew, while in a solo for the leading woman we sense the despair of someone cut off from love.

*At Midnight* was Feld's second ballet. He had made an immediate success with his first ballet for ABT, *Harbinger*, in 1967, and confirmed this with *At Midnight*, which was enhanced by the fine design of Leonard Baskin. In 1969 Feld founded his own ballet company and since then he has largely created for his ensemble.

*tor Barbee of American*
*llet Theatre in* At
dnight.

# Ballo della Regina

*Ballet in one act. Music by Giuseppe Verdi. Choreography by George Balanchine. Costumes by Ben Benson. First performed by the New York City Ballet at the State Theater, Lincoln Center, on January 17, 1978, with Merrill Ashley and Robert Weiss.*

*Ballo* takes its title from the dance sequence in Verdi's opera *Don Carlos*, whence comes its score. The plot for the ballet scene in the opera had to do with the quest for the perfect pearl, which was personified by the Queen of Spain. Hence the title *Ballo della Regina*—"the Queen's ballet"; hence, too, certain attitudes in the opening moments of this plotless ballet in which a corps de ballet of twelve girls are seen in poses that suggest the movement of water. What follows is a chain of solos and entrées for four female soloists and then the ballerina and her cavalier, which are of ebullient freshness. They seem somehow to evoke the grandiose attitudes of nineteenth-century opera ballets and the paraphernalia of transformations and crowds of supernumeraries, as if to say, "And here is where there are arches and processions and cohorts of dancers—only we do not need any of that." What the ballet needs and receives is the amazing speed and brilliance and joyous assurance of Merrill Ashley, whose gifts seem to have inspired something of *Ballo*'s radiance and the brilliant facets of its dances.

*Merrill Ashley and Robert Weiss of the New York City Ballet in* Ballo della Regina.

# La Bayadère

*Ballet in four acts. Libretto by Sergei N. Khudekov and Marius Petipa. Music by Ludwig Minkus. Choreography by Petipa. First performed at the Bolshoi Theatre, St. Petersburg, on February 4, 1877, with Yekaterina Vazem as Nikiya, Maria Gorshenkova as Gamsatti, Christian Johannsen as the Rajah, Lev Ivanov as Solor, and Pavel Gerdt as the solo dancer in Act III.*

*The corps de ballet of the Royal Ballet in the Kingdom of the Shades scene from* La Bayadère *is staged for the company at Covent Garden by Rudolf Nureyev.*

*La Bayadère* was one of the most successful of Petipa's middle-period ballets. In addition to its massive spectacular devices and its exoticism, so beloved of audiences of the time, it also contained a theme more serious than is usual for the ballet of the period. The work celebrated the skill of Petipa's favourite Russian ballerina, Vazem, but after her retirement in 1887 the work was neglected until 1900, when Petipa revived it for the young ballerina Kshessinskaya, and three years later revised it further for Anna Pavlova. By this time it was recognised as one of the choreographer's finest works, but following the Revolution in 1917, the ballet was truncated through lack of stage forces. The fourth (wedding) act was dropped and the ballet ended with the "Shades" scene. The work was further edited in its Leningrad staging by the great dancer Vakhtang Chabukiany in 1940. He made extensive cuts and reshaped the order of certain numbers. Even so *La Bayadère* continued to offer the most thrilling challenges as a dramatic and dance work for the leading Soviet ballerinas, and in 1961 when the Kirov Ballet first visited the Royal Opera House, Covent Garden, they presented the Kingdom of the Shades as a one-act ballet. There is every justification for considering this passage of symphonic dance as one of Petipa's most sublime achievements. The inexorable appearance of thirty-two Shades, the chain of superlative variations, the extraordinarily powerful imagery of the entire scene mark this as a jewel of choreography in which the perfection of the female corps de ballet is as vital as the stylistic excellence of the soloists.

For The Royal Ballet, Rudolf Nureyev provided a magnificent staging of this scene at Covent Garden in 1963 (and he later staged this scene for the ballet of the Paris Opéra). In 1974 Natalia Makarova produced a version of the "Shades" scene for American Ballet Theatre and in 1980 she revived the entire ballet for that same company.

## SYNOPSIS

### Act I
#### Outside an Indian temple

Solor, a young warrior, returns from a hunt with his companions. He orders that a tiger he has killed be taken as a gift to the Rajah Dugmanta. He sends his companions away and Magdaveya, a fakir, appears; Solor tells him to arrange a meeting with Nikiya, one of the temple dancers (bayadères). Priests emerge from the temple with the Grand Brahmin at their head, and Magdaveya leads his companions in a fire dance. Temple dancers perform, and then the Brahmin orders Nikiya to appear. As she prepares for the forthcoming rite the Grand Brahmin cannot conceal his passion for her, but Nikiya refuses him. After preparations for a ceremony, the priests re-enter the temple and Nikiya is told by Magdaveya that Solor awaits her. Solor tells Nikiya of his love, and she makes him swear, over the flames of the sacred fire, to be faithful to her. From the temple doorway the Grand Brahmin observes their interview and swears revenge.

### Act II
#### The Rajah's palace

Delighted with Solor's gift, the Rajah determines to betroth his daughter Gamsatti to Solor. Gamsatti is shown a portrait of Solor and admires it. Solor enters and is overwhelmed by Gamsatti's beauty. An entertainment has been ordered to celebrate the betrothal and temple dancers are brought in as part of a divertissement. The Grand Brahmin, present as an honoured guest, tells the Rajah of Solor's love for Nikiya, and Gamsatti's maid, Aiya, hears of this and tells her mistress. Gamsatti orders Nikiya to be brought to her and she tells Nikiya that Solor is destined to be her husband. Nikiya cannot believe this, but Gamsatti indicates the pomp and wealth that will be Solor's when he marries a princess. Goaded to distraction, Nikiya pleads, but Gamsatti is unmoved. Nikiya snatches up a dagger and makes as if to kill Gamsatti but is restrained by Aiya. Horrified at her own actions, Nikiya flees the palace.

### Act III
#### The garden of the palace

A procession of guests arrives and Gamsatti and Solor watch as an entertainment is given in their honour. They also participate in the dances and then Nikiya is brought on to dance. She complies reluctantly but Aiya presents her with a basket of flowers which supposedly have been sent by Solor. As she dances with the flowers a poisonous snake, concealed therein, bites her, for her death has been planned in this fashion by the Rajah and Gamsatti. The Grand Brahmin offers Nikiya an antidote if she will accept him, but she refuses, and, gazing despairingly at Gamsatti and Solor, she dies.

| | |
|---|---|
| *Act IV, Scene 1*<br>*The Kingdom*<br>*of the Shades* | The grief-stricken Solor is alone and Magdaveya brings him an opium pipe. As he smokes, Solor is transported to the Kingdom of the Shades. The ghosts of a troupe of bayadères appear out of the mists and the compassionate shade of Nikiya appears to him once more. At the end Solor awakens from his pipe dream. |
| *Scene 2*<br>*Inside the temple* | Preparations are made for the marriage of Gamsatti and Solor. As the temple dancers perform, the shade of Nikiya constantly interposes itself between Gamsatti and Solor. The Grand Brahmin prepares to perform the marriage ceremony but at this moment the temple is struck by lightning and celestial fire sent by the angry gods. The temple is utterly destroyed and everyone therein is killed.<br><br>In an apotheosis Solor and Nikiya are finally reunited. |

## American Ballet Theatre

*Ballet in three acts.*
*Choreography by*
*Natalia Makarova,*
*after Marius Petipa.*
*Music by*
*Ludwig Minkus,*
*arranged by*
*John Lanchbery.*
*Scenery by*
*PierLuigi Samaritani.*
*Costumes by*
*Theoni V. Aldredge.*
*First performed at the*
*Metropolitan Opera*
*House, New York,*
*on May 21, 1980.*

In this first Western staging of the complete *La Bayadère*, Makarova made use of the production as she had known it in Leningrad. But realising that this version was dramatically inconclusive, since it ends with the Kingdom of the Shades scene, Makarova decided to re-create the correct final act of the wedding and thus restore the proper dramatic shape that Petipa had intended. Her first-night cast included herself as Nikiya, Anthony Dowell as Solor, Cynthia Harvey as Gamsatti, Alexander Minz as the Grand Brahmin, and Victor Barbee as the Rajah.

In Makarova's production, Act I contains three scenes which are, in effect, the first three acts of Petipa's ballet, with the choreography somewhat edited to create a swift-moving action. Act II is her existing version of the Kingdom of the Shades scene. In Act III, Makarova relocates a celebrated lotus dance for the corps de ballet, turning it into a ritual candle dance for the bayadères. There follows a quartet for Gamsatti, Solor, the Rajah, and the vision of Nikiya, seen only by Solor. During this, a mysterious basket of flowers appears as a gift for Gamsatti. Terrified by this reminder of her guilt, Gamsatti urges the marriage ceremony foward. Gamsatti and Solor climb the stairs that lead to the altar where the Grand Brahmin is to perform the wedding ceremony. Solor is unable to make his vows of marriage because he is obsessed with the vision of Nikiya, and at this moment the temple is destroyed and everyone in it is killed. The gods have thus punished the evil-doers and a final apotheosis shows Nikiya leading Solor into a paradise of eternal love.

*Victor Barbee as the Rajah, Cynthia Harvey as Gamsatti, Anthony Dowell as Solor, and Natalia Makarova as Nikiya in La Bayadère for American Ballet Theatre.*

# Les Biches

*Ballet in one act. Music by Francis Poulenc. Choreography by Bronislava Nijinska. Scenery and costumes by Marie Laurencin. First performed by Diaghilev's Ballets Russes at the Théâtre de Monte Carlo, on January 6, 1924, with Bronislava Nijinska, Vera Nemchinova, Lubov Tchernicheva, Lydia Sokolova, Anatol Vilzak, Leon Woizikowski, and Nicholas Zverev.*

Les Biches *as revived by Bronislava Nijinska for The Royal Ballet, with Georgina Parkinson and David Blair on the left.*

*Les Biches* has been translated as "The House Party," though its correct rendering is "Does" (female deer), for it is a witty and ever-so-slightly naughty portrayal of amorous goings-on among the smart set of the 1920s. You can read the very worst—or nothing at all—into what you see. What matters is that this skilled social portrait is sustained by classical choreography of exceptional beauty, and exceptional demands—the writing for the figure in the blue jerkin calls for rare technical skill, especially in the pointe work. *Les Biches* epitomises a particular period in the history of the Diaghilev ballet when, with the collaboration of the best and most modish French musicians and designers, the Ballets Russes was the purveyor of "amusing" novelties for a fashionable audience. Most of the works of this period—such as *Le Train Bleu* and *La Pastorale*—are lost. *Les Biches* survives through the exceptional merits of its music, design, and choreography. In 1964 Bronislava Nijinska revived it for The Royal Ballet.

SYNOPSIS

The setting is an airy drawing room. Its occupants are a group of young girls, bright young things in pink dresses and ostrich plumes. There enter three athletic young men from the beach who excite the girls' interest. An androgynous figure in a blue velvet jerkin and white gloves appears and is courted by one of the bathers.

Two young girls dressed in grey exchange intimacies. The hostess appears, a woman of a certain age wearing a rope of pearls and making much of her cigarette holder. The characters all variously amuse themselves, and the curtain falls on an enchantingly frivolous picture of fashionable life in the 1920s.

# Billy the Kid

*Ballet in four scenes. Music by Aaron Copland. Libretto by Lincoln Kirstein. Choreography by Eugene Loring. Scenery and costumes by Jared French. First performed by Ballet Caravan at the Chicago Civic Theater, on October 6, 1938, with Eugene Loring as Billy, Marie-Jeanne as the Mother and Sweetheart, Lew Christensen as Pat Garrett, and Todd Bolender as Alias.*

*Eugene Loring as Billy in the original production of* Billy the Kid.

Billy the Kid is the first and best of those ballets dealing with the American West. Its hero is William Bonney, the outlaw, but its theme is less the

narrative of his life than a contemplation of the way in which the American West was opened up by pioneers, and how men like Bonney became part of its mythology. Billy was notorious for the fact that he had killed twenty-one men by the time he was twenty-one years of age: the ballet does not sentimentalise him as legend has done. He remains a nasty killer.

*Billy the Kid*, which survives in the repertory of American Ballet Theatre today, is the major work that remains from the creations inspired by American themes which were produced by the American Ballet and Ballet Caravan—two companies which preceded the eventual formation of the New York City Ballet. Lincoln Kirstein, so vital an influence on ballet in America, encouraged the production of several works on these native themes. They included *Alma Mater*, *Pocahontas*, *Yankee Clipper*, *Filling Station*, and *City Portrait*. *Billy the Kid*, with its attractive Copland score, showed how Western themes—later so popular in works like *Rodeo* and *Oklahoma!*—could be adapted for the ballet.

SYNOPSIS

*Prologue*
*The pioneers'*
*journey westward*

Along a path of light suggesting the westward-setting sun steps a man, Pat Garrett, who has been Billy the Kid's friend and who will become in due time the sheriff who is to kill Billy. His progress across the stage marks the journey of the pioneers to the new lands, their determination and aspiration. He is followed by men and women who tread in his path.

*Scene 1*
*A street, north of*
*the Mexican border*

A group of cowboys, Mexicans, townsfolk, saloon women pass by. A woman enters, her tall young son still holding her skirts. She is Billy's mother and her son's attitude reveals how devoted he is to her. A fight breaks out and Billy and his mother look on. One of the Mexican gunfighters misses his aim and kills Billy's mother. Billy is frozen in horror; then, taking a knife, he stabs him dead with a single blow. Billy flees. The townsfolk gather up the corpse of Billy's mother. The Mexican who has been killed will return later in the ballet as the figure identified as "Alias." He represents all the men Billy has killed, and the duplication of characters that is a thematic device of the ballet means that Pat Garrett is also present in this scene as the man who seeks to help Billy.

*Scene 2*
*In the desert*

The years have passed. Billy enters, a figure in black and white who is now a notorious outlaw and killer. In a solo he reveals his power and his quick, murderous skill in fighting, which is his way of life. Towards the end of the solo a posse of three horsemen arrive in search of Billy. Billy hides and succeeds in shooting the leader of the posse. Blackout. It is night and Billy is playing cards with Pat Garrett around a fire. Billy cheats at cards and is detected in this by Garrett. He denies the accusation, and when Garrett eventually leaves, Billy is joined by a group of friends. He is concerned because he did not kill Garrett. The arrival of a posse led by Garrett occasions a gunfight in which Alias is again killed by Billy. Billy is captured by Garrett and taken off to jail, while his Mexican sweetheart (danced by the artist who plays his mother) grieves for him.

*Scene 3*
*In jail*

Billy is playing cards with Alias, who is now his jailer. Seizing his moment he shoots Alias, and escapes to a hideout. Shielded by Mexican girls and then Alias (now an Indian guide), he is led away. A posse led by Pat Garrett passes by but does not see Billy. Billy sleeps, and in his dream his Mexican sweetheart appears to him. Pat Garrett, guided by Alias, finds Billy. Billy wakes on hearing a sound, but he does not see Garrett or Alias. He calls out "Quien es?" (Who is it?). He is nervous, then laughs at his fears and lights a cigarette. The flare of the match illuminates his face and Garrett fires, killing Billy. Mexican women grieve over his body.

*Scene 4*
*In the desert*

A final procession shows Garrett leading the pioneers ever forward as at the beginning of the ballet.

# Bolero

*Ballet in one scene. Music by Maurice Ravel. Choreography by Maurice Béjart. Scenery by Béjart. First performed by the Ballet du XXième Siècle at the Théâtre Royal de la Monnaie, Brussels, on January 10, 1961, with Duska Sifnios.*

*Bolero* was written for Ida Rubinstein, who had initially asked Ravel to orchestrate some piano pieces by Albéniz for her. Since the rights for orchestration had been given to another musician, Ravel felt impelled to produce some "Spanish music" to replace the Albéniz score. Hence *Bolero*, which was, as he himself observed, an exercise in orchestration, which was what Rubinstein had originally asked of him. The production for Rubinstein was choreographed by Bronislava Nijinska in 1928, and would appear to have had certain similarities with the Béjart version. The distinguished critic André Levinson described the setting as a dark Spanish tavern wherein is an immense table, lit from above, on which Rubinstein danced. She was surrounded by twenty men "fascinated by the dancer's bodily incantation: a theme which is gradually developed in tragic power. By the undulation of arms and the flexing of her waist, through the flare of her skirt and her foot's tracing of circles, the *danseuse* delineates the contours of the melody, that succinct magical formula. . . . The men, through the stamping of their feet and the clapping of their hands, mark the rhythm, providing drum beats of different timbres. They too restrict themselves, like an ostinato bass, to a limited vocabulary of steps, and always in unison—with stamping of the feet and pirouettes and that plunge onto the knee that is the soul of the Tango. . . . The leading man, Anatol Vilzak, crouches and twists, tormented by passion and by rhythm."

**SYNOPSIS**

The basic idea of Maurice Béjart's *Bolero* is very simple. The setting shows a large circular red table centre stage, while round the edge of the stage area are chairs. In the original production these chairs were occupied by a group of men who were gradually excited by the figure of a beautiful girl dancing on the table top as an impersonation of Ravel's ubiquitous little tune. Across the years Béjart has worked various permutations upon the components of the piece, offering a group of girls stimulated by the presence of a male dancer on the table and, most recently, providing an even steamier picture with a group of men becoming intoxicated by the presence of another chap on the table. *Bolero* remains obstinately popular.

*Jorge Donn of the Ballet du XXième Siècle in* Bolero.

83

# La Boutique Fantasque

*Ballet in two scenes. Music by Gioacchino Rossini, arranged by Ottorino Respighi. Choreography by Leonide Massine. Scenery and costumes by André Derain. First performed by Diaghilev's Ballets Russes at the Alhambra Theatre, London, on June 5, 1919, with Enrico Cecchetti as the Shopkeeper, Leonide Massine and Lydia Lopokova as the cancan dancers.*

*Moira Shearer and Leonide Massine as the cancan dancers surrounded by children in Massine's revival of* La Boutique Fantasque *for the Sadler's Wells Ballet in 1947.*

*La Boutique Fantasque*, one of the happiest of Massine's ballets, was the outcome of the wartime visits to Italy by Diaghilev and his entourage, which also produced another comedy work, *Les Femmes de Bonne Humeur* ("The Good-Humoured Ladies"). The idea of dolls coming alive is not a new one in ballet; Massine's ebullient treatment of it, and the combination of vivacity and true feelings in *Boutique*, make it an enduring masterpiece. One of its great attractions also is the inspired orchestration and arrangement of late Rossini piano pieces by Respighi. Revived by Massine for the Sadler's Wells Ballet when he came as a guest to Covent Garden in 1947, *Boutique* has remained in the repertory of The Royal Ballet ever since. It is also staged by the Ballet-Théâtre Français in Nancy.

SYNOPSIS

*Scene 1*
*A toyshop overlooking the Bay of Naples*

The shopkeeper and his assistant open the store and drive out an urchin who is trying to steal money. Prospective customers arrive, led by two English spinsters, followed by an American couple and their two small children and a Russian father and mother with their four daughters and son. The shopkeeper displays his toys: tarantella dancers; four court cards; a snob and a melon seller; a troupe of six cossacks led by a pretty girl; two dancing poodles; and, finally, a pair of cancan dancers. The children clamour for presents and the American family buy the male cancan dancer, while the Russians acquire his partner. The assistant places these two dolls in cylindrical covers and, as the customers leave, the shopkeeper and his assistant settle the books and close up the shop for the night. As midnight sounds the dolls come alive. Their revelry is shadowed by the fact that the cancan pair are to be separated, and, aided by the other toys, they flee.

*Scene 2*

In the morning the shop is reopened and the customers come to collect their purchases. Their fury and amazement that the packages are now empty is rudely interrupted by the irruption of the toys, who invade the shop, harass the customers, and eventually drive everyone out.

# The Cage

*Ballet in one act. Music by Igor Stravinsky (Concerto in D for string orchestra). Choreography by Jerome Robbins. Costumes by Ruth Sobotka. First performed by the New York City Ballet at the City Center, New York, on June 14, 1951, with Nora Kaye, Yvonne Mounsey, Nicholas Magallanes, and Michael Maule.*

*The Cage* had an immense, immediate success. The power of the music, the (then) sensationalism of its subject and style of gesture, and the impact of Nora Kaye, just arrived at the New York City Ballet from Ballet Theatre, all combined to give Jerome Robbins one of his biggest triumphs — and one that still obtains; this ballet has remained in the repertoire for thirty years, and still gives audiences new to it a *frisson* of horror.

The subject — a group of female humans/insects is inducting a novice into its mysteries. Two (male) intruders approach — and, despite a momentary impulse to romance, the female proves once again to be immeasurably deadlier than the male. For the females, Robbins created a brilliant vocabulary of inhuman movement. As he himself writes, "Sometimes the arms, hands, and fingers became pincers, antennae, feelers." But beneath this insectness, disturbing human psychological impulses project themselves — and they are no doubt what have carried the ballet, now that its first shock has diminished. But even thirty years ago, Robbins dismissed the sensationalism of his ballet as its mainspring: "I don't see why some people are so shocked by *The Cage*. If you observe closely you must realize that it is actually no more than the second act of *Giselle* in a contemporary visualization."

SYNOPSIS

In the first movement, the twelve women led by the Queen greet the Novice, who is veiled. The Queen rips the veil from her, and when the first male Intruder enters, demands that the Novice seduce and destroy him, which she easily does. To the second movement, the Novice and the second Intruder perform a love duet, in which she appears to give way to her softer feelings. Or is she only leading him on? Finally, to the urgent, driving third movement, she inflicts the first wounds — and consummates both their love and his death, to the satisfaction of the group, of whom she is now a true member.

# Cakewalk

*Ballet in one act. Music by Louis Moreau Gottschalk, arranged by Hershy Kay. Choreography by Ruthanna Boris. Scenery and costumes by Robert Drew. First performed by the New York City Ballet at the City Center, New York, on June 12, 1951, with Janet Reed, Patricia Wilde, Yvonne Mounsey, Tanaquil LeClercq, Beatrice Tompkins, Herbert Bliss, and Frank Hobi.*

Gottschalk was virtually unknown to the American public when Boris created *Cakewalk*, but the composer had a fan in George Balanchine, who had heard his music played often in Russia. Boris' idea of using a medley of his songs to support a balletic minstrel show proved an inspiration. Gottschalk's melodies and invigorating rhythms are irresistible, and they drive the ballet home free and clear. *Cakewalk* was a matinee staple at the City Ballet for many years and then entered the repertory of the Joffrey Ballet, where it usually induces even nighttime audiences to clap along during the final "gala cakewalk."

Boris' choreography is deftly moulded to a minstrel-show format, its standard bill of fare transformed into a series of cheerful *demi-caractère* variations. Particularly memorable are the ingénue's rendering of a "pathetic ballad" via droopy *pas de bourrée* and the interlocutor's "Sleight of Feet" number, which is casual in tone and exceedingly tricky in content. In the second part of the show the interlocutor becomes a conjuring magician; among his apparitions is the ingénue character, transformed into Hortense, Queen of the Swamp Lilies.

SYNOPSIS

The scene is a showboat, with the dancers seated at various levels of the deck. After a "grand introductory walkaround," several minstrel types perform, concluding with a "skip-away" for all. In the second part the interlocutor-magician, aided by the two endmen of the first part, invoke exotic creatures: Venus, the Three Graces, a wild pony, and lastly Hortense and her dying poet. The third part is a gala cakewalk, "in which all are invited to participate."

*Artists of the Joffrey Ballet in* Cakewalk.

# Carmen

*Ballet in five scenes. Music by Georges Bizet. Libretto by Roland Petit, based upon Bizet's opera. Choreography by Petit. Scenery and costumes by Antoni Clavé. First performed by the Ballets de Paris at the Prince's Theatre, London, on February 21, 1949, with Renée Jeanmaire, Roland Petit, Serge Perrault, and Gordon Hamilton.*

*Carmen* created a sensation at its premiere in London. The electric performance by Jeanmaire (who first cropped her hair ragamuffin fashion for the role and initiated a fashion), the no less potent performance by Petit as José, and the verve of the supporting performances—not least Serge Perrault's wonderful self-importance as Escamillo—were enhanced by designs by Clavé which both astonished and ravished the eye. Clavé knew exactly the effects to be obtained from vivid colours and vivid shapes.

   *Carmen* has been filmed and televised twice, most recently with Jeanmaire and Baryshnikov and the Ballet de Marseille. It is also in the repertory of the Royal Danish Ballet.

   Other balletic versions which batten on Bizet's masterpiece include John Cranko's production (1971) for the Stuttgart Ballet and Alberto Alonso's for the Bolshoi Ballet (1967) later staged also for the Cuban Ballet. In both cases Bizet's music was "rearranged"—an activity which amounted to a brutalisation—but in both cases the ballets were given a certain validity by the interpreters of the title role. Marcia Haydée was a spitfire Carmen in Cranko's production; in Alonso's *Carmen Suite*, Maya Plisetskaya unleashed megatons of temperament.

## SYNOPSIS

**Scene 1**
*A street in Seville*

The passing crowd is amused and amazed by a fight between two girls, workers from the local cigarette factory. Suddenly Don José comes in and separates the antagonists. He is on the point of arresting the victorious Carmen when he is suddenly a victim to her gypsy beauty, and instead of taking her to jail, he makes an assignation with her.

**Scene 2**
*In a tavern*

The customers are a thoroughly suspect crowd. When Don José enters he launches into the stamping Habanera, urged on by the crowd. Carmen now appears and dances seductively. At the end of her solo José is totally besotted and he carries her off to her bedroom above the bar, while the crowd returns to its revels.

**Scene 3**
*Carmen's bedroom the next morning*

José draws the curtains to let in the morning light. He washes, drying his hands on the curtains, then feels the first pangs of jealousy as he observes Carmen looking out into the street. There ensues a torridly erotic pas de deux. Three of Carmen's brigand friends enter and whisper to her. She nods to José and he willingly follows her out.

**Scene 4**
*A back street in Seville*

Carmen and her accomplices, including José, are cloaked and lurking in the darkness. Carmen gives José a dagger and tells him what he must do. A traveller comes by and José stabs him. Carmen and her friends snatch the man's money and flee, with José running after them.

**Scene 5**
*In front of a bullring*

Amid the milling crowd is Carmen, magnificently dressed. Escamillo, the toreador, enters in triumph and is attracted to Carmen when he sees her. Don José observes this, and when the crowd passes into the bullring, he dashes up to Carmen and makes as if to strangle her. There ensues a duel between them as intense as their love-making earlier. José stabs Carmen, and as her body sinks to the ground, cheers of delight come from inside the bullring and there is a rain of hats to celebrate Escamillo's victory. José stands agonised before Carmen's lifeless body.

# Chaconne

*Ballet in one act. Music by Christoph Willibald von Gluck. Choreography by George Balanchine. Costumes by Karinska. First performed by the New York City Ballet at the State Theater, Lincoln Center, on January 22, 1976, with Suzanne Farrell and Peter Martins.*

*Suzanne Farrell and Peter Martins of the New York City Ballet in* Chaconne.

Balanchine originally choreographed Gluck's ballet music in 1963 for a production of the opera *Orpheus and Eurydice* in Hamburg—a production which was revived at the Paris Opéra a decade later. In staging the work for his own company, Balanchine provided a duet for Suzanne Farrell and Peter Martins to open the ballet and then further added an initial *ballabile* for an ensemble the following season. The duet contains hints of the opera's narrative but thereafter the progress of the ballet—which ends with a chaconne—is a series of variations which, by their formal attitudes and devices, expose far more about the physical and emotional effects obtainable in the pre-Romantic opera-ballet than can be gleaned from most reconstructions of those actual dances. In *Chaconne* the theatrical life of the dance is strong, imaginatively stimulating: we understand the spirit of music and movement in Gluck's time. But this is no mere echo of the past. In the great pas de deux that lies at the heart of *Chaconne* Balanchine explores even further the possibilities of today's ballet's response to rococo music, in a profoundly innovative way.

# Checkmate

*Ballet in one act. Music and libretto by Arthur Bliss. Choreography by Ninette de Valois. Scenery and costumes by E. McKnight Kauffer. First performed by the Vic-Wells Ballet at the Théâtre des Champs-Elysées, Paris, on June 15, 1937, with June Brae as the Black Queen, Harold Turner as the Red Knight, and Robert Helpmann as the Red King.*

*Checkmate* is very much a ballet of its time, created when Europe was already darkened by approaching war. The ballet is a surely made commentary about the threats of totalitarianism, and the principal pieces in the game are recognisable as characters. Both score and design are distinguished and still extremely effective in the theatre, and de Valois' choreography reveals, especially in the last section, a skilled adaptation of folk-dance ideas into balletic language.

SYNOPSIS

*Beryl Grey, a notable Black Queen, is seen on the right in this Covent Garden staging from the 1950s. The body of the Red Knight is being borne away; the Red King is despairing on his throne, centre back; on the left, Death stalks the board.*

In a frontcloth scene, Love and Death prepare to play a game of chess. Love backs the red pieces to win, and Death the black.

The setting for the main action is a chess board. The red pawns dance and gradually all the red pieces assemble. Two black knights have already made a sortie and are followed by the Black Queen. Eventually the doddering Red King enters with his queen and from his throne at the back of the stage he directs the forthcoming battle. His pieces are attacked and overcome, and

the battle resolves into a duel between one of the red knights and the Black Queen. The Red Knight holds the advantage and is about to kill the Black Queen when he is unmanned by her beauty. Despite the Red King's commands he cannot kill, and turns away. The Black Queen arms herself with his sword as well as her own, and kills him. He is carried away by other red pieces and Death stalks the board. The Black Queen is triumphant. The Red King finally falls victim to the massed black forces.

# Cinderella

*Ballet in three acts. Music by Serge Prokofiev. Choreography by Frederick Ashton. Scenery and costumes by Jean-Denis Malclès (redesigned by Henry Bardon and David Walker in 1965). First performed by the Sadler's Wells Ballet at the Royal Opera House, Covent Garden, on December 23, 1948, with Moira Shearer as Cinderella; Michael Somes as the Prince; Frederick Ashton and Robert Helpmann as the Ugly Sisters; Pamela May as the Fairy Godmother; Nadia Nerina, Violetta Elvin, Pauline Clayden, and Beryl Grey as the fairies of the seasons; and Alexander Grant as the Jester.*

*Opposite: Moira Shearer as Cinderella on her way to the ball in the original production by the Sadler's Wells Ballet.*

The story of Cinderella has provided a theme for ballets for more than 150 years. There was an early version in London in 1822; Petipa's production was seen in Petersburg in 1893; Mikhail Fokine staged a version for the de Basil company in 1938, beautifully decorated by Natalia Goncharova; and in 1935, Andrée Howard produced a charming but miniature version for the Ballet Rambert. But it was the distinction of the Prokofiev score, written during the wartime years and first produced by Rostislav Zakharov at the Bolshoi Theatre, Moscow, in 1945, with Ulanova as the heroine, and mounted in the next year in Leningrad by Konstantin Sergueyev for Dudinskaya, which attracted Frederick Ashton to the ballet. This *Cinderella* is of great artistic significance. Ashton here created the first English full-length classical ballet. Despite the lack of balance in the musical structure—the first act is too long and the last act is too short, lacking a culminating grand pas de deux—he succeeded in adapting the form of the nineteenth-century full-length ballet to the demands of its new surroundings.

Ashton "naturalised" the story by making use of its pantomime traditions in Britain. The first act depends very much upon the skill of travesty playing for the two Ugly Sisters, who dominate the action. As taken by Ashton and Helpmann for thirty years, the timorous scuttlings of the former and the outrageous bravado of the latter made these characters rich in comic resource and wonderfully contrasted in feeling. In the purely classical inventions Ashton produced superlative writing for the seasonal fairies of the first act and for the corps de ballet of stars and of guests at the ball. The central role, intended for Fonteyn but first taken by Shearer because of Fonteyn's illness, is touched with humour but demands above all the lyric dignity and tenderness that were so inalienably Fonteyn's.

Both the major Soviet versions follow the traditional narrative. They differ from Western productions using this score by incorporating all the music which Prokofiev wrote, notably the travel scene in Act III, in which the Prince searches the world for his beloved, and in making the Ugly Sisters ugly in temperament rather than physique. In other respects the fairy tale remains a fairy tale.

**SYNOPSIS**

*Act I*
*A room in the house of*
*Cinderella's father*

Cinderella is seated by the fire as her Ugly Stepsisters make preparations for a ball that night and squabble. Cinderella's father looks disconsolately on. The sisters go to dress themselves for the ball and Cinderella dreams of going to the ball, from which she has been excluded. She places a candle in front of a picture of her dead mother and weeps in her father's arms. The stepsisters return and nag father and daughter. At this moment an old beggar woman appears and, despite the sisters' rudeness to her, Cinderella gives the old woman a crust. There is something mysterious about the old woman, however, for she strikes the bossier of the stepsisters

dumb in an unforgettable and hilarious moment. Attendants now arrive to dress the sisters in their madcap finery, and a dancing master falls victim to their predatory ways. All depart for the ball. Cinderella is alone and disconsolate. At this moment the old woman returns and is transformed into a fairy godmother. She shows Cinderella a divertissement by the four seasons, and promises that she shall attend the ball, warning her only that she must quit the dance before midnight sounds. A pumpkin is transformed into a coach and Cinderella, her rags exchanged for a ravishing dress, leaves in it for the ball as the curtain falls.

|  |  |  |
|---|---|---|
| *Act II*<br>*The ball* | Guests dance and the Jester leaps among them. The Ugly Sisters arrive *en grande toilette* and are given ill-assorted partners. The Prince arrives and shortly afterwards Cinderella makes her wondering entrance. Of course the Prince falls in love with her, and their bliss is | celebrated in a pas de deux. But midnight has caught Cinderella unawares. As the clock chimes she makes a desperate attempt to leave, and on the last stroke the ragged little figure runs from the scene, leaving a slipper behind. |
| *Act III*<br>*The house of*<br>*Cinderella's father* | An entr'acte shows Cinderella rushing home, the Ugly Sisters tottering homeward, and the Prince and his jester in pursuit of the mysterious beauty. Once more at the hearth, Cinderella wonders if she has been dreaming, but a jewelled slipper in her pocket tells her that what seemed a fantasy has been reality. The sisters return and recount their adventures. As they sit in hideous *déshabillé* the arrival of the Prince is announced. | They claw themselves back into their glad rags and determinedly try and fit on the slipper which the jester shows as clue to the identity of the Prince's lost love. But to no avail. Cinderella comes forward and her dance shoe slips from her pocket. The Prince recognises it as twin to the shoe he holds and also recognises Cinderella. The sisters are forgiven and hobble away. The Prince and Cinderella are blessed by the fairies and happily united. |

Opposite: *Sir Robert
Helpmann and Sir
Frederick Ashton as the
Ugly Sisters* en grande
toilette *at the ball.*

Above: *Merle Park in
Ashton's* Cinderella *for
The Royal Ballet. She is
dancing in the first-act
variation, when Cinderella
dreams of going to the ball.*

# Con Amore

*Ballet in one act. Music by Gioacchino Rossini. Libretto by James Graham-Luján. Choreography by Lew Christensen. Scenery and costumes by James Bodrero. First performed by the San Francisco Ballet at the War Memorial Opera House, San Francisco, on March 10, 1953, with Sally Bailey, Nancy Johnson, and Leon Danielian.*

Lew Christensen is that rarity among choreographers, a humourist. The special delight of *Con Amore* is that it encapsulates the clichés of nineteenth-century farce without being a cliché itself. Its bubbly pace and bustling plot line (three plots, actually) are fun in themselves and fun as commentary on Rossini, three of whose overtures are used: *La Gazza Ladra*, *Il Signor Bruschino*, and *La Scala di Seta*. Christensen develops each story with just the right amount of snap, breaks it off with a blackout at just the crucial moment, and ties it all together with just the right degree of implausibility.

Although *Con Amore* has always been associated with the San Francisco Ballet, of which Christensen is co-director, it had a healthy run at the New York City Ballet in the 1950s, with Edward Villella as a splendid bandit.

SYNOPSIS

*Scene 1*
*The Amazons and the Bandit*

While a company of Amazon soldiers drill in the woods, a bandit enters. He happens to be a virtuoso dancer as well, and so wins the captain's heart. He has no use for love, however. The soldiers capture him and the captain is about to shoot him when . . .

*Scene 2*
*The Husband's Return*

A rich lady receives a few too many lovers while her husband is out for the evening. Just as they come out from their hiding places, the husband returns. He is about to do something dreadful when . . .

*Scene 3*
*The Triumph of Love*

Amore visits the scene of each predicament. With her arrows she insures that everyone wins the heart of his or her desire.

Con Amore, *as performed by the New York City Ballet.*

# The Concert

*Ballet in one act. Music by Frédéric Chopin. Choreography by Jerome Robbins. Costumes by Irene Sharaff. First performed by the New York City Ballet at the City Center, New York, on March 6, 1956. Presented by The Royal Ballet on March 4, 1975, with two frontcloths by Edward Gorey.*

*The Concert* is a unique work in that its jokes are ever-fresh. No matter how many times we see the sextet of girls, for example, whose every convolution is marked by a hilarious mistake, the humour is bright and never ceases to amaze by its variety. Only at one moment—in the "Raindrop Prelude"—does comedy give way to a moment of quiet charm, which throws the zany finale into even greater relief.

SYNOPSIS

Subtitled *The Perils of Everybody*, the ballet presents an exteriorisation of the fantasies of people listening to a concert of Chopin music and of the dreadful winsomeness that is sometimes associated with it. A pianist enters, dusts the piano, and settles down to play as an audience assembles: a quiet man, a gloweringly intense girl, a pretty girl with a big hat, two dimwitted girls with rustling candy wrappers, a domineering lady with her husband, and finally a bemused young man with a ticket but no chair, all of whom are eventually accommodated. Then fantasy supervenes. The hen-pecked husband becomes a dashing hussar lusting after the girl with the hat; he also tries to stab his wife to the music of the sacrosanct *Sylphides* Prelude. More dancers appear and six girls are seen in a demure classical number in which one or another is always agonising out of step with her companions; a clogged ensemble finds a girl left holding a disembodied hand; a woman tries on hats and then meets another woman wearing the bonnet she has ultimately chosen; to the "Raindrop" Prelude the cast shelter under umbrellas; and finally everyone turns into butterflies, at which moment the outraged pianist turns into a lepidopterist and pursues them with a net. The curtain falls as the decorum of the concert room reasserts itself.

*lia Peters and Bart Cook*
*he New York City Ballet*
*The Concert.*

# Concerto

*Ballet in one act. Music by Dmitri Shostakovich (Piano Concerto No. 2). Choreography by Kenneth MacMillan. Scenery and costumes by Jürgen Rose. First performed by the Berlin Opera Ballet at the Deutsche Oper, West Berlin, on November 30, 1966, with Lynn Seymour.*

*Natalia Makarova and Donald MacLeary in the last movement of* Concerto *with The Royal Ballet.*

Kenneth MacMillan made *Concerto* soon after he arrived in Berlin to take up the direction of the Deutsche Oper Ballet. His intention was to produce a ballet—using the concerto that Shostakovich wrote for his son Maxim and the Moscow Youth Orchestra—which would help sharpen the classical work of his somewhat raw Berlin dancers. The ballet thus insists upon precision of corps de ballet work and a clear academic style. In the central movement MacMillan was inspired by the sight of Lynn Seymour, who had joined him in Berlin, warming up in class and practising *ports de bras* at the barre. The initial image of the lovely duet is of the female dancer doing just this, and from it evolves a sequence of movement which reflects the mood of Shostakovich's beautiful adagio.

The ballet was taken into the repertory of American Ballet Theatre in 1967 and in the same year was acquired by The Royal Ballet. It is now in the repertory of several other companies as well.

SYNOPSIS

*Concerto* is a plotless ballet in three movements. The mood of the first is joyful, with a male and female soloist leading the bright activities of three other couples and a supporting group of six girls. The lyrical second movement is a pas de deux with the three couples from the first movement who mirror some of the actions of the central pair. The third movement is introduced by a brilliant variation for a female dancer. A large corps de ballet then enters and the other dancers in the work join in the ebullient finale.

# Concerto Barocco

*Ballet in one act. Music by Johann Sebastian Bach. Choreography by George Balanchine. Scenery and costumes by Eugene Berman. First performed by American Ballet Caravan at Hunter College, New York, on May 29, 1941, with Marie-Jeanne, Mary Jane Shea, and William Dollar.*

*Suzanne Farrell and Kyra Nichols with artists of the New York City Ballet in Concerto Barocco.*

Set to Bach's Double Violin Concerto in D Minor, *Concerto Barocco* is the quintessential Balanchine ballet of its period, its manner entirely pure, its choreography no more (and no less) than an ideal response to its score. "If the dance designer sees in the development of classical dancing a counterpart in the development of music and has studied them both, he will derive continual inspiration from great scores." Thus Balanchine, discussing *Concerto Barocco*, and it is the most fitting comment upon this ballet. In the first movement of the concerto the two ballerinas may be understood to incarnate the violins while a corps de ballet of eight girls accompany them. In the second movement, the largo, the male dancer joins the leading female in a duet. In the final allegro the bright rhythms of the score inspire no less bright dancing in which Balanchine's classicism reflects exactly the syncopations and rhythmic vitality of the music.

Since 1951 *Concerto Barocco* has been danced in practice costume and without décor. It is today in the repertories of many companies, all of whom present it in similar undress.

# Coppélia

*Ballet in three acts. Music by Léo Delibes. Libretto by Charles Nuitter and Arthur Saint-Léon. Choreography by Saint-Léon. Scenery by Cambon, Despléchin, and Lavastre. Costumes by Paul Lormier. First performed at the Paris Opéra, on May 25, 1870, with Giuseppina Bozzacchi as Swanilda, Eugénie Fiocre as Franz, and Edouard Dauty as Dr. Coppélius.*

*Opposite: Inside Dr. Coppélius' workshop, in the New York City Ballet staging of* Coppélia, *Patricia McBride is seen as Swanilda with Shaun O'Brien as Coppélius. The sleeping Franz on the right is Helgi Tomasson.*

*Coppélia* is the last flower of the Romantic ballet, a masterpiece staged in the tragic summer that saw the end of the Second Empire. It was the final work produced by Arthur Saint-Léon (1815–1870), dancer, violinist, choreographer, and dance theoretician, whose career culminated in the decade of the 1860s when he was chief choreographer to the Imperial Ballet in St. Petersburg and also producer of several major works at the Paris Opéra. Delibes' superlative score was a commission which resulted from his success in contributing two scenes to an earlier Saint-Léon ballet, *La Source* of 1866. The role of Swanilda was entrusted to an exceptionally gifted Italian girl, Giuseppina Bozzacchi, who had been discovered at the age of fourteen in a Paris dancing class. When Saint-Léon's first choice, the outstanding ballerina Adèle Granzow, was unable to take the role, little Bozzacchi was groomed for a part which she created in her sixteenth year to immense acclaim. The outbreak of the Franco-Prussian war closed the Opéra; the subsequent hardships of the siege of Paris brought epidemics, and Bozzacchi died of smallpox on the morning of her seventeenth birthday. Saint-Léon, too, died in that same year, and before *Coppélia* celebrated its first birthday, Dauty, creator of the role of Coppélius, was also dead. The ballet was subsequently revived and, in various recensions, preserved at the Paris Opéra where, until the 1950s, the role of Franz was still retained as a travesty part. Most recently in Paris the 1973 production by Pierre Lacotte returned to the original sets and costumes and something like the original style.

The majority of Western stagings spring from the text established in St. Petersburg in 1884 by Petipa, which was extensively revised by Enrico Cecchetti ten years later. Reproduced for the Vic-Wells Ballet in 1934 by Nikolay Sergueyev, this basic text has been preserved by The Royal Ballet and is now given in an edition by Peter Wright. During the 1930s and 1940s *Coppélia*'s popularity was also manifest in the stagings presented by the various Ballet Russe companies, which had in Alexandra Danilova a supremely witty and enchanting interpreter of Swanilda.

Madame Danilova's association with the New York City Ballet has given that company a text for the first two acts which is very traditional. However, the third-act festivities have been rechoreographed, in this case by George Balanchine. The production, with designs by Rouben Ter-Arutunian, was first seen on July 17, 1974, in Saratoga Springs.

Many companies have versions of *Coppélia* which make various emendations to the basic outline described in the synopsis, but none of these departs from the traditional story line.

SYNOPSIS

## Act I

*A square in a small Galician town*

On one side of the square there is an inn and adjoining it the house where Swanilda lives; facing is the house and workshop of Dr. Coppélius. At curtain rise we see Dr. Coppélius, a toy-maker and scientist, placing the doll Coppélia at an open window of his house. Swanilda comes out into the square and, seeing the doll, greets her, for she believes her to be real. So does the young peasant boy Franz, who, although supposedly in love with Swanilda, has a roving eye. Dr. Coppélius contrives to make the doll throw a kiss to Franz, who is enraptured by her. Peasant boys and girls come on and the Burgomaster announces that at the dedication of a new bell each betrothed couple will receive a dowry. Swanilda seeks to test Franz's fidelity with an ear of corn: if the grains within it rattle, she will marry him. Alas, this seems not to be so and she leaves in tears. After some general dancing the peasant boys and girls disperse, and old Coppélius emerges from his house to go across to the inn for a drink. He locks the door of the house carefully, but a group of local lads start to make fun of him and after some skirmishing Coppélius is rescued by the innkeeper; as he mops his brow the key to his house falls unobserved to the ground.

Swanilda and her friends return to the square, discover the key, realise the door it fits, and determine to go and see the unknown girl who has been sitting immobile at Coppélius' window. Stealthily they enter the house. At the same time, Franz appears with a ladder: he proposes climbing up to the balcony to keep an assignation with the mysterious beauty. He is alarmed to see Coppélius return seeking his door key: dismayed, the old man sees his front door open and enters in pursuit of the intruders. Franz returns to the empty square, places his ladder against the balcony, and starts to climb as the curtain falls.

## Act II

*The workshop of Dr. Coppélius*

Swanilda and her friends enter the darkened chamber. They are terrified to discover mysterious figures lurking in the shadows, but are relieved when they find them to be automata. They are also vastly amused when, eventually, they bring out the mysterious beauty from a curtained alcove and discover that she too is nothing but a doll: Coppélia, the old scientist's newest creation. Suddenly Coppélius bursts in. The girls scatter and Swanilda takes refuge behind the curtain with Coppélia as her friends are driven out. As Coppélius settles down to survey the disorder, he is suddenly alerted to the presence of Franz, who creeps in by way of the window. When Coppélius confronts him, Franz admits that he has come to court Coppélia. The old man realises that he may profit from Franz's delusion about Coppélia. He gives the boy drugged wine and now brings out the doll from the alcove and prepares an alchemical experiment whereby he will transfer the life force from Franz to his beloved doll. What he has not realised is that Swanilda has taken the place of the doll, and the first success of his experiments in making the doll move enthralls him. His final success comes when he thinks that a heart and feeling have been warmed in the doll, and in a moment of beautiful seriousness, both musical and dramatic, he rejoices that his dream has come true. But the spirit of comedy reasserts itself as Swanilda starts to get out of hand. She demands to know the precise nature of all the dolls, and of the recumbent figure of Franz, and to distract her attentions Coppélius makes her dance a Scottish gigue and a Spanish dance. But Swanilda is not to be deterred, and she eventually succeeds in rousing Franz. As he comes to his senses, Swanilda wheels out the dummy Coppélia, whose dress she has been wearing, and, heartlessly mocking the old man, she and Franz go down to join their friends in the square while Dr. Coppélius grieves.

## Act III

*The square*

The peasants assemble for the festivities to mark the arrival of the new bell in the town. The local lord distributes dowries to happy couples, who now include the united Swanilda and Franz. Coppélius is awarded a purse of gold to compensate for the damage which has been done to his workshop. There is a divertissement which culminates in a grand pas de deux for Swanilda and Franz, and a final galop.

*Roland Petit as Coppélius with Karen Kain as Swanilda in the second act of his production for the Ballet de Marseille.*

## Ballet de Marseille

*Ballet in two acts.
Music by
Léo Delibes.
Choreography by
Roland Petit.
Scenery and costumes by
Ezio Frigerio.
First performed at the
Théâtre des Champs-
Elysées, Paris, on
September 18, 1975.*

In a programme note, Roland Petit observes: "The main idea is simple. Coppélia is created by Coppélius in Swanilda's likeness. Coppélius loves Swanilda. By running away from Swanilda it is in fact still Swanilda whom Franz seeks. And will find. All bliss is woven out of infidelities. . . . Every interpretation is both a sacrilege and a homage." Roland Petit's rethinking of *Coppélia* is a brilliant revision of an old classic. More Hoffmannesque than any other production (the original tale was adapted from one of E. T. A. Hoffmann's stories), it becomes a narrative about the heart's affections rather than a story about an old alchemist. Against a background of deliberately caricatured dances for soldiers and their girls, who become no more than doll-like backing for the action, the main characters have a resonance and wit to their choreography that make for irresistible pleasure in the theatre. In the first performance Karen Kain danced Swanilda, Roland Petit, Coppélius, and Denys Ganio, Franz. In the central role of Coppélius, Roland Petit gives a flawless performance as a man of elegance and true emotion.

In Act I, which takes place in a square in front of a barracks, the girls of the town are much occupied with the young soldiers. On a nearby balcony a mysterious girl hides her face behind a fan. Swanilda loves Franz and tells him of her love. But he looks at the girl on the balcony.

Coppélius, a middle-aged man about town, comes into the square and watches Swanilda, who looks at Franz, who looks at Coppélia, Coppélius' automaton, on the balcony. Coppélius drops the key of his house. Swanilda picks it up and enters with her friends. Franz, fascinated by Coppélia, decides to join her on the balcony.

In Act II, inside Coppélius' house, a table is laid for two. Swanilda enters and discovers that Coppélius makes automata. She is amazed to discover that Coppélia has a face exactly modelled on her own: Coppélius must be in love with her. She hides when Coppélius returns, and watches as he sits down and dines with the doll Coppélia, and then dances with her. Then, as he hears a noise made by Franz, Coppélius hides the doll behind a screen. Franz enters, is drugged, and Coppélius tries to transfer the young man's soul into the doll. To his amazement the doll appears, animated, from behind the screen. It is, of course, Swanilda. She dances, then awakens Franz, and Coppélius is eventually undeceived and stands amid the relics of his broken automaton. Franz realises that he loves Swanilda. The scene swiftly changes and the action is again in the square. Soldiers and their girls are happy; Swanilda is for a moment torn between Franz and Coppélius, but she turns to her young lover and Coppélius breaks his doll and at the end is left alone.

# Dances at a Gathering

*Ballet in one act. Music by Frédéric Chopin. Choreography by Jerome Robbins. Costumes by Joe Eula. First performed by the New York City Ballet at the State Theater, Lincoln Center, on May 8, 1969, with Allegra Kent, Sara Leland, Kay Mazzo, Patricia McBride, Violette Verdy, Anthony Blum, John Clifford, Robert Maiorano, John Prinz, and Edward Villella.*

In a letter to the New York magazine *Ballet Review*, then edited by its founder, Arlene Croce, Jerome Robbins said: "For the record, would you please print in large, emphatic, and capital letters the following: THERE ARE NO STORIES TO ANY OF THE DANCES IN *DANCES AT A GATHERING*. THERE ARE NO PLOTS AND NO ROLES. THE DANCERS ARE THEMSELVES DANCING WITH EACH OTHER TO THAT MUSIC IN THAT SPACE. Thank you very much." This *cri de coeur* was evidently prompted by the elaborate interpretations which had been imposed upon this set of dances from its very first performance. Because *Dances at a Gathering* had excited such enthusiasm, writers had inevitably sought to "interpret" Robbins' realisation of Chopin's piano music, and it must be said that there are strong emotional relationships existing between the performers. But there is no overriding theme, other than Robbins' own delightful response to the Chopin piano music and to the five women and five men for whom he made the ballet.

The work started from the idea of a pas de deux for McBride and Villella, and like Topsy "just growed" until it reached the sequence of eighteen numbers which comprise the final text.

*Dances at a Gathering* is a beautiful ballet that is simply about dancing. Robbins seems to find an ideal realisation of Chopin's pianistic manner in dancing, and the strong Polish character of the music is echoed by use of mazurka steps which serve to point out the refinement of the academic language. The way in which Chopin adapted national elements to the elegance of piano virtuoso writing is matched by Robbins' way of flavouring the classical academic style.

The work is ideally seen in performance by the New York City Ballet, who avoid any of the sentimentality and dramatic caprices which can cloud the choreography.

SYNOPSIS

Mazurka, Op. 63, No. 3: a male dancer enters walking; he dances and then leaves. Waltz, Op. 69, No. 2: a man and a woman dance together. Mazurka, Op. 33, No. 3: a lyrical, drifting duet for another couple. Mazurka, Op. 6, No. 4. A quickly moving solo for a girl who is then joined gradually by two men and two more girls and eventually another man, so that these six dancers are involved in ever-changing relationships to four more Mazurkas: Op. 7, Nos. 5 and 4, Op. 24, No. 2, and Op. 6, No. 2. The men go after one girl and then another, and the ensemble finally forms a series of groupings as if posing for family photographs. To the Waltz, Op. 42, a man and a woman are seen rivalling each other rather after the fashion of "Anything You Can Do I Can Do Better." They leave, the girl carried off on his shoulders, and three girls enter to the Waltz, Op. 34, No. 2. The Mazurka, Op. 56, No. 2, is a contest between two men who vie with each other, and try to upstage each other.

The Etude, Op. 25, No. 4, is a solo for a girl, and there follows a brilliant sextet to the Waltz, Op. 34, No. 1, which ends with the three girls being thrown ecstatically into the arms of their partners. The next Waltz, Op. 70, No. 2, finds a girl dancing alone. She tries to make each of three men dance with her in turn, but they are oblivious. To the Etude, Op. 25, No. 5, there is a duet and in the next Etude, Op. 10, No. 2, the male dancer has a brilliant solo. A darker mood is established with the first stormy notes of the Scherzo, Op. 20, No. 1, in which three women and three men are involved in intense emotional exchanges. Finally to the Nocturne, Op. 15, No. 1, the entire cast assemble on stage. They watch the sky, perhaps seeing a thunderstorm pass over; then the man who first entered places his hand on the ground. The dancers bow to each other and then link up in pairs as the curtain falls.

*Patricia McBride and Helgi Tomasson of the New York City Ballet in Jerome Robbins' Dances at a Gathering.*

# Dark Elegies

*Ballet in two scenes. Music by Gustav Mahler. Choreography by Antony Tudor. Scenery and costumes by Nadia Benois. First performed by the Ballet Rambert at the Duchess Theatre, London, on February 19, 1937, with Maude Lloyd, Antony Tudor, Walter Gore, John Byron, Agnes de Mille, Hugh Laing, Daphne Gow, Ann Gee, Patricia Clogstoun, Beryl Kay, and Celia Franca.*

*Dancers of the Ballet Rambert in the 1980 revival by Sally Gilmour of Tudor's* Dark Elegies. *Lucy Burge and Yair Vardi are the central couple.*

*Dark Elegies*, with no specific references, has always seemed a summation of grief at the loss of a child's life. The dances have a beautiful inevitability. At the end of the ballet the audience senses the depth of emotion that has been felt by the dancers. *Dark Elegies*, one of the great achievements of the young Ballet Rambert, has also been revived by Tudor for American Ballet Theatre, the National Ballet of Canada, and the Royal Swedish Ballet. In November 1980 *Dark Elegies* entered the repertory of The Royal Ballet.

SYNOPSIS The first scene of the ballet presents us with a group of simply clad men and women against a rocky, storm-tossed setting which suggests a coastal village. At one side of the stage a man similarly dressed is seated on a low stool as he sings the Mahler cycle—*Songs on the Death of Children*—which is a lament of bereaved parents. Singly, in pairs, or in groups, the dancers perform movement that will reveal the depths of their suffering. Before the final song they perform a round dance. As the last song begins, the scenery changes to a calmer landscape and the community finally walks quietly off in pairs, followed by the singer.

# Don Quixote

*Ballet in four acts and a prologue. Music by Ludwig Minkus. Libretto and choreography by Marius Petipa. First performed at the Bolshoi Theatre, Moscow, on December 26, 1869, with Anna Sobeshchanskaya as Kitri. Revived at the Bolshoi Theatre, St. Petersburg, on November 21, 1871, with Alexandra Vergina as Kitri and Lev Ivanov as Basil.*

The story of *Don Quixote*, or at least its narrative outline, has attracted choreographers since the days of Noverre. It was, however, the version which Marius Petipa staged in Moscow in 1869 that has provided a theatrically valid version which persists to this day. This Moscow staging was notable for its dramatic liveliness. When, two years later, Petipa produced the work in St. Petersburg it became altogether grander and less vivid in manner. It is to Moscow that we look for the perpetuation of this old ballet with its jolly score, for the Moscow ballet master Alexander Gorsky provided a much more dramatic and lively recension for the Bolshoi company in that city in December 1900 and it is this production which has persisted in the Soviet repertory and which is the basis for versions produced in the West. The best known of these is now that staged by Rudolf Nureyev for the Vienna Ballet in 1966 and subsequently revived for the Australian Ballet in 1970, both with designs by Barry Kay, while for a later Zürich Ballet version Nicholas Georgiadis provided the designs. Both Ballet Rambert and London Festival Ballet had versions produced for them by the Polish ballet master Witold Borkowski, and in 1978 Mikhail Baryshnikov produced his version for American Ballet Theatre with designs by Santo Loquasto (first given on May 2, 1978, at the Metropolitan Opera House, New York, with Gelsey Kirkland as Kitri and Baryshnikov as Basil). In this presentation Baryshnikov reversed the usual order of the tavern and the gypsy camp scenes so that the second act ends with Kitri and Basil tricking her father into allowing their marriage. Throughout, Baryshnikov tried to rationalise the bizarre and improbable incidents that have ever been part of the fabric of *Don Quixote*.

An important and completely different staging in three acts was made by George Balanchine for the New York City Ballet in 1965. This had a new score from Nicolas Nabokov, designs by Esteban Francés, and featured Suzanne Farrell as Dulcinea and Balanchine himself as the Don. The production was in every way a serious attempt to create a danced drama from incidents in Cervantes' novel.

There have been many other ballets inspired by themes from the novel; none has survived.

| | | |
|---|---|---|
| SYNOPSIS | | |
| *Prologue*<br>*Don Quixote's study* | The Don appears, reading a book of chivalry. He is lost in dreams and thinks he sees a vision of the fair Dulcinea, his ideal beloved. Sancho Panza enters, pursued by servants | from whom he has stolen a goose. The Don protects him and makes Sancho his servant for the adventures he intends seeking in the world. |
| *Act I*<br>*The marketplace in Barcelona* | Kitri, daughter of an innkeeper, is in love with the barber Basil. Kitri's father wishes her to marry the aristocratic ninny Gamache. Don | Quixote and Sancho Panza enter and amid general rejoicings the Don mistakes Kitri for Dulcinea. Kitri and Basil flee. |

| | | |
|---|---|---|
| *Act II, Scene 1*<br>*Inside a tavern* | Kitri and Basil join in the dances given by a troupe of merrymakers. Kitri's parents come in pursuit of their daughter and discover her. Basil | pretends to kill himself and somehow dupes Kitri's parents into allowing her to be betrothed to him. |
| *Scene 2*<br>*A gypsy encampment* | Outside a village near some windmills, gypsies and strolling players are encamped. Don Quixote and Sancho Panza appear and after some dances they are shown a puppet play in which the Don imagines the heroine is Dulcinea. He is so bemused that he | starts to fight the puppets and then mistakes the nearby windmills for giants, which he attacks with his lance. He is somewhat battered by the encounter and falls senseless at Sancho's feet. |
| *Act III*<br>*An enchanted forest* | The Don sees a vision of nymphs who surround Dulcinea, and watches them perform a classical ensemble. | |
| *Act IV*<br>*Inside a palace* | The local duke is giving a fiesta. The Don is still bemused and thinks that a maiden being protected by a mysterious knight is his Dulcinea. He challenges the knight to single combat and is defeated. The victorious knight | is revealed as Basil. He and Kitri now perform the final grand pas de deux amid a general dance, and as the lovers are united, the Don and his servant leave in search of further adventures. |

Opposite: *Suzanne Farrell as Dulcinea in George Balanchine's production of* Don Quixote.

Right: *Gelsey Kirkland as Kitri in Mikhail Baryshnikov's staging of* Don Quixote *for American Ballet Theatre.*

# The Dream

*Ballet in one act. Music by Felix Mendelssohn, arranged by John Lanchbery. Choreography by Frederick Ashton, based upon Shakespeare's* A Midsummer Night's Dream. *Scenery by Henry Bardon. Costumes by David Walker. First performed by The Royal Ballet at the Royal Opera House, Covent Garden, on April 2, 1964, with Antoinette Sibley as Titania, Anthony Dowell as Oberon, Keith Martin as Puck, and Alexander Grant as Bottom.*

In 1964, for the quatercentenary celebrations of Shakespeare's birth, The Royal Ballet put on a Shakespearean triple bill. It consisted of a revival of Helpmann's *Hamlet*; *Images of Love*, a new ballet by Kenneth MacMillan; and Ashton's *The Dream*. Inspired by the Victorian felicities of Mendelssohn's incidental music to the play, and by memories of Tyrone Guthrie's Old Vic production in 1937 with designs by Oliver Messel, Ashton decided upon a "Victorian" depiction of the central incidents of the play. The ballet totally captures the spirit of the play both in the airy poetry of the fairy scenes and in the delicious comedy of the lovers' quarrels and Bottom's caperings. The ballet was also important in that it launched the partnership of Antoinette Sibley and Anthony Dowell.

SYNOPSIS

In a wood outside Athens Oberon and Titania are quarrelling because Titania refuses to give a changeling Indian boy into the keeping of Oberon. To avenge himself on her, Oberon despatches Puck to fetch a magic flower whose juice, when dropped on the eyes of a sleeping person, will cause him to fall in love with the first person he sees on waking, for Oberon intends to humiliate Titania by making her fall in love with some ridiculous creature. To the sound of the lullaby "Ye spotted snakes" Titania goes to sleep in a bower. Oberon anoints her eyes with the juice of the flower and waits in the shadows.

Two pairs of lovers now appear: first Lysander and Hermia, who are happy in their love; next Helena and Demetrius, she pursuing, he fleeing. Puck comes across the sleeping Hermia and Lysander. Mistaking Oberon's instructions—the fairy king wished to unite the unhappy lovers—Puck squeezes the flower on Lysander's eyes. Helena and Demetrius return; Helena stumbles over Lysander, who is immediately infatuated with her. The lovers are set at odds and leave the scene. Then enter the "rude mechanicals": Bottom

the weaver and his friends, who have come to rehearse a play.

Puck puts an ass's head on Bottom and his companions flee in terror. Titania awakes and straightaway loves the ass. She and her attendants deck Bottom with garlands and she takes him to her bower. Oberon realises Puck's mistake; he conjures up a mist in which the four lovers are properly paired off, and the juice is used again so that when they awake in the morning Lysander will love Hermia and Demetrius will succumb to Helena. There follows a bravura passage of dancing for Oberon and Puck and four fairies, to the Scherzo from Mendelssohn's score. Titania is awakened and shown Bottom with his ass's head. She is reconciled with Oberon and cedes him the Indian boy. They leave the stage. Bottom is woken by Puck, who removes the ass's head, and he ponders on his dream. The lovers are now woken and happily united. Oberon and Titania return for a culminating pas de deux to Mendelssohn's great Nocturne, in which they are seen ecstatically together. The final curtain, as in the play, is for the mocking Puck.

*posite: Anthony
vell as Oberon surveys
esotted Titania
toinette Sibley), with
om in his ass's head
xander Grant). This is
sed photograph of the
artists who created the
; the pose does not occur
e ballet.*

# Duo Concertant

*Ballet in one act. Music by Igor Stravinsky. Choreography by George Balanchine. First performed by the New York City Ballet at the State Theater, Lincoln Center, on June 22, 1972, with Kay Mazzo and Peter Martins.*

The 1972 Stravinsky Festival, the summation of the Balanchine-Stravinsky collaboration, produced several very important works. *Duo Concertant*, by no means a large work, in its succinct yet oddly relaxed power (much implied, little stressed) is one of the most piercing comments upon the pas de deux as Balanchine has developed it.

At curtain rise we see the two dancers standing behind the piano (the musicians are placed at the side of the stage, to the audience's left). The dancers listen intently to the music, and after the first movement they seem seized by the score and start very gently to dance. The music's hold strengthens and their duet becomes tender and easy in manner. Occasionally they again listen, stationary, to the music, and their personalities seem happy and relaxed. But with the final movement, the Dithyrambe, the mood changes. The stage is darkened and the musicians spotlit, while another spot isolates the dancers. Tightly focused, the light catches the girl's hand—her gesture seems to hang in the air—and when eventually the male dancer kisses her hand he seems a creator saluting his Muse. At one moment it appears that he has lost her in the darkness of the stage, but she returns to him and the last moments unite them as if music and dance had found each other finally and perfectly—as they do in this ballet.

*Kay Mazzo and Peter Martins in* Duo Concertant, *created for them by Balanchine in 1972.*

# The Dying Swan

*Ballet solo. Music by Charles Camille Saint-Saëns (from* Carnival des Animaux*). Choreography by Mikhail Fokine. First produced at the Hall of Nobles, St. Petersburg, on December 22, 1907, with Anna Pavlova.*

The genesis of this, the most famous ballet solo in the world, was Pavlova's desire for a short dance to perform at a charity concert. Fokine records that he was so fond of the music and so impressed by the possibility of presenting Pavlova in a swan dance that he quickly devised this simple but extraordinary solo. Fokine described its creation as "almost an improvisation" as he and Pavlova worked together in a rehearsal room. The result was a dance based entirely on *pas de bourrée*, with the swan's movements becoming ever more faltering, until finally she expires. Pavlova's relentless touring meant that this solo became intimately associated with the image of the great star ballerina. She performed it countless times throughout the world, and though her version strayed from the original Fokine concept, it nevertheless always retained the extreme poetic intensity which Pavlova gave it and which has been partly preserved on film. Inevitably Pavlova had her imitators. The image of a ballerina became the image of a "dying swan," and Dame Ninette de Valois records that as a child dancer before the First World War, she danced *The Dying Swan*—"dying twice nightly on all the coastal piers, for my 'death' was always ferociously encored."

Since Pavlova's death nearly every great ballerina has essayed the swan's *bourrées*. The range of interpretation has varied widely—we would cite the contrasting interpretations of Galina Ulanova (happily preserved on film) and of Maya Plisetskaya. In the West, Alicia Markova learned the role from Fokine at his request, and her performances preserved the authentic image; this, too, has been fortunately saved for posterity on film.

*Maya Plisetskaya as the Dying Swan.*

# Echoing of Trumpets

*Ballet in one act. Music by Bohuslav Martinů (Fantaisies Symphoniques). Libretto and choreography by Antony Tudor. Scenery and costumes by Birger Bergling. First performed by the Royal Swedish Ballet at the Royal Theatre, Stockholm, on September 28, 1963, with Gerd Andersson, Svante Lindberg, A. Widersheim-Paul, and M. Mengarelli.*

After a period in which he had produced little major choreography Tudor, who was then working in Stockholm, found in this theme inspiration for a drama which once again explored the dreadful cruelties of man's inhumanity to man. As with *Dark Elegies* the incident is not specific—Tudor has denied the widely voiced assumption when the ballet was new that the action reflected the Lidice massacre—but it has a universal and terrible relevance. Staged for various companies, *Echoing of Trumpets* is still regularly performed by London Festival Ballet.

SYNOPSIS

Echoing of Trumpets *in the staging by Antony Tudor for London Festival Ballet. The fugitive is beaten up by the soldiers.*

The setting is a village ravaged by war. The action of this ballet is tragic and, tragically, can be seen as a constantly repeating incident wherever a country is at war and under the domination of an invading force. The women of the village grieve as the occupying soldiery move among them. The soldiers are unconcerned by the women's suffering. A partisan returns to see his wife. He is discovered by the soldiers and executed. His wife, inconsolable, clasps his body and dances a lament.

# Elite Syncopations

*Ballet in one act. Music by Scott Joplin, Paul Pratt, James Scott, Joseph F. Lamb, Max Morath, Donald Ashwander, and Robert Hampton, in various arrangements. Choreography by Kenneth MacMillan. Costumes by Ian Spurling. First performed by The Royal Ballet at the Royal Opera House, Covent Garden, on October 7, 1974, with Merle Park, David Wall, Monica Mason, Michael Coleman, Vergie Derman, and Wayne Sleep.*

*Peter Schaufuss in the National Ballet of Canada's production of* Elite Syncopations.

*Elite Syncopations* is a product of the ragtime boom of the early 1970s, a series of madcap moments in which The Royal Ballet lets its corporate hair down. The stage is opened up to the back wall of the theatre, showing whatever flats and props may be currently in the repertory. The band, wildly garbed, is placed centre back of the stage. Chairs on either side of the stage are there for the dancers to rest on—the entire atmosphere is very relaxed and as zany as the improbably decorated tights and lunatic hats that the cast wear with nonchalant charm.

*Elite Syncopations* has been a huge success with audiences everywhere, and was staged by the National Ballet of Canada in 1978. Part of its fun lies in the use of principal classical dancers of a company deploying their ballet technique in an atmosphere worthy of a New Orleans dive.

SYNOPSIS

After an opening general dance, three girls mooch through a number and then four boys zip and roar through "Hothouse Rag." A ballerina struts about as a "Ragtime Nightingale," and a pair of young lovers are innocently demure in the "Golden Hours Rag." Another ballerina is saucy with a cane, and a very tall girl is hilariously mismatched with a very small partner. The "Bethena Concert Waltz" contains some sardonic moments, and "Friday Night Rag" is a virtuoso solo for a male dancer. To the final "Cataract Rag" the company nip and tuck over the stage with great good humour.

# Enigma Variations

*Ballet in one act. Music by Edward Elgar. Choreography by Frederick Ashton. Scenery and costumes by Julia Trevelyan Oman. First performed by The Royal Ballet at the Royal Opera House, Covent Garden, on October 25, 1968, with Derek Rencher as Elgar, Svetlana Beriosova as his wife, Antoinette Sibley as Dorabella, Anthony Dowell as Troyte, Georgina Parkinson as Winifred Norbury, and Desmond Doyle as Jaeger.*

In a completely naturalistic setting Ashton performs a miracle of craft by linking a series of brilliant character variations to a central theme and thereby allowing us to understand the great dependence of a creative artist upon his friends. The creator may be isolated, but the love of wife and companions is here seen to be central to his existence. *Enigma Variations* is as essentially English as the music that inspires it. The original cast of the ballet remains unsurpassed.

Significantly, Lincoln Kirstein in his masterly book *Movement and Metaphor*, which surveys the development of ballet through an analysis of fifty seminal works, chooses *Enigma Variations* to represent the English school and contribution.

SYNOPSIS

The setting shows Elgar's house and garden in Worcestershire in the 1890s. Into this setting comes the succession of characters whom Elgar celebrated in his Enigma Variations, which the composer subtitled "My Friends Pictured Within." It is the quality of friendship which is so central to this ballet. Ashton presents each friend in a variation. The first three are eccentrics: Hew David Steuart-Powell on a bicycle; Richard Baxter Townshend on a tricycle; William Meath Baker banging about with a list of activities.

Next Richard P. Arnold and Isabel Fitton dance a romantic duet before she sinks back into a hammock, and then Arthur Troyte Griffith explodes over the stage in a bravura solo. Winifred Norbury's "gracious personality" is the subject of the next solo, which leads into the famous "Nimrod" variation, in which Elgar's close friend A. J. Jaeger joins Elgar in a contemplative duet, based on walking steps, in which they are joined finally by Elgar's wife.

The youthful Dorabella next appears, her choreography suggesting how the original, Dora Penney, had a slight stammer. George Robert Sinclair now appears in a dashing solo which relates to the music's theme of his bulldog Dan falling into the river. Basil G. Nevinson, a talented cellist, sits playing at the side of the stage while Elgar and his wife dance, expressing their mutual love and at the same time the isolation of the creative artist. The final solo is for Lady Mary Lygon, who was, at the time of the music's composition, away on a sea voyage, and she is presented by a dancer wearing floating draperies and appearing among swirls of mist.

For the finale a telegraph boy comes on and hands a telegram to Jaeger. It brings news that the conductor Hans Richter has agreed to undertake the first performance of the Enigma Variations. The good news is passed from one friend to another, and finally to Elgar. His wife arrives last on the scene and picks up the telegram that has fallen to the ground.

The entire group is finally immortalised in a photograph taken by Steuart-Powell.

# *Episodes*

*Ballet in one act. Music by Anton von Webern. Choreography by George Balanchine. First performed by the New York City Ballet and the Martha Graham Dance Company at the City Center, New York, on May 14, 1959, with Martha Graham, Bertram Ross, Helen McGehee, Ethel Winter, Sallie Wilson, and Paul Taylor of the Martha Graham Company; Violette Verdy, Jonathan Watts, Diana Adams, Jacques d'Amboise, Allegra Kent, Nicholas Magallanes, Melissa Hayden, and Francisco Moncion of the New York City Ballet.*

*Episodes*, as now presented by New York City Ballet, is the second half of a work which combined the forces of the Balanchine and Martha Graham companies in an evening devoted to choreography which used all of Webern's orchestral scores. *Episodes I*, which was choreographed by Graham, was a portrayal of the final moments in the life of Mary, Queen of Scots, and this section is now in the repertory of the Graham company. *Episodes II* begins with three sections that are among the most haunting and resonant choreography that Balanchine has made. The absolute compression and austerity of Webern's writing is mirrored in brief incidents for three couples which seem like Noh plays, filled with secrets, bizarre, succinct, battles of will and physique that we glimpse in the tightly compressed and allusive form that Balanchine adopts. The Symphony, Op. 21, is set for four couples, whose central pair are seen for part of the time linked hand to hand. The second duet, to the Five Pieces, Op. 10, is a night piece, the boy in black, the girl in white, in which the girl is manipulated, and finally placed in a bent position by the boy and left, in this seemingly incomplete pose, just as the music appears to leave our attention hanging in the air. The Concerto, Op. 24, is set as another pas de deux with an attendant group of four girls, in which the man seems to guide the woman's dancing, but their dialogue is always elegant, sardonic, a relationship of stylish and mysterious grace. In the final Ricercata from Bach's *Musical Offering* there comes the formal resolution of what may have seemed the uncertainties and perceptions that have been inspired by the preceding dancing—the progress of the choreography here is inevitable, serene, the perfect summation of the score.

Originally this Balanchine part of *Episodes* contained a solo for one of Graham's dancers, Paul Taylor, after the third duet, set to the Variations for Orchestra, Op. 30. Taylor, a magnificent dancer who is now one of the greatest of contemporary choreographers, was given a solo of exceptional difficulty, which has not been performed by any other interpreter.

The ballet is given in practice dress.

# Etudes

*Ballet in one act. Music by Knudåge Riisager, after Carl Czerny. Choreography by Harald Lander. First performed by the Royal Danish Ballet at the Royal Theatre, Copenhagen, on January 15, 1948, with Margot Lander, Hans Brenaa, and Svend Erik Jensen.*

The idea of danced tributes to the training of a dancer is not new. In a sense Bournonville's first scene in *Konservatoriet* is no more than an evocation of a ballet class: ballet training and the dancer's world have always had a fascination for audiences, and ballets have made capital of this—*L'Etoile* by Joseph Hansen at the Paris Opéra in 1897 is an early example. It was the Danish ballet master and choreographer Harald Lander who made the most successful and best-known classroom ballet in *Etudes*. Like the choreography, the score is a tribute to the ardours of daily practice: Lander commissioned an arrangement of pages from the piano student's one-time Bible, the exercises of Carl Czerny. Starting with the five positions of the feet and the simplest barre exercises, the ballet develops in difficulty and in brilliance to a final cascade of turns and leaps. To the central trio of two men and a ballerina fall the most demanding and most exciting moments.

*Etudes* is in the repertory of several companies, including the Paris Opéra Ballet, London Festival Ballet, and American Ballet Theatre.

In a similar vein, Asaf Messerer choreographed *Ballet School* for the Bolshoi Ballet, of which he was ballet master. This was first seen as a showpiece of the Bolshoi's training methods at the Metropolitan Opera House, New York, in 1962. The score uses music by Liadov, Glazunov, and Shostakovich. Like *Etudes*, it is a show-stopper.

*Mette Hønningen and dancers of the Royal Danish Ballet in Harald Lander's* Etudes.

# Façade

*Ballet in one act. Music by William Walton. Choreography by Frederick Ashton. Scenery and costumes by John Armstrong (redesigned in 1940). First performed by the Camargo Society, at the Cambridge Theatre, London, on April 26, 1931, with Lydia Lopokova as the Milkmaid, Alicia Markova in the Polka, and Frederick Ashton and Lopokova in the Tango.*

The Camargo Society was a private organisation founded by the critics and balletomanes Philip Richardson, Edwin Evans, and Arnold Haskell, and dedicated to providing subscription performances of ballet in the West End of London in the years immediately following the death of Diaghilev and the disappearance of the Ballets Russes. Everyone in British ballet was invited to participate, and a notable series of works were created during the four years (1930–1934) of the Society's existence. *Façade* was an early delight, a sequence of joking comments upon the popular dance forms of the period, which has never lost its public appeal. Its original cast is evidence of the demands that these lightweight dances make on their interpreters. Markova was never to be rivalled in the Polka—no other ballerina seems able to accomplish the final double *tour en l'air*—and later Robert Helpmann left an indelible stamp in the now suppressed Noche Espagnola, in which, with grey pinstripe suit and rolling eyes, he was the incarnation of opportunism and made a passing comment on Anton Dolin's celebrated *Bolero* solo. Sol Hurok insisted that the Sadler's Wells Ballet take it to New York in 1949; it was a smash hit.

## SYNOPSIS

The music for *Façade* was originally created as the partner and accompaniment to a sequence of poems by Edith Sitwell. Ashton selected certain numbers from the orchestral suite but there exists no other connection with the Sitwell text.

As currently performed by The Royal Ballet the ballet consists of the following numbers: Scotch Rhapsody for two girls and a boy; Yodelling Song for a milkmaid, her stool, and three young men in lederhosen; Polka, in which a ballerina sheds her skirt and embarks on a fiendishly difficult solo in bloomers and boater; Foxtrot for two Charlestoning couples; Waltz for four girls in candy-stripe frocks; Popular Song for two utterly bored music-hall dancers who, in boaters and blazers, do a soft-shoe; Tango, for a dim-witted debutante and a partner who is all hair oil and diamond rings; and a Tarantella finale for the whole company.

*Right: Margot Fonteyn and Frederick Ashton as the Tango dancers in the revival of Ashton's* Façade *staged by the Sadler's Wells Ballet 1941.*

117

# Fall River Legend

*Ballet in eight scenes and a prologue. Music by Morton Gould. Choreography by Agnes de Mille. Scenery by Oliver Smith. Costumes by Miles White. First performed by American Ballet Theatre at the Metropolitan Opera House, New York, on April 22, 1948, with Alicia Alonso as the Accused, Diana Adams as the Mother, Muriel Bentley as the Stepmother, Ruth Ann Koesun as the Accused as a Child, and John Kriza as the Pastor.*

*Nora Kaye as the Accused and Muriel Bentley as the Stepmother in Agnes de Mille's* Fall River Legend *for American Ballet Theatre.*

*Lizzie Borden took an axe*
*Gave her mother forty whacks;*
*When she saw what she had done,*
*Gave her father forty-one.*

This jolly New England verse is a reminder of the mystery surrounding the death of Lizzie Borden's father and stepmother in Fall River, Massachusetts, in 1892. In taking this subject for a ballet, Agnes de Mille produced a melodrama which has had continuing success.

*Fall River Legend* continued the exploration of American themes which had been initiated by Lincoln Kirstein's Ballet Caravan. Agnes de Mille's *Rodeo* and *Fall River Legend* are both theatrically effective examples of the genre. *Fall River Legend* offers a dramatic ballerina a splendidly meaty role, and it has been played with distinction by Nora Kaye, for whom it was created; by Alicia Alonso, who actually danced the first performance when Kaye became ill; and more recently by Sallie Wilson.

## SYNOPSIS

*Prologue*

A woman, the Accused, is seen facing prosecution for the double murder of her father and stepmother, and a gallows which forms part of the set reminds the audience of her fate. The set turns around and shows both the exterior and interior of a Victorian house with period furnishing.

*Scene 1*

The Accused watches as the past unfolds. She sees herself as a girl with her father and mother, and she sees the townspeople of Fall River. She also sees the rigid black-clothed figure of a spinster who seems friendly with her parents. Her mother becomes ill but recovers, and the girl dances with her parents and watches them dance together, while the Accused seems both observer and participant. The family's happiness is destroyed when the mother dies. The girl's grief is intensified by the fact that the spinster now assumes control over her father and her home and becomes her stepmother.

The Accused becomes distraught as she watches events unfold.

*Scene 2*
*Inside the house*

The Accused has grown up to womanhood and she is seen with her father and stepmother in their home. It is now a gloomy household and the Accused is unmarried and unhappy. She leaves the house and meets the local Pastor, a good-looking young man who sympathises with her evident distress of spirit and to whom she is attracted. Her father appears and puts an end to this meeting. The Accused re-enters the house and picks up an axe. Her stepmother is suddenly terrified, but the girl goes outside to chop wood and buries the axe blade in a chopping block. Nevertheless an idea has been planted in her mind.

*Scene 3*

The girl watches townspeople enjoying themselves. She feels that she is cut off from their happiness and she becomes obsessed with the axe. The Pastor appears and invites her to attend a dance with him. The girl becomes happy but her stepmother now intervenes and suggests to the Pastor that the girl is unbalanced. The girl is frenzied but eventually calms herself and manages to leave with the Pastor.

*Scene 4*
*A prayer meeting*

The girl is greeted by members of the congregation and by the Pastor. She dances ecstatically with him and her joy is complete until her stepmother appears and again insinuates to the Pastor that she is deranged. The girl becomes furiously angry and her stepmother leads her away.

*Scene 5*
*Inside the house*

The Accused watches the happy couples passing by. She surveys her father and stepmother inside the house and moves towards the chopping block. She takes the axe as the scene ends.

*Scene 6*

The crime has been committed. In a dream, the Accused stands in a blood-spattered shift; she is scolded by her mother, but eventually the mother consoles the child.

*Scene 7*

The Accused is seen running appalled from her home, as the neighbours are aroused by the dreadful events which they suspect have taken place. The axe is found and the white shawl which the girl associates with her mother. The Pastor arrives to console her and she collapses in his arms.

*Scene 8*

The Accused stands awaiting her execution with the Pastor at her side. Passers-by watch the event. The girl stands rigid; her head falls sideways to indicate that she has been hanged.

# Fancy Free

*Ballet in one act. Music by Leonard Bernstein. Choreography by Jerome Robbins. Scenery by Oliver Smith. Costumes by Kermit Love. First performed by American Ballet Theatre at the Metropolitan Opera House, New York, on April 18, 1944, with Harold Lang, John Kriza, Jerome Robbins, Muriel Bentley, Janet Reed, and Shirley Eckl.*

*Fancy Free* was the first ballet created by Jerome Robbins, and there probably has not been a more instantaneous smash hit début in choreography. Working with Leonard Bernstein, Robbins had prepared a detailed scenario which exactly explained the action and motivation of the piece. Here, for the first time, was the very stuff of contemporary urban living transferred to the ballet stage and given a huge theatrical efficiency which in no way destroyed its truthfulness. New York in 1944 teemed with similar incidents. The characters were absolutely real, absolutely comprehensible to the audience watching them. The dance language used the everyday idiom of social dance. The score reflected the musical idiom of the time. Yet by an extraordinary alchemy Robbins had produced from these mundane ingredients a work of the highest art which hid its skills under a seemingly casual and easygoing surface. It is a masterpiece and still invites admirable performances from its casts.

It is an extraordinary tribute to the ballet that it was to inspire the musical *On the Town*, which in turn inspired the no less successful film.

The sailors' variations were staged by Jerome Robbins for a gala performance of the New York City Ballet on May 8, 1979, with Mikhail Baryshnikov, Peter Martins, and Jean-Pierre Frohlich, and the complete ballet entered the NYCB's repertory the following season.

SYNOPSIS

The scene is Manhattan on a hot summer night. The time is "the present" of the ballet's creation in 1944. Outside a bar, three sailors on shore leave appear down the street. The world, and more especially this side street in Manhattan, is their oyster. They indulge in horseplay; then one enters the bar (where the bartender is idly reading an evening paper) and his two companions follow him. They order drinks. One of them, as always, is tricked into having to pay. They eye the bar, which is empty. They are bored and go outside. One chews gum and gives some to his friends. Suddenly outside the bar a girl walks past and the three sailors are at once in pursuit. They tease her by snatching her handbag and she feigns anger. Eventually she leaves and two of the sailors follow her. The third, bored, stays behind and is delighted when another girl appears, whom he contrives to pick up. He takes her into the bar and buys her a drink, tells her of his combat experience, and then

dances with her. This idyll is interrupted when his two friends return, bringing the first girl with them. Now, with three men and two girls, there are problems. The sailors agree to a dance contest. The girls shall judge it and the losing sailor will take off.

The first solo is a brilliant show-off display, so exhausting that at one moment the sailor dashes to the bar and gulps down a quick beer while at the same time miming pirouettes with his free hand before going back into the routine, which finishes on top of the bar. The second number is much quieter, more sentimental, and more immediately appealing to the girls' emotions. The third is a Latin American display of sinuosity. Far from settling the dispute the dance contest confuses the girls even further and the sailors start to fight among themselves in earnest. So engrossed are they in fisticuffs that they do not see the girls slip away. They eventually pick themselves up, dust themselves

*The original and unrivalled cast of* Fancy Free: *Jerome Robbins, John Kriza, and Harold Lang.*

off, and realise that they are alone. There is another round of drinks, the same cheating of the sentimental one into paying, and then they return to the street. They chew gum again, and resolve to avoid girls. At this moment another girl comes into sight, walking down the street in front of the bar. The sailors remember their vows of abstinence. They wander slowly in the opposite direction, then suddenly they turn and roar after her. Curtain.

# Far from Denmark

*Ballet in two acts. Music partly by Joseph Glaeser, with numbers by Louis Moreau Gottschalk, Hans Christian Lumbye, Edouard Dupuy, and Andreas Frederik Lincke. Choreography by August Bournonville. Scenery by Christian Ferdinand Christensen and Troels Lund. Costumes by Edvard Lehmann. First performed by the Royal Danish Ballet at the Royal Theatre, Copenhagen, on April 20, 1860.*

*The end of the party scene on board ship in the second act of* Far from Denmark. *The boy sailor is seen kissing the Danish flag in a moment of touching and entirely convincing patriotism so much a part of the fabric of this lovely ballet. Fredbjørn Bjørnsson is seen far left in Spanish costume; Kirsten Ralov stands centre as Rosita. The production is that staged in 1945.*

*Far from Denmark* affords extraordinary insight into the moral attitudes implicit in Bournonville's creativity. Characteristically, he provides charming genre pictures of Argentine life and shipboard festivities. But more significant, he shows the virtues of patriotism (a key moment comes when a young sailor kisses the Danish flag) and the necessity to resist temptation. Vilhelm's infatuation for Rosita must pass and he must return to a real world implied by the letter from his Danish sweetheart. He is unlike James in *La Sylphide*, who is lost to reason and reality, which is why *La Sylphide* is the least typical of Bournonville's ballets, an exercise in that Romantic extravagance which he so mistrusted. Like Gennaro in *Napoli*, like Ove in *A Folk Tale*, Vilhelm is put to a test—he has to dive into the sea to recover his engagement ring—and the happy outcome of each of these ballets is the result of loyalty to a sane ideal of love that avoids the lure of the exotic or the otherworldly. *Far from Denmark* is a vaudeville ballet: its mixture of pantomime and divertissement dance provides a rare and exceptional view of a balletic style of the mid-nineteenth century.

SYNOPSIS
*Act I*
*The house of*
*Fernandez*

A Danish frigate is anchored off the coast and Lieutenant Vilhelm is visiting the house of Fernandez, the Danish Consul, for he is infatuated with Rosita, the Consul's daughter. She has another suitor, Don Alvarez, and he is jealous of Vilhelm. Two cadets, Poul and Edvard (roles traditionally taken by girls), bring invitations to a costume ball on board the frigate, and Rosita and her friends are happy to receive them. The boatswain, Ole, arrives from the frigate with letters from home, but Vilhelm has no time for the letters from his fiancée in Copenhagen. One of the two cadets is homesick and plays a Danish air on the piano. Rosita contrives to take Vilhelm's engagement ring and she ties it to her fan. Two black servants appear with costumes for the ball and Poul and Edvard play for them before leaving to return to their ship.

*Act II*
*On the quarter-deck*
*of the frigate*

The Danish ship is decorated for the ball. The guests arrive and are entertained by the sailors, who are dressed as Neptune and his cohorts. The guests and the officers dance a quadrille, and there ensue character dances: an Eskimo pas de deux, a Chinese pas de cinq, a Bayadères' dance, and a Fandango. Vilhelm appears in Spanish costume, and Rosita promises her heart to the man who will fetch her fan, which she tosses into the ocean. Vilhelm knows that his engagement ring is still attached to it, and dives overboard. After some general disquiet Vilhelm returns, dripping, and hands the fan back to Rosita, while replacing the ring on his finger. Don Alvarez is accepted by Rosita and a final Indian war dance brings the party to a close. The guests leave and the Danish sailors dance and celebrate among themselves. From the shore the sound of a Danish song is heard—a gesture of thanks from the Argentineans. The sailors are moved by this and one of the cadets salutes the flag; when Vilhelm reappears in naval uniform he receives the letter from his fiancée which he had refused in the morning. The ballet concludes with a bonfire and a general dance.

*Lis Jeppesen (left) and Ann Kristin Hauge as the two cadets in the first act of* Far from Denmark, *during the 1979 Bournonville Centenary Festival. These two enchanting travesty roles are traditionally taken by aspirant ballerinas of the Royal Danish Ballet.*

# La Fête Etrange

*Ballet in one act. Music by Gabriel Fauré, selected by Ronald Crichton. Libretto by Crichton, based on Alain-Fournier's novel* Le Grand Meaulnes. *Choreography by Andrée Howard. Scenery and costumes by Sophie Fedorovitch. First performed by the London Ballet at the Arts Theatre, London, on May 23, 1940, with Maude Lloyd as the Châtelaine, Frank Staff as the Country Boy, and David Paltenghi as the Bridegroom.*

*Artists of Scottish Ballet in their staging of* La Fête Etrange.

Andrée Howard (1910—68) was one of the many talents fostered by Marie Rambert in the early 1930s. For the Rambert company she produced several important ballets, all of them distinguished by her own sensitivity and taste, both as designer and choreographer. *La Fête Etrange* is the only one of her ballets now in the current repertory, but it is a fitting memorial to a delicate but impressive talent. The emotional nuances of this adaptation of an early sequence from *Le Grand Meaulnes* are exquisitely judged and exquisitely in tune with the Fauré score and with Sophie Fedorovitch's muted and superlative décor.

**SYNOPSIS**

The setting is a wintry landscape. A schoolboy wanders into the park of a château where young people are preparing for a party. The boy is immediately attracted to the young Châtelaine and his affection for her disturbs her relationship with the young man she is to marry. At the ballet's end the boy is bewildered and alone, the Châtelaine and her fiancé are estranged.

# La Fille Mal Gardée

*Ballet in two acts. Music by Ferdinand Hérold, arranged by John Lanchbery. Choreography by Frederick Ashton. Scenery and costumes by Osbert Lancaster. First performed by The Royal Ballet at the Royal Opera House, Covent Garden, on January 28, 1960, with Nadia Nerina as Lise, David Blair as Colas, Stanley Holden as Widow Simone, Alexander Grant as Alain, and Leslie Edwards as Thomas.*

*La Fille Mal Gardée* was originally staged in Bordeaux in 1789 by Jean Dauberval. It marked an intriguing departure in the ballet of its time by abandoning the heroic conventions of the late-eighteenth-century dance in favour of a simpler and more natural theme and characters. The ballet's success was considerable and with various scores and in various choreographies it was performed throughout Europe during the next century—most importantly in Russia, where it was preserved in performance to post-Revolutionary times. Ashton's version owed much to the inspiration given the choreographer by Tamara Karsavina, who had danced the role of Lise in Petersburg at the Maryinsky Theatre and not only guided him but taught him Lise's celebrated mime reverie in Act II. The original score was located by the eminent ballet historian Ivor Guest, and John Lanchbery, working in close collaboration with Ashton, confected the delightful score we know now. For interpreters Ashton chose two brilliant young virtuoso principals of The Royal Ballet, Nadia Nerina and David Blair, as well as its two finest character dancers, Alexander Grant and Stanley Holden. The result was a masterpiece in the greatest pastoral traditions of English art. It combines bravura classical dancing with inspired comic characterisation, which in the case of Simone looks to the traditions of English pantomime and music hall, and for Alain combines true pathos with comic resource. The debt to English folk dance is seen in the corps de ballet work and the maypole dance. Ashton's *Fille* is the finest comedy ballet since *Coppélia*.

Although there are other versions of *La Fille Mal Gardée* extant, Ashton's had proved the definitive staging. It is in the repertory of companies throughout the world.

## SYNOPSIS

*Act I, Scene 1*
*The yard of*
*Simone's farm*

In the first light of dawn a group of young farm labourers go off to work. A cockerel and some hens jump down from their roost and dance. Lise, daughter of Simone, comes into the yard and sets about her tasks but she is dreaming of Colas, a young farmer whom she loves. Her mother makes a first appearance in wrapper and curlers, and Lise leaves a ribbon tied to a wall in a love knot so that Colas may know she has been thinking of him. When Colas enters the empty yard he searches for Lise, finds the ribbon, and dances exultantly. Simone tries to chase him away and sets Lise to work churning butter. Colas returns and hides in the hayloft, and, once Lise is alone, he joins her in a loving duet which makes much use of pink ribbons. Simone, however, sends him packing and thwarts Lise's attempts to escape with her friends, for she has plans for her daughter. These are made clear when Thomas, a wealthy farmer, arrives with his simpleton son Alain and bags of gold.

Simone and Thomas have decided that their children shall marry. Lise is very disconcerted by the simple-minded Alain's caperings with his red umbrella but eventually the party leave by pony cart for a picnic in the fields. A frontcloth scene shows the various characters on their way to the harvest field.

*Scene 2*
*The cornfield*

*This picture of the radiant
Nadia Nerina shows all
the quality that made her
creation of Lise in* La Fille
Mal Gardée *so thrilling.
She is seen in the ribbon
dance in the first scene.*

The harvesters have just finished gathering in the last sheaves of wheat. Colas arrives with two bottles of wine for refreshment and then Thomas, Simone, Lise, and Alain arrive. Thomas and Simone urge their children to dance together, but Colas contrives always to partner and embrace Lise as his friends distract Alain, and he carries her away. The harvesters tease Alain during a flute dance until he is rescued by his father. Now Lise and Colas return to celebrate their happiness in a grand pas de deux. At its end Simone scolds her daughter but she is mollified by being persuaded to do a clog dance.

The festivities continue with a maypole dance but storm clouds gather and the peasants are blown across the field by gusts of wind and rain. Lise and Colas seize a moment together again before the storm bursts out in greater fury and blows Alain away into the skies clutching his red umbrella.

### Act II
*Inside Simone's farmhouse*

*bove: Nadia Nerina as*
*ise miming the delights*
*¯looking after—and*
*olding—her children in*
*e second act of* Fille. *The*
*ime sequence of Lise's*
*eams of wedded bliss was*
*ught by Karsavina to*
*shton and incorporated*
*to the ballet, providing a*
*ecious link with* Fille's
*st history in the Imperial*
*ussian Ballet in St.*
*tersburg.*

Simone and Lise return soaking from the fields and they endeavour to warm themselves. All the time Lise tries to pilfer the front door key from her mother's key ring but she is constantly frustrated. Eventually her mother falls asleep over her spinning wheel and Lise is enraptured when Colas appears at the upper part of the farmhouse door. She hangs delightedly from his arms until Simone awakes. Farm workers now bring in the sheaves of wheat to dry and set them in the centre of the room. At the end of a lively stick dance the young men try to carry Lise away with them but Simone again frustrates this. Simone now has to leave and she locks Lise in the farmhouse. After a tantrum, Lise dreams of marriage and motherhood and places an imagined baby on the sheaves of wheat. From them erupts Colas. He dries Lise's tears of mortification over the dream scene he has obviously witnessed and the lovers are in each other's arms when Simone is seen returning. After a panicky search for a hiding place. Lise pushes Colas upstairs into her bedroom. Simone returns and soon suspects that something has been going on though she cannot discover what it is. But

there are more important matters on hand. The marriage contract is to be signed and she bundles the reluctant Lise upstairs to her bedroom to change into her wedding dress and locks the door on her.

Thomas and Alain arrive with the notary and his clerk and are followed by the farm workers and Lise's friends. The contract is signed and Alain is given the key to Lise's bedroom so that he may claim his bride. When he opens the door Lise and Colas are seen in close embrace. All hell breaks loose. Thomas rages, the contract is torn up, Simone faints, Alain is heartbroken and is dragged away by his father. The young lovers beg forgiveness and the notary persuades Simone that love matters more than riches. Amid general rejoicing Lise and Colas dance their love and the guests eventually dance everyone out of the house singing merrily. Then a figure climbs surreptitiously through the window. It is Alain. He stares round the room searching for something precious. Suddenly he darts across to one corner and snatches up his beloved red umbrella. Joyously he leaves as the curtain comes down.

# La Fin du Jour

*Ballet in one act. Music by Maurice Ravel. Choreography by Kenneth MacMillan. Scenery and costumes by Ian Spurling. First performed by The Royal Ballet at the Royal Opera House, Covent Garden, on March 15, 1979, with Merle Park, Jennifer Penney, Wayne Eagling, and Julian Hosking.*

Ravel at one time considered giving the title *Divertissement* to his Piano Concerto in G major: its crystalline brilliance and the jazz-flavoured finale suggest a playful mood that is only dispelled during the long-breathed adagio that is the middle movement. The concerto was composed in 1931, and its date and the spirit of the music suggested to MacMillan the idea of an elegy for the elegant, *sportif* world of fashion and fashion photographs that was lost forever in 1939. His view of this world, like that of his designer, Ian Spurling, is very stylised: the dancers appear in amusing, fantastical versions of the sports clothes of the period in the first two movements, their dances sometimes showing them as marionettes who flicker into life and then seem caught in modish poses. The Ravel concerto had been previously used by Jerome Robbins for his *In G Major*, created for the New York City Ballet's 1975 Ravel Festival.

SYNOPSIS

In the opening allegro, the central quartet are presented in an ingenious double duet. The two women are at first bathers, the men golfers, moving through choreography of great ingenuity with a frozen chic as they suddenly pause in hieratic poses. Everywhere there is a response of great sensitivity to Ravel's orchestral textures, so that at one moment the two women seem to be bathing in the shimmering sonorities of the music. The slow movement, with its serene *cantilena*, becomes a long adagio for the two women, each attended by five men. The choreographic device here is an ingenious canon in which the two voices slowly catch up with each other, then separate again, while the women are lifted and at one moment seem carried over the stage in chairs made from their cavaliers. The continuity suddenly breaks as the women freeze into poses, and the final bars of the movement find them alone, eddying over the stage in *pas de bourrée*.

With the last movement the cast is seen in evening dress. The two ballerinas are now like Jean Harlow and Jessie Matthews; the men, in tails, soar and roar over the stage. At the end dusk falls on the garden, which we see through an opening in the creamy setting, and the leading ballerina closes the door, as if to shut out the night that is descending over Europe.

*Artists of The Royal Ballet in the final movement of Kenneth MacMillan's La Fin du Jour.*

# The Firebird

*Ballet in two scenes. Music by Igor Stravinsky. Choreography by Mikhail Fokine. Scenery and costumes by Alexander Golovin; Firebird's and Tsarevich's costumes by Bakst (entire production redesigned by Natalia Goncharova in 1926). First performed by Diaghilev's Ballets Russes at the Paris Opéra, on June 25, 1910, with Tamara Karsavina as the Firebird, Mikhail Fokine as Ivan Tsarevich, and Alexei Bulgakov as Kastchei.*

*Tamara Karsavina as the Firebird in 1910. She is wearing the original costume designed by Leon Bakst.*

Diaghilev had wanted to present in the West a ballet based on Russian folklore, and after some delays and changes of collaboration the work was given during the second Russian season of 1910. It is marked by many distinctions: by Fokine's brilliant inventions for the Firebird and his use of Russian folk elements for the dance of the Princess and her maidens; by its designs, which in the case of Golovin were of great mystery, and in the later Goncharova decoration (provided when the original décor was ruined by damp) remain a powerful evocation of the magic of Russian fairy tales. Supremely, however, *The Firebird* marked the arrival on the ballet scene of Igor Stravinsky. It was characteristic of Diaghilev that he should have so soon recognised the genuis of the young Stravinsky, and should, through the three great scores he commissioned in these early seasons, have provided a wonderful showcase for the composer.

*The Firebird* in Fokine's production remained a regular feature of the several Ballet Russe companies that followed in Diaghilev's wake. The most important staging, however, was that supervised by Serge Grigoriev and Lubov Tchernicheva for The Royal Ballet in 1954, when Karsavina coached Margot Fonteyn and Michael Somes as the Firebird and Ivan.

Other versions proliferate; few choreographers can resist the wonders of the Stravinsky score. The most significant of these, inevitably, is that first made by George Balanchine in 1949 with designs by Marc Chagall for the New York City Ballet in consultation with his close friend and collaborator Stravinsky, which follows the original Fokine libretto. This has subsequently been extensively revised, and most recently in 1972 for the NYCB's Stravinsky Festival. Other interesting versions include those by Adolph Bolm for American Ballet Theatre in 1945, also with designs by Chagall (though in 1977 ABT acquired thc Fokine-Goncharova version); Lifar's for the Paris Opéra with designs by Wakhevich in 1954; and John Neumeier's for the Frankfurt ballet in 1970, which treated the story as science fiction.

The best known of the alternative stagings is that choreographed by Maurice Béjart.

SYNOPSIS

*Scene 1*   The curtain rises to reveal a mysterious garden. There is a flash of orange light and the Firebird darts in broad leaps through the garden. Over a wall appears the figure of Ivan Tsarevich. He is out hunting and has been attracted to this spot on seeing the bird. He hides himself behind a tree and watches the bird dart again through the garden. The bird now approaches a tree gleaming with golden apples. She snatches one and at this moment Ivan grasps her. Despite all her fierce efforts she cannot escape, and as Ivan finally subdues her she obtains her release by offering him one

Left: *Margot Fonteyn as the Firebird and Michael Somes as Ivan Tsarevich in a still from Paul Czinner's film record of* The Firebird *as staged by The Royal Ballet.*

Below: *The final moment of* The Firebird *as revived by Serge Grigoriev and Lubov Tchernicheva for the Sadler's Wells Ballet in 1954, with Svetlana Beriosova as the beautiful Tsarevna and Michael Somes as Ivan Tsarevich. The setting is that created by Goncharova for Diaghilev's 1926 revival of the ballet.*

of her feathers. Should he be in danger, let him wave it and she will come to his aid. Ivan accepts and the bird flies away. Now in the distance Ivan sees a group of young women. Again he hides, and sees eleven maidens attendant upon a princess. They enter the garden and dance, throwing and catching the golden apples. Ivan steps forward and bows to the princess. They are mutually attracted, but before long they are parted. A sudden noise disturbs the girls and they leave, warning Ivan of danger. He attempts to leave the garden but an enchanted barrier now comes down. As Ivan flings open the gates a horde of monsters and captives pour in and ring the stage; finally their lord and master also enters. He is the evil enchanter Kastchei. Ivan is a prisoner, and as Kastchei attempts to cast a spell on him Ivan reels, but remembering the Firebird's promise, he brings out the glowing feather from his tunic and waves it. The Firebird appears and immediately subdues Kastchei and his minions, leading them in an exhausting dance until they all collapse, at which moment she casts a spell of sleep. Kastchei alone is still awake. The Firebird tells Ivan to fetch Kastchei's soul, which is preserved in an enormous egg. Ivan brings a casket, takes from it the egg, and swings it into the air in front of the petrified Kastchei. The egg crashes to the ground and breaks, and darkness falls.

*Scene 2* The final scene is set against a backdrop of the myriad spires of Holy Russia. Priests and attendants appear and a procession of knights enters with the now-freed maidens. Finally Ivan and the Princess return in coronation robes. In the final pose Ivan raises his sceptre in majesty as he stands beside his bride.

*Paris Opéra Ballet*
*Ballet in one act.*
*Music by*
*Igor Stravinsky.*
*Choreography by*
*Maurice Béjart.*
*Scenery by*
*Joelle Roustan and*
*Roger Bernard.*
*First performed on*
*October 31, 1970.*

Béjart's radical version of *The Firebird* is a political ballet in which the Firebird becomes the spirit of revolution. A group of young revolutionaries are led by a young man who falls in battle, but he rises again and leads a reborn troupe of firebirds to triumph. The original cast included Michael Denard as the Firebird. On November 17, 1970, the Ballet du XXième Siècle first performed the ballet in Brussels with Paolo Bortoluzzi, a dancer of tremendous power, as the Firebird.

*aurice Béjart's version of
e Firebird as staged by
Paris Opéra.*

# A Folk Tale

*Ballet in three acts. Music by Niels Gade and J. P. E. Hartmann. Choreography by August Bournonville. (Revived 1979 by Kirsten Ralov with scenery and costumes by Lars Juhl.) First performed by the Royal Danish Ballet at the Royal Theatre, Copenhagen, on March 20, 1854.*

Bournonville thought *A Folk Tale* his "most perfect and finest choreographic work, especially as regards its Danish character." Morally it reasserts that constant theme of Bournonville's work, the triumph of good over evil; musically it has one of the finest scores made for Bournonville; dramatically it offers an extreme richness of mime and dance opportunities. Constantly preserved in the Royal Danish repertory, it is one of the great jewels of the Bournonville heritage.

SYNOPSIS

*Act I*
*In the park of a*
*noble estate*

The action takes place in medieval times. A hunting party from the noble estate of Holgarden is preparing for an *al fresco* meal. Birthe, the heiress to the estate, reveals her bad temper in the way she treats her cousin and fiancé, Junker Ove. She flirts with a neighbour, Sir Mogens. When the festivities are over, the hunting party disperses and Junker Ove remains alone, though he has been warned that nearby there is a hill which is the domain of trolls. As darkness falls the troll hill magically opens, revealing the trolls hammering the gold at which they work. From out of the hill steps a ravishing young girl, Hilda, who offers Ove a golden goblet and tries to lure him back into the hill with a magic drink. Ove avoids this danger, and the sorceress Muri, who lives in the hill, calls Hilda back into the trolls' underworld. She then summons up a group of elf maidens who whirl in the mist around Ove and drive him mad.

*Lis Jeppesen as Hilda dancing in the Troll scene of* A Folk Tale *during the 1979 Bournonville Centenary Festival in Copenhagen.*

*Lis Jeppesen as Hilda in*
A Folk Tale. *She is holding the goblet which will eventually prove her identity as heiress to the manor.*

*Act II*
*Inside the troll hill*

Two troll brothers, Viderik and Diderik, sons of Muri, are both courting Hilda. Diderik, the nastier of the two, is the elder and claims Hilda for his bride despite the protests of Viderik. They squabble and leave. Hilda falls asleep and dreams of a human nurse asleep by a cradle. She sees troll children who steal a human baby and replace it with a troll child.

They also steal a goblet. Hilda is further amazed in her dream to see a crucifix. When she awakens she makes a cross from two twigs, which terrifies Muri. Now Hilda's wedding to Diderik is to be celebrated and trolls assemble. They get hideously drunk and Hilda seizes the opportunity to enlist Viderik's support in escaping.

*Act III, Scene 1*
*On the edge of the forest*

Hilda and Viderik are discovered in a glade by a holy spring where sick people come to be healed. Hilda gives alms to the poor and then Ove appears, still deranged. Hilda takes him to the well and brings him to his senses with a draught of holy water. He recognises her as the beautiful girl with whom he has fallen in love. When the estate workers seek to chase Viderik and Hilda away, Hilda flees while Viderik delays the pursuers.

*Scene 2*
*Birthe's bedroom*

The fiery-tempered Birthe is bullying her servants and falls into a fit of bad temper. Hilda appears holding her goblet and is recognised as the rightful heiress, while Birthe, it is now realised, must be a troll changeling.

*Scene 3*
*In the gardens of the estate*

Birthe is recognised by her troll brothers Viderik and Diderik, and by Muri, not least because of her fiery red hair, and Sir Mogens is bought for her as a bridegroom with a huge treasure of gold. Hilda is united with Junker Ove, and as it is midsummer eve, a joyous divertissement ensues before the final curtain comes down.

# Four Schumann Pieces

*Ballet in one scene. Music by Robert Schumann. Choreography by Hans van Manen. Costumes by Jean-Paul Vroom. First performed by The Royal Ballet at the Royal Opera House, Covent Garden, on January 31, 1975, with Anthony Dowell.*

Four Schumann Pieces is set to Schumann's String Quartet in A Major, Op. 41, No 3. It is designed as a tribute to Anthony Dowell, to his unflawed classicism and to his elegant stage presence. It involves the dancer as a solitary figure caught up with five couples, and each movement of the quartet is conceived as an entity, unrelated save through the intensity and beauty of the male dancer's performance. The progress of the work shows this central figure in relation to both the men and women of the supporting ensemble—there are hints of loneliness, and also of self-sufficiency. The male costuming, alas, does nothing for the image of the male dancer, since it prettifies virility in baggy pink blouses.

The ballet has been revived for other companies and for other star performers, but the central role is essentially linked with the elegance of line and control of Dowell's technique.

*The five couples who surround the central male figure in The Royal Ballet's production of* Four Schumann Pieces.

# The Four Temperaments

*Ballet in one act. Music by Paul Hindemith. Choreography by George Balanchine. Costumes by Kurt Seligmann. First performed by Ballet Society at the Central High School of Needle Trades, New York, on November 20, 1946, with Gisella Caccialanza, Mary Ellen Moylan, Francisco Moncion, Tanaquil LeClercq, Todd Bolender, Lew Christensen, Elise Reiman, Beatrice Tompkins, Fred Danieli, and William Dollar.*

*The Four Temperaments* was commissioned for, and staged by, Ballet Society, the first effort made by Lincoln Kirstein and George Balanchine after the end of the war to re-establish their performing ensemble. Subscription audiences were shown a series of major works that culminated in the fifth programme in April 1948, which included the Stravinsky-Balanchine *Orpheus*. So important had been the society's activities that Morton Baum, Chairman of the New York City Center, offered to give Ballet Society a home, and it acquired a new identity and permanent status as the New York City Ballet at the City Center in October 1948.

*The Four Temperaments*, like *Agon*, presents an essential image of the New York City Ballet. Since 1951, it has been danced in practice dress. Plotless, though evocative of the bodily "humours" implicit in the title, it is above all a justification of the classical academic dance as Balanchine has shaped it in America.

SYNOPSIS

The ancient Greeks believed that the human body comprehended four temperaments, Melancholic, Sanguinic, Phlegmatic, and Choleric, which were in their turn associated with the four elements of Earth, Water, Air, and Fire. The score is divided into five sections: the statement of the theme, followed by the four "temperamental" sections. In the theme three couples are seen in pas de deux. There follows the Melancholic section, in which a male dancer is despondent and is then joined by two girls and later by four more female dancers. The succeeding Sanguinic section is a charming waltz for a couple, very bright in mood, in which they are accompanied by four more girls. The Phlegmatic section is for a male dancer who is joined by four girls and becomes cheerful. Finally the ballerina associated with the Choleric temperament storms onto the stage, eventually to be followed by the entire ensemble. The last image is of the dancers taking off in huge arcs of movement.

Right: *Bart Cook and Judith Fugate of the New York City Ballet in the Melancholic section of* The Four Temperaments.

# Frankie and Johnny

*Ballet in one act. Music by Jerome Moross. Choreography by Ruth Page and Bentley Stone. Costumes and scenery by Paul du Pont. First performed by the Page-Stone Ballet on June 19, 1938, with Ruth Page and Bentley Stone.*

*Frankie and Johnny* is a remnant of the WPA days. In 1938, under the auspices of the Federal Theater Project in Chicago, Ruth Page and Bentley Stone founded the Page-Stone Ballet and created for it this and other dances on American themes.

In earlier days *Frankie and Johnny* created a scandal, ostensibly because of its subject matter of a whore and her two-timing lover. The real reason was probably because Page and Stone treated the immoral tale immorally—that is, in a good-humoured manner. Certainly the ballet's burlesquing attitude toward the fabled lovers and other stock characters from American street life is the viable point today. The pace is brisk; the story, clearly told.

*Frankie and Johnny* survives largely because Frederic Franklin, a longtime associate of Page, revives it for regional ballet companies throughout America. It is currently performed by the Cincinnati Ballet.

SYNOPSIS

The scene is a back alley in Anytown, U.S.A., peopled by a policeman, bar girls, bums, and Salvation Army lasses. Frankie and Johnny dance a love duet. While Frankie is busy working in her house (of ill repute), Johnny takes up with Nellie Bly. Frankie finds out and shoots her lover in a full-fledged "mad scene." The mourners repair to the neighbourhood bar and stage a jolly wake. Frankie and Nellie kiss and make up. But, alas, Johnny's murder can't be undone. Frankie sits despondently by the coffin of the man who "done her wrong," and the Salvation Army girls chime that "you can't put no trust in any man."

# Giselle

*Ballet in two acts. Music by Adolphe Adam. Libretto by Théophile Gautier and Vernoy de Saint-Georges. Choreography by Jean Coralli and Jules Perrot, later revised by Marius Petipa. First performed at the Paris Opéra, on June 28, 1841, with Carlotta Grisi as Giselle, Lucien Petipa as Albrecht, Jean Coralli as Hilarion, and Adèle Dumilâtre as Myrtha.*

*Giselle*, the most celebrated ballet of the Romantic era, owed its creation to the French poet Théophile Gautier. Inspired by the legend of the Wilis, whom he had read about in a book by the German poet Heinrich Heine, Gautier was seized with an idea concerning the mysterious night dancers. He thought it would be an ideal vehicle for Carlotta Grisi, a new young star of the Paris Opéra to whom he was greatly attracted. With the assistance of the dramatist Vernoy de Saint-Georges he produced a scenario which offered two contrasting but complementary aspects of Romanticism—quaint local colour in Act I, and moonlit mystery in Act II. Carlotta Grisi was the pupil and protégée of Jules Perrot, great dancer and great choreographer of the Romantic age. Perrot hoped that her engagement at the Paris Opéra might also ensure his return to the theatre in which he had earlier shone as a dancer, notably in partnership with Marie Taglioni. In the event, he was only to be responsible for the choreography of Grisi's dances in the ballet. The choreography elsewhere was entrusted to Jean Coralli, official ballet master to the theatre. Perrot and Grisi were friends of Adolphe Adam, the composer, and their

*Galina Ulanova as Giselle in a scene from Paul Czinner's 1956 film* The Bolshoi Ballet.

common enthusiasm for the story meant that Adam produced his score in record time. First performed on Carlotta's twenty-second birthday, *Giselle* was a triumph and Grisi was hailed as the new star of the Opéra.

Versions of *Giselle* were mounted throughout Europe with exceptional speed; a pirated staging was presented in St. Petersburg by 1842. In 1848 Perrot himself arrived in Petersburg to start ten years of service as first ballet master. He mounted two versions there and was assisted by Marius Petipa. Carlotta Grisi danced the role in St. Petersburg, as did the other great Giselle of the age, the outstanding dramatic ballerina Fanny Elssler. Her magnificently acted interpretation still influences the way in which ballerinas today present the mad scene as a bravura mimetic passage. Although *Giselle* was dropped from the European repertory by the middle of the nineteenth century it was preserved in St. Petersburg, and Marius Petipa was responsible for several revisions during the latter years of the century. It was Diaghilev who, at the urging of Alexandre Benois, brought the ballet back to Western Europe in his second Russian season of 1910, when Tamara Karsavina and Vaslav Nijinsky danced the leading roles. All Western stagings stem from the St. Petersburg production.

In 1918 Nikolay Sergueyev, *régisseur* to the Imperial Theatres in St. Petersburg, left Russia, taking with him the notation of the entire repertory. Using these notes he was to provide productions for several companies, starting with the Paris Opéra in 1924. For that production, Giselle was the greatest incumbent of the role in this century, Olga Spessivtseva. Two years later, Sergueyev mounted the ballet for the Vic-Wells Ballet in London, when the Giselle was Alicia Markova, who was to prove a glorious interpreter of the role. Thereafter the ballet was to be found in many repertories, with Alicia Markova the inspiration for several stagings.

The popularity of *Giselle* is traceable both to the Vic-Wells staging and to the immense influence of Anna Pavlova, another great Giselle, who had danced the role in Russia and maintained a production with her own company until her death in 1931. Audiences have come to recognise *Giselle* both as a masterpiece of the Romantic dance and also as compelling theatre because of the tremendous opportunities offered to the interpreters of the two leading roles. Today every company having pretensions to a classical base feels impelled to present *Giselle*.

Most productions are traditional: Scottish Ballet, in the version prepared for them by Peter Darrell, gives the story a slight narrative twist which shows Albrecht as an unsympathetic character intruding into a close-knit village community. The continuity of performance in St. Petersburg/Leningrad since 1842 has meant that the Kirov staging remains an ideal realisation of this seminal work.

## SYNOPSIS

*Act I*
*A forest clearing
in the Rhineland*

Count Albrecht loves Giselle, a peasant girl, though she knows him only as a villager, Loys. Berthe, Giselle's mother, hopes that her daughter will marry Hilarion, a forester who is devoted to Giselle, and warns her against Loys. But Giselle disregards Hilarion, and joins with her beloved in the celebrations that mark the end of the grape harvest. When Albrecht's squire secretly warns his master of the approach of a hunting party, Hilarion observes them and manages to break into Loys's cottage, seeking to learn the secret of his identity. The hunting party arrives, led by the Duke of Courland and his daughter Bathilde, Albrecht's future bride, who are staying at Albrecht's castle. They seek rest in Berthe's cottage and Bathilde, charmed by Giselle, gives her a necklace. The Duke orders a hunting horn to be left that his courtiers may be summoned in due course, and this provides Hilarion with proof of Loys's identity as he compares the crests on the horn and on a sword he has found in Loys's cottage. Just as Giselle is crowned Queen of the Village, Hilarion reveals the truth about Loys. When Bathilde returns and claims Albrecht as her fiancé the shock unseats Giselle's reason. In her madness she relives her love for Loys and, seizing his sword, she kills herself.

*Act II*
*Giselle's grave
in the forest*

As midnight sounds, Hilarion keeps vigil by Giselle's grave, which lies in unhallowed ground by a forest lake. This is when the Wilis materialise—ghosts of young girls who have been jilted and have died before their wedding day; now they avenge themselves by dancing to death any man whom they happen upon during the hours of darkness. Myrtha, their Queen, summons her Wilis, and next Giselle is called from her grave to be initiated into their rites. When Albrecht enters, bringing flowers for Giselle's tomb, she appears to him. The Wilis pursue Hilarion, whom they drive to his death, and next fall vengefully upon Count Albrecht. Myrtha condemns him to dance until he dies, and though Giselle urges him to the safety of the cross on her grave, Myrtha commands Giselle to dance and lure Albrecht from the cross. Giselle tries to sustain him, but as the night wears on his dancing becomes more and more exhausted. Just as his death seems imminent, dawn breaks. Daylight destroys the Wilis' power and the ghostly dancers fade away; Giselle, too, melts away, leaving Albrecht sorrowing and alone.

*Above: Act II of The
Royal Ballet's production
of Giselle, with Margot
Fonteyn as Giselle, Alexis
Rassine as Albrecht, and
Pamela May as Myrtha.*

*Natalia Makarova and
Mikhail Baryshnikov in
the American Ballet
Theatre's production of*
Giselle.

# Gloria

*Ballet in one act. Music by Francis Poulenc. Choreography by Kenneth MacMillan. Scenery and costumes by Andy Klunder. First performed by The Royal Ballet at the Royal Opera House, Covent Garden, on March 13, 1980, with Jennifer Penney, Wendy Ellis, Wayne Eagling, and Julian Hosking.*

In the cataclysm of the First World War a generation was lost. Vera Brittain's autobiographical *Testament of Youth* was an elegy for that generation by one of its members, and a poem from *Testament* serves as a programme note to MacMillan's ballet. The poem speaks in part of *"The threatening woe that our adventurous feel/Would starkly meet."*

*Gloria*'s action takes place in no man's land. A skeletal iron framework stands on a rising slope that seems to overlook the abyss of the past whence appear the cast; soldiers in tatters of uniform, returned from death for a momentary contemplation of the past; their womenfolk grey and ghostly. As they relive earthly joys and earthly suffering the men are sometimes placed like troops on guard, gazing out over the unfathomable reaches of some war-scarred territory from which they have come. During the duet originally composed for Jennifer Penney and Julian Hosking, five men lie like sleepers or corpses upon the set's rising slope, as a counterpoint to the lyrical line of the pas de deux. Wayne Eagling makes a brutal entrance rolling down the incline of the set as if blasted by a shell, and the unease and anger that mark his role are implicit in his movement throughout a part that seems the embodiment of Housman's line: "Life, to be sure, is nothing much to lose; but young men think it is, and we were young."

## SYNOPSIS

Kenneth MacMillan's choreography uses a large cast but is centred upon a trio of a girl and two boys, and a quartet in which a girl is supported by three male dancers. There is no identification of relationships, though the book *Testament of Youth* may suggest certain parallels.

The beautiful soprano solo Domine Deus is a duet of clarity and grace, set for the leading girl and her partner; the succeeding Domini fili unigenite, musically joyous, is no less so in the writing for the second female soloist and her companions. The Miserere nobis finds the main trio caught in poses of sculptural beauty. Everywhere the choreography seeks to match both the gravity and the happier aspirations of the score, suggesting that these ghosts survey what was, and what might have been, with some dispassion. Any bitterness or regret and accusation is most clearly felt in the male role originally danced by Wayne Eagling, to whom falls the final section of the ballet when his companions have returned to their rest—like troops going over the top into action—and he makes a last tearing circuit of the stage before plummeting backwards out of sight.

# The Goldberg Variations

*Ballet in one act. Music by Johann Sebastian Bach. Choreography by Jerome Robbins. Costumes by Joe Eula. First performed by the New York City Ballet at the State Theater, Lincoln Center, on May 27, 1971, with Gelsey Kirkland, Sara Leland, John Clifford, Robert Maiorano, Robert Weiss, Bruce Wells, Karin von Aroldingen, Peter Martins, Susan Hendl, Anthony Blum, Patricia McBride, and Helgi Tomasson.*

*The Goldberg Variations* was composed by Bach for the harpsichordist J. T. Goldberg on a commission from Count von Kayserling, who hoped that hearing them played at night might alleviate the tedium of his insomnia. Robbins found a way of treating this monumental score so that the dance seems to exist side by side with it, appreciating and highlighting its qualities without battening on the music. He also suggests something about dancers and their life—as he does in *Afternoon of a Faun.* The first half of *Goldberg* has an innocence of spirit that contrasts with the more severe régime of the *danse d'école* in the second part.

*Merrill Ashley in The Goldberg Variations.*

**SYNOPSIS** In setting Bach's great sequence of variations, Robbins acquired a clearly ordered foundation to support the development of the dance incidents. A guiding formal device is provided by the dancers' costuming. The opening Aria presents the ground base that is the matter of the musical variations, and two dancers dressed in costumes that evoke the eighteenth century move calmly through a Sarabande. The group of sixteen dancers who are to play out the first of the ballet's two sections now appear in practice dress. When, after the sixteenth variation, the cast changes (and with it the ballet's mood), costuming is gradually adjusted to suggest baroque dress again. With the final variations (numbers 27–30) all the dancers from both halves are in an approximation of eighteenth-century dress. At the ultimate recapitulation of the Aria the two dancers who opened the ballet return, but now it is they who are in modern dress.

In the first part of the ballet movement seems characterised by an easy and unstressed camaraderie among the dancers. Robbins is obedient to Bach's musical forms, with contrasted gaiety and seriousness of writing, but his realisation has been free-flowing and relaxed in emotional mood. A quartet for two boys and two girls shows the boy-girl relationship melting without affectation into boy-boy and girl-girl partnership before returning to its initial grouping. A group of four boys and four girls, whose movements are complemented by an independent dance for another boy, are enlivened when the boy attracts one girl from the group, and their duet is contrasted with a no less happy patterning for the remaining septet. With the change at Bach's sixteenth variation, three new couples appear with supporting corps. The mood, like the first hints of period costuming, is more formal. Youthful play gives way to a stricter manner. The pas de deux which are given to each couple are more complex than in the earlier section.

At the end all the dancers form a group-photo pose; they salute the pianist, then disperse as the opening couple make their reappearance.

*elow: One of the final*
*oments of Robbins' 'The*
*oldberg* Variations, *as*
*rformed by the New York*
*ty Ballet.*

# Graduation Ball

*Ballet in one act. Music by Johann Strauss, arranged by Antal Dorati.
Choreography by David Lichine. Scenery and costumes by Alexandre Benois. First
performed by the Original Ballet Russe at the Theatre Royal, Sydney, on February
28, 1940, with Tatiana Riabouchinska and David Lichine.*

*Fredbjørn Bjørnsson as the
General leads the cadets into
the ballroom, where Lizzie
Rode as the Headmistress
waits with the schoolgirls.
Anne Marie Vessel and
Annemarie Dybdal are the
two leading junior girls in
this production by the Royal
Danish Ballet.*

David Lichine (1910–1972) was a leading figure, as dancer and
choreographer, with the Ballet Russe companies of the 1930s and 1940s,
for whom he created an impressive *Francesca da Rimini* in 1937 as
well as *Graduation Ball*, which is his best-known ballet. In post-war years
he made a notable contribution to the repertory of the Ballets des
Champs-Elysées with *La Rencontre* and *La Création* in 1948. *Graduation Ball*
is a work of great charm, all too easily dissipated by vulgar performance,
but when lovingly treated, as it is by the Royal Danish Ballet, for which it
was staged in 1953, it has endearing merits. It was staged for London
Festival Ballet in 1957.

SYNOPSIS The setting is a girls' school in Vienna
in the 1840s. Preparations are under
way for a party marking the end of the
school year, to which the cadets of a
neighbouring military academy have
been invited. The senior girls are
demure in long dresses; the junior
girls, in their shorter skirts and
pantalettes, are more excited and have
discovered a powder puff. The
headmistress (a role usually taken by a
man) enters and restores order. The
cadets now appear, led by their

commanding officer, an elderly
general, and various flirtations result
  Afterwards, as the ice is broken, the
schoolgirls and the cadets dance
happily together and one cadet serve
as postman, bringing notes from girl
to boys. There ensues a series of
divertissements which are introduce
by an ebullient junior girl with bounc
pigtails. First comes a drummer (a ro
unforgettably created by Nicholas
Orloff); then the Sylphide appears
with James, in an evocation of the

ballet of the period in which the action is set; next is an impromptu dance by a girl student; and then there is a dance-step competition in which two senior girls don tutus and unleash a cascade of turning steps. Originally there followed a sequence called "Mathematics and Natural History," which did not survive the first production, and the young people are finally caught up in the whirl of a perpetuum mobile.

When the students are absent from the ballroom there is a creaking mazurka flirtation between the headmistress and the general, which is interrupted when the girls and boys return. The general leads his young troops away in military formation, and the girls go disconsolately to bed. One of them creeps down to the ballroom—she has a tryst with a cadet—but their meeting is then rudely interrupted by the head-mistress, who sends the boy packing and the girl back to bed.

# The Green Table

*Ballet in one act and eight scenes. Music by Fritz Cohen. Libretto and choreography by Kurt Jooss. Costumes by Hein Heckroth. First performed by the Ballets Jooss at the Théâtres des Champs-Elysées, Paris, on July 3, 1932, with Jooss as Death.*

*The Green Table* was an instantaneous success. It won the prize in a choreographic competition organized by the Archives Internationales de la Danse in Paris, and its triumph led to the formation of a dance company built around its choreographer. Kurt Jooss had studied both music and drama in Germany and came under the influence of movement theorist Rudolf von Laban, and *The Green Table* is representative of the Central European school of movement. Jooss put down his roots in Essen, and a group of his dancers were the first cast of *The Green Table*. His company worked internationally, then found a home in England during the war. In 1951 Jooss returned to Essen, but the company did not survive long. Until his death in 1979, Jooss devoted his time increasingly to his Essen Folkwangschule, which offered all styles of dance and became world famous. Although his company did not survive, Jooss' choreography entered the repertories of several classical ballet companies in the postwar years, when such works as *The Big City* and *Ball in Old Vienna* were, like *The Green Table*, found to have continuing validity.

It is worth recording that Jooss stipulated that *The Green Table* should always be placed at the end of a program—for obvious reasons.

*The tableau that opens and closes* The Green Table, *in the original staging by the Ballets Jooss.*

SYNOPSIS The curtain rises in this "dance of death" on the eponymous green baize table around which ten politicians, in evening dress and grotesquely masked, are disagreeing. Their conference culminates in the moment when each pulls out a pistol and fires. War has been declared.

In the world outside the conference room young soldiers are called to the colours. Through all the subsequent action the figure of Death goosesteps

*Kurt Jooss as Death in the original production of The Green Table.*

the stage, claiming one victim after the other. There are scenes of farewell in which the soldiers leave their womenfolk. Battle commences; men die. Refugees flee; an old woman dies from exhaustion; a profiteer sells a young girl into a brothel. The war-stained soldiers return, but Death has claimed its portion and finally takes them all. The last scene returns to the green table. The politicians argue; the outcome will always be the same.

# Harlequinade

*Ballet in two acts. Music by Riccardo Drigo. Choreography by George Balanchine. Scenery and costumes by Rouben Ter-Arutunian. First performed by the New York City Ballet at the State Theater, Lincoln Center, on February 4, 1965, with Edward Villella, Patricia McBride, Suki Schorer, and Deni Lamont.*

*Harlequinade* is inspired by Balanchine's memories of Petipa's *Les Millions d'Arlequin*, first performed at the little Hermitage Theatre in St. Petersburg on February 10, 1900, and which later entered the repertory of the Maryinsky Theatre. The story is concerned with the antics of commedia dell'arte figures. Columbine and Harlequin are in love. Their desire to marry is thwarted by Columbine's father, who wishes his daughter to marry a wealthy and ridiculous old suitor. Pierrot and Pierrette, the father's servants, are told to keep the lovers from meeting, but they do not relish their task and Harlequin manages to obtain the key of Columbine's house. The father is suspicious and the house is searched. Harlequin is found, is torn limb from limb, and is thrown into a heap from an upstairs window. All seems lost, but the Good Fairy restores Harlequin to life, and also showers him with gold from a cornucopia. He is thus far richer than the old suitor, and he wins Columbine.

The ballet ends with celebratory divertissements, including dances for birds around a fountain and a final *ballabile* that includes hordes of young dance students. (This device is a reminder that as a student, Balanchine himself danced in St. Petersburg in the Petipa ballet, whose score he used in this present version.)

*Patricia McBride and Edward Villella in the New York City Ballet's production of* Harlequinade.

# Las Hermanas

*Ballet in one act. Music by Frank Martin (Concerto for Harpsichord and Small Orchestra). Libretto by Kenneth MacMillan, based on Federico García Lorca's* La Casa de Bernarda Alba. *Choreography by MacMillan. Scenery and costumes by Nicholas Georgiadis. First performed by the Stuttgart Ballet at the Württembergische Staatstheater, Stuttgart, on July 13, 1963, with Marcia Haydée as the Eldest Sister, and Ray Barra as the Man.*

In *Las Hermanas*, MacMillan produced a characteristically taut drama of sexual frustration. The ballet, in Georgiadis' economical monochrome design, brilliantly captures the atmosphere of rigid social and sexual convention. The characters, despite the conciseness of the action, are well rounded and have a vivid dynamic life. The role of the eldest sister, in particular, has produced exceptional performances from such artists as Marcia Haydée and Lynn Seymour. The ballet has entered the repertories of the Sadler's Wells Royal Ballet, the Australian Ballet, American Ballet Theatre, and Scottish Ballet.

SYNOPSIS

The setting is the interior of a house. Five sisters sit rocking in wicker chairs, fanning themselves. Their mother comes painfully down a staircase using a cane. This house of women is full of frustrations, typified by their interest in the wedding dress and veil which stand in the corner of the room. A man is introduced into the household. He is to be the bridegroom for the eldest sister, who already is entering upon desiccated middle age. She is both terrified by the man's obvious sexuality and jealously aware of her right to be married first. The man casts a glance at the lovely youngest sister and the middle sister is sardonically conscious of this fact. The scene moves to the outside of the house by night. The man returns and throws gravel at a window. The eldest sister appears.

The man's brutal demands on her body shock her, but she contrives to warm to him. Their meeting is interrupted by the middle sister; the eldest returns to the house. At this moment the youngest girl comes out and flings herself into the arms of the man. They leave. The middle sister, aware of what is going on, now arouses the household. The mother banishes the man from the house and after an agonised confrontation with the youngest girl she sends her to her room. The eldest sister is desperate; she is aware that she will never escape from this house. The mother locks the door and grimly surveys her prisoners. The youngest is missing. The mother limps upstairs to the girl's room and draws the curtain, to reveal her hanging dead. The curtain falls.

*The mother drives the man from the house in* Las Hermanas *as staged by Western Theatre (now Scottish) Ballet. Peter Cazalet is the man; next to him stands Robin Haig as the eldest sister.*

# Intermezzo

*Ballet in one act. Music by Johannes Brahms. Choreography by Eliot Feld.
Costumes by Stanley Simmons. First presented by the American Ballet Company at
the Teatro Nuovo, Spoleto, on June 29, 1969, with Christine Sarry, Elizabeth Lee,
Cristina Stirling, David Coll, John Sowinski, and Alfonso Figueroa.*

*Intermezzo* is a suite of dances for three couples dressed in tulle and velvet.
The prevailing tone is of young, tender love, yet Feld manages to work a
great variety of feeling into the dances. There are a boisterous polka, an
amusing episode in which a man is more intent on his dream lady than
on the very real and lovely lady beside him, and a pensive dance in which
a man seems to shield his lover from unpleasant dreams. Whatever the
character of the particular variation. Feld's choreographic invention
appears limitless and effortless.

Feld made *Intermezzo* early on in his career. People marvelled that so
young a person could create so mature a ballet. Many would agree today
that *Intermezzo* is still Feld's finest. It is a signature piece of the Eliot Feld
Ballet and for a time was in the repertory of American Ballet Theatre,
with which Feld was associated before he formed the first of his own
ensembles.

Intermezzo, *as performed
by Eliot Feld's American
Ballet Company.*

# The Invitation

*Ballet in one act. Music by Matyas Seiber. Libretto by Kenneth MacMillan, based on Colette's* Le Blé en Herbe *and Beatriz Guido's* The House of the Angel. *Choreography by MacMillan. Scenery and costumes by Nicholas Georgiadis. First performed by The Royal Ballet Touring Company at the New Theatre, Oxford, on November 10, 1960, with Lynn Seymour as the Girl, Christopher Gable as the Boy, Anne Heaton as the Wife, and Desmond Doyle as the Husband.*

*The Invitation* was unusual in its time for its honesty and poetic imagination in dealing with a sexual drama. MacMillan's choreography fixes with extreme precision both the shifting emotional currents of the characters and also the physical urgency that is so strongly a part of the ballet's fabric. The work offers four very fine dramatic roles which have received uniformly excellent interpretation from various Royal Ballet dancers; the role of the young girl launched Lynn Seymour as the outstanding dance actress of her generation.

SYNOPSIS

The setting is a house in some warm climate at the turn of this century. At curtain rise the mother is seen writing notes. In the garden a young boy is gazing at naked statues. The mother comes out with two of her daughters and they drape the statues in dust sheets. The boy is left alone in the garden and his young girl cousin enters. She does not understand the boy's first sexual feelings for her, and when they are joined by a group of other children she is shocked at their sexual precocity, and they tease her by making her kiss an undraped statue. Guests arrive at the house and are greeted by the mother and her daughters. Among them are a husband and wife whose marriage has become a mere convention. The husband is aware of the young girl; the wife glances briefly at the boy.

Left alone, the boy and girl dance and the girl gives him a fleeting kiss as she runs away.

Inside the house a dancing lesson for the young people is supervised by a governess. The boy is ungainly, and is embarrassed when the wife seeks to help him. The girl innocently shows off to the husband and asks him to dance with her. As she sways and soars in his arms her mother is appalled at the girl's forwardness and what seems the man's sexual interest.

Left alone, the husband and wife quarrel, he always rejecting her appeals for love and understanding. The girl and her cousin watch this. At nightfall the guests assemble in the garden. There is a feeling of hectic sexual anticipation. Three acrobats appear as entertainers, giving a display of two cockerels fighting for a hen. Amid the urgent flirtations of the guests the wife sits alone in the garden. When the boy appears she shows that she understands his sexual longings and she leads him away. The girl now slips through the garden in search of the husband. She meets him and seeks to re-establish the—to her—innocent mood of their dance. The man tries to resist her but succumbs and rapes her. The girl lies wounded on the ground as the husband staggers remorsefully away.

In the final scene the girl makes her way back to the house. Before she appears, the wife embraces the boy, whom she has seduced. She watches her distraught husband return. She understands what he has done but she forgives him and leads him away as the girl returns. The boy tries, uncomprehending, to console the girl, but she misinterprets his gentleness as yet another sexual assault. She angrily drives him away. She looks round the garden at the statues. Her body bends in pain and she walks rigidly forward towards an isolated and embittered future.

# Isadora

*Ballet in two acts. Music by Richard Rodney Bennett. Scenario by Gillian Freeman. Choreography by Kenneth MacMillan. Scenery and costumes by Barry Kay. First produced by The Royal Ballet at the Royal Opera House, Covent Garden, on April 30, 1981, with Merle Park and Mary Miller as Isadora, Derek Deane as Oskar Beregi, Julian Hosking as Edward Gordon Craig, Derek Rencher as Paris Singer, Ross MacGibbon as the Man on the Beach, and Stephen Jefferies as Sergei Esenin.*

Opposite: *Merle Park as Isadora Duncan in Kenneth Macmillan's* Isadora.

*Isadora* is not a ballet in the accepted sense. MacMillan's aim was to break with all the conventions which have been perpetuated from the big nineteenth-century ballets into the twentieth century's versions of these same spectaculars, in an attempt to reassert the "theatricality" of dance. To this end he employed speech and every resource available to him in the theatre to create a biographical fantasy about the life of the American modern dancer Isadora Duncan. Thus Duncan, the iconoclast, is celebrated in a work no less inconoclastic than her life. A key to MacMillan's approach was the fact that Duncan spoke extensively about her art, often interspersing her recitals with explanation and haranguing her audiences and the world in general about Life and Art—the capital letters implicit in her view. MacMillan therefore decided to divide the role of Isadora between an actress (originally Mary Miller), who is narrator and observer, and a dancer (originally Merle Park), who incarnates the lissom figure that Duncan believed herself to be.

The action of the piece is deliberately cinematic, and Barry Kay's design allows for considerable fluidity of narrative: he uses a bare stage into which properties can be introduced, plus an enormous silk curtain on a circular track which can enclose, conceal, or reveal incidents. MacMillan and his scenarist Gillian Freeman reached the conclusion that Duncan's life progressed through a series of "explosions."

## SYNOPSIS

*Act I*
We are introduced to the double Isadora figure. The Duncan tribe arrives in London, and Isadora gives her earliest recitals in society drawing rooms. (Isadora's dances are evocations by MacMillan of how he feels Duncan's style appeared to her contemporaries, just as Richard Rodney Bennett has provided pastiche Schumann and Brahms, rather than inserting authentic Duncan music, which would sit badly within the context of his own score.) There follow three scenes which are satiric views of the theatre dance of the time—the appalling Petit Ballet de Paris, the raucous Wadswa group of Spanish dancers, and a rehearsal of Loie Fuller's dancers. During the last, "Nursey," one of the Fuller *danseuses*, makes advances to Isadora. In the next scene Nursey's affections are even more explicitly stated, and as Duncan flees her the action moves to Budapest, where we see Isadora's first affair, with the actor Oskar Beregi. She next meets, and falls desperately in love with, Edward Gordon Craig, but there is a clash between their temperaments and their careers, and when she goes to Russia (where she sees the funeral of victims of the 1905 rebellion) the affair with Craig already seems doomed. The act ends with Isadora by the sea, in labour with her first child.

*Act II*
Isadora is now installed as mistress to Paris Singer, the millionaire whom she needed to finance her school (we have already seen her in Act I

recruiting children for the school, to be run by her sister). The infidelities implicit in this relationship are shown when Isadora flirts with a tango dancer (Ashley Page) and when, out of sheer boredom in England, she seduces the pianist André Caplet. We see her viewing the school run by Elisabeth Duncan and Max Merz, and aghast at the regimented style; premonitions of disaster to come are shown in a second sequence at a Russian train station, where she is haunted by a view of children's coffins. Projections on a screen show a motor car being pulled from the Seine and a newspaper headline announcing the death of her children. Paris Singer appears to tell her of their death, and after an agonised duet we see a rain-swept line of mourners watching the children's funeral procession, which ends with the tragic figure of Duncan walking past them in a trance of grief. There follows the most natural exteriorisation of this grief in two solos which Isadora dances.

She then consoles herself with an unknown young man on the beach, and her subsequent pregnancy occasions a vision scene in which her past lovers appear before her; she then gives birth to a child, who dies immediately.

Thereafter Isadora's decline is rapid. She goes to Russia, embraces the Revolution, and falls in love with the poet Esenin. She dances for the masses, and we are shown a celebrated incident in which a power failure in a theatre encourages her to dance to the singing of her audience.

A brief scene shows the drunken Isadora and the no less boorish Esenin with Maxim Gorky, and then comes the disastrous visit to the United States. Isadora dances the "Marseillaise" in a mass of scarlet draperies—this dance is performed by the actress Isadora, who accurately captures the statuesque style of Duncan's latter years—and, enraged by heckling and abuse from her public, she rounds on them and finally expresses her belief in Art by exposing her breast in a defiant gesture ("*This, this is Beauty*"). She is bundled away by the police.

The final scene shows Duncan in Nice, surrounded by an epicene court. She accepts a ride in the fateful Bugatti, and as it screeches to a halt the actress Isadora surveys the broken figure in the car and cries, "*Je vais à la gloire!*"

*Merle Park in the final scene of* Isadora.

# Ivan the Terrible

*Ballet in two acts. Music by Serge Prokofiev, arranged by Mikhail Chulaki. Choreography by Yuri Grigorovich. Scenery and costumes by Simon Virsaladze. First performed by the Bolshoi Ballet, Moscow, on February 20, 1975, with Yuri Vladimirov as Ivan and Natalia Bessmertnova as Anastasia.*

Grigorovich's drama is conceived in symbolic terms. The populace, the boyars, the bell ringers are convenient cyphers for an underlying theme of the struggle to unify the Russian state, a theme presented in a heavily expressionistic manner. Grigorovich extends many of the procedures he established with *Spartacus*: the succession of scenes in a general plan that intersperses big ensembles with soliloquies for his chief characters. Unlike *Spartacus*, though, *Ivan* is not a strict narrative. The demands of history and an overriding concern with the political rather than the personal shape the eighteen scenes to arrive—so says the programme—at a panorama of sixteenth-century Russia.

The score for the ballet is an elaboration and arrangement by Mikhail Chulaki of disparate Prokofiev music: from the film *Ivan the Terrible*, part of the Symphony No. 3, a section of *Alexander Nevsky*, and the Russian Overture. Brilliantly produced as spectacle, the drama yet fails to convince. In October 1976 *Ivan* was produced by its choreographer for the Paris Opéra Ballet.

| SYNOPSIS | | |
|---|---|---|
| **Act I, Scene 1**<br>*Moscow* | The bell ringers summon the people. The bells and their ropes are to be a leitmotif throughout the action. The | young Tsar, Ivan IV, has just mounted the throne and the bells announce this to the people. |
| **Scene 2**<br>*Ivan and the boyars* | The Tsar's hold on power is firm and he keeps the boyars on a short rein. The boyars are jealous of their power. | |
| **Scene 3**<br>*Arrival of the brides-to-be* | The Tsar is to marry. From thirteen young women presented to him he chooses Anastasia. Flattered and | already used to submission, she easily forgets Prince Kurbsky, leader of the boyars, who is in love with her. |
| **Scene 4**<br>*Kurbsky's despair* | Kurbsky is the most powerful of the boyars and a wily politician. He gives up his love for Anastasia and manages to control his first few weeks of despair | without too much pain. But he determines to be avenged on the Tsar by whatever means he can. |
| **Scene 5**<br>*The Tocsin* | The bells announce battle against invaders. The soldiers are summoned for fresh combat against the constant | danger of Tartar invasion. Ivan and Kurbsky lead their men into battle. |
| **Scene 6**<br>*Anastasia's meditation* | Anastasia wonders fearfully about her beloved Ivan and dreams tenderly of him and their future together. | |
| **Scene 7**<br>*The victory celebrations* | The Russians have been victorious. Festivities mark the general happiness of the populace. | |
| **Scene 8**<br>*Ivan's sickness* | The Tsar has been gravely ill for weeks. It is thought he will die. The boyars kneel before Ivan, who is in | torment on his throne. They are eager to regain their former power; each is certain that the throne should be his. |
| **Scene 9**<br>*"Ivan the Terrible"* | As the boyars plot, Ivan rounds on them, casting down one boyar who has sought to mount the throne. | Miraculously cured, Ivan turns upon the boyars and reasserts his complete dominion over them. |

*Jean Guizerix and Dominique Khalfouni as Ivan and Anastasia in the Paris Opéra Ballet's staging of Yuri Grigorovich's* Ivan the Terrible *in 1976.*

| | | |
|---|---|---|
| **Act II, Scene *1***<br>*Ivan's happiness* | Supreme master of his lands, having been made secure in his power by punishing the traitors and by the fear | he has inspired in them, Ivan is happy. Anastasia is the cause of his private happiness. |
| **Scene *2***<br>*The boyars' conspiracy* | The boyars and their womenfolk plan treachery. They pledge their loyalty with a cup of wine with which they decide to poison Anastasia. They offer | it to Kurbsky, who cannot take it, for he still loves Anastasia. But he does not prevent one of his peers from offering it. |
| **Scene *3***<br>*Anastasia's death* | Anastasia is given the cup. She drinks from it and collapses. She sinks into Kurbsky's arms, then rises and tries to | avenge herself by reaching out to the traitors before dying. |
| **Scene *4***<br>*The people's uprising* | The bell ringers give news of Anastasia's death to the people. The people revolt and this incident marks | the beginning of a long period of trouble and violence. |
| **Scene *5***<br>*Ivan weeps* | Ivan, half mad with grief, goes to mourn in the church where Anastasia lies. In his frenzy it seems to him that | Anastasia returns to him. She seems to offer him her blessing. |
| **Scene *6***<br>*Kurbsky's flight* | Kurbsky, compromised by his treacherous relations with foreign powers, flees to Poland. Ivan scourges | the drunken boyars and traps them with his soldiers. |
| **Scene *7***<br>*The boyars are hounded* | The boyars are pitilessly tracked down by the personal guard that Ivan has instituted as his tool of vengeance. Disguised as an evil clown, Ivan | derides and terrifies them. Kurbsky has been recaptured and is made to drink poison from the cup which killed Anastasia. |
| **Scene *8***<br>*Ivan's meditation* | The Tsar finds power is a dreadful burden. He climbs over figures which seem to threaten him with fears for his | mortality but he holds in his hands the lands of Russia—he is the first Tsar of all Russia. |
| **Scene *9***<br>*Epilogue* | Swinging from the bell ropes which dominate the scene, Ivan surveys the land of which he is absolute master. | |

# Jardin aux Lilas

*Ballet in one act. Music by Ernest Chausson (Poème for violin and orchestra). Choreography by Antony Tudor. Scenery and costumes by Hugh Stevenson. First performed by the Ballet Rambert at the Mercury Theatre, London, on January 26, 1936, with Maude Lloyd as Caroline, Hugh Laing as Her Lover, Antony Tudor as The Man She Must Marry, and Peggy van Praagh as An Episode in His Past.*

"Tudor was probing beneath the surface of actions and behaviour, trying to show the 'why' as well as the 'how,' and in so doing he was enlarging the frontiers of ballet and moving into a territory which he conquered completely in *Pillar of Fire* and into which very few choreographers have been able to follow." (*Dancers of Mercury* by Mary Clarke, London, 1962.)

When Antony Tudor was invited to join American Ballet Theatre in 1939 he staged *Jardin aux Lilas* for that company. In 1951 he also produced it for the New York City Ballet as (*Lilac Garden*), and The Royal Ballet presented it briefly in 1968. It has also been mounted for the National Ballet of Canada and the Royal Danish Ballet, among others. It remains one of the masterpieces of balletic psychology.

SYNOPSIS

Jardin aux Lilas, *as revived for The Royal Ballet in 1968, with the central quartet of Georgina Parkinson, Desmond Doyle, Svetlana Beriosova, and Donald MacLeary.*

In a garden overhung by lilac bushes an evening party is taking place. "Caroline, amidst the continuous interruptions of her friends, tries to take a last farewell of her lover before she is married to a man she does not love." Tudor's programme note indicates the essence of an action in which meetings and partings seem drenched by the scent of lilac and the swooning emotionalism of the score.

Caroline seeks to have a moment to say farewell to her lover, but they are forever thwarted by the presence of her prospective husband and the other guests. Similarly, another woman tries to snatch a last moment with the husband-to-be; she has obviously been his mistress. A crucial passage in the ballet comes when the action is frozen; Caroline alone can move out from among the motionless group of characters and survey past and future.

As Caroline bids a formal farewell to the guests, her lover presses a lilac sprig into her hand. Caroline leaves on the arm of the man she must marry. Her lover stands alone, his back to the audience, his body taut with grief.

# *Jewels*

*Ballet in three acts. Music by Gabriel Fauré, Igor Stravinsky, and Pyotr Ilyich Tchaikovsky. Choreography by George Balanchine. Scenery by Peter Harvey. Costumes by Karinska. First performed by the New York City Ballet at the State Theater, Lincoln Center, on April 13, 1967, with Violette Verdy and Conrad Ludlow in Emeralds, Patricia McBride and Edward Villella in Rubies, and Suzanne Farrell and Jacques d'Amboise in Diamonds.*

*Jewels* is three ballets linked by the idea of jewels: Balanchine had been shown a fine collection of precious stones in the New York showrooms of Van Cleef and Arpels. The opening ballet, *Emeralds*, is set to the incidental music that Fauré wrote for productions of *Pelléas et Mélisande* and *Shylock*. Ever obedient to his score, Balanchine provides dances that, by rarely rising above a dynamic *mezzo forte*, reflect all the quiet feeling of the music. The mood is romantic: there are hints at some of the "lovers'

*Stephanie Saland in* Emeralds.

*Patricia McBride and Mikhail Baryshnikov in* Rubies.

meetings" attitudes in Balanchine's earlier *Bourrée Fantasque*, and there is one exquisite solo, forever associated with the wonderfully musical dancing of its creator, Violette Verdy, which is set to the Spinning Song from *Pelléas*. *Rubies*, which follows, uses Stravinsky's 1929 Capriccio for Piano and Orchestra and is set for a central couple with an attendant female soloist and a corps de ballet of twelve dancers. Balanchine refracts the music through a ruby's facets to create a multi-rayed burst of dances that are intensely witty, glittering in cut, and as capricious as is the music itself. It is choreography of almost violent dynamic brilliance; the romantic feeling of the previous scene is replaced by a sharp-edged, exhilaratingly distorted classicism. The atmosphere is urban, tough, fast-pulsed. The dance insists upon a good-humoured and amused dislocation of traditional classical positions: sharp thrusts of the pelvis and athletic runs for the men; arms bent and fingers outspread as if imitating mad birds for the girls. For the male dancer Balanchine devised choreography of madcap virtuosity, supremely executed by Edward Villella. There is something about the bravura and verve of the dancing of the central couple that makes them look like fugitives from Broadway, for the piece pays nodding tribute to show business, turning the demotic of theatrical dance into something glittering and saucy.

*Suzanne Farrell and Peter Martins in* Diamonds.

*Diamonds* is Balanchine's tribute to his Petersburg past. It has been a convention to label Balanchine as heir to Petipa, which he indeed is in his development of the nineteenth-century's *danse d'école* as a tool for twentieth-century genius. Yet in *Diamonds*, which uses the last four movements of Tchaikovsky's Symphony No. 3 in D, we seem to see Balanchine as Ivanov rather than as Petipa. It is possible to view *Diamonds* as a homage to the Petersburg traditions in which Balanchine was educated, and to examine the "Russian to Russian" relationship of Tchaikovsky and Ivanov rather than the "Russian to French" manner of Tchaikovsky and Petipa. The two *ballabile* set to the symphony's Alla tedesca and its later Scherzo use fourteen girls to evoke the crystalline evolutions of the snowflakes in Ivanov's *Nutcracker*, rethought, but still catching an essential lyricism. Even more so the Andante elegiaco, which Balanchine made as a duet for the leading couple. It is a loving summation of the late-Romantic pas de deux, suggesting the Odette-Siegfried encounter in the second act of *Swan Lake*, with the same intensity and magnificent unfurling of the choreographic line. The symphony's final Polacca is Petipa, a polonaise for the entire cast, and it could serve as the closing sequence for *The Sleeping Beauty*: noble, Maryinsky-grand, and wonderful. If the entire Imperial Russian inheritance of ballet were lost, *Diamonds* would still tell us of its essence.

# Kammermusik No. 2

*Ballet in one act. Music by Paul Hindemith. Choreography by George Balanchine. Costumes by Ben Benson. First performed by the New York City Ballet at the State Theater, Lincoln Center, on January 26, 1978, with Karin von Aroldingen, Sean Lavery, Colleen Neary, and Adam Lüders.*

As is evidenced by *The Four Temperaments*, Hindemith's music sparks a wonderful response from Balanchine. In *Kammermusik No. 2*—composed in 1924 as Concerto for Piano and Twelve Instruments—the gritty academism of the score, its earnestness, and its moments of hushed poetic resonance are exactly matched in dances led by two women with partners and a corps de ballet of eight men—this last something of a departure for Balanchine. Karin von Aroldingen's style seems central to the work. She is a dancer with an abrasive, almost Amazonian manner here, "unfeminine" in conventional ballet terms, sometimes aggressive and brusque. This is very much the quality of the ballet. Von Aroldingen and Colleen Neary appear like movement and its reflection with canonic devices, echoes, parallelism, that suggest dancing seen "out of sync" or played in a "follow the leader" sequence a mere fraction of a second apart. The quick, urgent thrust of the women's dances is set against quirky writing for the male chorus, who curl and curve at moments in a linked chain of bodies or exit with arms bent at elbows and fingers splayed (a device that recalls Balanchine's *Rubies*). In a duet in the second movement, von Aroldingen dances as if hiding her face, and the image is unexpected, disquieting; but Balanchine has found a potent response to Hindemith in this uncompromising dance manner, with its absence of academic niceness and its nervous, athletic pulse.

*ean Lavery and Karin von roldingen of the New York ity Ballet in* Kammermusik No. 2.

# Kermesse in Bruges

*Ballet in two acts and four scenes. Music by Holger Simon Paulli. Choreography by August Bournonville. Scenery and costumes by Lars Juhl (1978 staging). First performed by the Royal Danish Ballet at the Royal Theatre, Copenhagen, on April 4, 1851.*

Kermesse, one of Bournonville's most joyous works, was originally a three-act production. As revived for the 1978–79 season in Copenhagen by Hans Brenaa it was in two hilarious acts. The richness of the Danish dramatic tradition is evident in that everyone is remarkable in the production. Every role, no matter how small, is played with total conviction.

## SYNOPSIS

**Act I, Scene 1**
*The marketplace of Bruges*

The action takes place in Bruges in the seventeenth century. A church fair—a kermesse—finds three brothers, Adrian, Geert, and Carelis, enjoying themselves. The older two are with their sweethearts, Johanne and Marchen; Carelis is with Eleonora, daughter of the alchemist Mirevelt. After a lovers' quarrel the three young men decide to find their fortunes in the world. Just as they leave they see Mirevelt being attacked by noblemen who wish to kidnap his daughter. The brothers save Mirevelt and are rewarded by three gifts: Geert receives a magic ring which causes everyone to fall in love with him; Adrian a sword which makes him invincible in battle; and Carelis a lute which will set everyone dancing to its magic tune.

**Scene 2**
*Mirevelt's study*

Johanne and Marchen want to know how their fiancés are faring in the world. A vision shows them Adrian successful in war and Geert successful with women. Suddenly they hear Carelis' lute. He urges them to go and seek out his brothers and tells Eleonora of his love for her.

**Act II, Scene 1**
*The house of Madame van Everdingen*

Geert has fallen on his feet. A rich widow, Madame van Everdingen, is besotted with him and has set him up in luxury. At a party the women cannot keep away from him. Adrian now appears, a hero in war, and soon Johanne and Marchen, with their mother, Trutje, appear. They are united with their true loves and the magic ring passes from hand to hand, finally ending up with Trutje. The two boys decide to get rid of their magic gifts but the authorities arrive and condemn them and Mirevelt to the stake as sorcerers, and they are led away by guards.

**Scene 2**
*The marketplace*

The three offenders are roped to the stake but Carelis appears and forces everyone to dance to the tune of his lute until they beg for mercy. Mirevelt, Adrian, and Geert are released in exchange for the lute, which is locked away in a chest to be played only at the annual kermesse. The lovers are reunited.

Opposite: *Ib Andersen and Mette-Ida Kirk of the Royal Danish Ballet as Carelis and Eleonora.*

# Konservatoriet

*Ballet in two acts. Music by Holger Simon Paulli. Choreography by August Bournonville. First performed by the Royal Danish Ballet at the Royal Theatre, Copenhagen, on May 6, 1849. Edited to one act in 1941 by Valborg Borchsenius and Harald Lander.*

Originally *Konservatoriet* was a two-act ballet set in Paris, in which Bournonville provided an amusing portrait of the man-hunting housekeeper of the principal of the Conservatoire, where Bournonville had studied dancing as a young man in the 1820s. The Ballet remained in the Royal Danish Ballet repertory until 1934. Seven years later its first scene was revived and revised to provide a divertissement view of the ballet class at the Conservatoire. This was Bournonville's homage to the great dancer and teacher Auguste Vestris (1760–1842), who was his professor and who entirely shaped him as a dancer. Thus Bournonville gives us a fascinating insight into the dance style of the old French school which was the basis of all his work. Extremely difficult to perform well, *Konservatoriet* is revered in Copenhagen: it offers brilliant choreography for both men and women, and allows the child pupils of the Royal Danish Ballet School to make a charming and unselfconscious appearance.

The ballet has been mounted for other companies, including the Joffrey Ballet in 1969 and London Festival Ballet in 1973 (in a careful staging by Mona Vangsaae), but authenticity of performance in this work can come only from years of schooling in the Bournonville manner.

*Dancers of the Royal Danish Ballet in* Konservatoriet; *the male dancers are wearing the flattering "Bournonville shoe" with its white "v" shape leading from the toes up to the arch of the foot.*

# The Lesson

*Ballet in one act. Music by Georges Delerue. Libretto by Flemming Flindt, based on Eugene Ionesco's play* La Leçon. *Scenery and costumes by Bernard Daydé. First performed on Danish television on September 16, 1963, with Josette Amiel and Flindt; revived at the Opéra-Comique, Paris, on April 6, 1964, with the same cast.*

The distinguished Danish dancer Flemming Flindt, who had a notable dance career not only in Copenhagen but also with the Paris Opéra Ballet and London Festival Ballet, came to choreography by way of television. He collaborated with Eugene Ionesco, first with *La Leçon* and later with *The Young Man Must Marry* and *The Triumph of Death* (based on Ionesco's *Jeu de Massacre*), all of which were originally conceived for television and then transferred to the stage, as was his version of *The Miraculous Mandarin* (1967). Flindt's gift for theatrical effect endowed these works with an immediacy which appealed very much to the younger audience in Copenhagen. In *The Triumph of Death*, to a commissioned pop score by Thomas Koppel, Flindt produced a characteristically brash yet often moving panorama of mankind as prey to plagues of various kinds. It enjoyed a long run in Copenhagen and was seen in London and New York. His *Salome*, to a score by Peter Maxwell Davies, was performed in a circus—Béjart fashion—in Copenhagen in 1979. Flindt was Director of the Royal Danish Ballet from 1965 to 1978, retiring early because of an injury.

**SYNOPSIS**

The scene is a ballet studio. A grim pianist is setting the room to rights, arranging furniture and tidying a dreadful muddle. The doorbell rings and we see the figure of a young girl waiting outside the door of the studio. The pianist draws the curtains. The bell rings again. Only now, when the room is tidy, does the pianist go to the door and let in the girl who has come for a ballet lesson. The girl is ushered into a changing room and returns ready for class. Now the ballet master appears, a grey-haired figure whom we immediately recognise as being disturbed. Just how disturbed is only revealed as the lesson progresses. The demands he makes upon the girl in her exercises become increasingly manic, and as the girl puts on her pointe shoes the teacher loses control. He strangles his pupil, and his relationship with the warden-pianist becomes clear: he turns to her like a naughty child to its mother when it knows it has behaved badly. The girl's corpse is removed and the ballet master retires.

The pianist draws the curtains and sets about tidying the room in readiness for the next lesson. The doorbell rings. . . .

Right: *Rudolf Nureyev as the ballet master and Anne Marie Vessel as the pupil in Flemming Flindt's* The Lesson.

# Liebeslieder Walzer

*Ballet in one act. Music by Johannes Brahms. Choreography by George Balanchine. Scenery by David Hays. Costumes by Karinska. First performed by the New York City Ballet at the City Center, New York, on November 22, 1960, with Diana Adams and Bill Carter, Melissa Hayden and Jonathan Watts, Jillana and Conrad Ludlow, and Violette Verdy and Nicholas Magallanes.*

Liebeslieder Walzer, *as performed by the New York City Ballet.*

The waltz, which has ever inspired Balanchine, seems here to reach an apotheosis—quite as much as in the grander scheme of *Vienna Waltzes*. Modest in scale, *Liebeslieder Walzer* is a work of the most exquisite construction, with an exceptional brilliance in the way that Balanchine, in the first part, transcends the inherent problems of treating the waltz in more sober and social form, as opposed to its freer, more theatrical style in the second part. In doing so, he creates choreography of the most heart-stirring grace and ease.

SYNOPSIS  Brahms' *Liebeslieder* waltzes and the subsequent set of *Neue Liebeslieder* waltzes are settings of love poems for vocal quartet and piano duettists. They are chamber music, intended for the delight of nineteenth-century drawing rooms. On this musical foundation Balanchine has created a masterpiece about the nature of the waltz and about intimate feeling, for a group of four couples. The nature of the music dictates both form and development, as always with Balanchine's work.

At curtain rise we are in a drawing room, where four couples listen to the singers and pianists who are placed at the side of the stage. The beguiling waltz seizes the dancers. They move sweetly, almost decorously to its pulse in the first half of the ballet, for the women are in long satin dresses and low-heeled shoes, the men in evening dress. The ingenuities of pattern and phrase, of step and pose, that Balanchine creates from the lilt of triple time are ceaseless, fresh, absolutely at one with the domestic and emotional nature of the music. The couples flirt gently, but the sense of good manners and social convention is never lost—these are people from a clear historical period and their dances are masterly both in the wealth of choreographic invention and in the choreographer's acceptance and use of convention.

At the end of the first set of waltzes, the lights fade, the dancers walk out of the drawing room into the summer night, and the curtain falls. When it rises again the dancers have moved out under the stars. Gone are the women's heeled shoes and satin dresses; they are now idealised versions of their earlier selves in tulle and pointe shoes, and the dance has become the more idealised form of ballet. The horizons of the work are larger. The dancers, freed from social convention, become lighter, faster, more intoxicated by the possibilities of the waltz's rhythm and of movement itself. They respond to the feeling with more vivid emotion. The choreography soars.

But as the *Neue Liebeslieder* set ends, the stars fade from the sky, the candles gleam again in the drawing room, and the couples return to the stage clad as in the first section.

The final song is sung and the pairs of lovers, in turn, take their ease and listen quietly, immobile, to the last notes of the music. They applaud gently as the curtain falls.

# Lifeguards of Amager

*Ballet in two scenes. Music by Wilhelm Christian Holm. Choreography by August Bournonville. Scenery and costumes by Valdemar Gullich. First performed by the Royal Danish Ballet at the Royal Theatre, Copenhagen, on February 19, 1871, with Valdemar Price as Edouard du Puy and Laura Stillmann as his wife. Revived by Hans Brenaa in 1971 with scenery and costumes by Bjørn Wiinblad.*

*Lifeguards* is based upon Bournonville's own recollections of a childhood in which he visited the island of Amager, with its country community (of Dutch origin) where many old customs and costumes were preserved. In 1848, at the time of the Schleswig-Holstein war, Bournonville had joined the volunteer corps; his ballet combines memories of this and the earlier experiences of his childhood. Like *Far from Denmark*, *Lifeguards* is a fascinating survival of the "vaudeville ballet" in which mimetic narration plays a very important part. This is not dumbshow, but a gestural language possible only to the highly trained bodies of dancers. As with *Far from Denmark*, the early part of the ballet is largely pantomime—an art of which the Royal Danish dancers alone seem master—while the final section is an explosion of dancing.

SYNOPSIS

*Scene 1*
*Inside Tønnes farmhouse*

The ballet is set on the island of Amager, which is linked to Copenhagen by a bridge. It takes place in the house of a wealthy farmer, Tønnes, just before Lent in 1808. The lifeguards—a corps of volunteers—are quartered here in anticipation of an attack by the English fleet. A Shrovetide party is being prepared in the farmhouse and the central character, Edouard, a lieutenant (based on the well-known singer and womaniser Edouard du Puy), flirts with two local girls, Else and Trine. The sound of gunshot from an English vessel calls the volunteers away, and the two Amager girls have a disagreement with their local boyfriends, Jan and Dirk. A group of guests arrive from Copenhagen to celebrate carnival on the island and they include Edouard's wife Louise and her two friends Sophie and Andrea. When Jan and Dirk speak about the flirtatiousness of the volunteers, the ladies think it must be two young men, Otto and Emil, who are engaged to Sophie and Andrea, but Trine and Else point out that it is Edouard, and this news distresses Louise. She decides to teach her errant husband a lesson.

*Scene 2*
*A large room in the farmhouse*

In the entertainment that ensues on the volunteers' return, Louise is disguised as a *vivandière*, and she teases the mystified Edouard, who is immediately attracted to this stranger. There follow some divertissements which include a classic pas de trois, a sailor's reel, a molinasque and a quadrille in which the volunteers pose as characters from the comedies of the famous Danish dramatist Ludvig Holberg, with Louise as the central figure. Edouard swears his love, and Louise now reveals to him that he has been flirting with his own wife. She forgives him and the ballet concludes with a joyous galop.

# Le Loup

*Ballet in one act. Music by Henri Dutilleux. Libretto by Jean Anouilh and Georges Neveux. Choreography by Roland Petit. Scenery and costumes by Jean Carzou. First performed by the Ballets de Paris at the Théâtre de l'Empire, Paris, on March 17, 1953, with Violette Verdy, Roland Petit, Claire Sombert, and George Reich.*

*Le Loup* is a characteristic Petit work both in the distinction of the collaborators involved and in the sound theatrical argument which sustains the action. Petit has in many ballets been concerned with the idea of a physically blemished but heroic central figure, forever doomed to love unhappily. (His *Cyrano de Bergerac*, *Le Fantôme de l'Opéra*, *Notre Dame de Paris*, and *Le Rendezvous* all offer variations upon this theme.) Visually *Le Loup* is a work of haunting theatrical beauty. As always with Petit the importance of fine design is an integral part of his creations.

SYNOPSIS

The story takes place in a fantastical medieval period. In a clearing in the forest a group of peasants surround a travelling entertainer and his caravan. The entertainer—an animal trainer—and a gypsy girl watch a group of young men and girls who have come to see a wolf, which performs for them. The animal trainer is also a magician. He passes a black cloth in front of the face of a young girl, who suddenly acquires a wolf's mask. It is then removed by another pass of the cloth. The trainer repeats this trick on a bridal party who now appear, making the handsome bridegroom wolf-like, and then again removing the spell. The gypsy girl has already danced with the bridegroom and shown her interest in him. The bridegroom has to rejoin his bride, but shortly he contrives to return to see the gypsy girl once again, and to facilitate their liaison the animal trainer now transforms the wolf into a semblance of the bridegroom.

The bride and her wolf-groom now dance together. The bride is suddenly terrified when she sees that the groom has fangs and claws and a furry body, but she comes to realise that she loves him, and he her. Their mutual joy is disturbed by the return of the crowd with the gypsy girl and the animal trainer, who reveal the way in which the bride has been duped. The wolf is dragged away and the bridegroom goes to join his bride, but she rejects him. She goes to the wolf and they dash away into the forest.

The bride and the wolf flee through the forest and seek shelter from the outraged and pursuing villagers. They are trapped and surrounded by men and women who menace them with viciously shaped rakes and farm instruments. The wolf is attacked and mortally wounded. The girl, seeking to protect him, is also injured. The couple die in each other's arms. The girl's body is borne away. The animal trainer drags the carcass of the wolf away by the legs.

# Mam'zelle Angot

*Ballet in three scenes. Music by Charles Lecocq, arranged by Efrem Kurtz.*
*Choreography by Leonide Massine. Scenery and costumes by Mstislav Dobuzhinsky*
*(1943). First performed by American Ballet Theatre (as* Mademoiselle Angot*)*
*at the Metropolitan Opera House, New York, on October 10, 1943, with Nora Kaye,*
*Rosella Hightower, André Eglevsky, and Leonide Massine. Revived and revised*
*with scenery and costumes by André Derain for the Sadler's Wells Ballet at the Royal*
*Opera House, Covent Garden, on November 26, 1947, with Margot Fonteyn, Moira*
*Shearer, Michael Somes, and Alexander Grant.*

Opposite: *André Derain's*
*setting for the first scene of*
*the Sadler's Wells*
*production of* Mam'zelle
Angot.

Mam'zelle Angot is based upon the celebrated operetta *La Fille de*
*Madame Angot*, which was first performed in 1872. Massine staged the
ballet, based on his own adaptation of the operetta's libretto, for American Ballet Theatre in New York in 1943. When he came to work with the
Sadler's Wells Ballet at Covent Garden in 1947 he revised the
choreography and also commissioned superb new designs by André
Derain, who himself painted some of the decorations on the scenery. The
American version of the ballet soon disappeared, but *Angot* is still retained in the repertory of The Royal Ballet. In casting Alexander Grant
in his own created role of the barber, Massine launched the career of this
greatest of English character dancers.

*Margot Fonteyn as*
*Mam'zelle Angot and*
*Alexander Grant as the*
*Barber in the first scene of*
Mam'zelle Angot *as*
*staged by Leonide Massine*
*for the Sadler's Wells*
*Ballet in 1947.*

## SYNOPSIS

**Scene 1**
*The market*

Vendors are busy arranging their wares as Mam'zelle Angot arrives. She is the daughter of a shopkeeper and is betrothed to a Barber. The Barber is seen with his friends and he complains of Mam'zelle Angot's infidelity when she is attracted to a new arrival in the market, a handsome and dashing Caricaturist. While Angot dances with him, the Barber mopes in the arms of his friends. Matters are complicated when an elderly Government Official arrives with a beautiful Aristocrat on his arm. She is his mistress, but the Caricaturist is nevertheless attracted to her and makes a rude drawing of the Government Official. The Official orders the Chief of Police to arrest the Caricaturist, but he persists in his suit of the lady and follows the couple from the square.

Mam'zelle Angot has also incurred the police's displeasure by mocking the airs and graces of the Aristocrat and is arrested by two gendarmes. A frontcloth scene shows her outwitting the gendarmes and escaping.

**Scene 2**
*The salon of the Aristocrat's house*

One of the Aristocrat's friends is playing the harp while the others dance. The Caricaturist arrives and is hastily concealed by being put in place of a marble bust. The Government Official and the Chief of Police dance with the young girls, and the Caricaturist has fun with the Chief of Police before he recognises him and tells the Government Official. They exit. Mam'zelle Angot enters, followed by her Barber, to explain her conduct. She and the Aristocrat suddenly realise they are old acquaintances and embrace. Soldiers arrive pursuing the Caricaturist. The Aristocrat dances with their officer and pleads for a last reunion with the Caricaturist. They dance a love duet. A frontcloth scene shows revellers on the way to a fancy dress ball.

**Scene 3**
*A carnival*

The masked revellers dance and all the principal characters arrive for a resolution of the action. The Government Official is disillusioned about the fidelity of his mistress. The beautiful Aristocrat finally departs in the Caricaturist's arms and Mam'zelle Angot at last acknowledges her love for the Barber.

# *Manon*

*Ballet in three acts, based on Abbé Prévost's novel. Music by Jules Massenet, arranged and orchestrated by Leighton Lucas and Hilda Grant. Libretto by Kenneth MacMillan. Choreography by MacMillan. Scenery and costumes by Nicholas Georgiadis. First performed by The Royal Ballet at the Royal Opera House, Covent Garden, on March 7, 1974, with Antoinette Sibley as Manon, Anthony Dowell as Des Grieux, David Wall as Lescaut, Monica Mason as his mistress, and Derek Rencher as Monsieur G.M.*

*Opposite: David Wall as Lescaut and Derek Rencher as Monsieur G. M. in the first scene of* Manon.

*Overleaf: Natalia Makarova as Manon and Anthony Dowell as Des Grieux in the first scene of* Manon.

**Manon** was Kenneth MacMillan's third full-length ballet. Although its score is by Massenet it uses nothing from that composer's opera of the same name. Originally written for Antoinette Sibley, Anthony Dowell, and David Wall, the ballet offers three superlative lyrical pas de deux in which the love of Manon and Des Grieux is celebrated, and a tour de force of comedy in the drunken duet in Act II for Lescaut and his mistress—a hilarious catalogue of balances only just held, of holds only just grasped. The progress of the narrative is well maintained and the ballet's dramatic strength has been proved by the number of impressive changes in cast that have followed its fine first performance—with, most notably, Natalia Makarova and Dowell, Jennifer Penney and Wayne Eagling as the lovers, and an exceptional switching of roles in which David Wall was Des Grieux, and Anthony Dowell and Lynn Seymour were the Lescaut siblings, united in their predatory progress through the ballet.

## SYNOPSIS

**Act I, Scene 1**
*The courtyard of an inn near Paris*

At curtain rise a black-cloaked figure is seated on the ground. He surveys the world like a predator. As the inn yard fills with people he is revealed as Lescaut, awaiting the arrival of his young sister, Manon, who is due to enter a convent. When she alights from a coach she is attended by a lecherous old gentleman, but Manon's beauty catches the eye of the wealthy Monsieur G. M., who has arrived with a group of actresses. Manon has also become an object of interest to the madame of a house of pleasure. Most importantly, Des Grieux, a young seminarian, has seen her and has fallen in love with her. She responds to his love and they flee to Paris while her brother arranges with G. M. to procure his sister in return for gold.

**Scene 2**
*Des Grieux's lodgings*

Des Grieux is writing a letter requesting money to his father, but he and Manon are passionately in love and dance ecstatically together. When Des Grieux leaves to mail the letter Lescaut arrives with G. M., who buys Manon with jewels and fine clothes. Lescaut awaits the return of Des Grieux and tries to calm his anguish with the prospect of the money which Manon's new relationship will bring them.

**Act II, Scene 1**
*Madame's residence*

A party is in progress and Manon enters, gorgeously dressed, on the arm of Monsieur G. M., as whores and their clients drink and gamble. Des Grieux appears with Lescaut, who dances a drunken pas de deux with his mistress. When all the guests have gone to supper Des Grieux reproaches Manon for her unfaithfulness. She eventually suggests that he should play cards and cheat, thereby winning enough money to enable them to escape together. This ruse is discovered and a fight ensues during which Des Grieux and Manon manage to get away.

**Scene 2**
*Des Grieux's lodgings*

The lovers are packing, preparing to flee, with Des Grieux objecting to the fact that Manon still wears G. M.'s jewels. G. M. now enters with soldiers who have arrested Lescaut. Before Manon's horrified gaze her brother is shot; she is arrested as a prostitute, and must await deportation.

| | | |
|---|---|---|
| *Act III, Scene 1*<br>*The port of New Orleans* | A shipboard of prostitutes arrives, deported to the Americas. Manon is among them and Des Grieux has contrived to stay with her by declaring | himself to be her husband. The jailor of the penal colony is attracted to Manon. |
| *Scene 2*<br>*The jailor's office* | Manon is summoned to the jailor and he makes love to her. She collapses in despair. The jailor gives her a bracelet. | At this moment Des Grieux enters and kills the jailor, then flees with Manon. |
| *Scene 3*<br>*The Louisiana swamps* | Manon and Des Grieux are running from their pursuers but Manon is now burning with fever. In her delirium she | seems to see the events from her past life and after a final agonised duet she dies in Des Grieux's arms. |

# Mayerling

*Ballet in three acts. Music by Franz Liszt, arranged and orchestrated by John Lanchbery. Libretto by Gillian Freeman. Choreography by Kenneth MacMillan. Scenery and costumes by Nicholas Georgiadis. First performed by The Royal Ballet at the Royal Opera House, Covent Garden, on February 15, 1978, with David Wall as Crown Prince Rudolf, Lynn Seymour as Mary Vetsera, Merle Park as Countess Larisch, Georgina Parkinson as the Empress Elisabeth, Michael Somes as the Emperor Franz Josef, Wendy Ellis as Princess Stephanie, and Graham Fletcher as Bratfisch.*

The action of MacMillan's *Mayerling* covers a period of eight years between the Crown Prince Rudolf's marriage and his death at Mayerling. It is a story that has been the subject of books, films, and endless speculation. MacMillan's purpose, and that of his scenarist, the novelist Gillian Freeman, is to cut away much of the spurious romanticism that surrounds this tragic and psychologically complex event to suggest something nearer the truth of what happened. To be able to do so successfully in dance, and to create so gripping a dramatic narrative, is a tribute to MacMillan's choreographic skill and also to the quality of his interpreters. Naturally, in the process of transference to the stage, history has been edited and given viable theatrical form. The result is first and foremost an outstanding dramatic ballet, which is also a remarkable study of a man trapped by society and by his own morbid psyche. In its very complexity the ballet demands that its audience prepare themselves beforehand by acquiring some knowledge of the intricacies of the political and social world of the Austro-Hungarian Empire. But even without prior knowledge, *Mayerling* is gripping theatre. It enshrines several exceptional roles, most notably that of Rudolf, which presents the most massive challenges to a male dancer.

No less intriguing are the women who surround him: his mother, his wife, his mistresses. With none of them is his relationship happy; none of them understands the demands he makes upon them. And it is curious that the Countess Larisch, who so fatally manipulates him, also seems to be the one who best understands him. The ballet received superlative performances from its original cast. As Rudolf, David Wall gave an interpretation magnificent in its sensitivity, in its dignity, and in its power to keep our sympathy despite the moral and physical degeneration of the character.

**SYNOPSIS**

*Prologue*

In the cemetery at Heiligenkeuz, just before dawn, a coffin is lowered into the ground in a secret burial.

*Act I, Scene 1*
*The ballroom of the Imperial Palace, Vienna*

A ball is being given to celebrate the marriage of Crown Prince Rudolf to Princess Stephanie of Belgium. Rudolf causes some comment by flirting with his new wife's sister. Left alone in the ballroom, he meets his former mistress, the Countess Larisch, and is introduced to a young girl, Mary Vetsera, by her mother. He also meets four Hungarian officers who wish to involve him in a separatist conspiracy for their country. Countess Larisch is eager to revive the one-time relationship she had with Rudolf. The Emperor Franz Joseph, returning with the court to the ballroom, is shocked by Rudolf's behaviour and orders him to think of his bride.

| | | |
|---|---|---|
| *Scene 2*<br>*The Empress Elisabeth's*<br>*apartments* | The Empress is surrounded by her ladies-in-waiting when Rudolf appears on his way to his bride. He makes a desperate appeal for understanding to | his mother, for her sympathy in his enforced marriage and his loneliness. Elisabeth does not respond to his entreaties. |
| *Scene 3*<br>*Rudolf's apartments* | The terrified Princess Stephanie awaits her husband. When he appears he frightens her even more by | threatening her with a revolver and by showing her a skull. He then brutally assaults her. |
| *Act II, Scene 1*<br>*(some years later)*<br>*A tavern* | Accompanied by his faithful driver Bratfisch, Rudolf has brought Stephanie to a low tavern in which he meets his erstwhile mistress Mitzi Caspar. Bratfisch, a popular entertainer, tries to distract Stephanie and eventually leads her away. A group of whores dance and then Mitzi and the four Hungarian officers join in an exultant display. A police raid ensues, but Rudolf, Mitzi, and the | Hungarian officers are able to hide. In despair at what he feels is the way he is hounded by the police. Rudolf suggests to Mitzi that they should commit suicide, but she refuses. Then Count Taafe, the Prime Minister, enters, having learned that Rudolf is in the tavern. Rudolf hides but Mitzi tells Taafe of his whereabouts and leaves with him. Rudolf and the Hungarians go also. |
| *Scene 2*<br>*Outside the tavern* | Rudolf is intercepted by Countess Larisch, who introduces Mary Vetsera, now a young woman in | society, whom she is chaperoning, and whom she feels will attract and be attracted to Rudolf. |
| *Scene 3*<br>*The Vetsera household* | Mary is dreaming over a portrait of Rudolf when Countess Larisch arrives. She tells Mary's fortune and deludes | her into thinking that Rudolf will love her. Mary gives Larisch a letter to Rudolf. |
| *Scene 4*<br>*Inside the*<br>*Imperial Palace* | A family party is being held to celebrate the Emperor's birthday. Count Taafe shows Rudolf a pamphlet advocating the Hungarian cause which implicates him. The Empress's admirer, the Englishman Colonel | "Bay" Middleton, makes Rudolf laugh by giving Taafe a joke cigar. The Empress presents her husband with a portrait of his mistress, the actress Katherina Schratt, who then sings to the assembled guests. During her so |

Rudolf despairingly surveys his world. As a firework display progresses in the gardens of the palace, Countess Larisch gives Rudolf Mary's letter.

**Scene 5**
*Rudolf's apartments*

Mary has been smuggled into the palace. She appears wearing only a nightdress under her coat; she and Rudolf become lovers.

**Act III, Scene 1**
*A winter countryside*

The court is at a shooting party. Rudolf's gun accidentally fires, narrowly missing the Emperor and killing a member of the court. The Hungarian officers are suspected of treason.

**Scene 2**
*Rudolf's apartments*

The Empress Elisabeth is furious when she discovers the Countess Larisch with Rudolf, who is by now a morphine addict. She orders Larisch to leave, but before she departs Larisch ushers in Mary. Rudolf suggests that they should die together.

**Scene 3**
*The hunting lodge at Mayerling*

Rudolf drinks with two companions, then dismisses them. Bratfisch brings in Mary. The lovers have decided to kill themselves, and after making passionate love to Mary and injecting himself with morphine, Rudolf leads her into a bedroom. A shot is heard. Rudolf emerges but dismisses his companions who come running in. Rudolf shoots himself, and his friends and his valet return to discover the bodies of the lovers.

**Epilogue**

At the cemetery of Heiligenkreuz the body of Mary, fully dressed, is lifted from a cab by Bratfisch, laid in a coffin, and buried.

*Opposite: Crown Prince Rudolf on his wedding night with his bride, Princess Stephanie: David Wall and Wendy Ellis.*

*Right: David Wall as Rudolf and Lynn Seymour as Mary Vetsera in the death scene at Mayerling.*

# A Midsummer Night's Dream

*Ballet in two acts. Music by Felix Mendelssohn. Choreography by George Balanchine. Scenery and lighting by David Hays. Costumes by Karinska. First performed by the New York City Ballet at the City Center, New York, on January 17, 1962 (revised version at the State Theater, Lincoln Center, on January 16, 1981) with Arthur Mitchell as Puck, Jillana as Helena, Edward Villella as Oberon, Melissa Hayden as Titania, Patricia McBride as Hermia, and Gloria Govrin as Hippolyta.*

*Gloria Govrin as Hippolyta in the original staging of* A Midsummer Night's Dream *by the New York City Ballet.*

Although Balanchine has noted that his ballet is inspired by the incidental music that Mendelssohn wrote for the play, he skillfully contrives to give an edited account of Shakespeare's drama in his first act. Since the Mendelssohn music is not adequate to sustain a full-length ballet, other music by the same composer has been used: the overtures to *Athalie, The Fair Melusine,* and *The First Walpurgis Night,* as well as *Son and Stranger* and the Symphony No. 9. The quicksilver Puck is a very well-realised character; the four lovers are drawn with tenderness and humour; and the role of Oberon contains some of Balanchine's most challenging male choreography, with its nonstop beaten steps. The second act is pure dance, a ceremonial affair ostensibly to celebrate the three weddings: of Theseus to Hippolyta, of Hermia to Lysander, and of Helena to Demetrius.

# Monotones I and II

*Ballet in two parts. Music by Erik Satie. Choreography by Frederick Ashton. Costumes by Ashton. First performed by The Royal Ballet at the Royal Opera House, Covent Garden, on March 24, 1965, with Vyvyan Lorrayne, Anthony Dowell, and Robert Mead (I), and on April 25, 1965, with Antoinette Sibley, Georgina Parkinson, and Brian Shaw.*

*Derek Deane, Vergie Derman, and Mark Silver in Ashton's Monotones II.*

*Monotones* started as a trio for a gala at the Royal Opera House. The dancers in white all-over tights and white caps were seen in calm movement to the hushed serenities of Satie's *Trois Gymnopédies*. This brief poem stole all the thunder of the gala. Its popularity was such that a month later, Ashton added a second *Monotones*, to Satie's *Trois Gnossiennes* and *Prélude d'Eginhard*, with the dancers costumed in pale almond green all-over tights. This trio is similar in style to the first, which it now precedes in performance, since both *Monotones* are usually given together. Ashton's mastery is everywhere apparent in the seamless flow of this apparently simple yet miraculous choreography.

179

# A Month in the Country

*Ballet in one act. Music by Frédéric Chopin, arranged by John Lanchbery. Libretto by Frederick Ashton. Choreography by Ashton. Scenery and costumes by Julia Trevelyan Oman. First performed by The Royal Ballet at the Royal Opera House, Covent Garden, on February 12, 1976, with Lynn Seymour as Natalia Petrovna and Anthony Dowell as Beliaev.*

*A Month in the Country*, coming after a period in which Ashton had created very little, showed his mastery of economic dramatic structure to be as sure as ever. He had abstracted from Turgenev's play its central incident and cast it into dancing that mingled skilled character solos with magnificently expressive emotional writing. The central role of Natalia Petrovna, superlatively created by Lynn Seymour, is that of a mature woman, and it treats of her emotions with maturity. The difficult role of the ingénue Vera is beautifully conceived in dance terms and was admirably taken by Denise Nunn, who was chosen from the corps de ballet by Ashton for this, her first major role. In the role of Beliaev, Anthony Dowell captured both the sexual charm and the headstrong youthfulness of the immature but irresistible tutor whose presence so disrupts the household.

*Lynn Seymour and Anthony Dowell of The Royal Ballet as Natalia Petrovna and Beliaev.*

*The closing moments of* A Month in the Country, *when Beliaev (Anthony Dowell) returns to take a last, unseen farewell of Natalia Petrovna (Lynn Seymour).*

SYNOPSIS

The scene is the country house of the Yslaev family. At curtain rise Natalia is seated on a chaise longue with her admirer Rakitin while her husband reads and her ward Vera plays the piano (the score is the Variations on "Là ci darem" from *Don Giovanni*) and her son Kolia writes at a desk. Each character is introduced in a short solo: a capricious variation for Natalia; a bouncy entry for Kolia, and a wild fluster as Yslaev searches for some lost keys. Then to dramatic chords in the score Beliaev the tutor enters. We sense immediately Natalia's interest in him and also Vera's girlish adoration. Natalia admits her feelings to Rakitin and she walks into the garden with him. Vera expresses her love for the tutor but he contrives, with great gentleness, to escape from her entreaties. When Natalia learns about this she seeks to dismiss Vera's feelings as mere girlish infatuation. But then, her jealousy breaks through and she slaps the girl's face. Immediately conscience-stricken, she goes into her room. Beliaev flirts momentarily with a maid, Katia, but

left alone he betrays his feelings for Natalia as he holds the shawl she has left behind. Her return—and Ashton's use of the Andante spianato and grande polonaise—produces an impassioned duet which suggests the depth of Beliaev's love and Natalia's mingled attraction and fear of the young man's infatuation. Vera enters, surprises them, and rouses the household. Natalia tries to laugh off the incident and goes into her bedroom for the moment.

Rakitin persuades Beliaev that they must both make their departure and they take farewell of Yslaev and Kolia; Yslaev leads his son away and Natalia returns to the empty room. She stands lost in sorrow with her back to the doors, which are open to the garden. Beliaev returns and walks quietly into the room; unnoticed, he kisses the ribbons of Natalia's peignoir and throws the rose she had earlier given him at her feet before darting silently away.

Natalia awakes from her reverie and picks up the rose.

# The Moor's Pavane

*Dance in one act. Music by Henry Purcell, arranged by Simon Sadoff. Libretto by José Limón, based on Shakespeare's Othello. Choreography by Limón. Costumes by Pauline Lawrence. First performed by José Limón and Company at the Palmer Auditorium, Connecticut College, on August 17, 1949 with Limón as the Moor, Betty Jones as His Wife, Lucas Hoving as the Friend, and Pauline Koner as the Friend's Wife.*

*The Moor's Pavane* makes a miniature of an immense play, and in so doing derives a power of its own. Designed for only four dancers plus a handkerchief, the text is organised into a series of dance meditations on the nature of love, fear, jealousy, bitchery, and remorse. By using courtly music and by emphasising quadrille patterns, Limón juxtaposed formal politeness and decorum with seething passions. The feeling of outward elegance is heightened by the women's long gowns, but as the dance progresses the costumes and very notion of pavanes and minuets become increasingly ironic. Even at the moment of murder Limón maintains this tension between manner and deed.

*The Moor's Pavane* is universally considered Limón's masterpiece. Although it bears no resemblance to ballet, and although critics have consistently maintained that it is more truly performed by modern dancers, many ballet companies have found it a useful addition to their repertories, among them American Ballet Theatre, the Joffrey Ballet, and the National Ballet of Canada.

The Moor's Pavane, *as performed by the Limón company.*

# Mozartiana

*Ballet in one act. Music by Pyotr Ilyich Tchaikovsky (Suite No. 4). Choreography by George Balanchine. Costumes by Rouben Ter-Arutunian. First performed by the New York City Ballet at the State Theater, Lincoln Center, on June 4, 1981, with Suzanne Farrell, Ib Anderson, and Christopher d'Amboise.*

For the opening night of the 1981 Tchaikovsky Festival, George Balanchine created his fourth version of *Mozartiana*—to the music with which Tchaikovsky paid tribute to his great predecessor. The title and the music (in a somewhat different order) are unchanged from Balanchine's early versions, but the ballet is completely new—and a work of extraordinary subtlety, elegance, and surprise.

It begins with the Preghiera, or Prayer, in which the ballerina, dressed in black, is attended by four young girls. There follow an energetic, almost humorous solo by the second male lead, a dance for four women, and then an amazing series of alternating variations for the ballerina and her partner, at the end of which they finally dance together. Only after this do the young girls, the older girls, and the three principals come together in a finale.

The entire ballet is characterized by an extraordinary fecundity of invention. Within a limited area of the stage, employing a small group of dancers, and restricting the range of steps (but not the variety), Balanchine has succeeded in creating a unique work—complex, ardent, moving, like Mozart himself.

*Suzanne Farrell in the Preghiera from Balanchine's Mozartiana.*

# Napoli

*Ballet in three acts. Music by Niels Gade, Edvard Helsted, Holger Simon Paulli, and Hans Christian Lumbye. Choreography by August Bournonville. Scenery by Christian Ferdinand Christensen. First performed by the Royal Danish Ballet at the Royal Theatre, Copenhagen, on March 29, 1842, with Bournonville, Caroline Fjeldsted, and Stramboe.*

Opposite: *Eva Kloborg and Flemming Ryberg dancing in the final celebrations of* Napoli. *On the bridge can be seen some of the pupils from the school of the Royal Danish Ballet. It is on this bridge that nearly every Danish dancer makes a first acquaintance with Bournonville's radiant masterpiece.*

*Napoli* is Bournonville's happiest masterpiece and one of the greatest achievements of nineteenth-century ballet. It gives some indication of Bournonville's ability to incorporate his travel experiences and affection for national dances into his ballets. He adored Italy and found the themes for several of his ballets in that sunny land. *Napoli* is typical of Bournonville's work both in its moral integrity and in the joyous richness of its dances set in the framework of a well-told narrative. Its last act is sometimes given by itself as an explosion of joy.

In Copenhagen the ballet is danced with total authority. The Danish Ballet is rich both in mime artists able to round out the several character roles with exceptional veracity (and comic resource) and in male dancers able to bound and soar through the ardours of the final act. We must salute in particular the performances of Niels Kehlet as Gennaro.

In 1978 Poul Gnatt staged a scrupulous production of *Napoli* for Scottish Ballet as part of a continuing process of acquiring Bournonville works for this company's repertory.

## SYNOPSIS

### Act I
*The wharf and square of Santa Lucia, Naples*

The scene is crowded with local inhabitants mingling with tourists and artists. The widow Veronica appears with her daughter Teresina, who is being courted by Giacomo, a macaroni vendor, and by Peppo, a lemonade seller. Teresina, however, is not interested; she is waiting for the return of her beloved Gennaro, a young fisherman. Gennaro arrives and there is bickering about the catch he has brought back. Veronica will not allow her daughter to be betrothed to Gennaro, and the young lovers have a quarrel, which is soon mended. Teresina and Gennaro give alms to Fra Ambrosio, a monk, and he blesses them, while Peppo and Giacomo try to spread slanders about Gennaro, accusing him of being in league with the devil. The young people of the town perform a general dance, after which the lovers set out for a sail by moonlight. The crowd is entertained first by the street singer Pascarillo and then by a puppeteer. Suddenly a storm breaks out. Gennaro is washed up in his boat, unconscious. Everyone thinks Teresina has been drowned. Veronica curses him, but he is consoled by Fra Ambrosio, who gives Gennaro a medallion of the Virgin and tells him not to despair but to go and seek his beloved.

### Act II
*The Blue Grotto in the Island of Capri*

The naiads bring the lifeless form of Teresina into the grotto, where Golfo, the sea spirit, is enraptured by her beauty and transforms her into a naiad. She has lost all memory of her earthly existence and when Gennaro rows into the grotto and finds her guitar she no longer recognises him. But the medallion of the Virgin defeats Golfo's powers and Teresina returns to her human form. Golfo and the sea nymphs have to acknowledge the power of Christianity. Gennaro and Teresina can leave, and Golfo, abandoning his designs on Teresina, gives the young couple treasures as they set out to return to the city of Naples.

*Act III*
*The Shrine of Monte*
*Virgine near Naples*

Pilgrims come to a shrine of the Virgin. Gennaro is shunned by the crowd, who believe him to be in league with the devil. But after he has been blessed by Fra Ambrosio, and Veronica has appeared with the rescued Teresina, a festival begins. The ballet culminates in a tremendous sequence of dances, including a sextet, a tarantella, and a wild finale as Teresina and Gennaro are fêted in a bridal cart to the sound of muskets being fired.

# Les Noces

*Ballet in one act. Music and text by Igor Stravinsky. Choreography by Bronislava Nijinska. Scenery and costumes by Natalia Goncharova. First performed by Diaghilev's Ballets Russes at the Théâtre Gaîté-Lyrique, Paris, on June 13, 1923, with Felia Dubrovska as the Bride and Leon Woizikowski as the Bridegroom.*

Above: *A design by Natalia Goncharova showing the bride's attendants holding one of her plaits.*

Below: *The corps de ballet of the Teatro la Fenice in the second scene, the Blessing of the Groom.*

Igor Stravinsky had started work on *Les Noces* in 1914 when he had taken up residence in Switzerland. The work was intended as an abstraction of the traditional ceremonies associated with a Russian peasant wedding, Stravinsky selecting the material of the text from collections of folk poetry. Diaghilev heard part of the score during the period of its composition and was profoundly moved by it, but it was not until 1922 that he eventually decided that the work could be staged. For choreography he turned to Bronislava Nijinska, whose recent work on *The Sleeping Princess* persuaded Diaghilev that she had creative ability. The design was entrusted to Goncharova, who created colourful designs; these were replaced, at Nijinska's insistence, by the austere design which reflects exactly the grand simplicity of her choreography. *Les Noces* is one of the masterpieces of twentieth-century ballet because of the architectural dignity of Nijinska's invention and the extraordinary rhythmic complexity by which she reflects the intricacies of Stravinsky's score for four pianists, percussion, and a group of singers. The Nijinska production of *Les Noces* is unchallenged. Both Jerome Robbins and Maurice Béjart have also choreographed ballets to Stravinsky's score.

In 1964 and 1966 Sir Frederick Ashton, then Director of The Royal Ballet, decided to repay a debt which he felt he owed to Bronislava Nijinska, from whom he had learned his craft of choreography, by inviting her to restage her two masterpieces, *Les Biches* and *Les Noces*, for The Royal Ballet. Those members of the Diaghilev Ballets Russes present at the Royal Ballet revival—Tamara Karsavina, Lydia

Sokolova, Lubov Tchernicheva, and Serge Grigoriev among them—were unanimous in hailing the authenticity of the staging.

## SYNOPSIS

Above: *Svetlana Beriosova as the Bride and Robert Mead as the Groom in the final scene of The Royal Ballet's production of* Les Noces.

The four scenes of the ballet are the Blessing of the Bride, the Blessing of the Groom, the Departure of the Bride and the Wedding Feast.

In the first scene the Bride is seen surrounded by a group of friends who are braiding her long tresses. The second scene shows the Bridegroom surrounded by a group of friends. In the third scene the Bride departs for her new home and leaves her mother mourning behind. In the fourth scene the two families are seen waiting on an inner stage while below them the massed corps de ballet of men and women dances in celebration. As the sound of bells rings out in the score, the bride and groom withdraw to the marriage chamber. A final pose shows the guests in a celebratory pyramid.

# The Nutcracker

*Ballet in two acts. Music by Pyotr Ilyich Tchaikovsky. Libretto by Marius Petipa. Choreography by Lev Ivanov. Scenery by M. I. Botcharov. First performed at the Maryinsky Theatre, St. Petersburg, on December 17, 1892, with Antonietta dell'Era as the Sugar Plum Fairy, Pavel Gerdt as the Prince, and Serge Legat as the Nutcracker.*

In 1891 Tchaikovsky was commissioned to produce a double bill for the Maryinsky Theatre which comprised his one-act opera *Iolanthe* and the two-act *Nutcracker*. The story of the ballet was based upon the tale of "The Nutcracker and the Mouse King" as adapted by Alexandre Dumas *père* from the original by E. T. A. Hoffmann. Marius Petipa drafted the scenario, but was then taken ill, and the ballet was eventually choreographed by his assistant, Lev Ivanov. Tchaikovsky was unhappy with the theme; nevertheless this, his last completed ballet score, contains some of his noblest music for the stage. When finally produced in 1892 the ballet was thought a failure through the flimsiness of its action and the poor opportunities it gave the ballerina. However, for the snow scene and for the grand pas de deux of the Sugar Plum Fairy and her cavalier, Ivanov had created magnificent choreography.

In the very early days of The Royal Ballet, then known as the Vic-Wells Ballet, Nikolay Sergueyev, former *régisseur* at the Maryinsky Theatre, staged the Ivanov *Nutcracker* under the title *Casse-Noisette* with considerable authenticity. This production, first seen at the Sadler's Wells Theatre on January 30, 1934, with Alicia Markova and Harold Turner, was a staple of the company's repertory for many years, and its choreography was to provide the text to which many other productions referred. The production did not survive the war.

The attraction of the score and the suitability of the subject for Christmas entertainment has meant that many choreographers have made their own versions of the ballet. The original Ivanov choreography is now, alas, no longer performed.

## SYNOPSIS

*Act I, Scene 1*
*The drawing room of Dr. Stahlbaum's house*

Dr. Stahlbaum and his wife are giving a Christmas party. With their guests they are decorating a Christmas tree. The doors of the drawing room open and a group of children come in, including Clara and Fritz, the Stahlbaums' daughter and son. Then another guest is announced: the mysterious Herr Drosselmeyer. He orders servants to bring in mechanical toys which he gives to the children. To Clara he also gives a toy nutcracker, which delights her. All the children play with their Christmas presents, and during the mêlée Fritz breaks Clara's new toy. She is heartbroken and Drosselmeyer repairs it. The guests join in a formal "Gross Vater" dance ("Grandfather" dance, the traditional end to the festivities at a private party), and then leave. Clara and Fritz are sent to bed by their parents and the room is deserted, lit only by moonlight. Clara returns in her nightgown to find her nutcracker toy, but she is frightened to hear the sound of mice squeaking and scratching. The clock strikes midnight and she is amazed to see that the figure of the owl which decorates the clock has turned into Drosselmeyer. Now mice appear and the Christmas tree begins to grow to enormous size. Terrified, Clara watches a battle

*Opposite: Dancers of the New York City Ballet in the snow scene from Balanchine's Nutcracker.*

189

which ensues between a regiment of toy soldiers and squadrons of mice led by the Mouse King. In order to save her Nutcracker, the leader of the soldiers, from attack by the Mouse King she throws a slipper at the enemy, who falls dead. The Nutcracker turns into a handsome prince and leads Clara on a magical journey.

*Scene 2*
*A fir forest in winter*

Amid snowy trees, Clara watches the snowflakes dance in swirling patterns.

*Act II*
*The palace of the Sugar Plum Fairy in the Kingdom of Sweets*

Clara and the Nutcracker Prince are welcomed by the Sugar Plum Fairy. She is told how Clara has saved the Nutcracker and there follows a divertissement in her honour: Chocolate is a Spanish dance: Coffee is an Arabian dance, and Tea is a Chinese dance. There follows a Trepak which is a Russian dance; a dance of the flutes; and then Mère Gigogne), a fairy-tale character, appears with little children climbing from under her skirts. Finally there is the Waltz of the Flowers. The Sugar Plum Fairy and her cavalier dance a grand pas de deux and there follows a big ensemble for all these characters.

## New York City Ballet

*Ballet in two acts.*
*Music by Pyotr Ilyich Tchaikovsky.*
*Choreography by George Balanchine.*
*Scenery by Rouben Ter-Arutunian.*
*Costumes by Karinska.*
*First performed at the City Center, New York, on February 2, 1954. Revised with costumes and scenery as above on December 11, 1964, at the State Theater, Lincoln Center.*

George Balanchine danced in *The Nutcracker* when he was a pupil at the ballet school in Petrograd. For his own company he accepted the original scenario, though amplifying it with some reference to its original Hoffmann story. The opening scene presents the interior of the wealthy bourgeois household of Dr. Stahlbaum. Marie and Fritz, the Stahlbaum children, are asleep in the hallway of their home as the Doctor and his wife decorate a Christmas tree in the drawing room, for it is Christmas Eve. The children awaken and await the arrival of guests, who eventually turn up with more children, and all enter the drawing room, where Dr. Stahlbaum organises his young visitors and their parents for games and dances. As the children examine their presents the owl on top of an old grandfather clock flaps its wings and an old family friend, Herr Drosselmeyer, appears. He is Marie's godfather and he is also an inventor of automata. He has brought with him three large boxes and also his dashing young nephew, who immediately appeals to Marie. The boxes turn out to contain mechanical dolls—a Harlequin, a Columbine, and a Toy Soldier—who dance to everyone's delight. But for Marie there is a special nutcracker toy, shaped like a soldier. Fritz is upset by this favouritism and breaks the toy. Drosselmeyer's nephew chases him off and Drosselmeyer comforts Marie by bandaging the nutcracker's head with his handkerchief. Marie and her friends play with their dolls, despite some boisterous interruptions from the boys,

and Marie puts her nutcracker to bed. The children are now getting drowsy and after a final dance for the guests everyone departs and Marie bids farewell to Drosselmeyer's nephew.

The room darkens and at midnight Marie returns in her nightgown. She seeks out her nutcracker and takes him to the sofa, cradled in her arms. Now Drosselmeyer appears and without waking the sleeping Marie mends the nutcracker. At this moment the lights on the Christmas tree flash and Marie awakens and runs to put the nutcracker back in his own bed. Suddenly, terrified, she sees Drosselmeyer like an owl on top of the clock, and as she hides a large mouse appears. Now everything in the room seems to grow: tree, toy soldiers, even the room itself, and there is an invasion of mice. The soldiers protect Marie and battle with the mice but these toy troops seem in danger of losing the battle. Help is at hand. The Nutcracker, now full size, leads the soldiers in battle; a cannon fires sweets at the mice and Marie stuns the Mouse King with her shoe so that the Nutcracker can run him through with his sword. Marie collapses onto the Nutcracker's bed—now also full size—which glides from the room into the snowy night where the snowflakes dance.

Act II takes place in "Confituerenburg," which resembles the inside of a enormous box of sweets. Twelve little angels glide across the stage. The Sugar Plum Fairy dances a variation, for she is ruler of this kingdom. Variations are also danced by Hot Chocolate, Coffee, Tea, Candy Canes

*Opposite: Anthony Dowell as Drosselmeyer in the party scene of Rudolf Nureyev's staging of* The Nutcracker *for The Royal Ballet.*

Marzipan Shepherdesses, Mother Ginger and her Polichinelles, and a Dewdrop leading a Waltz of the Flowers. Now Marie arrives with her Nutcracker Prince in a walnut boat. The Prince tells the Sugar Plum Fairy all the events of the battle and of Marie's bravery. As a reward, the Sugar Plum Fairy presents a divertissement for their delight. At its culmination the Sugar Plum Fairy and her cavalier dance the grand pas de deux. Now all of the sweets return to salute Marie and her Prince and bid them farewell, for a sleigh drawn by reindeer has arrived to take them up into the sky as the curtain falls.

It was Balanchine's enterprise in reviving this much-loved ballet as a seasonal entertainment that has led to its present popularity throughout the United States in a variety of stagings. Maria Tallchief danced the Sugar Plum Fairy in the original cast.

## The Royal Ballet

*Ballet in two acts.*
*Music by*
*Pyotr Ilyich*
*Tchaikovsky.*
*Choreography by*
*Rudolf Nureyev.*
*Scenery and costumes by*
*Nicholas Georgiadis.*
*First performed at the*
*Royal Opera House,*
*Covent Garden, on*
*February 29, 1968.*

In his version of *The Nutcracker*—which was first staged for the Royal Swedish Ballet in 1967—Rudolf Nureyev reworked the dramatic element in the tale to try and make the ballet more suited to an adult audience. His production follows the original story line at first but during the party Clara falls asleep and dreams of the mouse battle and her rescue of the nutcracker, who is turned into a Prince. In the snowflake scene at the end of Act I there is an interpolated pas de deux for Clara and the Prince.

At the start of the second act, Clara finds herself alone being attacked by huge bats, but these turn—such is the Freudian nature of the staging—into the members of her family, and when Drosselmeyer disappears he turns out, perhaps unsurprisingly, to be the Nutcracker Prince. The statutory divertissement is given in Clara's toy theatre by her dolls, and by members of her family, and Clara and the Prince dance the grand pas de deux, entirely rechoreographed by Nureyev. After the Waltz of the Flowers we find ourselves back at the party as Clara awakes to see the guests leaving; and, dashing to the front door of her home, she sees Drosselmeyer walking away down the snowy street.

## Bolshoi Ballet

Ballet in two acts.
Music by
Pyotr Ilyich
Tchaikovsky.
Choreography by
Yuri Grigorovich.
Scenery and costumes by
Simon Virsaladze.
First performed at the
Bolshoi Theatre,
Moscow,
on March 12, 1966.

Yuri Grigorovich, when he became director of the Bolshoi Ballet in Moscow, produced a charming (albeit visually dismal) staging to supplant the earlier production by Vainonen. It follows the traditional scenario, differing only in making Drosselmeyer

a jovial eccentric who eventually takes Masha (as the girl is called in all Soviet productions) and her Nutcracker Prince off into the skies in a balloon. Masha, who is a young girl, is a full-scale ballerina role.

Vladimir Levashev as Drosselmeyer in the closing moments of Yuri Grigorovich's staging of The Nutcracker for the Bolshoi Ballet.

## San Francisco Ballet

Ballet in two acts.
Music by
Pyotr Ilyich
Tchaikovsky.
Choreography by
Willam Christensen
(1944);
Lew Christensen (1954,
1967).
Scenery and costumes by
Robert O'Hearn (1967;
second act redesigned
1980).
First performed at the War
Memorial Opera House,
San Francisco,
On December 24, 1944.

The San Francisco Ballet mounted the first full-length production of *The Nutcracker* in the United States, and it has been an annual Christmas extravaganza for San Franciscans every year since its première in 1944. Willam Christensen, then director of the company, received advice for his *Nutcracker* from George Balanchine and Alexandra Danilova, both of whom had danced in it as children. "One evening . . . George described the Maryinsky production: how the big doors opened on the tree, the mime with Drosselmeyer. . . . We worked all night, and this is how I got my first *Nutcracker*," wrote Christensen. And this is why the San Francisco production bears so strong a family resemblance to the one Balanchine mounted for the New York City Ballet.

In 1954, Willam's brother—Lew Christensen—rechoreographed the ballet, and he revised this version himself in 1967.

The story is traditional—with such differences from Balanchine's as having Drosselmeyer's dancing mechanical toys represent a doll and a brown bear (instead of two dolls followed by a toy soldier), and having Clara and the young prince greeted by the Snow King and Queen as they enter the Land of Snows. There are also individual conceptions of the dances that take place in the palace of the Sugar Plum Fairy—Chinese Tea is a fiery dragon, and there are Ribbon Candy dancers, as well as a magician who makes the pretty Arabian Coffee disappear.

## American Ballet Theatre

Ballet in two acts.
Music by
Pyotr Ilyich
Tchaikovsky.
Choreography by
Mikhail Baryshnikov.
Scenery by
Boris Aronson.
Costumes by
Frank Thompson.
First performed at the
Kennedy Center,
Washington, D.C., on
December 21, 1976.

The Nutcracker as
staged by Mikhail
Baryshnikov for American
Ballet Theatre with, left
to right, Baryshnikov as
the Prince, Marianna
Tcherkassky as Clara,
and Alexander Minz as
Drosselmeyer.

Commenting on his staging of *The Nutcracker* in an interview in the *Washington Post*, Baryshnikov observed: "This is Drosselmeyer's evening. It is his ballet. He makes this experience of the dream for Clara because he likes her. He wants to help her grow up, but he also wants to protect her from tragedy." At the Stahlbaum Christmas party the family and their guests are offered a puppet show by Drosselmeyer in which the tale of a beautiful young princess and her two suitors—a Prince and a Mouse King—is performed. The Prince is the successful suitor, and after Drosselmeyer has presented three life-size and magical dolls, he gives Clara a toy nutcracker which she asks him to make life-size like the three other puppets. But the toy nutcracker is broken and Clara has to bind up its jaw with her handkerchief. As the party ends Clara is made to leave her new toy under the Christmas tree.

In the second scene Clara comes down at midnight to seek her nutcracker, and is terrified to find that Drosselmeyer is still there and that the guests at her parents' party have turned into enormous mice. Now Drosselmeyer makes the Christmas tree grow and the nutcracker doll becomes life-size, leading an army of toy soldiers in battle with the mice.

After Clara saves the Nutcracker from the Mouse King, Drosselmeyer turns him into a handsome young Prince who will take Clara into a dreamland. The snowflakes appear amid a wintry forest to lead Clara and the Prince to his kingdom.

In the second act the Prince introduces Clara to his subjects, tells them how she saved him, and causes his puppet courtiers to spring to life and dance for Clara. All join in the Waltz of the Flowers, and then the atmosphere changes. The courtiers melt away and Clara is distressed when Drosselmeyer tells her that her dream is over and she must go home. To the music of the grand pas de deux, the Prince and Clara seek to prevent Drosselmeyer from bringing the dream to an end. They are successful, but even so, as a procession of the Prince's court passes by, Clara's dreamworld melts away and she finds herself awakening to the morning sunlight.

This version, like many others staged in recent years, seeks to discover the Hoffmannesque atmosphere which was ignored from the very beginning of *The Nutcracker's* ballet life. The first night's cast included Baryshnikov as the Nutcracker-Prince, Marianna Tcherkassky as Clara, and Alexander Minz as Drosselmeyer.

# Ondine

*Ballet in three acts. Music by Hans Werner Henze. Choreography by Frederick Ashton. Scenery and costumes by Lila de Nobili. First performed by The Royal Ballet at the Royal Opera House, Covent Garden, on October 27, 1958, with Margot Fonteyn, Michael Somes, Julia Farron, and Alexander Grant.*

*Margot Fonteyn in the last act of* Ondine—*a still from Paul Czinner's film of The Royal Ballet's production.*

Ashton's programme note for Ondine reads: "This is the story of Palemon and Ondine telling how Palemon wedded with a water-sprite and what chanced therefrom and how Palemon died and she returned to her element beneath the Mediterranean sea."

For his libretto Ashton turned to the story of Ondine as published in 1811 by Friedrich de la Motte Fouqué. This narrative had attracted the attention of several Romantic choreographers, the most famous being Jules Perrot, who created a ballet on the theme in 1843 for Fanny Cerrito. It was in this that Cerrito danced the celebrated shadow dance, the *pas de l'ombre*. Ashton included a charming reference back to the Perrot staging by inserting a shadow dance in the first scene. His ballet, though, is a totally new conception, filled throughout by the haunting presence of water. The role of Ondine is the supreme statement about the Ashton-Fonteyn partnership; water seems the very life of the character, from her first appearance sporting in the fountain. The work was distinguished by the magnificent designs of Lila de Nobili and the fine score of Hans Werner Henze. Happily, this ballet was filmed, and the result is an absolutely authentic record of Fonteyn's interpretation.

## SYNOPSIS

### Act I, Scene 1
*Before Berta's castle*

Berta and her companions are returning from the chase. Palemon is in love with Berta, but she rejects the amulet which he offers her. When the hunting party enters the castle Palemon is left alone. Suddenly he sees the mysterious figure of a water sprite laughing amid the waters of a fountain. She comes into the courtyard to play and suddenly is aware that she has a shadow. She dances with her shadow in the moonlight and the enraptured Palemon stands behind her, mingling his shadow with hers. Ondine is both fascinated and terrified when she sees him; she feels his heart beating, and flees into the forest. Palemon follows in pursuit. Berta and her friends then set out in pursuit of Palemon.

### Scene 2
*A mysterious forest*

Tirrenio, Lord of the Mediterranean, surveys the water sprites who live in the rivers of the forest. When Palemon and Ondine arrive, he warns Palemon that if he should be unfaithful to Ondine he will die. Ondine has now fallen in love with Palemon and together the lovers defy Tirrenio and seek out an old hermit, who marries them. Ondine has now acquired a soul and has ceased to be a water sprite. Tirrenio leads the sprites and the spirits of the forest in harrowing Berta in her pursuit of the lovers.

### Act II
*On board a ship*

Ondine and Palemon arrive at a port and embark on a ship. Berta has followed them and she takes passage on the same vessel. She is jealous, and when Palemon gives the amulet to Ondine, who accepts it, Berta is furious. Ondine offers the amulet to Berta, but Tirrenio, who has been watching, snatches the jewel from Berta, and to replace it Ondine puts her hand in the sea and brings out some mysterious jewels. Berta is terrified at this and she rejects the gift. She now incites the sailors against this frightening creature from another world. The sailors threaten Palemon and Ondine, and to protect Ondine Tirrenio causes a great storm to arise. The ship is wrecked, Ondine is taken back to her natural element by Tirrenio, and Palemon and Berta find refuge upon a rock.

### Act III
*Inside Palemon's castle*

Palemon and Berta are married and are awaiting guests for a celebration of their wedding. Berta has given Palemon a portrait of herself. Left alone for a moment Palemon gazes at it; suddenly the figure of Berta is replaced by that of the grieving Ondine. When the guests arrive a troupe of entertainers are brought on, but as their divertissement ends the palace is invaded by creatures from the sea. Tirrenio appears and Berta and all her guests are driven away. Ondine is first seen floating and diving in the sea; then she approaches. Palemon realises that she loves him, but she warns him that should he kiss her, he will die. They embrace and he falls dead at her feet. She clasps him in her arms below the waves.

# Onegin

*Ballet in three acts. Music by Pyotr Ilyich Tchaikovsky, arranged by Kurt-Heinz Stolze. Libretto by John Cranko, based on Pushkin's poem* Eugene Onegin. *Choreography by Cranko. Scenery and costumes by Jürgen Rose. First performed by the Stuttgart Ballet at the Württembergische Staatstheater, Stuttgart, on April 13, 1965, with Marcia Haydée as Tatiana. Ray Barra as Onegin, Egon Madsen as Lensky, and Ana Cardús as Olga.*

Cranko's work in Stuttgart was enhanced by the great devotion he inspired from his dancers. His achievement within the decade of the 1960s would not have been possible were it not for the fact that he provided an emotional focus for the aspirations and creative lives of many gifted dancers. Perhaps the most potent statement about this very important aspect of a ballet company's life is contained in the ballet *Initials R.B.M.E.*, set to the Brahms Piano Concerto No. 2, which was inspired by the common affection of Cranko and his four principals at that time, whose initials give the ballet its title: Richard Cragun, Birgit Keil, Marcia Haydée, and Egon Madsen. In Haydée, particularly, Cranko found a muse. For her he created several full-length roles—Juliet, Kate in *The Taming of the Shrew*, Tatiana, and Carmen—as well as mounting productions of *Giselle* and *Swan Lake*.

*Marcia Haydée as Tatiana dreaming over her book at the beginning of the ballet.*

*The Australian Ballet in the ball at Prince Gremin's palace in the last act of Cranko's* Onegin.

*Onegin* inevitably has gained much of its lustre in performance from the beauty of Marcia Haydée's interpretation of Tatiana, which marvellously suggests the development of the character from dreaming girlhood to worldly beauty. Onegin himself acquired exceptional intensity in the performance of Heinz Clauss (in a slightly revised version in 1967), while Egon Madsen personified the romantic ardour of Lensky. The ballet contains two party scenes in which Cranko vividly made the distinction between the provincial atmosphere of Tatiana's home in Act II and the grandeur of Prince Gremin's palace in Act III. The score, though arranged from Tchaikovsky's works, owes nothing to the composer's opera *Eugene Onegin*.

## SYNOPSIS

**Act I, Scene 1**
*Madame Larina's garden*

Madame Larina and her daughters, Tatiana and Olga, are seen on the eve of Tatiana's birthday party. Friends arrive. Lensky, a poet engaged to Olga, introduces his friend Onegin, who is bored but elegant. Tatiana, her head filled with romantic dreams, falls immediately in love with Onegin.

**Scene 2**
*Tatiana's bedroom*

Tatiana tries to write a letter of passionate avowal to Onegin. She imagines that he enters her room and dances with her.

**Act II, Scene 1**
*Tatiana's birthday party*

Provincial society is assembled and the guests discuss Lensky's affection for Olga. Onegin is contemptuous of what he thinks to be Tatiana's childish infatuation and he tears up her letter and returns it to her. He tries to relieve the tedium of the evening by flirting with Olga. Lensky is deeply angry at this and challenges him to a duel.

**Scene 2**
*The duel*

Tatiana and Olga try to prevent the men from fighting. Onegin is willing to be reconciled but Lensky obstinately insists upon his honour being satisfied. Lensky is killed.

**Act III, Scene 1**
*A ball in Prince Gremin's palace*

Onegin, after years of travel, returns to the capital and visits his friend Prince Gremin. He is astounded to find that Gremin's beautiful young wife is Tatiana. Onegin is appalled at the mistake he made in rejecting her love and he seeks an interview so that he may tell her of his passion.

**Scene 2**
*Tatiana's boudoir*

Tatiana is reading a letter from Onegin. He enters and tells her of his love for her. But Tatiana, disillusioned, orders him away. When Onegin has left she collapses, grief-stricken.

# Orpheus

*Ballet in one act. Music by Igor Stravinsky. Choreography by George Balanchine. Scenery and costumes by Isamu Noguchi. First performed by Ballet Society at the City Center, New York, on April 28, 1948, with Nicholas Magallanes as Orpheus, Maria Tallchief as Eurydice, and Francisco Moncion as the Dark Angel.*

*Opposite: Peter Martins of the New York City Ballet as Orpheus.*

*Orpheus* was conceived as the second part of a trilogy of Stravinsky-Balanchine collaborations. Its first part was the seminal *Apollo*; its third part would come a decade later with *Agon*. *Orpheus* was the culminating achievement of the Kirstein-Balanchine Ballet Society subscription performances in New York. Shortly after the première of *Orpheus* Morton Baum, Chairman of the Executive Committee of the City Center, invited Kirstein and Balanchine to establish their company there thus giving them a home and a name—the New York City Ballet.

In passing we should note that in 1936 Balanchine and Kirstein had been involved with Gluck's *Orpheus and Eurydice* when their American Ballet had been engaged to work at the Metropolitan Opera House, New York. Produced and choreographed by Balanchine, and superlatively designed by Pavel Tchelitchev, the production failed totally to please the jewelled canary-fanciers of the Diamond Horseshoe.

In decorating the Stravinsky *Orpheus*, the New York City Ballet acquired some of the finest designs in its history. Noguchi, the eminent Japanese-American sculptor, provided decorative ideas as resonantly beautiful as the music and choreography, not least in the huge white silk curtain which billows down to divide the scenes.

## SYNOPSIS

**Scene 1**
*Eurydice's grave*

After a musical prologue, Orpheus is seen weeping at the grave of Eurydice. Friends try to console him but he ignores them. Then, taking up his lyre, he dances his distress of spirit. Next, placing his lyre on the grave, he strikes its strings, and forest creatures are moved by his music. Heaven answers Orpheus' prayers and the Angel of Death appears to lead Orpheus into the underworld where he may again see Eurydice. He places a gold mask over Orpheus' eyes and, taking up his lyre, he leads him on the journey to Hades. In an interlude we see Orpheus led by the Angel into the realm of the dead.

**Scene 2**
*In the underworld*

The Furies threaten Orpheus and the Angel when they appear, but they cannot attack them. The Angel now gives Orpheus his lyre and encourages him to play it. The souls of the dead who throng the place are consoled by Orpheus' music. Pluto now appears, bringing with him Eurydice. She and Orpheus are allowed to meet but he must not look upon her, and his eyes are bound. Orpheus and Eurydice dance but she longs to know that Orpheus can see her and she tries to make him remove his mask; but he refuses. As their pas de deux continues their longing for each other increases and eventually Orpheus is impelled to disobey Pluto's instruction that he not look at Eurydice. He tears off the mask. Eurydice falls dead at his feet and the underworld reclaims her.

Orpheus returns to the upper world and meets a group of bacchantes who taunt and finally attack and kill him.

**Scene 3**
*Orpheus' grave*

The god Apollo takes up from the grave Orpheus' gold mask and tries to summon music from it. Then Orpheus' lyre arises from the grave and Apollo shows the poet's song as eternally beautiful for the world as the lyre rises into the air.

# *Paquita*

*Ballet in two acts and three scenes. Music by Ernest Deldevez. Choreography by Joseph Mazilier. First performed at the Paris Opéra, on April 1, 1846, with Carlotta Grisi and Lucien Petipa.*

*Paquita* was a vehicle created for Carlotta Grisi, with a narrative set in Spain during the Napoleonic occupation in which a gypsy girl saves the life of a French officer. The year after its creation Marius Petipa arrived in St. Petersburg as a *premier danseur*. For his début he appeared in *Paquita*, which had been staged there by his father, Jean Petipa, and a ballet master, Frédéric. The ballet was maintained in both Petersburg and Moscow, and it was Marius Petipa who was to be responsible for an important version, much revised, which he produced in St. Petersburg in 1881 for his favourite ballerina, Yekaterina Vazem. In this production, he interpolated a *grand pas* with music by Ludwig Minkus, official composer to the Imperial Ballet. It is this *grand pas* which has been so lovingly preserved in Petersburg/Leningrad until today, as an exultant display piece for a ballerina and a *premier danseur*, with six first soloists and eight second soloists. The *grand pas* has always been seen as one of the jewels of the Petipa repertory, demanding a cast of the very first quality. In her memoirs Mathilde Kshessinskaya records meeting Anna Pavlova in the early 1920s. Pavlova observed: "How happy I am to see you! We ought to put on the *grand pas* from *Paquita* together like in the old days in St. Petersburg! Tata Karsavina, Vera Trefilova, Sedova, Egorova, and Preobrazhenskaya are in Paris. You'll have the main part, and we'll dance behind you. It will be lovely." How lovely we shall never know, but it is some indication of the quality of dancing required that six prima ballerinas were considered proper to appear behind the only official Russian *assoluta* of the Imperial Ballet.

It is this *grand pas*, or excerpts from it, which has been presented in the West in various stagings. The Kirov Ballet, naturally enough, dance it ideally well. They present it as light-hearted choreography, but the company's distinction of style avoids any tinselled or cheap moments. This Kirov staging can on occasion include a virtuoso trio for two girls and a boy, which was first given public currency in the West in a revival by Balanchine for the Grand Ballet du Marquis de Cuevas on August 9, 1948, at Covent Garden. This subsequently entered the repertory of the New York City Ballet on February 18, 1951, at the New York City Center. For the Ballet Russe de Monte Carlo in 1949 Alexandra Danilova staged a version of the *grand pas*, and Rudolf Nureyev has produced his own recension for American Ballet Theatre in 1971.

The most recent stagings are those by Galina Samsova for the Sadler's Wells Royal Ballet, first produced on April 17, 1980, with designs by Peter Farmer, and by Natalia Makarova for her season at the Uris Theatre, New York, first presented on October 7, 1980, with designs by Rouben Ter-Arutunian. It was also staged by Oleg Vinogradov for the ballet of the Paris Opéra in 1980.

The form of the divertissement varies slightly with each staging, but the *grand pas* from *Paquita* remains thrilling testimony to Petipa's genius.

# Parade

*Ballet in one act. Music by Erik Satie. Choreography by Leonide Massine. Libretto by Jean Cocteau. Scenery and costumes by Pablo Picasso. First performed by Diaghilev's Ballets Russes at the Théâtre du Châtelet, Paris, on May 18, 1917, with Leonide Massine as the Chinese Conjuror.*

It is significant that in the middle of World War I Diaghilev could make it possible for this adventurous work to be created. Cubism was still a fresh and vital artistic movement, with Picasso its most brilliant exponent. Erik Satie's score, with its sirens and typewriters, was also firmly in the avant-garde. Massine's manipulation of the constructed managers (he had been fascinated by the skyscrapers he had seen on his first visit to New York in the previous year) was something entirely new in ballet. *Parade*, indeed, typified the renewed vitality of the Ballets Russes at this most difficult time, thanks to Diaghilev's determination to launch Massine as a new choreographer. Largely masterminded by Jean Cocteau, *Parade* also represents the beginning of Diaghilev's turn towards the School of Paris in painting and music. After the demise of the Diaghilev company in 1929. *Parade* was not seen again until it was revived by Massine in 1973 for the Joffrey Ballet in New York, and for London Festival Ballet the following year. Its value lay chiefly for art historians interested in Picasso's theatre work.

## SYNOPSIS

*The New York Manager, John Travis and Loma Rogers as the Acrobats, and Kerrison Cooke as the Chinese Conjuror in London Festival Ballet's staging of* Parade.

A *parade* in the French popular theatre is the equivalent of a sideshow. In this Cubist extravaganza two managers, one American and one French (both massive Cubist structures worn by dancers), introduce a series of variety turns: a Chinese conjuror, a little American girl who impersonates Charlie Chaplin and also mimes the sinking of the *Titanic*, two acrobats, and a pantomime horse.

Despite the performers' skill and the exhortation of the managers, no public appears to attend the proper show and at the end the dancers are disconsolate and the horse collapses to the ground.

# Pas de Deux

Most principal dancers worth their salt have a repertory of "party pieces" which they perform at galas.

Extracts from full-length ballets—the Black Swan pas de deux from Act III of *Swan Lake*; that final pas de deux known as "Don Q" which ends the Petipa *Don Quixote* in a blaze of fouettés and fireworks; the great pas de deux from the last acts of *The Nutcracker* and *The Sleeping Beauty*—are standard fare. But there are also some duets which are all that now survive in regular performance from old ballets, and others which have been created specially for an occasion, and have remained popular favourites. Five of the most famous are described below.

## Flower Festival in Genzano

*Music by Edvard Helsted and Holger Simon Paulli. Choreography by August Bournonville. First performed by the Royal Danish Ballet on December 19, 1858.*

Bournonville's ballet *Flower Festival in Genzano* was a fruit of his Italian travels. It was based on an incident concerning the love of a young girl and a marksman. Nothing has survived of this ballet except the enchanting love duet in which the girl's sweetness is set off by the ebullience and virtuosity of the male dancer. This pas de deux is sometimes now interpolated into the last act of *Napoli* in order to give Teresina and Gennaro an extended duet. As with all Bournonville choreography, the niceties of style and grace of manner are only to be captured by dancers trained in the Danish school, although few virtuoso dancers can resist attempting it.

## Le Corsaire

*Music by Adolphe Adam and others. Choreography by Joseph Mazilier and others. First performed at the Paris Opéra on January 23, 1856.*

One of the great triumphs of the late-Romantic ballet, *Le Corsaire* was a three-act extravaganza based upon Lord Byron's poem *The Corsair*. In 1858 Jules Perrot produced a version in St. Petersburg which introduced the ballet to the Russian stage. Thereafter it was maintained, acquiring additional music by Pugni and Minkus; revived by Petipa in 1868; and considerably revised thereafter. It remained one of the most important dramatic works in the Imperial Ballet repertory for many years—its shipwreck was a celebrated theatrical spectacle. (Tamara Karsavina late in life included the pantomimic scene from this shipwreck in her incomparable lecture-demonstrations on the art of ballet mime.) Fresh music and fresh choreography continued to be added, and the pas de deux which is now seen as a concert item has music provided late in the nineteenth century by Riccardo Drigo. Extracts from the ballet are still preserved in Leningrad but the West knows best the duet, which features slave-like yearnings for a male dancer in baggy gold trousers, and whatever virtuoso tricks a ballerina may have.

Opposite: *Helgi Tomasson and Patricia McBride in* Tchaikovsky Pas de Deux.

*Peter Schaufuss in* Le Corsaire.

### Tchaikovsky Pas de Deux

*Music by Pyotr Ilyich Tchaikovsky. Choreography by George Balanchine. Costumes by Karinska. First performed by Violette Verdy and Conrad Ludlow at the City Center, New York, on March 29, 1960.*

The music for this duet is the original pas de deux which was placed in the third act of *Swan Lake* at its first Moscow production. It owes its presence there to the fact that the second Odette-Odile of this Moscow staging, Anna Sobeshchanskaya, was unhappy with the duet she had been given, and went to Petersburg, where she acquired a pas de deux from Petipa, to music by Minkus. Tchaikovsky was unwilling to allow another composer's music in his score and promptly provided new music to accompany the rhythmic pattern of Petipa's choreography. The pas de deux was later dropped and the score

lost, but it came to light some thirty years ago in the music library of the Bolshoi Theatre in Moscow. When Vladimir Bourmeister staged his radical new *Swan Lake* for the Stanislavsky and Nemirovich-Danchenko Theatre Ballet in 1953, he incorporated this music. The score was brought to the notice of Balanchine and he conceived the brilliant duet that we know today. It is choreography that demands exceptional speed and even more exceptional musical understanding—qualities that marked Violette Verdy's dancing, and are the hallmark of New York City Ballet style today.

203

## Tarantella

*Music by
Louis Moreau
Gottschalk.
Choreography by
George Balanchine.
Costumes by
Karinska.
First performed by
Patricia McBride and
Edward Villella at the
State Theater,
Lincoln Center, on
January 7, 1964.*

The Tarantella is a dance from southern Italy in 6/8 time. Balanchine used Gottschalk's Grande Tarantelle, in an orchestration by Hershy Kay, for a fizzing demi-caractère duet which demands exceptional speed and high spirits, and an ability to beat a tambourine while dancing full out. The original performers made it stunningly their own.

## Other Dances

*Music by
Frédéric Chopin.
Choreography by
Jerome Robbins.
Costumes by
Santo Loquasto.
First performed by
Natalia Makarova and
Mikhail Baryshnikov
at the Metropolitan
Opera House,
New York,
on May 9, 1976.*

Jerome Robbins had already made three other ballets using Chopin's music by the time he came to write for the very special gifts of the two ex-Kirov stars Makarova and Baryshnikov.

An opening Mazurka found the couple almost dreaming their way through the steps, floating and soaring, happy together. Their second Mazurka brought Baryshnikov bounding on in a solo replete with virtuoso steps and jumps in which his legs were tucked up under him and then allowed to beat while he stayed airborne. Despite the ferocious demands of the solo, the rhythmic pulse of the Mazurka was never allowed to flag. There followed a Waltz for Makarova, her arms drifting, her torso bending to the melody before she sailed off the stage in a broad, ecstatic jump. Then came a daring and lovely idea from Robbins: another Mazurka, set first for Baryshnikov, and then repeated, slightly more *piano*, for Makarova, with gentle suggestions, which run throughout the whole piece, of Polish dance attitudes. Finally, and more daring still, there came the hallowed *Les Sylphides* Mazurka, but here reidentified as a Polish court dance for both artists. Their Leningrad education taught them how to treat this number: not as something folksy but as an aristocratic expression of national feeling.

Top: *Patricia McBride and Edward Villella in* Tarentella.

Right: *Mikhail Baryshnikov and Natalia Makarova in* Other Dances.

# Pas des Déesses

*Ballet in one act. Music by John Field. Choreography by Robert Joffrey. Costumes by Anver Bey Khan. First performed by the Robert Joffrey Ballet Concert at the Kaufmann Auditorium, New York, on May 29, 1954, with Lillian Wellein, Barbara Gray, Jacquetta Keith, and Michael Lland.*

Joffrey's "dance of the goddesses" harkens back to an event less famous now but in its time no less a great publicity coup than Jules Perrot's *Pas de Quatre* of 1845, which brought together on the same stage the greatest dancers of the Romantic era—Lucile Grahn, Fanny Cerrito, Marie Taglioni, and Carlotta Grisi. One year later Perrot fashioned a variation on this quartet by presenting Grahn, Cerrito, and Taglioni with the *danseur noble* Arthur Saint-Léon. Tactfully, Perrot called this *Pas des Déesses*.

The contemporary *Pas des Déesses* is tactful too. Each of the ballerinas has a full pas de deux with the cavalier, and each has a solo exhibiting her special talents and charms. Joffrey's choreography refers to the Romantic style of Perrot and to the feelings of rivalry attributed to the celebrated dancers. The reluctance with which each ballerina leaves the stage after her solo adds a humourous underside to the piece. Basically, however, *Pas des Déesses* is a straightforward interpretation of a perhaps mythical past.

*Dancers of the Joffrey Ballet in* Pas des Déesses.

# Les Patineurs

*Ballet in one act. Music by Giacomo Meyerbeer, arranged by Constant Lambert. Choreography by Frederick Ashton. Scenery and costumes by William Chappell. First performed by the Vic-Wells Ballet at the Sadler's Wells Theatre, London, on February 16, 1937, with Harold Turner, Margot Fonteyn, and Robert Helpmann.*

*Pamela May, Margot Fonteyn, and June Brae in the original Vic-Wells production of* Les Patineurs.

*Les Patineurs*, like so many others in the first decades of Britain's national ballet, owes much to the musical guidance and artistic taste of Constant Lambert, composer, conductor, and musical conscience of the company. It was he who suggested the music from Meyerbeer's operas *Le Prophète* and *L'Etoile du Nord* as source material for the score. (In passing we would note that in 1849, when *Le Prophète* was staged at the Paris Opéra,

the ladies of the corps de ballet put on roller skates to impersonate the milkmaids gliding over a frozen lake to bring provisions to the Anabaptist soldiery during the religious uprising of 1534.) It was Ninette de Valois who originally intended using the score, but she did not find much inspiration in it and Frederick Ashton was delighted to take over the production of a ballet that offered an impressive picture of the technical standards of the Vic-Wells Ballet in 1937. The "Blue Skater" was a tribute to the virtuosity and high spirits of Harold Turner, and his two partners in brilliance were Mary Honer and Elizabeth Miller as the whirling girls in blue. The "White" pas de deux—all the roles have gained enduring if unofficial titles from William Chappell's pretty costumes—was made for Margot Fonteyn and Robert Helpmann, and the two girls in red whose sudden collapse reveals them as newcomers to the ice were taken by Pamela May and June Brae.

The ballet was first staged by American Ballet Theatre in 1946 with John Kriza, Nora Kaye, and Hugh Laing, in unbecoming designs by Cecil Beaton, and has since been seen in the repertories of many other companies, including the Joffrey Ballet.

*Dancers of The Royal Ballet in* Les Patineurs.

SYNOPSIS  The scene is a Victorian park at night, with a frozen pond surrounded by Chinese lanterns. Onto the ice come a group of skaters, some expert, some less so. The corps de ballet appears first gliding along, couple by couple; then appear two girls in red, two girls in blue, a couple in white, and the star figure, the Blue Skater, a role for a virtuoso male dancer. The delights and occasional mishaps of a skating party are the entire action of the ballet; the choreography makes excellent capital from skating imagery throughout. At the end as snow begins to fall the skaters whirl away, leaving the solitary spinning figure of the blue boy.

# *Petrushka*

*Ballet in four scenes. Music by Igor Stravinsky. Choreography by Mikhail Fokine. Scenery and costumes by Alexandre Benois. First performed by Diaghilev's Ballets Russes at the Théâtre du Châtelet, Paris, on June 13, 1911, with Vaslav Nijinsky as Petrushka, Tamara Karsavina as the Doll, Alexander Orlov as the Moor, and Enrico Cecchetti as the Charlatan.*

*Vaslav Nijinsky as Petrushka.*

*Petrushka* remains the supreme example of the artistic collaborations that Diaghilev masterminded. Score, action, décor and choreography blended totally, because they were created in the same artistic impulse. The result was a ballet generally acknowledged as the greatest masterpiece of the Diaghilev era. It owes much to Benois' wish to evoke the old fairs of St. Petersburg; it owes even more now to Stravinsky's score. However threadbare productions are today, the dramatic intensity and rich theatrical colour of the score seem to impel belief in the audience. The ballet remains a magnificent example of Fokine's ideal of expressive dramatic action realised through truthful dance totally in accord with music and decoration.

In 1970 Maurice Béjart produced his own version of *Petrushka*, initially as a vehicle for Vladimir Vasiliev, star of the Bolshoi Ballet. Béjart's argument is based upon a sound theatrical idea: Petrushka putting on the masks of puppet, then blackamoor, then doll, and becoming gradually confused by their identities when he enters the mirrored booth of the charlatan. As a result, he doubts his own identity and all other human relationships. The theme is an interesting reworking of the Petrushka tale but its realisation proved, in fact, to be unilluminating, although Vasiliev was greatly admired in the role, and in later performances Jorge Donn was a tremendously committed interpreter.

*The first scene of* Petrushka *as danced by London Festival Ballet for Herbert Ross' film* Nijinsky, *with Jay Jolley as the Moor, Patricia Ruanne as the Doll, and George de la Pena as Petrushka.*

SYNOPSIS
*Scene 1*
*Butterweek Fair*
*in Admiralty Square,*
*St. Petersburg, 1830*

A crowd is milling in front of the booths that are the chief attraction of the fair. Two little street dancers vie for attention amid the bustle. Suddenly two drummers still the crowd and an old Charlatan emerges from the central booth. He plays a flute and the curtains of the booths draw back to reveal three puppets—Petrushka, the oppressed fool; the vapidly pretty Doll; and the brutish, splendid Blackamoor. To the Charlatan's pipings they start to dance and then emerge into the crowd to act out the drama in which Petrushka mimes his love of the Doll and is trounced by the Blackamoor. They exit.

*Scene 2*
*Petrushka's cell*

Petrushka grieves over his fate; he mimes his terror of the Charlatan, whose portrait is on the wall. Suddenly the Doll is pushed into his cell but his frantic reception of her drives her out at once. Petrushka beats his head against the walls of his prison and then flings his body half through the wall as the curtain falls.

*Scene 3*
*The Moor's cell*

The Moor is playing with a coconut. The Doll enters playing a trumpet. The Moor dances an awkward pas de deux with her but their courtship is interrupted when the Charlatan pushes Petrushka into the cell. The Moor bullies Petrushka again and boots him out.

*Scene 4*
*The fair*

The crowd is excited as evening draws nigh. Coachmen perform a stamping dance and then there comes a contrast with the gliding steps of a group of nursemaids. More carnival revellers appear as snow gently starts to fall. Suddenly Petrushka rushes in with the Blackamoor and the Doll in pursuit. The Blackamoor kills Petrushka and then stealthily creeps away with the Doll as the crowd gathers round the dying puppet. He makes one last gesture of appeal and a guard brings in the Charlatan. He shows the crowd that the dead body is no more than a straw-filled puppet. Wonderingly they disperse. The Charlatan makes his way across the empty square, dragging the puppet behind him. At this moment there appears above the booth the ghost of Petrushka, screaming defiance at the old man, who flees, terrified. Petrushka's ghost collapses forward as the curtain falls.

*A drawing showing one of the Butterweek Fairs in the mid-nineteenth century in Russia which inspired Alexandre Benois' designs for* Petrushka.

# Piano Concerto No. 2

*Ballet in one act. Music by Pyotr Ilyich Tchaikovsky. Choreography by George Balanchine. Scenery and costumes by Mstislav Dobuzhinsky. First performed (as* Ballet Imperial*) by American Ballet Caravan at Hunter College, New York, on May 27, 1941, with Marie-Jeanne, Gisella Caccialanza, and William Dollar.*

*Piano Concerto No. 2* is a work which has undergone several changes in the years since it was first created. It was initially staged as *Ballet Imperial* for a tour of South-America during the war, at a time when it was thought politic to show the classic dance traditions of North America. To this end Balanchine created choreography that was overtly a homage to the Imperial Ballet of his childhood in St. Petersburg, while the Dobuzhinsky designs echoed the grandeur of the Imperial city.

After its initial staging for American Ballet Caravan, *Ballet Imperial* was acquired by the Denham Ballet Russe de Monte Carlo in 1945 and then in 1950 Balanchine staged it for the Sadler's Wells Ballet at Covent Garden. This production was superbly designed by Eugene Berman, who placed it firmly in a St. Petersburg setting, and it was very carefully prepared by Balanchine himself. (The production in fact was a prelude to the first appearance in London later that summer of Balanchine's own New York City Ballet.) A triumph with the discerning public, it remained in the Royal Ballet repertory for a considerable number of years. Tragically, in 1963, at Balanchine's insistence, the Berman designs were rejected and replaced by new ones by Carl Toms in "Maryinsky blue." Later still even these were abandoned and the ballet was shown as *Piano Concerto No. 2* in a glum abstract setting. The New York City Ballet revived the work in 1964 as *Ballet Imperial*, with designs by Rouben Ter-Arutunian which still evoked St. Petersburg, but in 1973 all formal design was jettisoned at Balanchine's request and the work itself became known as *Piano Concerto No. 2*. Balanchine observes in his *Complete Stories of the Great Ballets* that he simplified the design and the pantomime gesture which once featured in the second movement "because times have changed since the ballet was first done. . . . We see dancing better than we used to and prefer to see it directly, unencumbered." For once we must disagree with Mr. Balanchine. The Berman designs were among the most distinguished that The Royal Ballet has ever had and represent that company's only link with this great designer. The world they evoked was that of the music as well as of the original choreography, and we must concur with a dancer from the very first production who insists that *Ballet Imperial* is "a tutu ballet," and with Nadia Nerina, a lustrous incumbent of the ballerina role, who said that "in Leningrad, standing in the Great Hall of the Winter Palace with massive gold columns and huge chandeliers, I got exactly the same feeling as I had had in *Ballet Imperial*."

It is a ballet which requires grandeur of manner and a meticulously schooled corps de ballet to support its principals.

SYNOPSIS

From the opening moment of the first movement of the concerto, when we see two diagonals of dancers facing each other and the line of men salute the women, we are in a world of palaces and balletic dignity. The chief figures are a ballerina and her cavalier, and a secondary ballerina with two male attendants. The progress of the first movement is an exhilarating display of bravura dancing in which the ballerina's virtuosity is often identified with the prodigies demanded of the piano soloist. The second movement—the Andante non troppo which is performed in Siloti's shortened version—suggests a balletic prince to whom appears a vision in the form of the ballerina. The final Allegro con fuoco brings on the entire cast, flashing with diamond glitter to match the sparkling music.

Right: *Sean Lavery and Suzanne Farrell of the New York City Ballet in* Piano Concerto No. 2.

Below: *The first staging by the Sadler's Wells Ballet of* Ballet Imperial *with Michael Somes, left, Beryl Grey, kneeling centre, as the second ballerina, and Moira Shearer, right, in arabesque, as the principal ballerina. Berman's setting is clearly to be admired.*

# Pierrot Lunaire

*Ballet in one act. Music by Arnold Schoenberg. Choreography by Glen Tetley. Scenery by Rouben Ter-Arutunian. First performed at the Fashion Institute of Technology, New York, on May 5, 1962, with Glen Tetley, Linda Hodes, and Robert Powell.*

Tetley provides the following programme note to his *Pierrot Lunaire*: "In the antiquity of the Roman theatre began the battle of the white clown of innocence with the dark clown of experience. Pierrot and Brighella are their lineal descendants, and Columbine their eternal feminine pawn." This argument he develops using Schoenberg's melodrama as a musical rather than a literary basis (he ignores most of the Beardsleyesque imagery in Albert Giraud's poems, which are the vocal text of the score).

*Pierrot* was among Glen Tetley's earliest ballets, and its immediate success brought him international renown. Shortly after its creation by his own company, Tetley came to Europe, where he became an influential figure in the new wave of choreography associated with the Nederlands Dans Theater, of which he was a director, which sought to find common ground between the classical academic and contemporary dance forms. When Ballet Rambert was reorganised in 1966 in the image of NDT, Tetley staged *Pierrot Lunaire* for the company, who danced it for the first time on January 26, 1967. It was Christopher Bruce's performance as Pierrot on this occasion which announced him as one of the most gifted dance actors of his generation. The ballet has been staged for several other companies, notably the Royal Danish Ballet, which found a great Pierrot in Niels Kehlet. While Pierrot is, of course, the central figure, the roles of Brighella and Columbine are also rewarding. The ballet needs a trio of skilled dramatic interpreters to succeed.

## SYNOPSIS

The setting is a skeletal white tower of scaffolding on which we see the white-clad figure of Pierrot swinging. Pierrot is the eternal dreamer, the moody, introverted clown, innocently puppyish, forever wounded by experience, always deceived by reality which destroys his dreams. To him, in a series of incidents that recall *Petrushka*, come the other two characters in the ballet: Brighella, who is experience, the bully and guide to the world; and Columbine, who is a mistress, a mother figure, and always cruel and beyond Pierrot's reach. These two tease, goad, and manipulate him, initiating him into the harshness and cruelty of the world. Eventually they strip Pierrot of his clothes and invade the tower which is his world. Mocked, derided, Pierrot suddenly finds strength to come to terms with them, and the final pose finds him clasping Brighella and Columbine to his body, pressing their heads against his breast.

Right: *Niels Kehlet and Vivi Flindt as Pierrot and Columbine in Glen Tetley's* Pierrot Lunaire *as staged by the Royal Danish Ballet.*

# Pillar of Fire

*Ballet in one act. Music by Arnold Schoenberg (*Verklärte Nacht*). Choreography and scenario by Antony Tudor. Scenery and costumes by Jo Mielziner. First performed by American Ballet Theatre at the Metropolitan Opera House, New York, on April 8, 1942, with Nora Kaye as Hagar, Hugh Laing as the Young Man from the House Opposite, Antony Tudor as the Friend, Lucia Chase as the Eldest Sister, Annabelle Lyon as the Youngest Sister.*

In *Pillar of Fire* Tudor explored further the world of psychological inquiry which he so movingly charted in *Jardin aux Lilas* in 1936. In 1939 Tudor had gone to America to work for the newly formed Ballet Theatre. For them he staged some of his earlier ballets, but with *Pillar of Fire* he made his first major piece for this company. The ballet was blessed with a magnificent cast and in the central role Nora Kaye became immediately established as a leading dramatic ballerina.

SYNOPSIS

The setting shows two houses facing each other; the period is the beginning of this century. At curtain rise Hagar sits brooding on the steps of her house, motionless, her hands clenched in her lap. She is the central, unhappy figure of the dramatic incident which follows. She watches a world filled with characters identified as Lovers in Innocence and Lovers in Experience. She thinks that the man whom she loves (the Friend) does not return her affection. Her Eldest Sister delights in making her unhappy by urging the youngest of the three sisters to flirt with the Friend. Hagar, in despair, gives herself to the worthless and sexually opportunist Young Man from the House Opposite. Hagar is then distraught with shame. Rejected by everyone, she finally finds love and compassion in the Friend, who has, in fact, loved her throughout, and the ballet ends with their walking away together to a happy future.

*Pillar of Fire in its original production for Ballet Theatre with, left to right, Norma Vance as the Youngest Sister, Antony Tudor as the Friend, Lucia Chase as the Eldest Sister, Nora Kaye as Hagar, and Hugh Laing as the Young Man.*

# Pineapple Poll

*Ballet in one act. Music by Arthur Sullivan, selected and arranged by Charles Mackerras. Choreography by John Cranko. Scenery and costumes by Osbert Lancaster. First performed by the Sadler's Wells Theatre Ballet at Sadler's Wells Theatre, London, on March 13, 1951, with Elaine Fifield as Poll, David Blair as Captain Belaye, David Poole as Jasper, Stella Claire as Blanche, and Sheilah O'Reilly as Mrs. Dimple.*

*Pineapple Poll* was the work that finally confirmed the fact that John Cranko was a master of comic choreography. The adaptation of a story from W. S. Gilbert's *Bab Ballads* and its marriage to some of Sullivan's most beguiling music resulted in a work intensely English, extremely funny, and brimful of brilliant character dancing. Its original cast has never been bettered although subsequent interpretations in several repertories have revealed how sound is its structure and enduring its good humour. The Osbert Lancaster designs are as ideally and wittily English as the score and dances, and as resourceful in establishing personalities. They are affectionate exaggerations of types, as are the characters.

*This moment from the opening scene of* Pineapple Poll *shows David Blair as the dashing Captain Belaye surrounded by members of the crew of HMS* Hot Cross Bun *while sweethearts and wives swoon adoringly at the sight of the irresistible Captain. On the far right, Elaine Fifield is seen as Pineapple Poll. This photograph is of the original production at the Sadler's Wells Theatre.*

**SYNOPSIS**

*Scene 1*
*Portsmouth Harbour,*
*outside the*
*Steampacket Public*
*House*

Sailors and their girlfriends are assembled in the square while Jasper the potboy plies the men with ale. Poll, a bumboat girl who earns her living selling pretty trinkets to sweethearts and wives, enters. Jasper adores her but she mocks him. Suddenly the dashing Captain Belaye appears and at once every woman on stage faints away in hopeless passion from his good looks. Poll is particularly affected. He chucks her under the chin, beats off the attention of the women, and upbraids his men for indiscipline. When the outraged sailors and their womenfolk have departed Belaye has his hands full yet again with his idiot fiancée, the adorable Blanche, and her garrulous aunt and chaperone Mrs. Dimple.

*Scene 2*
*The quayside, below*
*HMS* Hot Cross Bun

Poll has followed Belaye to his ship. She changes into midshipman's clothes and tittups up the gangplank. She is followed by a succession of "sailors," all with a curious gait. Jasper comes in search of Poll. He finds her discarded dress and stockings and, believing her drowned, grieves.

*Scene 3*
*On board HMS*
*Hot Cross Bun*

The ship's company are involved in their tasks with Poll muddling the issue. Belaye enters and orders the gun to be fired, which causes a pretty confusion. He then goes ashore and the curious antics of the crew perplex Poll. Her suspicions are confirmed when Belaye returns with Blanche, now his bride, and Mrs. Dimple. At this moment the "crew" tear off their rig to reveal the feminine curves of the adoring sweethearts. Belaye is aghast, but matters are resolved when the real crew return and eventually forgive their girlfriends. Belaye is promoted to Admiral and hands his captain's uniform to Jasper, who is so enhanced that Poll willingly transfers her affections to him. In an apotheosis Mrs. Dimple becomes Britannia.

# Prince Igor
## (Polovtsian Dances)

*Ballet in one act. Music by Alexander Borodin. Choreography by Mikhail Fokine. Scenery and costumes by Nicholas Roerich. First performed by Diaghilev's Ballets Russes at the Théâtre du Châtelet, Paris, on May 18, 1909, with Adolph Bolm as the Polovtsian Chief.*

Below: *Dancers of London Festival Ballet in the Polovtsian Dances from* Prince Igor *as staged for Herbert Ross' film* Nijinsky.

The scene in the Polovtsian camp from the second act of Borodin's opera *Prince Igor* was presented by Diaghilev on the opening night of his historic ballet and opera season in Paris in 1909. More than any other work in that season, the *Polovtsian Dances* astounded the Parisian public: the ferocious horde of warriors reasserted the image of the male dancer as virile and, in this case, brutally thrilling. Preserved in the repertories of the various Ballet Russe companies during the 1930s, *Prince Igor* is still performed, London Festival Ballet retaining an acceptable version.

SYNOPSIS

The scene is a camp of the Polovtsian tribe on the steppes of Central Asia. A line of dome-shaped tents and smoke from campfires are on the horizon. The men and women of the tribe dance, led by their Chief. A group of captive Persian women are brought in and are caught up in the general dance which ends with a hectic and frenzied display of male dancing.

# The Prodigal Son

*Ballet in one act. Music by Serge Prokofiev. Choreography by George Balanchine. Scenery and costumes by Georges Rouault. First performed by Diaghilev's Ballets Russes at the Théâtre Sarah Bernhardt, Paris, on May 21, 1929, with Serge Lifar as the Prodigal and Felia Dubrovska as the Siren.*

Overleaf: *Mikhail Baryshnikov as the Prodigal leaps away from home in the first scene of* The Prodigal Son *with the New York City Ballet.*

The Prodigal Son was the final ballet created by Diaghilev's Ballets Russes. Balanchine's choreography is very different from the classical harmonies of *Apollo*: he is here using an acrobatic, expressionist manner of great dramatic intensity. The writing for the Siren, in particular, has a chilling erotic force of exceptional power, while the role of the Prodigal insists upon athletic bravura and highly emotional acting.

Though there have been other versions choreographed to the score, Balanchine's staging is universally recognised as definitive. The New York City Ballet has presented this since 1950; in 1973 both The Royal Ballet and the Paris Opéra Ballet also acquired this version, and in 1981 it entered the repertory of American Ballet Theatre.

SYNOPSIS

*Scene 1*
*The Prodigal's home*

Outside the Prodigal's home his two servants are preparing wine jars as if for a journey. The Prodigal enters, an excited and eager youth. His father, a patriarchal figure, appears with his two daughters and makes the Prodigal join the group in prayer. But the Prodigal is impatient to be away, and despite his family's entreaties the headstrong youth leaves with his servants, leaping over the low fence which is to feature importantly later in the action.

*Scene 2*
*A distant country*

A group of revellers, bald-headed and bizarre, scuttle over the stage. The Prodigal enters with his companions, and they are eagerly greeted by these new companions, who encourage them to drink. There now appears the mysterious figure of the Siren, crowned with a white mitre-shaped headdress and trailing a long wine-coloured cloak. She dances, winding the train round her body in a fiercely erotic manner, and finally subsides on the floor, hidden beneath her train. The Prodigal lifts it from her and there ensues an acrobatic pas de deux in which she completely dominates him through her potent sexuality. The fence of the first scene now becomes a table which forms an integral part of the choreography, and as the increasingly drunken Prodigal loses all sense, the table becomes a pillar against which he stands in drunken stupor while his servants, the Siren, and her minions strip him. They leave, and the Prodigal crawls away. The Siren and her companions return and the table becomes a boat into which they load the Prodigal's treasure and sail away, with the Siren becoming the figurehead and her train streaming behind.

*Scene 3*
*The return home*

The setting is the same as in the first scene. The Prodigal, dirty, ragged, and exhausted, drags himself home with the help of a wooden staff. He reaches out towards the gate but collapses. His sisters discover him there and bring him lovingly back to the parental home. His father emerges and his son falls abjectly at his feet. He pulls himself up towards his father's arms; his father enfolds his son in his arms and pulls his cloak around him.

# Push Comes to Shove

*Ballet in one act. Music by Joseph Lamb and Franz Josef Haydn. Choreography by Twyla Tharp. Costumes by Santo Loquasto. First performed by American Ballet Theatre at the Uris Theatre, New York, on January 9, 1976, with Mikhail Baryshnikov, Martine van Hamel, Marianna Tcherkassky, Kristine Elliott, and Clark Tippet.*

Overleaf: *Mikhail Baryshnikov and Marianna Tcherkassky in Twyla Tharp's* Push Comes to Shove.

Below: *Baryshnikov with Martine van Hamel and dancers of American Ballet Theatre in* Push Comes to Shove.

*Push Comes to Shove* entered Baryshnikov's life when the process of his Americanization was well under way but in need of a grace note. Tharp's first work for American Ballet Theatre provided it for him and gave the company a smash hit as well. This ballet gives us a Baryshnikov of many seasonings: beebopper, man-about-the-town (in derby hat), roughneck, street crazy, nice guy, and premier danseur. Perhaps the most winning part of Tharp's tribute to him is a solo in which just about every Russian ballet included in this book gets a poke in the ribs, in a few minutes flat.

The Baryshnikov factor isn't the only factor, though the ballet does lose some of its point when he doesn't appear in it. Its combination of popular and classical music (a Lamb rag and Haydn's "Bear" symphony) is a satisfying surprise. A big ensemble dance for women is remarkably lambent, considering all the jokes that get strewn about the stage. And its feeling of romp and joy is sustained until the last measures, when the original derby mysteriously multiplies. *Push Comes to Shove* ends with hats flying into the air. They could be champagne corks.

**SYNOPSIS**   As a teaser, the three principal dancers jive and fool around with a derby hat to Lamb's "Bohemian Rag 1919." The front curtain lifts, the Haydn begins: solo for male principal. There's some sideline skirmishing to silence and then the female chorus enters for the adagio. More bits of squabble and on comes another ensemble, led by a svelte lady and a cavalier. After a mock courtly dance the leads engage in a funny competitive duet. The finale begins with all the dancers trooping on for bows, some of them very much in the style of certain star dancers, who shall remain nameless. More flourish, fanfare, posing for pictures perhaps, and much tossing of that hat.

# The Rake's Progress

*Ballet in six scenes. Music by Gavin Gordon. Libretto by Gordon, after William Hogarth. Choreography by Ninette de Valois. Scenery and costumes by Rex Whistler, after Hogarth. First performed by the Vic-Wells Ballet at the Sadler's Wells Theatre, London, on May 20, 1935, with Walter Gore as the Rake, Alicia Markova as the Betrayed Girl, and Harold Turner as the Dancing Master and the Man with a Rope.*

In the formative years of the Vic-Wells Ballet, Ninette de Valois was called upon to be choreographer, director, and dancer. Her ballets of this period reveal her concern with creating dramatic works on specifically English themes—*Job* (1931), inspired by Blake's drawings, was an early example. *The Rake's Progress* survives not least through the excellence of its construction; its score is theatrically potent; its design is the only surviving example of the theatrical genius of Rex Whistler, who was killed in action in 1944; its choreography captures the essence of the Hogarth paintings which inspired the ballet; its principal roles still offer dramatic and emotional challenges to dance artists performing today.

*Robert Helpmann as the Rake in the first scene of The Royal Ballet's production of* The Rake's Progress.

| SYNOPSIS | | |
|---|---|---|
| **Scene 1**<br>*The rake's house* | A young man, having newly inherited a fortune, is the prey of a variety of characters: a jockey, a fencing master, a music master, a dancing master, a hired assassin, and a tailor. He | dismisses them except for the Dancing Master. A girl whom he has betrayed is brought in by her mother. He spurns them and they leave. |
| **Scene 2**<br>*A brothel* | After a frontcloth scene for the Dancing Master and a little blackamoor servant girl, we are in a house of ill fame where the young Rake | now enjoys wine, women, and song, and not least a girl with bright red stockings. |
| **Scene 3**<br>*A street* | The Rake is faced with his creditors. The young girl gives them money, but he ignores her. | |
| **Scene 4**<br>*A gaming house* | The Rake attempts to recover his lost fortune at cards. He loses everything including his reason. | |
| **Scene 5**<br>*A street* | The Betrayed Girl, still faithful, is embroidering as she waits for the Rake's release from debtor's prison. | |
| **Scene 6**<br>*Bedlam* | The Rake is flung into a madhouse, surrounded by people from his past who have come to a similar end; they include a macabre figure of a man who dances obsessively with a piece of rope. | The girl enters in search of him. She appeals to some strangers who have come to view the lunatics, but to no avail. The Rake now goes into convulsions, and dies at the girl's feet. |

*Rex Whistler's design for the frontcloth of* The Rake's Progress *is an outstanding example of his understanding of historical period.*

# Raymonda

*Ballet in three acts. Music by Alexander Glazunov. Libretto by Lydia Pashkova and Marius Petipa. Choreography by Petipa. First performed at the Maryinsky Theatre, St. Petersburg, on January 19, 1898, with Pierina Legnani as Raymonda, Sergei Legat as Jean, and Pavel Gerdt as Abdérâme.*

Although *Raymonda* is blessed with a magnificent score—Glazunov producing music entirely worthy of the Tchaikovsky tradition—it had from the first been crippled by the improbabilities of its story. The eighty-year-old Petipa poured into the ballet a superlative sequence of dances culminating in the justly celebrated final Hungarian divertissement. Despite the inadequacies of plot and characterisation, *Raymonda* has survived in Soviet Russia; it was massively edited to try and rationalise its action, most notably by Konstantin Sergueyev for the Kirov Ballet.

In 1935 the Lithuanian Ballet presented a complete staging by Nicholas Zverev which featured the technically brilliant Vera Nemchinova as Raymonda. In New York in 1946 Alexandra Danilova and George Balanchine mounted a short version for the Ballet Russe de Monte Carlo, but it is Rudolf Nureyev who has enabled the work to have its widest showings in the West. In 1964 he made a first version for The Royal Ballet's touring group at Spoleto; in 1965 he mounted it for the Australian Ballet; and in 1972 he produced it for the Zurich Ballet.

In an attempt to dignify the story Nureyev shows us Raymonda reluctant to marry. Half of the first act and the entire second act become a dream sequence in which the opposing forces of Jean and Abdérâme—courtly love and a darker, more sexual passion—are in conflict and eventually bring about her marriage. The third act becomes the conventional wedding divertissement. This production was also staged for American Ballet Theatre in 1975; in 1980, Mikhail Baryshnikov assembled a divertissement from Acts II and III of *Raymonda* for American Ballet Theatre.

"The treasure chest of music titled *Raymonda*," as a New York City Ballet programme describes it, has been used three times by Balanchine. Earliest of his stagings was *Pas de Dix* in 1955, which was an overt homage to the Petipa original. In 1961 came *Raymonda Variations*, a splendid series of variations for a ballerina and her cavalier with attendant soloists and a small corps de ballet. Finally, in 1973, came *Cortège Hongrois*, a farewell tribute to Melissa Hayden, who was retiring.

*...ght: Marina Semyonova
...aymonda, with Alexei
...gakov as the Comte de
...is, in the second act of
...Bolshoi Ballet's revival
...etipa's* Raymonda *in
...5.*

*...erleaf: Doreen Wells
...David Wall with
...bers of The Royal
...let Touring Company in
...ast act of* Raymonda
*...aged by Rudolf
...eyev in 1964.*

SYNOPSIS
*Act I, Scene 1*
*The Château de Doris*
*in Provence*

Raymonda is betrothed to Jean de Brienne, who is away at the Crusades, and she celebrates her birthday at the castle of her aunt, the Countess Sybille. Jean sends her a tapestry portrait of himself and announces his imminent arrival. A Saracen lord, Abdérâme, arrives to court Raymonda and offers her valuable presents.

*Scene 2*
*The castle terrace*

Left alone on the terrace of the castle by moonlight, Raymonda dreams of Jean, who appears in a vision and dances with her. The statue of the White Lady, one of Raymonda's forebears, has led her into this enchanted garden where she meets Jean, and when Abdérâme's vision appears to renew his advances, Raymonda appeals to the spectral White Lady for help. Goblins and fireflies fill the stage and dance. Raymonda faints and is carried by her companions into the castle.

*Act II*
*The courtyard*
*of the castle*

Guests arrive and Raymonda is awaiting Jean's return. She is horrified when Abdérâme appears with a troupe of Moorish and Spanish entertainers. As they dance, Abdérâme tries to abduct Raymonda, but Jean enters with King Andrew II of Hungary, with whom he has been fighting the Saracens. The King orders that Jean and Abdérâme shall fight in single combat. The ghost of the White Lady intervenes and causes Abdérâme to falter. He is slain and Raymonda and Jean are united.

*Act III*
*The garden of*
*Jean's castle*

Festivities in Hungarian style mark the wedding of Jean and Raymonda.

# Les Rendezvous

*Ballet in one act. Music by Daniel François Auber, arranged by Constant Lambert. Choreography by Frederick Ashton. Scenery and costumes by William Chappell. First performed by the Vic-Wells Ballet at the Sadler's Wells Theatre, London, on December 5, 1933, with Alicia Markova, Stanislas Idzikowski, Pearl Argyle, Ninette de Valois, and Robert Helpmann.*

*Les Rendezvous* was the first ballet which Ashton made specifically for the young Vic-Wells Ballet—a company he was to join as choreographer eighteen months later. Of *Les Rendezvous* he observed: "It has no serious portent at all; it is simply a vehicle for the exquisite dancing of Idzikowski and Markova." The ballet has endured to this day by reason both of its charm and of the superbly crafted dances. Its first American production took place in 1980 when Mikhail Baryshnikov chose it to open his first season as artistic director of American Ballet Theatre.

Its score is an early example of Constant Lambert's taste for rediscovering otherwise forgotten composers and his skill in adapting their work for the ballet stage. For *Les Rendezvous* he turned to Auber's opera *L'Enfant Prodigue*. Lambert was nothing if not catholic in his musical taste and far in advance of musical opinion of his time in his affection for and understanding of the byways of nineteenth-century music. His book of criticism, *Music Ho!*, which appeared in 1934, is still a stimulating and worthwhile parade of opinions. In it he wrote of Auber: "The vulgarities of Auber have already taken on a period charm, like Victorian woolwork. . . ."

SYNOPSIS

The setting is a park in which we witness the happy meetings and partings of young lovers. There are roles for a ballerina and her virtuoso partner, and a pas de trois of lightly tripping brilliance and humour for a girl and two boys.

*Doreen Wells as the ballerina and Donald Britton, right, as the principal male dancer in* Les Rendezvous *as staged by the Sadler's Wells Theatre Ballet.*

225

# Requiem

*Ballet in one act. Music by Gabriel Fauré. Choreography by Kenneth MacMillan. Scenery and costumes by Yolanda Sonnabend. First performed by the Stuttgart Ballet at the Württembergische Staatstheater, Stuttgart, on November 28, 1976, with Marcia Haydée, Richard Cragun, Egon Madsen, Birgit Keil, and Reid Anderson.*

"This danced Requiem is dedicated to the memory of my friend and colleague John Cranko, Director of the Stuttgart Ballet." Thus Kenneth MacMillan prefaces his setting of the Requiem that Gabriel Fauré wrote in memory of his father, a setting of part of the Mass for the Dead, whose gravity reveals depths of belief without excessive dramatics or vehemence.

It is ironical but fitting that this beautiful ballet should have been created in Stuttgart when MacMillan was still Director of The Royal Ballet. Eleven years before, he had staged *Song of the Earth* for the Stuttgart Ballet because the Covent Garden authorities lacked confidence in MacMillan's ability to realise the music. Cranko believed, and thus acquired a masterpiece. Similarly Stuttgart acquired *Requiem*—to a score which MacMillan had long contemplated—and the work both honoured Cranko's memory in noblest fashion and reminded people once again of his belief in MacMillan.

## SYNOPSIS

The stage picture is austere: six square columns of misted glass rise into the flies, lit from above, with a white backcloth and wings. The dancers, save for two principals, are in flesh-coloured tights, decorated on the trunk with striations and patterns that recall the musculature and veining of the body as seen in drawings by Pavel Tchelitchev and William Blake. Blake's drawings may also have provided certain initial poses that MacMillan has developed to feed his dances: the drama implicit in Blake's figures in *Milton, Job,* and *The Inferno* is exactly what the choreography presents and extends through movement. MacMillan avoids traditional pietism to seek something directly communicative in the text of the Mass. The ballet begins with a shock. A large cast shuffle on stage at the initial Requiem Aeternam, fists raised heavenwards in grief and supplication. The leading ballerina, her angelic nature suggested by a dress of white chiffon, is held high above the opening group and rolled to and fro on a sea of hands, and as the Kyrie ends there are five reclining bodies on the stage while a central group remains caught in a supplicating pose.

The Offertorium finds a male dancer grieving and alone, wearing a simple loincloth and looking very like Patinir's John the Baptist. To him comes the ballerina as a hope of liberation from the pains of hell, and there follows a tender duet. With the baritone solo at Hostias et Preces the man is again alone, and the prayer for the redemption of the soul is exemplified by a solo in which his body is sometimes curled on the ground, then swept in broad spans of energy. At the recapitulation of the Domine Jesu Christe the man kneels in supplication while the girls of the corps de ballet are carried on as if in realisation of the prayer. The Sanctus which follows opens with another shock: the ballerina launches herself in a joyous leap into the arms of a male dancer, and with the closing Hosannas she seems to float beatifically, supported on the knees of her reclining partner. The Pie Jesu engenders a feeling of absolute trust and childlike innocence as the ballerina is sometimes seated on the ground or moves across the stage, contemplating the earth far below. In the Agnus Dei a second female dancer incarnates both the hope of peace an

*Kenneth MacMillan's* Requiem *as staged by the Stuttgart Ballet, with Marcia Haydée supported by Richard Cragun and Reid Anderson.*

sacrificial aspect of the Lamb. On the orchestral tutti that precedes the choral Requiem Aeternam she is held inverted above the stage and this pose is resolved when the leading ballerina enters as the representation of consolation. The Libera Me is given to another male dancer and a group of men, their bodies flung and tossed by their awareness of the day of wrath, and when the leading male dancer is carried off the ballerina is carried behind him as the promise of redemption. The final In Paradisum has the girls of the corps lifted high over the stage. The entire cast then walk to form a central group which divides in two as the stage is brilliantly illuminated from above. They stand motionless, then exit, some walking, others carried, as the ballerina is lifted high and triumphant by two men, to suggest the last feeling of eternal rest and peace.

# Rhapsody

*Ballet in one act: Music by Sergei Rachmaninov. Choreography by Frederick Ashton. Scenery by Ashton. Costumes by William Chappell. First performed by The Royal Ballet at the Royal Opera House, Covent Garden, on August 4, 1980, with Mikhail Baryshnikov and Lesley Collier.*

*Rhapsody* had a double inspiration for its creation. It is dedicated to Her Majesty Queen Elizabeth The Queen Mother and received its first performance on the evening of her eightieth birthday, an evening which Her Majesty spent at the Royal Opera House accompanied by Her Majesty The Queen and the immediate Royal Family. It was an evening remarkable for the extreme affection shown by the audience to The Queen Mother, which ranged from a chorus of "Happy Birthday to You" to a final shower of silver confetti from the blue and gold ceiling of the Royal Opera House. A second inspiration for Ashton was the guest appearance, for the third time, of Mikhail Baryshnikov with The Royal Ballet. Rachmaninov's Rhapsody on a Theme of Paganini has been given two other notable choreographic treatments. One of Mikhail Fokine's last ballets was *Paganini*, which he staged for the de Basil Ballet Russe at Covent Garden in 1939 with scenery and costumes by Sergei Soudeikin. This, Fokine's last successful ballet, had been suggested to him by the composer, and it maintained its place in the de Basil repertory until the demise of the company. Another version, with choreography by Leonid Lavrovsky, was staged by the Bolshoi Ballet. Like the Fokine version, this production stressed the diabolic aspects of Paganini's art and the consolation he derived from a muse and a beloved.

SYNOPSIS

*Rhapsody* is a plotless series of dances which, like the score, depends on contrasts of mood and texture. The ballet is set for a central pair with an attendant group of six couples. In the writing for the male dancer, who opens and closes the ballet, Ashton acknowledges the virtuoso Rachmaninov's tribute to the virtuoso Paganini in his writing for a great *danseur*. (There is even a passing hint at violin playing in a gesture given to the male dancer.) For the ballerina Ashton has created choreography demanding exceptional speed and brilliance of footwork; for the attendant soloists there is complex choreography which challenges them at every moment; inevitably the luscious eighteenth musical variation becomes a pas de deux. The work ends with a gesture from the man—like that of the "Blue Skater" in Ashton's *Les Patineurs* and Puck in *The Dream*—which seems to express amusement at the technical ardours that had gone before.

Opposite: *Mikhail Baryshnikov in Ashton's* Rhapsody *for The Roya Ballet.*

# The Rite of Spring

*Ballet in one act. Music by Igor Stravinsky. Choreography by Kenneth MacMillan. Scenery and costumes by Sydney Nolan. First performed by The Royal Ballet at the Royal Opera House, Covent Garden, on May 3, 1962, with Monica Mason as the Chosen Maiden.*

"I wanted the whole of the composition to give the feeling of closeness between men and earth, the community of their lives with the earth, and I sought to do this in lapidary rhythms. The whole thing must be put on in dance from beginning to end. I give not one measure for pantomime. Nijinsky directs it with passionate zeal, forgetting himself." So wrote Stravinsky in a letter in December 1912. The scandal and sensation caused by the first performance of Stravinsky's score and Nijinsky's choreography for Diaghilev's Ballets Russes in Paris on May 29, 1913, is part of balletic and musical history. This third ballet created by Nijinsky provided an astounding and innovative realisation of the violence with which the Russian earth cracks open at the arrival of spring. Like the harsh rhythms of the score, the turned-in and percussive nature of Nijinsky's choreography offended and bemused most of the audience at the first performance. Tragically, because of the rupture with Diaghilev in the year of its creation, Nijinsky's version was lost. Seven years later Leonide Massine made a version, also lost. It was not until after the Second World War that other choreographers turned to the score, among them Mary Wigman in Berlin in 1957, Maurice Béjart in Brussels in 1959. Vladimir Vasilyov and his wife Natalia Kasatkina in Moscow in 1965, Erich Walter in Düsseldorf in 1970, Pina Bausch in Wuppertal in 1975, and, in an innovative version which turns it into a detective story and uses the two-piano version of the score, Paul Taylor in New York in 1980. In the spring of 1981 Richard Alston also used the two-piano reduction for a version for Ballet Rambert.

The MacMillan production for The Royal Ballet is deservedly famous. The choreographer has sought to give it more universal implications by avoiding any specific Russian connotations: indeed, the design of the Australian painter Sydney Nolan suggests an aboriginal world. Without seeking an obviously ethnic language, MacMillan yet devised patterns and chains of movement which admirably convey the intensity of this tribal ritual. In the role of the chosen maiden Monica Mason has shown unquestioned greatness by the power of her dancing and the dignity with which she shows the maiden accepting fate.

Of the other versions, that by Maurice Béjart has reached the widest audience. Though he maintains a certain tribal theme, Béjart's view is that the act of human love is the fundamental attitude of the rite. His version presents the two separate forces of a group of men and a group of women. The culminating moment is the union of a virginal man with a virginal woman.

Glen Tetley has also made a version of the Stravinsky score. His staging was first presented by the Bavarian State Opera Ballet in Munich on April 17, 1974, and later by the Stuttgart Ballet and American Ballet theatre with Mikhail Baryshnikov in the leading role. His theme is the sacrifice of a chosen youth who is the incarnation of men's hopes

*Opposite: The culminating moment in Maurice Béjart's staging of* The Rite of Spring *for the* Ballet du XXième Siècle.

and sins and sufferings. He is killed as a scapegoat, but is reborn with the spring and represents the hope and promise of a new life. The ballet takes place in a mysterious grove—designed by Nadine Baylis—in which the youth is first seen in a variation which features contractions, broken poses, and eager, questing leaps. Thereafter a group of men and women join in the ritual, and at their heart Tetley places a couple who represent experience and whose actions are of explicit erotic power. Tetley's treatment of the score is more concerned with its emotional and animal drive than with its rhythmic structure; from it he extracts an imagery of harsh coupling in unquenchable sexual hunger for the couples and an identity both frenzied and somehow innocent for the chosen youth. In a final *coup de théâtre* he is whisked heavenwards in an explosion of energy.

SYNOPSIS

*Monica Mason in Kenneth Macmillan's* The Rite of Spring *as staged by The Royal Ballet.*

MacMillan's ballet is in two tableaux. In the first, The Adoration of the Earth, members of a tribe—adolescents, men, and women—are involved in group dances preparatory to the annual spring rite. In the second tableau, The Sacrifice, the scene changes from a desert setting to a space dominated by an immense golden phallic tree. The elders of the tribe watch a group of six maidens dancing and choose one of them. Amid the urgent participation of the tribe the chosen maiden moves through her ritual dance and finally collapses; at the end, her body is tossed heavenwards.

# Robert Schumann's "Davidsbündlertänze"

*Ballet in one act. Music by Robert Schumann. Choreography by George Balanchine. Scenery and costumes by Rouben Ter-Arutunian. First performed by the New York City Ballet at the State Theater, Lincoln Center, on June 12, 1980, with Karin von Aroldingen and Adam Lüders, Suzanne Farrell and Jacques d'Amboise, Kay Mazzo and Ib Andersen, and Heather Watts and Peter Martins.*

The fullness of this ballet's title is some indication of the importance which Balanchine attaches to his musical text and its reference to Schumann's private mythology of the League of David—what Balanchine calls "a conspiracy of himself alone" against the Philistines. Further, there are the indications in Schumann's score: nearly all of these eighteen piano pieces bear the inscription of the letter "E" for Eusebius or "F" for Florestan, those two aspects of Schumann's personality: respectively the lyric and dreaming Eusebius and the impassioned Florestan.

"*Davidsbündlertänze*" is a ballet without a story. Four couples and a pianist, dressed in approximations of mid-nineteenth-century costume, inhabit an undefined drawing room. In fact, the audience can hardly be sure that it is a room at all: there are no edges, the stage is hemmed in by white drapery set at an angle; the backcloth is a blurred vision of a Gothic cathedral which rises out of an expanse of water (at one time Balanchine wanted to have a flood engulf the stage to wash away all the inimical figures in Schumann's life—his critics and his enemies, including his father-in-law Wieck). There is less pure dancing and more "atmosphere" than in many of Balanchine's previous ballets. The music clearly hints at love, attachment, parting, sorrow, and joy, all on an intimate scale. In a rare interview Balanchine suggested that he had certain episodes of Schumann's life in mind when he created the ballet. Clearly there is at least one male solo that hints at the composer's madness, and the final duet could be interpreted as Schumann and his wife parting forever as he sinks to an early death.

The chosen incidents in the composer's life are not treated explicitly but one of the couples—originally Karin von Aroldingen and Adam Lüders—may be identified as Clara and Schumann. The other couples, who are more or less equal in the amount they have to do, can be seen to represent other aspects of love or human relationships—perhaps possibilities that existed for the Schumanns. In the choreography for these couples, the Florestan or Eusebius qualities in the music are revealed in dances by turns ardent or contemplative. For the first part of the ballet the women wear heeled slippers (as in *Liebeslieder Walzer*). They change to pointe shoes later in the piece. The most explicitly dramatic and emotional writing is for von Aroldingen and Lüders, and at one moment Lüders has a solo indicative of Schumann's encroaching mental disturbance, during which he is visited by five, black-clad figures—the Philistines who seek to destroy the artist. Order seems restored and the dances continue, but at last the Schumann figure is seen to be more

*Karin von Aroldingen and Adam Lüders in* Robert Schumann's "Davidsbündlertänze."

and more unable to accept the conventions expressed in the social dance attitudes of the choreography. He escapes from the protective Clara figure and is drawn into the watery depths of madness present in the setting, while Clara weeps.

# Rodeo

*Ballet in one act. Music by Aaron Copland. Choreography by Agnes de Mille. Scenery by Oliver Smith. Costumes by Kermit Love. First performed by the Ballet Russe de Monte Carlo at the Metropolitan Opera House, New York, on October 16, 1942, with Agnes de Mille as the Cowgirl, Frederic Franklin as the Champion Roper, and Casimir Kokitch as the Head Wrangler.*

*Rodeo* was a turning point in the career of Agnes de Mille. In her admirable volume of autobiography *Dance to the Piper* de Mille describes how she was called upon to prepare this vivid piece of Americana for the touring, émigré Ballet Russe de Monte Carlo, instilling into a classical company the earthy activities of Wild West characters. That she was so successful meant that the ballet had a triumph, and it remains a staple of the repertory of American Ballet Theatre, which acquired the production in August 1950. Very importantly for de Mille's career, it led to her being commissioned to provide the dances for the musical *Oklahoma!* the following year.

SYNOPSIS

### Scene 1
*The corral*

A blazing Saturday afternoon. Cowboys are getting ready for the ritual rodeo that marks the end of the week. The men dance, evoking the bucking motions of horses, and one tomboyish Cowgirl (who is attracted to the Head Wrangler) tries repeatedly to join in. She is prevented from doing so by the men, but their attention is soon distracted by a group of young girls from the city, prettily dressed and consciously feminine in contrast to the trousered, dusty Cowgirl. The men display their skills, not least the Champion Roper. The Cowgirl tries to ride on and display her abilities but she is thrown by her supposed mount and is humiliated in front of the girls and cowhands. As evening falls the rodeo ends and everyone prepares for the Saturday evening dance. The Cowgirl is disconsolate.

In a frontcloth scene a caller guides four couples through the patterns of a square dance.

### Scene 2
*The party at the ranch house*

The cowboys and their girls are dancing and enjoying themselves. The men are showing off their best clothes. The Cowgirl, still in her blue jeans, is alone. She does not know how to dance but the Champion Roper tries to smarten her up and also show her how to behave at the dance. When the Head Wrangler appears, the girl is overcome by her infatuation and starts to mope. She dances with the Champion Roper, but her pleasure dissipates when she sees the Wrangler dancing with another girl. She runs away, and soon returns in a vivid red dress. The men are somewhat amazed, as are the other guests, and the Wrangler and Roper try to dance with her. The girl is torn between them. Suddenly she realises that she loves the Roper as much as he loves her, and at curtain fall they look lovingly into each other's eyes as the dance continues.

# Romeo and Juliet

*Ballet in three acts. Music by Serge Prokofiev. Libretto by Sergei Radlov, Prokofiev, and Leonid Lavrovsky, based upon the play by William Shakespeare. Choreography by Lavrovsky. Scenery and costumes by Pyotr Williams. First performed by the Kirov Ballet in Leningrad, on January 11, 1940, with Konstantin Sergueyev and Galina Ulanova.*

*Costume design by Eugene Berman for American Ballet Theatre's staging of Romeo and Juliet with choreography by Antony Tudor to music of Frederick Delius, first performed in 1943.*

*Opposite: Lynn Seymour and Christopher Gable, the artists for whom Kenneth MacMillan created his version of Romeo and Juliet for The Royal Ballet 1965. At the ball, Juliet plays her lute so that her friends may dance and Romeo, enraptured with Juliet, dances among them.*

The initial idea for this balletic version of *Romeo and Juliet* came from two Soviet writers, Sergei Radlov and Adrian Piotrovsky, in 1934. Their scenario included a happy ending in which Friar Laurence prevented Romeo from stabbing himself so that when Juliet awakens the Friar can hide the reunited lovers behind a rosebush before summoning the Capulet and Montague factions by beating a gong. Prokofiev had started composing the score before some good sense prevailed and the production was abandoned. In 1936 the ballet was again scheduled for production, two years hence, as part of the bicentennial celebrations of the Kirov Ballet. In the event, the score was first produced outside Russia, when the Czechoslovak choreographer and dancer Vania Psota mounted a version in Brno in 1938.

The Kirov then decided to stage the work in the following year, with choreography by Lavrovsky. Prokofiev had strengthened the score, ridding it of its happy ending and darkening its emotional tone. With Radlov, Lavrovsky and Prokofiev also devised an amended scenario. But the composer refused to write more music and he was only to be won round to expanding the score by the sight of some completed choreography and by further discussions with Lavrovsky. In January 1940 the ballet eventually reached the stage of the Kirov Theatre with Galina Ulanova as Juliet and Konstantin Sergueyev as Romeo. Six years later, at the war's end, when Ulanova was transferred as ballerina to the Bolshoi company, the ballet was staged in Moscow. The production was a triumphant assertion of the basic ideals of Soviet ballet. In its heroic impulse, its massive force of dancers, its choreographic directness and literalism of manner, it remained a signature ballet for the Bolshoi for many years. With it, the Bolshoi made its first triumphant appearance in the West, at the Royal Opera House, Covent Garden, in 1956 and three years later took it to New York. On both occasions Ulanova was the incomparable Juliet, with Yuri Zhdanov as her Romeo.

In later years the production wilted, losing much of its urgency and fire, following the death of Lavrovsky in 1967. His successor as director of the Bolshoi Ballet, Yuri Grigorovich, produced his own version of the ballet for the Paris Opéra in February 1978, and his decision to supplant the Lavrovsky version in the Bolshoi repertory caused a near revolt in the company.

A major Western staging of *Romeo and Juliet*, using the Prokofiev score, was that made by Frederick Ashton for the Royal Danish Ballet, first produced in Copenhagen on May 19, 1955, with Henning Kronstam and Mona Vangsaae. This production, which followed the main outline of the Soviet libretto, enjoyed great success not only in Denmark but also in Edinburgh and the United States, when the Royal Danish Ballet presented it on tour. Interestingly, it was a production made before the West had had any sight of the Lavrovsky staging, which has since been such a strong influence upon all subsequent versions. Unhappily, the Ashton ballet has been lost from the repertory.

SYNOPSIS

*Prologue*

The marriage of Romeo and Juliet is blessed by Friar Laurence in a triptych-like tableau.

*Act I, Scene 1*
*A square in Verona*

Romeo, son of Lord Montague, wanders through the square. Servants from the house of Capulet enter and are soon involved in a fight with servants from the Montague household—the two households are bitter enemies. Involved in the fighting are Benvolio, nephew to Montague and friend to Romeo, and Tybalt, nephew to Lady Capulet. Paris, who is to be married to Capulet's daughter Juliet, observes the fighting and Capulet and Montague now join in the fray. The ringing of a bell when the brawling is at its height brings more citizens to the square and Escalus, Prince of Verona, enters with his guard. The fighting stops and Escalus orders that such violence cease forthwith. A frontcloth scene shows Juliet's Nurse scolding servants during preparations for a ball.

*Scene 2*
*Juliet's room*

Juliet is playing with her Nurse. Her mother, Lady Capulet, enters and tells her that she is to be married to Paris. She ignores Juliet's pleas that she is too young and shows her daughter that, physically, this is not so. Another frontcloth scene shows preparations for the ball continuing.

*Scene 3*
*Outside the Capulets' house*

Guests arrive for the ball. In a frontcloth scene Romeo's companions Mercutio and Benvolio decide to go to the Capulet ball in disguise and they induce Romeo to join them.

*Scene 4*
*The ballroom of the Capulets' house*

Juliet receives a bouquet from Paris and as the guests arrive the ball commences with a formal cushion dance. Juliet also dances. Romeo and his friends enter, all masked. Romeo is thrilled by Juliet's beauty. Mercutio distracts the guests when Paris becomes suspicious. Romeo and Juliet now dance and Romeo's mask falls off so that Juliet can see him. Tybalt realises that Romeo is a member of the hated Montagues and tells Lord Capulet. Romeo puts on his mask and Mercutio prevents Tybalt from attacking Romeo. In a frontcloth scene Juliet tells her Nurse that she has fallen in love with Romeo, son of her father's greatest enemy.

*Scene 5*
*The garden of the Capulets' house*

Juliet stands on the balcony of her room after the ball. It is a moonlit night and she cannot sleep. Romeo appears in the garden below; Juliet goes to join him and they declare their love.

*Act II, Scene 1*
*The square in Verona*

The crowd is enjoying itself. A religious procession passes by. Benvolio and Mercutio are paying court to girls from an inn. Juliet's Nurse enters in search of Romeo. When he enters she gives him a message from Juliet. In a frontcloth scene Romeo reads a letter in which Juliet agrees to marry him.

*Scene 2*
*Friar Laurence's cell*

Romeo arrives and asks the Friar to marry them. Juliet enters and Friar Laurence performs the wedding ceremony. In a frontcloth scene the tension between the Capulets and Montagues bursts out in further skirmishing.

*Scene 3*
*The square*

The crowd is dancing lightheartedly. Tybalt engineers a duel with Mercutio and although Romeo tries to pacify the pair Tybalt succeeds in making Mercutio fight. Mercutio is wounded and dies. Mercutio's body is borne away and Tybalt's braggart air impels Romeo to fight him. Tybalt is killed. Romeo takes flight and the Capulets appear and grieve over the body. Lady Capulet is borne on the bier with Tybalt's body in a paroxysm of grief. Prince Escalus banishes Romeo from Verona.

| | |
|---|---|
| **Act III, Scene 1**<br>*Juliet's bedroom* | Romeo and Juliet are together but Romeo must leave with the dawn. They dance a desperate duet of farewell. Juliet's parents enter with Paris and her Nurse to make preparations for the wedding. Juliet is |
| | distraught and her parents rage against her. Alone, Juliet decides to seek help from Friar Laurence. In a frontcloth scene the cloaked figure of Juliet is seen running to Friar Laurence. |
| **Scene 2**<br>*Friar Laurence's cell* | The Friar offers Juliet a sleeping potion which will make it seem that she is dead. Her family will thus place |
| | her body in the family vault and Friar Laurence will warn Romeo to rescue her and escape from Verona. |
| **Scene 3**<br>*Juliet's bedroom* | Juliet consents to marry Paris. Her parents are delighted and the Nurse brings Juliet a wedding dress. Left alone, Juliet drinks the draught given to her by Friar Laurence. Her friends |
| | enter with musicians to greet her on her wedding morning. Paris enters and the family assemble but Juliet lies motionless on the bed. Believing her to be dead, they mourn. |
| **Scene 4**<br>*Mantua* | Romeo is distressed at his separation from Juliet. His servant now appears with the news of Juliet's death. He has made the journey more quickly than |
| | Friar Laurence's messenger and Romeo is heartbroken. He decides that he must return to see Juliet one last time. |
| **Scene 5**<br>*Inside the Capulet vault* | Mourners watch as Juliet's body is placed in the family tomb. When they leave, Romeo appears and embraces Juliet's body. He then drinks poison |
| | and dies. Juliet awakes and discovers Romeo's corpse. Seizing his dagger, she kills herself. |
| **Epilogue** | The Montagues and Capulets standing by the bodies of the young lovers swear eternal peace. |

*...is photograph depicts ...detail and vividness of ...Bolshoi's early ...formances of the ...rovsky production of ...meo and Juliet. ...dina Ulanova as Juliet is ...ted at centre holding a ...let.*

## The Royal Ballet

*Ballet in three acts.*
*Music by*
*Serge Prokofiev.*
*Choreography by*
*Kenneth MacMillan.*
*Scenery and costumes by*
*Nicholas Georgiadis.*
*First performed at the*
*Royal Opera House,*
*Covent Garden,*
*on February 9, 1965.*

Although the Royal Opera House felt the need to give the first performance of MacMillan's *Romeo and Juliet* with Fonteyn and Nureyev in the title roles, the ballet was written and conceived for two very different artists: Lynn Seymour and Christopher Gable, whose youth and lyric intensity were the entire justification for the ballet when they were seen in it on the second night. Seymour was the clear inspiration for the work; her impassioned account of the role— Juliet as the driving force of the action—explained the approach which MacMillan had taken. Given courage to make his own version by the scale and manner of Cranko's Stuttgart presentation, MacMillan saw the ballet as a story to be told as truthfully as possible in dance terms. The result is one of the greatest successes The Royal Ballet has known, a work which celebrated the beauty of Seymour as the finest dance-actress of her time, a unique and thrilling performer. It is regrettable that the filmed record of the ballet—albeit made when the production was still fresh and the original cast was largely available—should have featured the unconvincing portrayals of Fonteyn and Nureyev rather than the beautiful and powerful readings of Seymour and Gable.

*Act I, scene 1. The marketplace in Verona.*
Rosaline appears with two attendants, followed by the adoring Romeo. She leaves and Romeo joins his friends Mercutio and Benvolio as the morning market comes to life. Three harlots are among the crowd. Feuding begins between Capulets and Montagues and a fight soon ensues with Romeo and Tybalt at the heads of the opposing forces. Lord Capulet and Lord Montague join in the fray. Escalus, Prince of Verona, now appears with his guards and orders both parties to lay down their swords, which are placed in front of the piled-up corpses of the slain. The families stand facing each other in an uneasy truce.

*Act I, scene 2. An anteroom in the Capulets' house.*
Juliet is playing with a doll and teasing her Nurse. Her parents bring in Paris, who is to be her bridegroom. When they leave, Juliet seeks to play again with her doll but her Nurse shows her that she is no longer a child.

*Act I, scene 3. Outside the Capulets' house.*
Guests arrive for a ball. Romeo and his friends sport among the company and Romeo courts Rosaline yet again, to Tybalt's annoyance. When the guests have gone into the house the three young men dance a spirited trio and then put on masks, take up lutes, and enter the house to join the party.

*Act I, scene 4. The ballroom.*
The guests dance. Juliet enters and is presented to the assembly. Romeo and his friends appear and he seeks out Rosaline. Suddenly Romeo and Juliet come face to face. As Juliet plays a lute for her friends, Romeo dances for her. When Juliet dances, Romeo joins her. Tybalt is shocked that she should neglect Paris. Mercutio and Benvolio distract everyone's attention from what is going on, and as the guests leave for supper Juliet indicates that she feels faint and asks to be left alone. Romeo joins her and eventually takes off his mask and the young lovers gaze at each other, enraptured, and then dance ecstatically. Tybalt sees this encounter and confronts Romeo. A fight between them is prevented by Lord Capulet, who insists on their making peace. When the guests return for a general dance, Romeo and Juliet meet again briefly but Mercutio and Benvolio urge Romeo to leave.

*Act I, scene 5. Outside the Capulets' house.*
The guests are leaving; Tybalt follows Romeo from the house, as the three young men depart.

*Act I, scene 6. The garden of the Capulets' house.*
Juliet is on her balcony. A noise announces the appearance of Romeo. He gazes up at Juliet. She runs down a flight of steps into the garden and the lovers are united in an impassioned pas de deux.

*Act II, scene 1. The marketplace.*
Amid the hubbub of the market, Romeo dreams of Juliet. A wedding procession appears which the crowd greets with pleasure. A group of young men dance with mandolins. Juliet's Nurse enters, seeking Romeo. After some comic byplay with Mercutio and Benvolio, a letter which she brings from Juliet is handed to Romeo. He rushes away in an access of joy.

*Act II, scene 2. Friar Laurence's chapel.*
The Friar enters in prayer. Romeo dashes in and shows him Juliet's letter. Juliet appears with her Nurse and the lovers are married.

*Act II, scene 3. The marketplace.*
The wedding procession is still a focus of attention; when Romeo returns,

Tybalt tries to make him fight, but Romeo—now Tybalt's kinsman by marriage—refuses. His friends are amazed, and Mercutio embarks upon a duel with Tybalt. Mercutio mocks him, but as he turns laughing to his friends, Tybalt stabs him in the back. Mercutio first jokes, then gradually succumbs to the wounds. He curses the houses of both Montague and Capulet, and then dies. Distraught, Romeo now takes up his sword and kills Tybalt. Lady Capulet enters, and grieves in wild despair over Tybalt's body. Romeo tries to beg her forgiveness; she in turn tries to attack him with a sword. Romeo leaves: Lady Capulet clasps the dead Tybalt in her arms.

*Act III, scene 1. Juliet's bedroom.*
The lovers wake, and Romeo prepares to leave. Juliet tries to shut out the dawn light, and takes an impassioned farewell of Romeo. Her Nurse and her parents enter, with Paris. He is presented to Juliet as her future bridegroom. She rebels against this, and her parents rage at her. They leave her so that she may try and mend her obstinate ways, and Juliet sits motionless for a long moment on her bed, trying to summon up strength for some action. She puts on a cloak and rushes away.

*Act III, scene 2. The chapel.*
Friar Laurence enters, and Juliet runs in, begging for his help. He offers her a sleeping potion, which she eventually accepts.

*Act III, scene 3. Juliet's bedroom.*
Juliet hides the potion under the bolster on her bed. When her parents return with Paris, she endeavours one last time to make them cancel her wedding. At last she agrees to marry Paris, and dances like a ghost in his arms. Her parents and Paris leave, and the Nurse is ordered to follow them.

*The letter scene in Act II of MacMillan's* Romeo and Juliet *with the authentic cast. David Blair as Mercutio supports Gerd Larsen as the collapsing Nurse, while Christopher Gable reaches for Juliet's letter. On the right, Anthony Dowell is the amused Benvolio.*

Left alone, Juliet finds the courage to take the sleeping draught, and crawls onto her bed. Her friends enter with flowers to greet her on her wedding morning. They are made uneasy by her immobility. The Nurse enters with Juliet's wedding dress, and discovers that the girl is apparently dead. Juliet's parents enter and mourn at her bedside.

*Act III, scene 4. The Capulet vault.*
Hooded monks progress through the vault, where Juliet lies on her bier. The family take a last farewell of her, and Paris stands grieving by. From the shadows a figure emerges, and throws off a cloak. It is Romeo. He stabs Paris, then clasps the senseless Juliet in his arms and dances with her. Laying her back on the bier he takes poison and dies. Juliet gradually stirs. She wakes, gazes in horror round the vault, and then discovers Romeo's body. In total despair she seizes his dagger and kills herself, her body falling over the bier, arms outstretched to the lifeless figure of Romeo.

## American Ballet Theatre

*Ballet in one act.
Music by
Frederick Delius,
arranged by
Antal Dorati.
Choreography by
Antony Tudor.
Scenery and costumes by
Eugene Berman.
Incomplete version first
performed at the
Metropolitan Opera
House, New York,
on April 6, 1943;
completed version
presented four days
later.*

Tudor's version of the Shakespearean tragedy has many merits. The story is told in dancing of extreme intensity which compresses the full-length action into one-act form without any deformation of proportion. The characterisations are succinct and have the kind of emotional resonance which we associate with Tudor's finest work. The ballet is further enhanced by superlative designs from the Russian-born neo-Romantic painter Eugene Berman, who provided a permanent set which evoked all the grandeur of Renaissance architecture which he peopled with beautifully apposite costumes. The score was made up from works by Delius ("A Walk to Paradise Garden" from *A Village Romeo and Juliet, Eventyr, Over the Hills and Far Away*, and *Brigg Fair*) and the Englishness of the music became essentially right for the drama. In wartime New York, this production became a very English affair with Alicia Markova as Juliet, Hugh Laing as a highly poetic Romeo, Tudor as Tybalt, and, at certain performances, Sir Thomas Beecham invited to conduct a score by the composer for whom he was so magnificent an advocate.

At the first performance the choreography was incomplete— Tudor is a perfectionist—but this did not detract from the beauty of the work. Four days later, the production was completed. Despite the over-shadowing bulk of the Prokofiev score in its many versions, the Tudor-Delius-Berman staging retains all its poetic power and clarity.

*Prologue. Before the Palace in Verona.*
Romeo steps out of an arch and pays court to Rosaline, who follows him. The Montagues and Capulets, led by Mercutio and Tybalt, start to brawl. The Lord Montague and the Lord Capulet order them to stop and the crowd disperses. Romeo and Mercutio turn again to Rosaline.

*Scene 1. The ball at the Capulets' house.*
The guests are dancing. Juliet appears. She is shy but is encouraged to accept Paris as her suitor. Suddenly she sees Romeo and he gazes at her, though the formal patterns of the dance separate them. Left alone they are able to declare their love. Juliet's Nurse warns her charge against Romeo, and Tybalt threatens him.

*Scene 2. In the Capulet orchard.*
Romeo and Mercutio enter. Mercutio chides his friend for his attentions to Juliet and urges him to come to a tavern. Romeo hides from passers-by. Juliet appears at her balcony, and eventually Romeo expresses his love to her.

*Scene 3. Friar Laurence's cell.*
The Friar marries the young lovers.

*Scene 4. A street.*
Juliet and Romeo are seen, but fighting again breaks out and Mercutio is killed by Tybalt. Romeo avenges his friend's death by killing Tybalt and he is urged to flee from Verona. Juliet sees what has happened and grieves for Tybalt, but realises that her love for Romeo transcends this family feud.

*Scene 5. Juliet's bedroom.*
The young lovers are together. Juliet is at first happy, then weeps as Romeo prepares to leave. After a passage of time, Juliet's friends enter to make her ready for her marriage to Paris. Juliet is in despair and she appeals to her father to release her from the betrothal. He refuses and Juliet is dressed for her wedding. When Friar Laurence appears he gives her a potion which will render her seemingly dead. She drinks it and collapses.

*Alicia Markova as Juliet and Hugh Laing as Romeo with Dimitri Romanoff as Friar Laurence in Antony Tudor's production for American Ballet Theatre. Something of the quality of Berman's designs is apparent in this scene.*

*Scene 6. The procession to the tomb.*
Juliet's body is taken to the Capulet vault.
*Scene 7. The vault.*
Juliet lies on her bier. Romeo enters in despair and takes poison. When Juliet regains consciousness she discovers Romeo and tries to revive him. Briefly she succeeds, but he expires, and Juliet, taking his dagger, stabs herself.

### The Stuttgart Ballet

*Ballet in three acts.*
*Music by*
*Serge Prokofiev.*
*Choreography by*
*John Cranko.*
*Scenery and costumes by*
*Jürgen Rose.*
*First performed at*
*the Württembergische*
*Staatstheater, Stuttgart, on*
*December 2, 1962.*

Cranko first staged his *Romeo and Juliet* for the ballet company of the Teatro alla Scala, Milan, who performed it in Venice on July 26, 1958. In its initial Italian staging, and in the very successful revisions which he incorporated when mounting the ballet for his own Stuttgart company in 1962, with Marcia Haydée and Ray Barra, Cranko found a way of reducing the scale of the forces involved without losing the urgency of Shakespeare's tragedy which had characterised the Bolshoi staging. The Stuttgart Ballet has toured this production with great success and it was acquired by the National Ballet of Canada in 1964. It was also staged by the Bavarian State Opera Ballet in Munich in 1968.

*Act I, scene 1. A street in Verona.*
Romeo, son of Montague, is in love with Rosaline. He flirts with her, then joins with his friends Mercutio and Benvolio in a brawl with members of the Capulet household. Their fighting is stopped by the Duke of Verona, who threatens the death penalty for anyone who disturbs the peace.

*Act I, scene 2. The garden of the Capulets' house.*
Juliet is playing with her Nurse when her mother brings in the dress she is to wear at a ball that night.

*Act I, scene 3. The entrance to the Capulets' house.*
Guests are arriving for a ball; they are joined by the masked figures of Romeo, Mercutio, and Benvolio.

*Act I, scene 4. The ballroom.*
Juliet learns that she is to marry Paris. As she dances with him she sees Romeo and falls in love with him. They manage to snatch a few moments together but Tybalt, Juliet's cousin,

realises who Romeo is and tries to fight with him. Lord Capulet intervenes and when the guests depart Benvolio and Mercutio search for Romeo.
*Act I, scene 5. The garden of the Capulets' house.*
Juliet is dreaming on her balcony and sees Romeo in the garden. They declare their love in a pas de deux.
*Act II, scene 1. A street in Verona.*
Amid the milling crowd Juliet's Nurse seeks Romeo and gives him a note from Juliet telling him that Friar Laurence will marry them.
*Act II, scene 2. Friar Laurence's cell.*
The lovers are married.
*Act II, scene 3. A street in Verona.*
The crowd is involved in joyous dancing. Tybalt seeks out Romeo but Romeo, now married into the Capulet clan, wishes to avoid a duel. Mercutio takes up his sword and is killed by Tybalt. Romeo avenges his friend and kills Tybalt. Lady Capulet mourns the death of her nephew and Romeo flees.

*Act III, scene 1. Juliet's bedroom.*
Romeo and Juliet part at dawn. Juliet's parents appear with Paris to arrange for his forthcoming marriage to their daughter. In great distress Juliet hurries to Friar Laurence to seek advice.
*Act III, scene 2. Friar Laurence's cell.*
Friar Laurence gives Juliet a potion which will induce a catatonic sleep.
*Act III, scene 3. Juliet's bedroom.*
Juliet drinks the potion and falls insensible onto her bed. When her bridesmaids enter with flowers for her, and Lady Capulet and the Nurse arrive to prepare her for the wedding, they all believe her to be dead.
*Act III, scene 4. The Capulet vault.*
Juliet's body has been placed in the family tomb. Paris mourns beside her. Romeo enters and, unaware of Friar Laurence's plan, kills Paris, and then takes his own life. When Juliet awakens she finds Romeo dead beside her and she kills herself.

## London Festival Ballet

*Ballet in three acts.
Music by
Serge Prokofiev.
Choreography by
Rudolf Nureyev.
Scenery by
Ezio Frigerio.
First performed at the
London Coliseum,
on June 2, 1977.*

Rudolf Nureyev's version of *Romeo and Juliet* was staged by London Festival Ballet during the ten-year period of Beryl Grey's directorship and it has given the company a production which it has been able to tour extensively. In making his version Nureyev looked carefully at the text of the play and at the actualities of life during the Renaissance—a period handsomely evoked in Frigerio's beautiful settings and costumes. The result is a presentation which offers many strong dramatic moments, notably the fight scenes and the sense of grievance which infuses all the feuding between the families, as witness the moment when the Capulets plunge their swords into a flag during the ball.

Nureyev danced Romeo in the first cast with Patricia Ruanne as Juliet, Nicholas Johnson as Mercutio, and Friedrich Werner as Tybalt.
*Act I, scene 1. The market square in Verona.*
A group of dice players is seen; a cart carries away the corpses of plague victims; Romeo pays court to Rosaline; the feuding retainers of Montagues and Capulets fight and brawl in the street, and while Benvolio, of the Montague faction, tries to pacify his men, Tybalt, the Capulet leader, urges his followers on to do battle. Mercutio, a friend to both factions, is happily engaged in

fighting on both sides. The Prince of Verona appears and commands order and peace.
*Act I, scene 2. The anteroom to Juliet's bedchamber.*
Juliet is seen with her companions and her Nurse. Her parents bring in Paris, the husband they have chosen for her.
*Act I, scene 3. Outside the Capulets' house.*
Guest arrive for a banquet. Romeo still pursues Rosaline, and Mercutio and his friends mock Romeo. Capulet invites Mercutio and his friends to join the festivities; they put on masks and enter the house, followed by Romeo.
*Act I, scene 4. The ballroom of the Capulets' house.*
Lady Capulet and Tybalt open the ball; the guests demonstrate their hatred of the Montague faction by striking with swords at a banner. Juliet dances with Paris, but when Mercutio and his companions arrive, chance brings about an encounter between Romeo and Juliet. They are immediately attracted, and when Romeo is recognised, Tybalt seeks to drive him from the ballroom. Lord Montague intervenes, and the company join in a wheel of fortune dance.
*Act I, scene 5. The Capulets' garden.*
Romeo hides below Juliet's bedchamber. His friends seek him, but Tybalt drives them away. Romeo and Juliet declare their love for each other.

*Opposite: Mercutio's death in Rudolf Nureyev's production of* Romeo and Juliet *for London Festival Ballet. Nureyev as Romeo holds the dying Mercutio (Nicholas Johnson) as Benvolio (Jonas Kåge) looks on.*

*Dominique Khalfouni as Juliet being dressed for her wedding to Paris in Yuri Grigorovich's production of* Romeo and Juliet *at the Paris Opéra in 1978.*

*Act II, scene 1. The market square.*
Juliet's Nurse brings a letter for Romeo. Eventually she delivers it and, as the square becomes crowded with acrobats and entertainers, Romeo receives Juliet's suggestion of marriage.

*Act II, scene 2. Friar Laurence's chapel.*
The lovers are married.

*Act II, scene 3. The market square.*
The Montague and Capulet factions rival each other in displays of dancing. Mercutio and Benvolio are provoked by Tybalt, who seeks Romeo. When he finds him, he tries to challenge him to fight. Romeo refuses, and Mercutio eagerly challenges Tybalt instead. They fight and Mercutio is mortally wounded; his friends think he is joking, and are only aware of the truth when they find him to be dead. Romeo avenges Mercutio's death by killing Tybalt. The Prince of Verona enters with Juliet, who sees that her new husband is the murderer of her cousin. Romeo is banished to Mantua.

*Act III, scene 1. Juliet's bedroom.*
Juliet's parents talk about her forthcoming marriage to Paris, while Juliet sits fearfully in her bedroom. Romeo appears, and they express their passion for each other. Romeo leaves for Mantua, and Juliet's parents enter to urge her to marry Paris.

*Act III, scene 2. Friar Laurence's chapel.*
The Friar gives Juliet a potion which will make her sleep. He tells her of his plan whereby her parents will think her dead, and she will be interred in the family crypt. Friar John, meanwhile, will have alerted Romeo of events, and he will come and claim his bride.

*Act III, scene 3. Juliet's bedroom.*
Juliet accedes to her parents' commands. When they leave she drinks the potion.

*Act III, scene 4. The anteroom to Juliet's bedchamber.*
Paris arrives with a group of musicians and dancers to meet Juliet. They discover Juliet apparently dead and Benvolio rushes away to tell Romeo.

*Act III, scene 5. The road to Mantua.*
Friar John, bearing Friar Laurence's letter to Romeo, is robbed and killed.

*Act III, scene 6. Mantua.*
Romeo dreams of Juliet, unaware of her plans. He is woken by Benvolio, who tells him that Juliet is dead. Romeo rushes to Verona.

*Act III, scene 7. The Capulet vault.*
Juliet has been placed in the family vault. Mourners pass by, then Romeo appears, kills Paris, and, deranged with grief, kills himself. Juliet gradually awakens and, finding Romeo dead, kills herself.

## Paris Opéra Ballet

*Ballet in two acts.*
*Music by*
*Serge Prokofiev.*
*Choreography by*
*Yuri Grigorovich.*
*Scenery and costumes by*
*Simon Virsaladze.*
*First performed at*
*the Paris Opéra,*
*on February 24, 1978.*

"Why restage *Romeo and Juliet?*" wrote Yuri Grigorovich in a programme note for the Paris Opéra, when he produced his version for the first time. "I felt the desire to do so from the first moment that I heard Prokofiev's score. I was a dancer with the Kirov Ballet when I fell in love with this music. But there was the Lavrovsky version, a great spectacle, in which I often danced in Leningrad and which I also found in Moscow when I was nominated artistic director of the Bolshoi Ballet. It is one of the pillars of our repertory, a vital landmark in our theatrical history. So I turned towards other scores, realised other projects. . . . Some of the most famous choreographers, throughout the world, have been tempted by this grandiose score. Many choreographic memories are now linked to it. And yet it seemed to me that there was still something to attempt, something very direct, very frank, very simple. If one turns back to the history of this ballet, to the circumstances surrounding its creation and Prokofiev's autobiographical notes, one sees that the composer was somewhat contradicted in his usual taste for swift, laconic, energetic expression by his collaborators. He always tended, as we know so well, to orientate his musical language on essentials. But he had here to adapt to the exigencies of a scenario perhaps too careful not to neglect the least details of Shakespeare's tragedy. Whence come the musical repetitions, especially in the third act. One must respect the letter, but even more so the spirit. . . . I decided, after mature reflection, to condense the entire action into two acts of roughly one hour each, instead of the three acts which are the form adopted by Prokofiev in the final version of his work. To prune many details in the action, much of the pantomime. To suppress, for example, the Duke, inevitably a static character. To focus everything on the salient features. I wished to show—have I succeeded?—the love of these two beings amidst hatred and cruelty. There is no question here of Verona and its ramparts, of street scenes, of genre pictures and historical evocation. Ballet has nothing to gain from wanting to rival the cinema. It has its own extremely effective means of expression and these suit it better to deal in quasi-abstract fashion with a story well known to everyone, and one whose central theme alone interests us today. Love and hatred. The death of love. Its apparent defeat."

Grigorovich's introductory comments indicate that his *Romeo and Juliet*, which also entered the repertory of the Bolshoi Ballet in 1979, is a far from conventional presentation of either story or score. The action is framed by the dreadful scampering which afflicts carnival revellers in ballet; the fight scenes are excellent; the lovers are almost invisible abstractions of Shakespearean characters. Their credibility is in no way helped by dull and prosaic choreography, and even the illustrious Muscovite Natalia Bessmertnova's intensity as Juliet—as a second cast at the Paris Opéra—could not infuse any credible passion into the choreography. The first cast included Dominique Khalfouni as Juliet, Michael Denard as Romeo, and Jean Guizerix as Tybalt.

The action is shown in the following scenes:

*Prologue*
*Act I*
*Scene 1:* Carnival in Verona.
    *2:* Quarrel and fight between Capulets and Montagues.
    *3:* Carnival scene.
    *4:* Juliet prepares for the ball.
    *5:* Romeo and Mercutio, wearing masks, get into the Capulet ball.
    *6:* Arrival of the guests.
    *7:* Ball at the Capulet house.
    *8:* After the ball: first meeting of Romeo and Juliet.
*Act II*
*Scene 9:* In Friar Laurence's cell: the marriage.
    *10:* The carnival at its height.
    *11:* Meeting and duel between Romeo, Mercutio, and Tybalt.
    *12:* Lamentation over the deaths of Mercutio and Tybalt.
    *13:* Farewell of Romeo and Juliet.
    *14:* Paris asks for Juliet's hand in marriage.
    *15:* Despair and flight for Romeo.
    *16:* "Take this potion. It will send you to sleep. They will think you dead."
    *17:* Betrothal to Paris.
    *18:* Death of Romeo and Juliet.
*Epilogue*

# Scènes de Ballet

*Ballet in one act. Music by Igor Stravinsky. Choreography by Frederick Ashton. Scenery and costumes by André Beaurepaire. First performed by the Sadler's Wells Ballet at the Royal Opera House, Covent Garden, on February 11, 1948, with Margot Fonteyn and Michael Somes.*

In 1944 the American impresario Billy Rose decided to present a revue on Broadway whose title *The Seven Lively Arts* indicated its all-embracing aim. Its cast included Beatrice Lillie, Bert Lahr, Benny Goodman, and Alicia Markova and Anton Dolin, who were then the most celebrated balletic partnership. At Markova's suggestion Igor Stravinsky was asked to provide a score. He completed it rapidly during the summer of 1944 and the ballet, with choreography by Dolin, was first performed in Philadelphia on November 24, prior to its New York opening on December 7.

On November 30 Stravinsky received a telegram from Dolin which began "Ballet great success" and went on to ask if certain re-orchestrations could be made "to insure greater success. . . ." Stravinsky wired back a laconic "Satisfied great success." Dolin's choreography was an evocation of the Romantic manner of the ballet *Giselle* (a work forever associated with Markova).

Ashton's production found in Stravinsky's music allusions to a more classical style, and has an elegance which was also found in the first designs by the young French designer André Beaurepaire. These, unfortunately, have been much reduced, but nothing can dim the formal excellence of Ashton's choreography.

SYNOPSIS

*Scènes de Ballet* is a plotless sequence of dances. Its manner pays homage to the grandeur of the late-nineteenth-century Russian repertory. Within the brief span of the ballet can be seen, in miniature scale, many of the splendid procedures of the Petipa *ballet à grand spectacle*: the adagio in which the ballerina is partnered and lifted by the five cavaliers seems a modern restatement of Petipa's Rose Adagio in *The Sleeping Beauty*. At the time he created the ballet Ashton was fascinated by Euclidean geometry and he devised floor patterns which would be effective seen from any angle.

*John Hart and Moira Shearer in Ashton's* Scènes de Ballet *as originally staged by the Sadler's Wells Ballet. The Beaurepaire set is shown as it was edited for the ballet's later performances. Moira Shearer gave an interpretation of exceptional brilliance and poise in the leading role.*

248

# Schéhérazade

*Ballet in one act. Music by Nikolay Rimsky-Korsakov. Choreography by Mikhail Fokine. Scenery and costumes by Léon Bakst. First performed by Diaghilev's Ballets Russes at the Paris Opéra, on June 4, 1910, with Vaslav Nijinsky as the Golden Slave, Ida Rubinstein as Zobeide, Enrico Cecchetti as the Chief Eunuch, and Serge Grigoriev as the Shah.*

*Schéhérazade* created a sensation at its first performance, not only because of its torrid action but also because of the glory of its design by Bakst. And it is this magnificence of hue—in which the emotional power of colour establishes the vivid passions which are unleashed in the claustrophobic splendour of the harem—which preserves the ballet in performance today. It is a ludicrous work, and one whose text is now very suspect, but it contains characters who can be compelling. No one can ever rival the animal allure that Nijinsky plainly had—a quality quite clear in Baron de Meyer's photographs—nor the phenomenal beauty and pride of Ida Rubinstein. However, even without these dancers *Schéhérazade* remained a staple work of the Ballets Russes and its successor companies.

## SYNOPSIS

*Mikhail Fokine as the Golden Slave and Vera Fokina as Zobeide in Fokine's* Schéhérazade *in 1914.*

*Ida Rubinstein as Zobeide.*

The Shah is seated in his harem with his brother, surrounded by his wives. Despite the Shah's evident affection for his chief wife, Zobeide, his brother suggests that the women are unfaithful, and to test their fidelity the men pretend they are going on a hunting expedition. As soon as they have left, the women bribe the waddling Chief Eunuch to open the doors which bar the male slaves from the harem. Two doors are opened, the men rush in, and soon the women and the slaves are enjoying each other's favours. Zobeide remains aloof and then forces the reluctant Eunuch to open the last door, whence emerges the Golden Slave. He becomes the central figure in a whirling orgy. Suddenly the Shah and his brother return with attendant guards. A massacre ensues and the Golden Slave is the last to be killed. The angered shah surveys the scene and is about to pardon the contrite Zobeide when his brother kicks the body of the Golden Slave to remind the Shah of her infidelity. Zobeide must die. Unable to accept this dishonour, she snatches a dagger from a guard and kills herself at the Shah's feet.

# Serenade

*Ballet in one act. Music by Pyotr Ilyich Tchaikovsky* (Serenade in C for Strings). *Choreography by George Balanchine. Scenery by Gaston Longchamp. Costumes by Jean Lurçat. (Now performed without scenery and with costumes by Karinska.) First performed by students of the School of American Ballet, on December 6, 1934, in Hartford, Connecticut.*

*Joseph Duell and Heather Watts of the New York City Ballet in Balanchine's* Serenade.

*Serenade* was the first ballet created by Balanchine in the United States. It was made as an exercise to show his first group of students the essential differences between classroom work and performance. A plotless ballet, it is Balanchine's loving response to the music. Such incidents as emerge are best explained by Balanchine's own comment that he introduced

into the choreography events which occurred during the creation of the ballet. Thus the numbers of dancers involved varies because Balanchine choreographed on whatever bodies happened to be in the studio on any particular day. A girl fell in class and this was incorporated into the text, as was the fact that boys gradually came to attend ballet class. The ballet begins, perhaps symbolically, with a group of girls standing with their feet together and pointing straight ahead and one arm raised, which they gradually bring down to their forehead. Their feet turn out in first position. This can be interpreted today as a fundamental statement about implanting classical academic dance in America. Dance incidents then ensue which culminate in a boy appearing at the back of the stage and coming forward to join a girl who has arrived. The second movement is a Waltz in which this couple are joined by the other dancers. In the third movement of the ballet (fourth in the score) five girls are seen seated on the stage, linking arms. A joyous folk melody impels them into the dancing but at the end one girl is again left alone, lying on the stage. With the final movement a man enters, his eyes masked by the hand of a girl who walks behind him. He bends over the recumbent girl and dances first with her, then with the other. But she will finally guide him away again: the incident seems highly dramatic, but any interpretation of it must be subjective. The ballet ends with the solitary girl borne high in the air by three supporting boys in a procession that moves diagonally towards the back of the stage.

Since its first performance, *Serenade* has become one of the signature ballets for what is now the New York City Ballet. It has been mounted for many other companies who give it an individual and often very attractive flavour—as the ballet grew out of a school, it inevitably reflects the schooling of the company which dances it. Thus The Royal Ballet dances it with an English lyric flavour. The New York City Ballet dances it with bold emotional and technical effects, not least on those occasions when the leading ballerinas have worn their hair loose.

*One of the final moments of* Serenade, *as danced by the NYCB.*

# The Sleeping Beauty

*Ballet in a prologue and three acts. Music by Pyotr Ilyich Tchaikovsky. Chore-*
*ography by Marius Petipa. Libretto by I. A. Vsevolozhsky. Scenery by Mikhail*
*Bocharov, Andreyev, K. Ivanov, Levogt, and Shishkov. Costumes by Vsevolozhsky.*
*First produced at the Maryinsky Theatre, St. Petersburg, on January 15, 1890, with*
*Carlotta Brianza as Aurora, Pavel Gerdt as Prince Désiré, and Enrico Cecchetti as*
*Carabosse and the Blue Bird.*

*The Sleeping Beauty*, the supreme ballet of the nineteenth century, owes
everything to its librettist, Vsevolozhsky. As Director of the Imperial
Theatres from 1881 to 1899, this charming, cultivated, and much-loved
man encouraged Petipa and befriended Tchaikovsky. It was his idea to
produce this elaborate homage to the ideals of an absolute monarchy by
evoking the age of Louis XIV, and it was his enthusiasm that brought
Tchaikovsky to work on a second ballet score after the failure thirteen
years before of *Swan Lake*. But on this occasion Tchaikovsky was working with the sure genius of Petipa. He composed the score to the exact
demands—dance by dance, scene by scene, and sometimes, it must
seem, bar by bar—of the choreography; and against all probability, it is
the greatest ever written for ballet. Despite this musical magnificence
and the prodigality of Petipa's genius in the dances, the ballet was not an
immediate success. But it soon found a devoted audience that it has
never lost. Its first cast indicates the influence of Italian virtuoso dancing
in Petersburg: Carlotta Brianza was a delightful young star, one of the
several Italian guest ballerinas who illuminated the Imperial Ballet by
their technical prowess in the last decades of the century. Enrico
Cecchetti was a tiny, bouncing, and prodigious technician whose virtuosity is enshrined in the dances for the Blue Bird and whose great
mimetic gifts were deployed in the travesty role of Carabosse. Among the
earliest devotees of the ballet were Alexandre Benois and Leon Bakst.
Their enthusiasm was in turn communicated to a young man whom they
greatly influenced—Serge Diaghilev. Thirty-one years after the Petersburg première, Diaghilev was to present a superlative staging of the
ballet, designed by Bakst, in London.

Meticulously preserved in Leningrad, which to this day honours its
illustrious past—the Kirov Ballet's presentation is still the ideal production of this masterpiece—the ballet is also handsomely staged by the
Bolshoi Ballet in a version edited in 1973 by Yuri Grigorovich.

In the Western world the most influential staging was that presented by
Diaghilev in London in 1921. It was only eighteen years later that *The
Sleeping Beauty* received its first proper Western staging when Nikolay
Sergueyev mounted the work for the Vic-Wells Ballet. Decoratively a
disaster, the production was nevertheless very important, not least for
the musical standards obtained by Constant Lambert, musical director
of the company, and for the dancing of Margot Fonteyn as Aurora. Its
popularity has never waned with the British public. Grandly redesigned
by Oliver Messel, it brought the company to reopen Covent Garden after
the war in February 1946. Since that time the ballet has been restaged
and recostumed, but has always sought to remain faithful in spirit to the
version as mounted by Sergueyev.

In 1975 Rudolf Nureyev produced a version with designs by Nicholas Georgiadis, in which, characteristically, he has massively elaborated the Prince's role, effectively distorting the Vision Scene and diminishing the role of Aurora. This production was staged for the National Ballet of Canada and the ballet of the Teatro alla Scala, Milan.

For the Stuttgart Ballet, Rosella Hightower provided a production in 1976 which was based upon an extravagant staging, in which she had starred, presented by the Grand Ballet du Marquis de Cuevas in 1960. The choreographic text is indifferent, as also is the version mounted by Alicia Alonso for the Paris Opéra Ballet in 1974.

*Margot Fonteyn as Aurora in the first act of the 1968 Royal Ballet production of The Sleeping Beauty.*

American Ballet Theatre has a version originally prepared in 1976 by Mary Skeaping and using Oliver Messel designs. For the Australian Ballet Sir Robert Helpmann, the Prince of the original Vic-Wells staging, mounted a production, designed by Kenneth Rowell, in 1973.

**SYNOPSIS**

*Prologue*
*The Christening*

Courtiers assemble in the palace of King Florestan XXIV for the christening of his baby daughter, the princess Aurora. Catalabutte, the court chamberlain, supervises the guests. The King and Queen arrive, and there next enter a group of fairies with their cavaliers, the Lilac Fairy at their head. They are Aurora's godmothers. Each in turn dances and then proceeds to bestow gifts upon the child. Just as the Lilac Fairy is about to approach the cradle, a peal of thunder announces the arrival of the wicked

Opposite: *Irina Kolpakova in the first act of* The Sleeping Beauty *as staged by the Kirov Ballet.*

fairy Carabosse. In a carriage drawn by grotesque attendants, she appears in a blazing temper. She has been omitted from the guest list. She rounds on Catalabutte and then announces her gift to Aurora: she will grow up and be beautiful, but one day prick her finger—and die. Amid the court's consternation, the Lilac Fairy steps forward. She has not yet bestowed her gift. She cannot avert Carabosse's curse, but she can convert the threat of death into the promise of a sleep of one hundred years, from which Aurora shall eventually be awakened by a prince's kiss. Carabosse storms out and the curtain falls on a tableau as the royal couple advances towards the cradle over which the Lilac Fairy hovers protectively.

### Act I
#### The Spell

In the palace garden courtiers and peasants are rejoicing: it is Aurora's twentieth birthday. Among their number are three women who have, despite the royal ban on all pointed objects, retained their knitting needles and are busily at work. Catalabutte discovers them and, aghast, seizes the needles; when the royal party enters he shows the needles to the King, who orders that the knitting women be hanged, but the Queen intercedes for them and so as not to cloud the happiness of the day, they are pardoned. The peasants now dance a Garland Waltz and four princely suitors for Aurora's hand await her arrival. She enters and is told by her father that she must be betrothed. She dances for the princes, each of whom in turn offers her roses and declares his love. (This Rose Adagio is the supreme challenge of nineteenth-century classical choreography by reason of its demands on both technical skill and stamina, and, even more important, on mastery of pure classical style.) She then dances among her friends but suddenly is aware of a mysterious old woman who taps her stick to attract her attention. She runs to her and the old woman produces a gift; it is a spindle. Aurora takes it happily and dances gladly around the stage despite her parents' dismay. Suddenly, as she waves the spindle, she pricks her finger. She falters, but the injury seems minor and she continues to dance. But now her movements have become frenzied and giddy; watched by the horrified court, she circles the stage and then collapses. The old woman throws off her disguise and is revealed as Carabosse. Exultantly she proclaims that her curse has come true. Amid general confusion she disappears and at this moment the Lilac Fairy appears to fulfill her promise. She orders Aurora to be carried into the castle, and as she waves her wand a spell of sleep descends upon the court, and a magic forest grows.

### Act II
#### The Vision

The hundred years have passed and Prince Désiré is hunting near the enchanted forest. Members of his entourage dance and amuse themselves, as do a group of peasants. The hunt moves off but the Prince decides to remain alone with his thoughts. His mood is melancholy and he is amazed when an enchanted boat appears bearing the Lilac Fairy. She is his godmother and she shows him a vision of Aurora. Enraptured, Désiré begs to meet her, and Aurora's vision now appears to dance with him amid a group of nymphs. She then disappears and Désiré implores the Lilac Fairy to take him to the real princess. They embark on the boat and journey to the castle. Désiré makes his way through rooms covered in cobwebs to the place where Aurora is sleeping. Prompted by the Lilac Fairy, he kisses Aurora and thus awakens her. The whole court now returns to life and King Florestan gladly bestows his daughter's hand upon Désiré.

### Act III
#### The Wedding

Fairy-tale characters join the court to celebrate the marriage of Aurora and Désiré, the most celebrated of these divertissements being the pas de deux for the Blue Bird and Princess Florine. The ballet culminates in the grand pas de deux for Aurora and her prince, and in the final tableau the Lilac Fairy returns to bless the marriage.

### New York City Ballet

The Garland Dance
*from* The Sleeping Beauty

*Music by
Pyotr Ilyich Tchaikovsky.
Choreography by
George Balanchine,
after Petipa.
First performed
(as part of* Tempo di
Valse*) at the State
Theater, Lincoln Center,
on June 9, 1981.*

*The Garland Dance, as
performed by the New York
City Ballet.*

For many years American ballet-lovers have been hoping for a full-length *Sleeping Beauty* from George Balanchine. In June 1981, the New York City Ballet mounted a two-week Tchaikovsky Festival, for which it commissioned an extraordinary set, an "ice palace," from the famous architect Philip Johnson (who had designed the State Theater itself). Among the works presented during the festival was *Tempo di Valse*, a moveable feast of old and new works to Tchaikovsky waltz music. And the first section of *Tempo di Valse* was the famous Garland dance from *The Sleeping Beauty*, which in most Western productions presents a large group of peasant boys and girls holding garlands of flowers and dancing in celebration of Aurora's birthday.

But Balanchine's Garland Dance clearly went back for its inspiration to the Maryinsky production of his childhood, in which he himself had danced. The stage filled with chains of small girls in pink from the School of American Ballet, interweaving and forming the most charming patterns with the large group of company dancers already on stage. In a very few minutes, Balanchine managed to suggest the texture, the grandeur, the brilliance of *The Sleeping Beauty* as Petipa and Tchaikovsky created it; yet in no way did this dance appear to be a museum piece—the steps were basic and minimal, but the style of performance was classic New York City Ballet, and stylistically appropriate. The Garland Dance left Balanchine's admirers even more avid for his complete *Beauty*.

# Soldiers' Mass

*Ballet in one act. Music by Bohuslav Martinů* (Field Mass). *Choreography by Jiří Kylián. Scenery and costumes by Kylián. First performed by the Nederlands Dans Theater at the Circustheater, Scheveningen, on June 13, 1980.*

*Soldiers' Mass* is written for twelve men, clad in khaki-green shirts, with trousers that end in vestigial gaiters. They are treated for the most part as a military squad. By insisting upon groupings that evoke the disciplined formations of men in battle and a consequent community of feeling, the occasional emergence of a single figure from the urgent racing of the men conveys the loneliness and dread of the individual in combat. The choreographic style, as in several Kylián ballets, is one of teeming energy, dance dedicated to the proposition that bodies are to be used to the full. The high-voltage action of *Soldiers' Mass* explores the tensions of war. A closing *coup de théâtre*, in which the men tear off their sweat-soaked shirts and stand motionless, stresses their vulnerability, which is further accentuated when they clasp their faces in agonised prayer and collapse to the ground. Made with undeniable zeal, *Soldiers' Mass* invites unsparing, dedicated performance. One soloist is isolated as a victim of the tempest of battle, and the no less tempestuous matters of faith that are the text of the Mass. He seems especially piteous as he dashes among his companions and then swings from the arms of two comrades.

Soldiers' Mass *by Jiří Kylián as performed by the Nederlands Dans Theater.*

# Song of the Earth

*Ballet in one act. Music by Gustav Mahler. Choreography by Kenneth MacMillan. First performed by the Stuttgart Ballet at the Württembergische Staatstheater, Stuttgart, on November 7, 1965, with Marcia Haydée as the Woman, Ray Barra as the Man, and Egon Madsen as the Messenger of Death.*

Gustav Mahler wrote this symphony for tenor and alto voices and orchestra using as his text German translations of the poetry of the eighth-century Chinese poet Li Tai Po. Kenneth MacMillan used the imagery of the poems to provide six dance scenes which are concerned with the transitory nature of worldly joy and worldly suffering, and the self-renewal of life itself after death. At the end of the text Mahler provided his own postscript: "The dear Earth blossoms in the spring and buds anew/Everywhere and forever the luminous blue of distant space/Forever . . . forever . . . forever. . . ."

There are no sets and costumes other than the barest and simplest necessities for *Song of the Earth*, yet it is so rich in visual imagery that one might swear that the incidental surroundings of the poems—little pavilion, horses, lotuses—all exist. It is a profoundly serious ballet and profoundly moving in performance. MacMillan is nowhere specific about his theme, yet we everywhere understand the transitory nature of the world and of human feeling, and also the inevitability of death as an accompaniment to man's every activity. The final passage offers a mood of serene acceptance and hope born of the cyclic nature of life.

*Song of the Earth* is a ballet very difficult to perform well. It has received its most exceptional performances from the artists of the Stuttgart Ballet—Marcia Haydée, Richard Cragun, and Egon Madsen—whose performances in the central roles seem inspired by a common artistic impulse and a unique community of feeling. It entered the repertory of The Royal Ballet, with designs by Nicholas Georgiadis, in 1966.

SYNOPSIS

The first song is "The Drinking Song of Earthly Woe." It shows the Man sporting with his companions, but at the end the character conveniently identified as the Messenger of Death claims him. In the second song, "The Lonely One in Autumn," the Woman and three girls dance with four men. At the end the woman is left alone. The next song, "Of Youth," finds a group of young people surrounding a pool in which stands an imagined pavilion of green and white porcelain. They are delightfully happy, but the Woman is finally claimed by the messenger. In the next song, "Of Beauty," girls are gathering lotuses by a river bank when a group of young horsemen arrive. The final pose shows the young people standing in couples. "The Drunkard in Springtime," which follows, shows the Man with three companions. They have caroused all night, but birdsong at dawn cuts through the fumes of alcohol and at this moment the Man falls into the arms of the Messenger, who is one of his companions. The final section of the work is the lengthy "Farewell." In this the Man, the Woman, and the Messenger come together. After an impassioned duet for the Man and the Woman, the Messenger takes him away. The Woman eddies over the stage in desolation of spirit, but the Messenger brings the Man back. He is now wearing a half-mask similar to that which has been worn by the Messenger throughout the ballet. In the closing moments of the work, as the alto sings "Forever . . . forever," the three principal dancers advance slowly towards the front of the stage as if moving into eternity.

# La Sonnambula

*Ballet in one act. Music by Vittorio Rieti, after themes of Vincenzo Bellini. Libretto by Rieti. Choreography by George Balanchine. Scenery and costumes by Dorothea Tanning. First performed (as* Night Shadow*) by the Ballet Russe de Monte Carlo at the City Center, New York, on February 27, 1946, with Alexandra Danilova as the Sleepwalker, Nicholas Magallanes as the Poet, and Maria Tallchief as the Coquette.*

Overleaf: *Allegra Kent as the Sleepwalker and Nicholas Magallanes as the Poet in the New York City Ballet's* La Sonnambula.

*La Sonnambula* is a superb piece of Gothick Romanticism. Bellini's themes provide a vivid accompaniment; Balanchine's dances create an atmosphere of hectic and menacing eroticism. The heart of the ballet is the great duet between the Sleepwalker and the Poet, in which a stream of *pas de bourrée* for her are directed by the very touch of his hand, so that her white figure seems to float on the ground like a flower on water. The ballet has been staged by many companies—the Royal Danish Ballet, London Festival Ballet, and, of course, the New York City Ballet—in designs by such artists as André Delfau, Peter Farmer, Bernard Daydé, and Esteban Francés. Of the various productions, that by the Royal Danish Ballet deserves a special commendation for its dramatic power. However, the performances by the Grand Ballet du Marquis de Cuevas in the 1950s are unforgettable because of the interpretation by Nina Vyroubova, the great Franco-Russian ballerina, as a somnambulist of uniquely beautiful poetry and mystery. With the New York City Ballet, Allegra Kent has also given an outstanding interpretation.

## SYNOPSIS

The scene is a masked ball in the garden of a splendid house. The Baron, who is the host, greets the various guests, among whom is his mistress, the Coquette. After a general dance a new guest arrives. He is a Poet, and the Coquette shows an immediate interest in him. To amuse the guests an entertainment now takes place which includes a peasant dance, a Moorish dance, and an eccentric Harlequin. When the divertissement is over the guests move out of the garden, and the Poet and the Coquette are left together for a brief time before the Baron returns with some of the guests, claims the Coquette as his supper partner, and leads the party back to the house.

The Poet is left alone. He is suddenly aware of a light moving down the stairs inside the château, one side of which can be seen from the garden. Amazed, he observes a mysterious figure emerging. It is a beautiful woman in a white nightgown, her hair streaming down her back and holding a lighted candle in front of her. He is excited by her mysterious, unseeing progress through the garden, but then swiftly falls under the spell of her beauty. He realises that she is a somnambulist and there ensues a pas de deux in which he manipulates and impels the sleepwalker through the garden so that she seems to drift over and round his body. He follows her as she leaves the garden, but the Coquette has seen this meeting and when the Baron returns she tells him of the incident. The Baron is furiously jealous—we are to understand that the white-clad figure is his wife. During a general dance he leaves the garden clutching a dagger and enters the house.

As a final divertissement takes place the guests are appalled to see the Poet stagger back into the garden mortally wounded. He falls to the ground dead. The Sleepwalker appears again, eddying through the night. Her steps are impeded by the body of the Poet. The guests pick up the corpse and place it in her outstretched arms. Carrying the body, she seems to drift back into the house; the guests watch the light of her candle slowly ascending through the windows of the house.

259

# Spartacus

*Ballet in three acts. Music by Aram Khachaturian. Libretto by Yuri Grigorovich. Choreography by Yuri Grigorovich. Scenery by Simon Virsaladze. First performed by the Bolshoi Ballet in Moscow, on April 9, 1968, with Vladimir Vasiliev as Spartacus, Ekaterina Maximova as Phrygia, Maris Liepa as Crassus, and Nina Timofeyeva as Aegina.*

*Spartacus* was originally staged in Leningrad by the Kirov Ballet on December 27, 1956, in a version by Leonid Jacobson. The production was not entirely successful and two years later a version by Igor Moiseyev for the Bolshoi Ballet was even less successful. Ten years was to pass before Yuri Grigorovich, the recently appointed director of the Bolshoi company, produced his very effective reworking of the ballet. By clever editing of the narrative, and with some alterations to the score, Grigorovich produced a work which seems to epitomise the new Soviet style of ballet. In its political message, in its enormously energetic style, and with its bold and simplistic choreography, *Spartacus* has a theatrical efficiency which is hard to deny. No small part of its success lies in the lush and bombastic score. But the ballet supremely celebrates the massive resources of the Bolshoi troupe and, above all, the heroic splendour of Vladimir Vasiliev and Mikhail Lavrovsky as Spartacus.

Structurally, Grigorovich broke new ground by contrasting the mam-

*Ekaterina Maximova and Vladimir Vasiliev in Yuri Grigorovich's production of Spartacus for the Bolshoi Ballet.*

moth effects of crowd scenes and huge tableaux with the intimacies of the monologues in which the leading characters are allowed to display their inner feelings. *Spartacus* represents the most popular manifestation of the Soviet ballet ideal since Lavrovsky's *Romeo and Juliet*, and it has inevitably been produced extensively throughout Eastern Europe. A particularly interesting alternative version is that choreographed in 1968 by László Seregi for the Budapest Opera Ballet, later staged by the Australian Ballet.

SYNOPSIS

*Act I, Scene 1*
*Rome*

The war machine of the Roman Empire straddles across its conquered lands. It is led by the arrogant, pitiless Roman general Crassus. After the invasion of Thrace, prisoners are brought back in chains and these include Spartacus and his wife Phrygia.
Spartacus' monologue:
A freeborn man, he will never be reconciled to slavery.

*Scene 2*
*The slave market*

Below the walls of the Capitol, slaves are offered for sale, and to improve chances of a good price, Phrygia is separated from Spartacus.
Phrygia's monologue:
She grieves at her separation from her husband and the uncertainty of her fate.

*Scene 3*
*The orgy at Crassus' house*

Phrygia has been bought by Crassus and taken to his villa. Aegina, Crassus' mistress, mocks Phrygia's fears. She cares only for power and debauchery and the gold which serves to whet her appetite. An orgy takes place and to entertain the guests two blindfolded slaves, who have been trained as gladiators, are brought in to fight to the death. One eventually triumphs. He takes off his mask. It is Spartacus, and he is distraught to see that he has killed a fellow slave.
Spartacus' monologue:
He has been forced to kill a fellow man. What more will he be called upon to do? What can he do? What does he wish to do?

*Scene 4*
*The gladiators' barracks*

Spartacus rallies his fellow prisoners. He tells them that they must fight for liberty, for their homeland, for their loved ones. The gladiators swear to follow Spartacus and they flee the barracks.

*Act II, Scene 1*
*On the Appian Way*

Shepherds are dancing. The rebellious slaves arrive and the shepherds are urged to join the revolt. Other slaves join them: there is now an army to fight against Rome and Spartacus is hailed as its leader.
Spartacus' monologue:
Shall he accept leadership of this army? He must not become like Crassus. His first task is to find Phrygia and free her.

*Scene 2*
*Crassus' triumph*

Spartacus discovers Phrygia and is reunited with her. Crassus is giving a banquet and Aegina is present with a host of guests. Spartacus and Phrygia escape.
Aegina's monologue:
Crassus wants to dominate the world; she wants to dominate Crassus. He uses force and cruelty; she uses guile and treachery. But their aim is the same—they both want to have wealth, power, and glory.

*Scene 3*
*Crassus' villa*

The guests at Crassus' party celebrate his magnificence. But their pleasures are interrupted by the news that Spartacus and his slave army encircle the villa. Crassus, Aegina, and the patricians flee, leaving the slaves in command of the villa.
Spartacus' monologue:
Rome's power resides in the arms of its legions and the docility of conquered races. Romans are cowards and every rebel must learn this.

*Scene 4*
*The defeat of Crassus*

Crassus is captured and brought before Spartacus. The rebels wish to kill Crassus, who recognises in Spartacus his former gladiator. But Spartacus insists that Crassus shall undergo the same trial to which he was subjected: single combat. But he shall not be blindfolded. Spartacus and Crassus fight and Crassus is defeated. He pleads for mercy; the cowardice of the Patrician excites Spartacus' contempt and he lets him go.

| | |
|---|---|
| *Act III, Scene 1*<br>*The conspiracy* | The disgraced Crassus swears to make his enemy pay dearly for having dishonoured him. Aegina urges him on and Crassus reassembles his legions once again.<br>Aegina's monologue:<br>She expresses her hatred for Spartacus and vows to be revenged. |
| *Scene 2*<br>*The camp of Spartacus* | Aegina slips into the slave camp by night. Phrygia is uneasy and Spartacus tries to calm her. A messenger announces that the Roman legions are marching against the slave army. Spartacus proposes a battle plan and asks his lieutenants to swear fidelity. The daring of the plan alarms the weaker among them. If his lieutenants dissent, then the battle will be lost, but death is to be preferred to slavery.<br>Aegina's monologue:<br>She determines to be avenged on Spartacus, who has shaken her position of power as mistress to Rome's leading general. |
| *Scene 3*<br>*Treason* | Spartacus' faithful men await the battle signal and, having received it, set out. The backsliders will soon follow, but Aegina now appears bringing wine and women which corrupt the weaker troops and turn them into traitors to the slaves' cause. Crassus' advancing army captures the slaves—Aegina will be rewarded for bringing about their downfall.<br>Crassus' monologue:<br>Spartacus shall pay with his life, for Crassus cannot forgive the humiliation of having his life spared by the scornful slave. He will destroy the whole of Spartacus' army. |
| *Scene 4*<br>*The final battle* | The Roman legions surround the rebel slaves. The weakened slaves are still inspired by Spartacus but the Romans contrive to trick him and he is captured and raised high on the legionnaires' spears. Phrygia comes to seek her husband on the battlefield and mourns over his dead body. |

*Vladimir Vasiliev and Ekaterina Maximova in the slave market scene from the first act of Grigorovich's Spartacus for the Bolshoi Ballet.*

# Le Spectre de la Rose

*Ballet in one scene. Music by Carl Maria von Weber. Libretto by Jean-Louis Vaudoyer. Choreography by Mikhail Fokine. Scenery and costumes by Leon Bakst. First performed by Diaghilev's Ballets Russes at the Théâtre de Monte Carlo, on April 19, 1911, with Tamara Karsavina and Vaslav Nijinsky.*

*Le Spectre de la Rose* was inspired by a line from Théophile Gautier: "Je suis le spectre d'une rose/Que tu portais hier au bal." *Le Spectre* is a duet of intense emotional grace, conceived for the unique talents of two great artists. In its original performances it was perfect: a dance poem contained within the beautiful mime sequences for the girl. It is impossible today to expect either its delicate perfume or its prodigious technical and artistic demands to be met, though in Mikhail Baryshnikov the spirit of the rose seems to live again. Any design which departs from Bakst's sensitive original decoration destroys the ballet utterly.

## SYNOPSIS

The setting is a young girl's bedroom, its windows open to the night. The girl returns from her first ball holding a rose. Removing her cloak, she sinks into an armchair and in her reverie the spirit of the rose that she has worn comes to her. In her dream they dance, and as she sinks back into the chair once again the spirit soars away into the night. The girl awakens and, lifting the rose, recalls her dream.

Opposite: *Mikhail Baryshnikov and Marianna Tcherkassky in American Ballet Theatre's production of* Le Spectre de la Rose. *Neither the setting nor his costume is authentic, but Baryshnikov, whose performance is preserved in a television production, probably came nearest of all to recapturing the magic of Nijinsky's role.*

*Tamara Karsavina and Vaslav Nijinsky, the original cast of* Le Spectre de la Rose.

# Stars and Stripes

*Ballet in one act. Music by John Philip Sousa, adapted and orchestrated by Hershy Kay. Choreography by George Balanchine. Scenery by David Hays. Costumes by Karinska. First performed by the New York City Ballet at the City Center, New York, on January 17, 1958, with Allegra Kent, Diana Adams, Robert Barnett, Melissa Hayden, and Jacques d'Amboise.*

"Sousa?" To which Balanchine replied, "Yes, and why not? It makes me feel good." If America's March King is a far cry from Stravinsky, Vivaldi, and Gounod, whose music Balanchine had used immediately prior to the Sousa ballet, *Stars and Stripes* is not all that different in terms of its concerns. It is a perfectly serious exposition of music and classical technique, with many vintage examples of Balanchine's ingenious management of large ensembles and including as brilliant a pas de deux as he has ever made. The attitude behind *Stars and Stripes* is not quite so straightforward or familiar, however. It is both frankly patriotic and a bit teasing. References to drum majorettes and Rockettes infiltrate the choreography. The women wear proper tutus—and anklet socks. Depending on who is dancing "Liberty Bell" and "El Capitan," the pas de deux can range from Petipa-like glamour to campy satire. The audience's response to the ballet has varied too. During the Vietnam War, for example, many found its gaiety and the final unfurling of the flag offensive. In happier times, that huge flag which rises just at the peak of the finale strikes one as a wonderful *coup de théâtre*.

*Linda Homek, Deni Lamont, and Debra Austin with artists of the New York City Ballet in* Stars and Stripes.

*Colleen Neary and Adam Lüders in the pas de deux from Balanchine's* Stars and Stripes.

**SYNOPSIS** *Stars and Stripes* is described as a "ballet in five campaigns." The first campaign, to "Corcoran Cadets," is for an ensemble of girls led by a baton-twirling ballerina. "Rifle Regiment" is also for girls; the music is relatively lyrical and the dancing less robust. Men take over for the third campaign, "Thunder and Gladiator," an all-out razzle-dazzler, an American version of a British tattoo. The fourth campaign is the pas de deux, to the "Liberty Bell" and "El Capitan" marches. All the "regiments" participate in the fifth campaign, to "Stars and Stripes." The flag rises, the dancers salute, and the curtain falls.

# The Stone Flower

*Ballet in three acts. Music by Serge Prokofiev. Libretto by Mira Prokofieva, based on folktales collected and edited by Pavel Bazhov. Choreography by Yuri Grigorovich. Décor and costumes by Simon Virsaladze. First performed by the Kirov Ballet, Leningrad, on April 27, 1957, with Irina Kolpakova, Alla Ossipenko, Yuri Gribov, and Anatoly Gridin.*

*The Stone Flower* was Prokofiev's final ballet score. Its first staging was in Moscow in 1954 with choreography by Leonid Lavrovsky. This was superseded in the Russian repertory by the version which the then young dancer Yuri Grigorovich made in Leningrad in 1957, a production notable for its clarity of staging and absence of the usual earnest Soviet *verismo* in decoration and presentation. It was with this production that the Kirov Ballet made its first appearances in the West at Covent Garden in 1961 with Yuri Soloviov, a dancer of angelic grace and prodigious technique, as Danila, and Alla Sizova as Katerina (Ossipenko and Gridin repeated their performances as the Mistress of the Copper Mountain and Severyan). The piece has not become a favourite with Western audiences: it shows rather obviously its political and aesthetic biases, but Grigorovich's use of the corps de ballet in the gypsy and village scenes showed his early ability to manipulate large forces of dancers.

SYNOPSIS

*Act I*   Danila is a young stonecutter who is obsessed with the idea of creating a perfect malachite vase. He meets his fiancée Katerina and at a celebration of their betrothal, an overseer, Severyan, tries to purchase the vase Danila has made—and also pays unwelcome attentions to Katerina. Danila breaks the vase and sets to work afresh on a new piece of stone. A fantastic being appears: she is the spirit of the stone and she suggests how he may create something ideal by showing him a beautiful vase from the malachite he is working. Danila seeks to keep her with him, but she eludes him, then finally tells him that she is the Mistress of the Copper Mountain. She leads Danila to her subterranean kingdom and there he sees the spirits of the precious stones in the earth.

*Act II*   Katerina is alone, and Severyan seeks to make her his. Danila is still obsessed with the arts that the Mistress of the Copper Mountain is showing him. Katerina goes to a village fair where she again rebuffs Severyan as she looks for Danila. The Mistress of the Copper Mountain appears and bewitches Severyan and causes his death.

*Act III*   Katerina is seeking Danila in the forest: as she rests by a fire, a spirit appears and leads her to the Copper Mountain. Inside the Copper Mountain Danila has at last succeeded in making a perfect stone flower. The Mistress of the Copper Mountain seeks to persuade him to stay with her, showing him the dances of the various precious stones, but Danila now has thoughts only for Katerina. To punish him, the Mistress of the Copper Mountain decides to turn him to stone. The fire spirit now arrives with Katerina and there ensues a dramatic confrontation between Danila and these two women who love him. He knows that he must be true to Katerina, and the strength of their love persuades the Mistress of the Copper Mountain that she must yield to them. Danila is permitted to leave the mountain with Katerina. They return to their village where he can reveal to the people the artistry he has acquired in working stone. The Mistress of the Copper Mountain returns to wish them well.

# Stravinsky Violin Concerto

*Ballet in one act. Music by Igor Stravinsky. Choreography by George Balanchine. First performed (as* Violin Concerto*) by the New York City Ballet at the State Theater, Lincoln Center, on June 18, 1972, with Karin von Aroldingen and Jean-Pierre Bonnefous, Kay Mazzo, and Peter Martins.*

*Stravinsky Violin Concerto*, like the Stravinsky-Balanchine *Symphony in Three Movements*, comprises two ensembles which frame duets. The initial Toccata is bright, sharp, almost staccato. There follows the first Aria, which is angular, uneasy, a view of a physical relationship that is strained and contorted. It made fine capital of Karin von Aroldingen's sometimes harsh style, stressing the abrasive and dominating force of her presence and ending in a pose of dark poetry as the male dancer lies on the stage facing the back-curving figure of von Aroldingen. There could be no greater contrast, despite some choreographic similarities, than with the lyricism of the second duet. In this, as in *Duo Concertant*, which was written for the same dancers, Peter Martins seems a creator working with his muse, guiding and watching Kay Mazzo's lovely evolutions: the effect is of a tender reflection of the earlier duet. The final Capriccio is a dazzling exercise in often small-scale movement which depends upon exceptional sophistication of rhythm and dynamics and subtle dislocations of line.

Balanchine had already used the Violin Concerto once before, in 1941, for *Balustrade*, which he created for the Original Ballet Russe.

*Pierre Bonnefous and in von Aroldingen in the aria of* Stravinsky lin Concerto.

# Suite en Blanc

*Ballet in one scene. Music by Edouard Lalo. Choreography by Serge Lifar. First performed by the Paris Opéra Ballet in Zürich, on June 19, 1943, with Solange Schwarz, Yvette Chauviré, Lycette Darsonval, and Serge Lifar.*

The score for *Suite en Blanc* is taken from the two-act ballet *Namouna*, which Edouard Lalo wrote for the Paris Opéra, and which received its first performance with choreography by Lucien Petipa in 1882. With the German occupation of France during World War II, Serge Lifar, the Opéra's ballet master, was much concerned with maintaining the activities of his company, and he secured performances and tours which did much to help preserve the company's identity. In Lalo's score Lifar found a glorious excuse for a prodigious technical display—of the richness of the Opéra schooling, and the ingenuities of his own neoclassical style.

When given by its parent company, *Suite en Blanc* remains a heady and thrilling experience, calling upon cohorts of well-trained dancers and a central group of principals who must be of the finest quality. For many years it was a staple of the repertory of the touring Grand Ballet du Marquis de Cuevas (under the title *Noir et Blanc*), and at the Opéra it still receives exultant performances. Lifar's grandiloquent style must be presented with total conviction and an idiomatic security if it is to make full theatrical sense. The solos have long been treasures for ballerina performance, notably by such artists as Yvette Chauviré and Nina Vyroubova. *Suite en Blanc* entered the repertory of London Festival Ballet in 1966.

## SYNOPSIS

The opening finds the cast ranged on raised platforms at the back of the stage. When they leave, three girls in long tutus dance the Siesta. There follows an exhilarating pas de trois for a female soloist with two men, and this in turn gives way to the Serenade for a ballerina and a corps de ballet of eight girls. In the succeeding quintet, four male dancers perform beaten steps around another ballerina, and there ensues the enchanting Cigarette variation (whose title refers back to the original action of *Namouna*, a story of slaves and pirates in Corfu). The leading male dancer now has a Mazurka, followed by a pas de deux for the principal ballerina and her cavalier, and then the second ballerina has a solo with flute accompaniment. The ballet ends with a general dance.

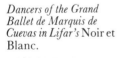

*Dancers of the Grand Ballet de Marquis de Cuevas in Lifar's* Noir et Blanc.

# Swan Lake

*Ballet in four acts. Music by Pyotr Ilyich Tchaikovsky. Choreography by Marius Petipa and Lev Ivanov. Scenery and costumes by Mikhail Bocharov and Heinrich Levogt. First performed at the Maryinsky Theatre, St. Petersburg, on January 27, 1895, with Pierina Legnani as Odette-Odile and Pavel Gerdt as Siegfried.*

Before achieving the form in which it is so widely known—that created by Petipa and Ivanov, and described above—*Swan Lake* went through several previous versions. This, Tchaikovsky's first ballet score, was commissioned by the Bolshoi Theatre in Moscow and was first seen there in 1877, with choreography by Julius Reisinger. Tchaikovsky's inexperience in ballet resulted in a score lacking formal balance. Reisinger's lack of distinction as a choreographer produced an entirely dull version, in no way enhanced by second-rate Moscow casts. The production was a failure, yet in 1880 the Belgian choreographer Joseph Hansen made another staging for the Moscow company and revised this again two years later. But the ballet did not find public favour and was abandoned. When, in St. Petersburg, Tchaikovsky's two later ballet scores, *The Sleeping Beauty* and *The Nutcracker*, had been produced under Petipa's régime, the existence of *Swan Lake* was recalled. Before Tchaikovsky could be encouraged to work again on the score he died, and the second act was presented with choreography by Lev Ivanov, Petipa's assistant and the choreographer of *The Nutcracker*, at a memorial performance in 1894. At the beginning of 1895, Petipa supervised the staging of the entire work. The score was edited by Riccardo Drigo, conductor for the Imperial Ballet. Ivanov's second act was retained and he provided the choreography for Act IV, while Petipa was responsible for Acts I and III. It is this production which was to establish the ballet in public favour. Subsequently there were many different stagings in Russia itself, most notably the four produced by Alexander Gorsky in Moscow, which remain a basic text for most Russian stagings. The Petipa-Ivanov version was brought to the West through the choreographic notations used by Nikolay Sergueyev. In 1934 he mounted the ballet for the Vic-Wells company, who had in Alicia Markova a ballerina capable of sustaining the great central role of Odette-Odile.

This full-length production was unique in the West for many years; several companies, however, included the second act in their repertories. The Royal Ballet has maintained the Sergueyev version in spirit, although over the years alterations and additions have been made and in particular new choreography for Act IV has been created by Frederick Ashton to replace what was recognised as a suspect original text. Inevitably *Swan Lake* has attracted the attentions of many producers. The Soviet choreographer Vladimir Bourmeister provided an influential staging in 1953 for the Moscow Stanislavsky and Nemirovich-Danchenko ballet company in which he returned to the original 1877 score and somewhat amplified the libretto. He also mounted this staging at the Paris Opéra (where it is in part preserved) and for London Festival Ballet. *Swan Lake*—the most popular of ballets—has an irresistible attraction for both companies and producers. The extraordinary appeal of the Tchaikovsky score must inevitably account for a certain popularity of the work; in addition, the acceptance of the idea of full-length ballets from the nineteenth-century repertory as the essential ballet experience has meant that ballet companies have been able to guarantee their existence by keeping this ballet—in no matter what form—in performance. The public image of ballet is still closely linked to the idea of the ballerina in swan costume dancing to Tchaikovsky. Traditionally the role of Odette-Odile was one of the great challenges for a leading ballerina—Fonteyn, Plisetskaya, and Makarova have proved this. Lately, however, a kind of "princes' " lib has emerged with the male stars of the post-war years. Productions by Erik Bruhn and Rudolf Nureyev have typified a trend that seeks to make Siegfried the leading character. The ballet is thereby distorted, for nineteenth-century classics were all conceived for the glorification of the female dancer (the Bournonville repertory being the only real exception).

Of stagings which offer alterations to the basic narrative we would cite that of John Cranko for the Stuttgart Ballet, in which Siegfried is finally killed in a flood and Odette is left alone, and that of Erik Bruhn for the National Ballet of Canada, in which Von Rothbart becomes a Black Queen and the psychological confusion in Siegfried's mind finally brings about his suicide and Odette is again abandoned. This version is largely rechoreographed and suffers thereby.

*Natalia Makarova as Odile in the third act of American Ballet Theatre's production of* Swan Lake.

## SYNOPSIS

### Act I
*The palace gardens*

It is Prince Siegfried's twenty-first birthday and a group of courtiers and peasants are celebrating the event. Siegfried enters to find his tutor Wolfgang and his friend Benno among the revellers. Toasts are drunk and a pas de trois for two girls and a boy is danced in the Prince's honour. The appearance of the Prince's Mother with attendant ladies causes the drinking goblets to be hidden. She gives Siegfried a crossbow and announces that the time has come for him to marry; at a ball he will be introduced to prospective fiancées. Siegfried is aghast. His mother leaves. As a peasant dance begins, Siegfried moves away, lost in thought. At the end of the dance the peasants leave and Siegfried's depression is lifted only when one of his companions suggests that they go to hunt swans. Dusk falls as Siegfried leaves with his companions; Wolfgang is left alone.

### Act II
*The lakeside*

The huntsmen enter and Benno indicates a flight of swans. Siegfried orders his companions away. He is surprised to see a swan alight and is then amazed to see it change into a beautiful girl. He hides amid the trees and sees the appearance of Odette, who now runs into the glade. He approaches her; terrified, she runs from him. He assures her that he means no harm, and there follows the celebrated mime passage in which he promises not to shoot her and she then tells him that she is queen of the swans under the spell of the enchanter Von Rothbart, and that the lake is made of her mother's tears. The spell can only be broken if a man promises to love her and be faithful. Siegfried at once swears this, but no sooner has he done so than Von Rothbart in the form of a giant owl appears on a nearby crag. Siegfried seizes his crossbow and aims at him, but Odette runs in front of Von Rothbart to protect him, for if he should die the spell will never be broken. Von Rothbart leaves, and Odette runs away, followed by Siegfried. Now her swan maidens appear, circling the glade. Benno and the other huntsmen see them and make ready to shoot. Siegfried dashes on and bids them stay their fire; then Odette, too, enters and pleads for their safety. Siegfried and the huntsmen acquiesce and Odette again disappears among the swan maidens. The swans dance the celebrated Waltz and at its end Siegfried returns, seeking Odette among them. She appears and there ensues the great adagio in which their tragic love is expressed. There follows a pas de quatre for four little swans, and a dance for two leading swans. Odette enters and performs a solo; at its coda she is joined by the other swan maidens and its final moment finds her held again in Siegfried's arms. Dawn is now breaking and the maidens must reassume their swan identity. Odette bids them leave and she takes farewell of Siegfried, who is left alone.

### Act III
*The palace ballroom*

Guests have assembled and a majordomo marshals the court. The Princess Mother and Prince Siegfried appear and six prospective fiancées dance. Siegfried dutifully partners each in turn, but his thoughts are on Odette, and at the end of the dance he tells his mother that he cannot marry any of them. At this moment trumpets sound and two mysterious guests appear. They are Von Rothbart, now in human guise, and his daughter Odile, whom he has transformed into the semblance of Odette. The enraptured Siegfried greets Odile and leads her from the ballroom. The Princess Mother and Von Rothbart watch with the rest of the court a divertissement of national dances: Spanish, Hungarian, Neapolitan, and Polish. Siegfried returns with Odile in an exultant pas de deux (the famous "Black Swan" pas de deux). It is interspersed with moments of high drama as the real Odette appears grieving at the castle window, at which point Von Rothbart casts a spell which bemuses Siegfried and all the guests so that they cannot see Odette. Odile imitates the swan queen's movements further to beguile Siegfried, and Von Rothbart instructs her in this impersonation. The duet reaches its brilliant climax with a series of thirty-two *fouettés* from Odile and at its end Siegfried declares that he wishes to marry her. His mother is gratified and Von Rothbart demands that he swear an oath to be true. He does so. With peals of mocking laughter Von Rothbart and Odile reveal their true identities and flee the ballroom. Siegfried dashes away to find Odette.

*Act IV*
*The lakeside*

The swans are grieving the absence of their queen, who then enters in despair. Siegfried has broken his vow and she will kill herself. The swans prevent this and a sudden storm sweeps the lake. At its climax the distraught Siegfried enters in search of Odette. He finds her and begs forgiveness. This she grants, but says that she must die. Von Rothbart endeavours to drive Siegfried away and keep Odette for his own but the lovers determine to defy him and die together. After a passionate embrace, Odette flings herself into the lake and Siegfried follows. Von Rothbart, mortally wounded by this act of love, dies. In an apotheosis the swan maidens watch Odette and Siegfried journeying to a land of everlasting happiness.

*Natalia Makarova as Odette.*

## Bolshoi Ballet

*Ballet in four acts.*
*Music by*
*Pyotr Ilyich*
*Tchaikovsky.*
*Choreography by*
*Yuri Grigorovich,*
*after Petipa and Ivanov.*
*Scenery by*
*Simon Virsaladze.*
*First performed at the*
*Bolshoi Theatre, Moscow,*
*on December 25, 1969.*

In his new staging for the Bolshoi company Yuri Grigorovich retained the basic outlines of the story, but in common with many producers over the last decades he saw the action as centred on Siegfried. His other concern was to preserve as much as possible of the 1877 score, excising the later interpolations by Drigo for the 1895 Petersburg version. To focus interest upon Siegfried, Grigorovich created an almost "abstract" choreographic surrounding for him. In the same way the settings are more gauzy hints at Gothic magnificence than specific settings for the court, and the lakeside acts are placed in a rocky chasm.

At curtain rise Siegfried soars across the stage with his tutor and a jester in attendance. (In passing we must note the Jester—a detestable figure in all ballets—was first introduced into *Swan Lake* as a positive character by Alexander Gorsky, thus initiating the distracting capers of a completely unnecessary intruder into the ballet's action.) The court assembles during the progress of the Waltz and vassal lords present the young prince with a sword and chain that indicate their obedience to his suzerainty. The pas de trois is danced by Siegfried and two court ladies and the final dance allows the court to leave the stage. Now Siegfried is alone, and indulges in a mournful solo. He is vouchsafed a vision of a swan before he, too, leaves the stage.

The second act respects much of the Ivanov-Gorsky choreography, with the important exception that Von Rothbart is now a figure more nearly symbolising Siegfried's fate than the evil enchanter of the original. The role is an important dancing one and throughout the action he haunts Siegfried, often doubling his steps. He must be understood as an aspect of the Prince's own personality that constantly interposes itself between him and the possibility of true love.

Act III is conceived as a dazzling display of dancing. Grigorovich recasts the five national dances as a classical divertissement, each dance led by one of the prospective fiancées. Siegfried enters to dance with each princess in turn and then Von Rothbart and Odile appear. The production makes good sense by showing Odile first surrounded by six black cygnets, and she dances to the oboe melody known as "The Prince's Song" from the 1877 third-act divertissement, while Von Rothbart also has a variation from the same musical source. The effect is to show Siegfried, obsessed by memories of Odette, gradually succumbing to Odile's power; the "Black Swan" duet which follows becomes both logical and dramatically effective. The variations for Odile and Siegfried are also taken from the original third-act *pas des fiancées* but the coda is the traditional one: the duet hereby seems far more of a piece and musically more distinguished than the usual grab bag of salon pieces. As Siegfried prepares to swear his love for Odile he is suddenly aware of Von Rothbart's trickery. The feeling of a hero fighting against his fate is very clear. Von Rothbart and Odile make a quiet exit and Siegfried, despairing, rushes in search of Odette.

For the fourth act Grigorovich uses the score exactly as Tchaikovsky first conceived it. His choreography treads hopefully in the steps of Ivanov's original conception. The crisis comes when Siegfried and Odette swear their love again. This defeats Von Rothbart, who collapses and dies with splendid promptitude. This optimistic ending is characteristic of Soviet art's positive view of ballet.

Overleaf: *Darci Kistler of the New York City Ballet in Balanchine's version of* Swan Lake. Page 276, *with Sean Lavery;* page 277, *with Stephanie Saland and Maria Calegari.*

## New York City Ballet

*Ballet in one act.*
*Music by*
*Pyotr Ilyich Tchaikovsky.*
*Choreography by*
*George Balanchine,*
*after Ivanov.*
*Scenery and costumes by*
*Cecil Beaton; revised 1964*
*by Rouben Ter-Arutunian.*
*First performed at the*
*City Center, New York,*
*on November 20, 1951.*

Balanchine's *Swan Lake* was the first of his rescensions of major nineteenth-century works for the New York City Ballet. He chose to present only Act II, the first of the two "white" acts, following in the tradition of the post–Diaghilev Ballet Russe companies. Balanchine's *Swan Lake* has undergone many changes in its thirty-year history—Benno has disappeared, together with the four cygnettes; male variations have come and gone; a pas de trois has been replaced by the Valse Bluette—but its essential character has remained consistent and imposing: it is musical and formal, rather than narrative and atmospheric—except in the finale, for which Balanchine borrowed music from Act IV to build to an intensely dramatic climax.

The original Odette was Maria Tallchief; the original Prince Siegfried, André Eglevsky. These roles have been performed by most of the principals of the company since then, the latest Odette being sixteen-year-old Darci Kistler, at the time of her début still a member of the corps de ballet. The Balanchine *Swan Lake* continues to be highly popular with the New York City Ballet audience.

# La Sylphide

*Ballet in two acts. Music by Herman Løvenskjold. Libretto by Adolphe Nourrit. Choreography by August Bournonville. First performed by the Royal Danish Ballet at the Royal Theatre, Copenhagen, on November 28, 1836, with Lucile Grahn as the Sylph and Bournonville as James.*

*This bronze by Auguste Barre dates from 1837 and celebrates the popularity of Taglioni's impersonation of the sylph. Artistic licence gives her bare feet, but the costume is authentic, and the facial likeness remarkable.*

On March 12, 1832, Marie Taglioni appeared in *La Sylphide* at the Paris Opéra. It had been choreographed for her by her father, Filippo Taglioni, and it was her performance in this ballet which marked the triumph of the Romantic movement on the ballet stage and proved Marie Taglioni's right to being considered the supreme ballerina of her age. In the role of the sylph all Marie Taglioni's qualities, so novel and so greatly admired at this time, were revealed. Her lightness, her grace, the demure charm of her personality, and her prodigious technical skill, which made her seem a creature truly of the air, were displayed. Her performance is a landmark in balletic history, announcing the beginning of female domination of the ballet stage in the nineteenth century.

Bournonville, who considered Taglioni his "ideal" dancer, saw *La Sylphide* in Paris in 1834, when he took his fifteen-year-old pupil Lucile Grahn to watch this peerless ballerina. Although he disapproved of the ballet's fevered, unwholesome theme, in which evil triumphs, as well as the debasement of the male dancer into a purely supporting role, Bournonville yet saw that *La Sylphide* would make an ideal vehicle for Grahn, with whom he was in love. Consequently, two years later in Copenhagen he staged his own version of the work. In it he provided choreography which reasserted the essential balance between male and female dancing, and he used a score from the young Norwegian composer Herman Løvenskjold instead of the too-expensive original Schneitzhoeffer score. It is Bournonville's version which has been preserved in continuing performance by the Royal Danish Ballet, while the Taglioni original has been totally lost.

In 1972 Pierre Lacotte, through the use of choreographic notes and programme materials, conceived a television presentation which sought to restore something of Filippo Taglioni's original version. Lacotte's staging was presented at the Paris Opéra later in that same year, and it offers a not very convincing alternative to the beauty and dramatic good sense that mark the Bournonville production.

Many producers have provided stagings of the Bournonville text for ballet companies outside Denmark. Nevertheless, as with every one of his ballets the ideal staging is inevitably that presented by the Royal Danish Ballet in Copenhagen. Here a continuing artistic tradition of interpretation, not least in the mime roles, and the authenticity of the style of dancing passed down from generation to generation, means that we find the real voice of Bournonville still strong, still convincing and still beautiful.

In 1964 the great Danish dancer Erik Bruhn was responsible for a production of *La Sylphide* for the National Ballet of Canada, and in 197 he edited the version mounted for American Ballet Theatre by Harald Lander in 1964. Neither of these productions achieves the period charm or the dramatic integrity of the original text, but they are popular with

*The Sylphide (Anna Laerkesen) appears at the window of the farmhouse to James (Flemming Flindt) in Act I of the Royal Danish Ballet's production of La Sylphide. This pose is immortalised in Chalon's lithographs of Marie Taglioni.*

audiences, in addition to providing an excellent role for a ballerina. The part of James offers a challenge which has been taken up by many of the greatest dancers of our day.

Today Scottish Ballet has an admirable version reproduced by Hans Brenaa, and in 1979 London Festival Ballet acquired a production by the outstanding Danish dancer Peter Schaufuss. He restored musical material which had been excised from the Copenhagen staging during the course of more than 140 years of performance, and incorporated steps from Bournonville classes and ballets to fill out this new music, with the aim of expanding the production for the larger stages on which Festival Ballet plays.

SYNOPSIS

*Act I*

*The interior of a farmhouse in Scotland*

James, a young farmer, is asleep in a chair by the fireside, and kneeling at his feet is the sylph who gazes up at him. In the shadows some of James's friends are also dozing. The sylph dances happily and expresses her affection for James by kissing his forehead. He awakes but feels he is still dreaming: he is to be married today to Effie, his fiancée, but now the sylph has appeared to him and he is captivated by her ethereal beauty. He runs after her but she disappears up the chimney. The preparations for the wedding at the farm begin, and Effie's friends appear with gifts. A cloud upon the general happiness is caused by Gurn, another young farmer, who declares his love for Effie. In the midst of the happy young people a sinister figure appears—it is Madge, an old soothsayer, who is seen crouching over the fire. James tries to drive her away, but the rest of the guests beg her to tell their fortunes. She gulps down two glasses of whiskey and then reads the palms of several girls. She predicts that Effie will marry Gurn and this infuriates James, who drives her from the house. As she leaves, Madge

curses him.

Effie retires with her mother and her friends to dress for the wedding and James is left alone. The sylph now materialises again on the windowsill, gazing wistfully at James. She drifts into the room and tells James that she has loved him long, and begs him to come away with her. A sudden noise alarms James and he hides the sylph in the armchair, covering her with his plaid. Gurn witnesses this but when he denounces James's encounter with the sylph and snatches away the plaid, the chair is empty. The wedding festivities begin with general dances, which include two brilliant male solos set in the framework of a reel for the company. The sylph appears yet again to James and he is completely beguiled by her charms. She snatches his wedding ring and then, plucking his bonnet from a peg, entices him away. He cannot resist. When the guests raise their glasses to toast the groom he is no longer there. Gurn and his friends rush out of doors and return with the news that James has fled with the sylph. Effie weeps in her mother's arms.

Below: *Eva Evdokimova as the Sylphide enchanted by the scarf that Peter Schaufuss as James is holding. A scene from the second act of Schaufuss' production of* La Sylphide *for London Festival Ballet.*

**Act II, Scene 1**
*The witches' glen*

**Scene 2**
*The forest glade*

Above: *The death of the Sylphide. Lis Jeppesen as the Sylphide takes farewell of Arne Villumsen as James in the Royal Danish Ballet's production of La Sylphide.*

Amid the dark of night Madge and her cronies prepare a mysterious scarf in a cauldron. At dawn they disappear.

A group of sylphs appear in the morning light. James enters with the sylph, who shows him her kingdom. She brings him strawberries and water, but avoids him when he tries to hold her. The sylphs dance, with James joining them in a grand divertissement, but the sylph still eludes his grasp. James pursues her, and at this moment Gurn enters the glade seeking James. He finds James's bonnet but Madge appears, hides the bonnet, and urges Gurn to propose to Effie, who has just arrived with her mother. Believing James to be lost forever, Effie accepts Gurn. They leave the scene and when James returns, Madge is alone. She shows him the

bewitched scarf and tells him that it will make the sylph absolutely his. James begs it from her, and when the sylph returns she is, indeed, enraptured by the scarf. As instructed by Madge, James binds it around her arms. At once tragedy strikes—the sylph's wings fall off; the chill of death is on her. She returns James his wedding ring and expires in the arms of her companions. Madge triumphantly returns. James watches in the distance the bridal procession of Effie and Gurn, and then witnesses the sylph being borne to heaven by her companions. He collapses lifeless and Madge exults over James's body.

# Les Sylphides

*Ballet in one act. Music by Frédéric Chopin (variously orchestrated). Choreography by Mikhail Fokine. Scenery and costumes by Alexandre Benois. First performed by Diaghilev's Ballets Russes at the Théâtre du Châtelet, Paris, on June 2, 1909, with Anna Pavlova, Tamara Karsavina, Alexandra Baldina, and Vaslav Nijinsky.*

*Les Sylphides* was one of the ballets shown by Serge Diaghilev in his first Paris season of 1909 and it was the great impresario's favourite of all the ballets he presented during the twenty years' existence of his company. *Les Sylphides* is one of the revolutionary works of this century; it reasserted the lyrical and poetic qualities of ballet at a time when brilliantly faceted virtuosity contained in the setting of mammoth full-length ballets by Petipa was the norm. Fokine created it as a statement of his belief in the expressive nature of dance. As originally staged for students of the Imperial Ballet School in St. Petersburg, and named *Chopiniana*, the ballet was a series of dramatic scenes which included the famous Waltz as an evocation of the gentler manner of the Romantic age. From this there evolved an entire ballet set in this genre for Fokine's girl pupils, with one male soloist. When Diaghilev organised his first Russian season in Paris he chose it as part of a repertory of Fokine ballets and decided that a more poetic title had to be found—hence *Les Sylphides*.

Since then *Les Sylphides* has been performed throughout the world: in Russia it retains its original title and the original overture, which was the Polonaise Militaire, with an alternative Mazurka for the male dancer. On January 20, 1972, the New York City Ballet presented a controversial staging by Alexandra Danilova; all decoration was removed and the ballet was given in practice dress to the original piano music.

Les Sylphides *as danced by* The Royal Ballet.

Galina Ulanova (left),
Boris Khokhlov. and Nina
Timofeyeva in
Chopiniana (the original
title for Fokine's Les
Sylphides) as staged by
the Bolshoi Ballet in
Moscow in 1961.

**SYNOPSIS** The setting is a glade beside a ruined abbey by moonlight. At curtain rise the dancers are seen in an opening group which finds the one male dancer supporting the prima ballerina and one other leading soloist while the other soloist reclines at their feet. The women are all dressed in white, wearing the long Romantic tarlatans immortalised by Marie Taglioni in *La Sylphide*; the man wears a black velvet jerkin over a voluminous white blouse and white tights. The action of the ballet is a series of plotless dances to Chopin music. After the overture Prelude (Op. 28, No. 7) comes a general dance to the Nocturne (Op. 32, No. 2). There follow four solos: to the Waltz (Op. 70, No. 1) for a soloist; to the Mazurka (Op. 33, No. 2) for the ballerina; to the Mazurka (Op. 67, No. 3) for the man; and to the Prelude, which has been the overture, for the other soloist. There follows the Waltz (Op. 64, No. 2) as a duet for the ballerina and the male dancer, and the ballet ends with an ensemble to the Waltz (Op. 18, No. 1) which brings on the entire company. At the end the opening pose re-forms, but as the curtain falls two groups of the corps move to the footlights, thus opening out the picture to fill the stage.

# Symphonic Variations

*Ballet in one act. Music by César Franck. Choreography by Frederick Ashton. Scenery and costumes by Sophie Fedorovitch. First performed by the Sadler's Wells Ballet at the Royal Opera House, Covent Garden, on April 24, 1946, with Margot Fonteyn, Pamela May, Moira Shearer, Michael Somes, Brian Shaw, and Henry Danton.*

Ashton had initially considered creating a ballet with a reasonably explicit theme about love, which was to be the first British ballet created at Covent Garden. However, an injury to the leading male dancer, Michael Somes, meant that the work's first performance was postponed for five weeks. Thus it was that the honour fell to Robert Helpmann's *Adam Zero*; thus, too, it was that Ashton's *Symphonic Variations* was revised extensively before its first performance. Dame Margot Fonteyn records: "When we started to rehearse it all again Fred took out a lot of things and simplified and purified the choreography. . . . I think that's one reason why it turned out to be one of his masterpieces."

The action of the ballet presents three female and three male dancers on stage throughout a performance of Franck's celebrated work for piano and orchestra. The choreography is a beautifully apt realisation of the different moods of the score, finishing with a sense of completeness achieved by the final union of the men and women.

*Symphonic Variations* is the most positive statement made by Ashton about the English lyric style of classical dancing. Returning to the Sadler's Wells Ballet after wartime service, Ashton provided a declaration about how he understood the classical academic tradition and the qualities that he wished to encourage in English dancing: harmony, musicality, and technical excellence that is never overstated. The original cast was blessed with three ballerinas of wonderfully complementary gifts. At the centre was the radiant Fonteyn; on one side, the blonde Pamela May, with her nobility and purity of line; on the other, the auburn beauty Moira Shearer, with her exceptional lightness. The ballet has remained exclusively in The Royal Ballet repertory.

*Five members of the original cast of* Symphonic Variations, *(left to right): Moira Shearer, Michael Somes, Margot Fonteyn, Brian Shaw, and Pamela May. The missing figure is Henry Danton, who stood to the left of Shearer.*

# Symphony in C

*Ballet in one act. Music by Georges Bizet. Choreography by George Balanchine.
Scenery and costumes by Léonor Fini (since 1950, costumes by Karinska). First
performed (as* Le Palais de Cristal) *at the Paris Opéra, on July 28, 1947, with
Lycette Darsonval, Tamara Toumanova, Micheline Bardin, and Madeleine Lafon.
Revived for Ballet Society, New York, on March 22, 1948, with Maria Tallchief,
Tanaquil LeClercq, Beatrice Tompkins, and Elise Reiman.*

In 1947 Balanchine was invited to work as guest choreographer at the
Paris Opéra and he revived *Apollo, Le Baiser de la Fée,* and *Serenade* before
creating a work especially for the troupe. On his return to New York,
Balanchine revived the work for Ballet Society, and it became a staple of
the New York City Ballet repertory thereafter.

Each of the movements of the Bizet Symphony (a student work written
when he was a laureate of the Prix de Rome, and only rediscovered and
published in the 1930s) is cast round a central couple. The first is a
brilliant sequence to the allegro vivo; the second is an adagio in which
the leading ballerina becomes associated with the oboe melody of the
score; the third movement is an ebullient entry to the allegro vivace; and
for the fourth movement, also an allegro, the three leading couples of the
previous movements join in competing with the fourth couple in an
exuberant finale which involves the entire cast of fifty-six dancers. When
danced well, the effect of *Symphony in C* is as intoxicating as champagne.

*Suzanne Farrell and Peter
Martins in the second
movement of* Symphony
in C *as danced by the New
York City Ballet.*

# Symphony in Three Movements

*Ballet in one act. Music by Igor Stravinsky. Choreography by George Balanchine. First performed by the New York City Ballet at the State Theater, Lincoln Center, on June 18, 1972, with Sara Leland, Marnee Morris, Lynda Yourth, Helgi Tomasson, Edward Villella, and Robert Weiss.*

"Speaking for myself I can only say that Stravinsky's music altogether satisfies me. It makes me comfortable. When I listen to a score by him I am moved—I don't like the word inspired—to try to make visible not only the rhythm, melody and harmony, but even the timbre of the instruments. For if I could write music it seems to me that this is how I would want it to sound." Thus Balanchine wrote about Stravinsky in 1947, and a quarter-century later he reaffirmed this intense sympathy in art during the New York City Ballet's Stravinsky Festival. On that occasion audiences could see more clearly than ever before the depth of Balanchine's sympathy with Stravinsky and the way in which his understanding of music is manifest not just in his ballet but in the way his artists are trained at the School of American Ballet. We see this in their quickness of physical response, in their total avoidance of any interpretative caprices other than those attitudes which Balanchine has sanctioned, because they are already there in the music, and by showing these attitudes Balanchine can make the music more clear to us. Stravinsky wrote: "I do not see how one can be a choreographer unless, like Balanchine, one is a musician first." Watching a Balanchine-Stravinsky work we are shown the music, its pulse, rhythms, melodic contrivances, textures. In the resultant theatrical image there is nothing that strains the coordination between our ears and our eyes.

In June 1972 the New York City Ballet presented a week of performances in homage to Igor Stravinsky at which thirty-one ballets to Stravinsky scores were presented, the majority by Balanchine. The Stravinsky Festival celebrated the life and work of the composer, who would have been ninety years old on the opening night. As Balanchine observed: "In Russia we don't cry when a person dies. We are very happy.... So you are all invited to come to see our festival, our party." The festival included twenty-one new ballets, and the vital factor of it was the tremendous upsurge in Balanchine's choreographic creativity.

## SYNOPSIS

Stravinsky's score dates from the mid-1940s and is a work of intense energy. It is this dynamism which, naturally enough, inspires and shapes the choreography. The ballet opens with an ensemble of violent physical imagery and proceeds very much in the same style. The first and third movements are massive in their power and they frame a mysterious, almost puppet-like pas de deux. The effects of the big ensembles is of large forces manipulated with daring and almost dangerous precision—one misjudgement and you sense that the cogs of this machine would grind together and the entire enterprise come to a terrifying halt. The final movement starts with pounding, driving force and it finishes with a moment in which the male dancers are placed on the forepart of the stage like runners ready to start some further arduous sprint. It is possible to make a comparison with *Symphony in C*: the sunlit exuberance of Balanchine's realisation of Bizet can be contrasted with the bold and percussive response to Stravinsky.

# Symphony of Psalms

*Ballet in one act. Music by Igor Stravinsky. Choreography by Jiří Kylián. Scenery by William Katz. Costumes by Joop Stokvis. First performed by the Nederlands Dans Theater at the Circustheater, Scheveningen, on November 24, 1978.*

*Symphony of Psalms* is cast for eight men and eight women. At curtain rise the men are seated on chairs at the back and on one side of the stage while the women kneel facing the backcloth, which is an extraordinary screen made of Persian carpets. The theme of the ballet is that struggle between belief and doubt which is an essential matter of faith. The action of the ballet contrasts passages of solemn and deliberate walking, or a progress across the stage on knees, with passages of exultant and ferocious dynamic energy as the dancers roar over the stage. In manner, the dance seems to combine academic attitudes with the freer outlines of contemporary style; recurring through it are moments when one or another of the dancers seems to secede from group activities and is then drawn back into the corporate feelings of the ensemble—indication perhaps of the doubt which can isolate an individual from his faith. At the end of the ballet the stage darkens and the back wall of Persian rugs begins to rise. Certain of the dancers walk through the hanging decoration and then rejoin the group. Eventually all the dancers move into the darkened recesses at the back of the stage as the carpets disappear into the flies, and shafts of light flash out in the shape of a cross—as an indication of a final hope.

*řı́ Kylián's production of ymphony of Psalms by ravinsky for the ederlands Dans Theater. he design by William atz features a great panel pendant carpets.*

# Tales of Hoffmann

*Ballet in three acts with prologue and epilogue. Music by Jacques Offenbach, arranged and orchestrated by John Lanchbery. Libretto by Peter Darrell. Choreography by Darrell. Scenery and costumes by Alistair Livingstone. First performed by Scottish Ballet at the King's Theatre, Edinburgh, on April 6, 1972, with Peter Cazalet, Patricia Rianne, Hilary Debden, Marian St. Claire, and Elaine McDonald. Restaged for American Ballet Theatre with sets and costumes by Peter Docherty at the State Theater, Lincoln Center, on July 12, 1973, with Jonas Kåge as Hoffmann and Cynthia Gregory as all four heroines.*

*Elaine McDonald as Giulietta with Graham Bart as Hoffmann and Gordon Aitken, on the ground, as Dapertutto, in the third act of Scottish Ballet's production of Tales of Hoffmann.*

In Peter Darrell's dance realisation of Offenbach's opera, the theme of the artist haunted by a many-faced adversary (Lindorf, Spalanzani, Doctor Miracle, and Dapertutto) provides two strong roles for male dancers with a firm character bias, set against three ballerina roles. As always with Darrell, a skilled dramatic structure is the basis for lively characterisations. *Hoffmann* is no great ballet, but has proved an enduring popular success, not least because of the public's familiarity with the Offenbach original. Peter Darrell's scenario follows the general outline of Offenbach's opera but reverses the order of incidents in the last two acts of the ballet.

*Gordon Aitken as Doctor Miracle, Graham Bart and Patricia Rianne as Hoffmann and Antonia, and Gavin Dorian as Antonia's father in the second act of Scottish Ballet's production of* Tales of Hoffmann.

| | | |
|---|---|---|
| **SYNOPSIS** *Prologue* | Hoffmann awaits the arrival of La Stella, with whom he is in love. His friends ask him the meaning of souvenirs which lie on the table. La Stella gives a note for Hoffmann to her maid, which is taken by Councillor | Lindorf. Hoffmann is sufficiently drunk to begin telling the story of his three loves, represented by the pair of spectacles, the shoe, and the crucifix, which lie on the table before him. |
| *Act I* | Spalanzani, an inventor, shows his friends his latest creation, the mechanical doll Olympia. The young Hoffmann is attracted to Olympia, and when Spalanzani declares that she will dance for his guests, he makes Hoffmann put on a pair of magic spectacles. Hoffmann falls under | Olympia's spell and wants to marry her, which delights Spalanzani. Hoffmann dances ecstatically with the doll but his magic spectacles fall off and he is suddenly aware that Olympia is no more than a disintegrating automaton. |
| *Act II* | Hoffmann, now ten years older, is a student of Antonia's father, a composer. Antonia flirts with Hoffmann and dances for him, but when her father sees this he warns his daughter that such exertions may kill her. The sinister Doctor Miracle | arrives and offers to cure Antonia. He hypnotises her and she believes that she is a ballerina. She insists that Hoffmann play for her so that she may dance for him, and Doctor Miracle urges Hoffmann to do so. Antonia dies in his arms. |
| *Act III* | After a passage of years, Hoffmann has turned to a life of religious contemplation. In Dapertutto's Venetian salon he is unimpressed by the worldliness of the guests, but the appearance of the courtesan Giulietta so amazes him that he falls in love with | her. But he realises that he has lost his immortal soul when he discovers that he no longer can see his reflection in a looking glass. In despair he prays for forgiveness; his reflection is restored to him, and Giulietta and Dapertutto disappear. |
| *Epilogue* | Hoffmann, having told his stories, becomes increasingly drunk as Lindorf offers him more wine. When La Stella comes to look for him he is collapsed in a drunken stupor, and she is led sadly | away by Lindorf. Coming to his senses, Hoffmann realises that he has again fallen victim to the evil forces which have destroyed all his past happiness. |

# The Taming of the Shrew

Ballet in two acts. Music by Kurt-Heinz Stolze after Domenico Scarlatti. Libretto by John Cranko, based on the play by Shakespeare. Choreography by Cranko. Scenery and costumes by Elizabeth Dalton. First performed by the Stuttgart Ballet at the Württembergische Staatstheater, Stuttgart, on March 16, 1969. with Marcia Haydée as Katherine and Richard Cragun as Petruchio.

Opposite: *Marcia Haydée as Kate splendidly at odds with Richard Cragun as Petruchio in the first act of the Stuttgart Ballet's production of* The Taming of the Shrew.

Cranko's wonderfully resourceful comic writing is everywhere apparent in this clever adaptation of the basic theme of Shakespeare's play. He had a particular gift for character vignettes—thus Bianca's three suitors become lively roles for dancers—and even the small scene in which Petruchio shows his servants how he wants them to greet Kate as twitching monstrosities is full of comic invention. Inevitably the ballet is dominated by Kate and Petruchio. Gorgeously funny for much of the time, it yet has a seriousness of feeling which prevents it from being merely farcical. Marcia Haydée and Richard Cragun responded to Cranko's ideas with performances of immense good humour but also true sincerity of emotion. The ballet has been performed by other troupes but nothing has yet rivalled the ensemble playing of the Stuttgart company.

## SYNOPSIS

**Act I, Scene 1**
*Outside Baptista's house*

Three suitors—Hortensio, a ninny; Lucentio, a foolish student; and Gremio, an ageing *roué*—serenade Bianca, younger daughter of Baptista. His elder daughter, Katherine, storms from the house and belabours everyone in sight, for she must be married first. Neighbours are appalled at the uproar.

**Scene 2**
*A tavern*

Petruchio, charming but penniless, is fleeced by two whores while blissfully drunk. Bianca's three suitors promise him wealth if he will marry Katherine.

**Scene 3**
*Inside Baptista's house*

Bianca is being bullied by Kate when Petruchio arrives with Bianca's three suitors disguised so that they may gain admittance to the house. Petruchio and Kate find that each is the other's match in temperament, and Kate, attracted to Petruchio, agrees to marry him.

**Scene 4**
*A street*

Neighbours are amused at the news of Kate's marriage; each of the three suitors hopes soon to win Bianca for himself.

**Scene 5**
*Inside Baptista's house*

Kate, in bridal dress and carrying a lily (which she uses as a truncheon), and the assembled guests await the bridegroom. He appears in shocking disarray, ludicrously garbed. Nevertheless they are married.

**Act II, Scene 1**
*Inside Petruchio's house*

Petruchio prepares a horrid reception for Kate. His servants are made to behave like lunatics. Kate is frustrated in her quest for food and is left to sleep curled up by the fireplace.

**Scene 2**
*A carnival*

Lucentio disguises two whores in cloaks so that they look like Bianca, and he arranges for Hortensio and Gremio to marry them, thus leaving the field free for himself.

**Scene 3**
*Inside Petruchio's house*

The bemused Kate is further teased by Petruchio about her clothes. She finally capitulates to him, and finds him tender and loving.

**Scene 4**
*Bianca's wedding day*

Kate is riding behind Petruchio on his horse. He tests her good nature even more but she has learned how to love him and how to humour him.

**Scene 5**
*Inside Baptista's house*

Kate teaches Bianca and the whores and their three bridegrooms the rules for a happy marriage. She and Petruchio are blissfully happy.

# Tchaikovsky Suite No. 3

*Ballet in one act. Music by Pyotr Ilyich Tchaikovsky. Choreography by George Balanchine. Scenery and costumes by Nicola Benois. First performed by the New York City Ballet at the State Theater, Lincoln Center, on December 3, 1970, with Karin von Aroldingen, Anthony Blum, Kay Mazzo, Conrad Ludlow, Marnee Morris, John Clifford, Gelsey Kirkland, and Edward Villella.*

Opposite: *Kyra Nichols in "Theme and Variations," the last movement of Balanchine's* Tchaikovsky Suite No. 3, *with the New York City Ballet.*

If the collaboration between Balanchine and Stravinsky has begot great things, no less vivid is the choreographer's response to the music of Tchaikovsky. Settings of the second and third piano concertos, of the greater part of the third symphony (as *Diamonds*), and of two orchestral suites and several shorter works are evidence of his belief that "Tchaikovsky composed a great deal of music ideal for dancing." *Suite No. 3* is an unusual work which seems at first to be split in two, its second part—the Tema con variazioni which is the suite's last movement—having already existed as a ballet since 1947. This *Theme and Variations*, created for Ballet Theatre, was first seen at the City Center, New York, on November 26, 1947, with Alicia Alonso and Igor Youskevitch. In 1960 Balanchine staged this ballet for his own company, with Violette Verdy and Edward Villella, and in 1970 he set the preceding three movements—"to listen to them is to think immediately of dancing," he once said of the Tchaikovsky suites—casting them in ecstatic style. They differ in every way from the "virtuosity in tutus" of *Theme and Variations*, which culminates in a polonaise which could well be used as the final sunburst for *The Sleeping Beauty*, but their mood is dictated unerringly by the drenched emotionalism of the score.

The opening Elégie is filled with musical echoes from the "Vision Scene" of *The Sleeping Beauty* in its yearning melody. Thus the setting of this section as a nocturnal incident, in which a group of women in drifting draperies, hair floating unbound, feet bare, appear like visions to a young man, seems apt. Among them the youth seeks, finds, and loses a beloved. In the following Valse mélancolique the dislocated pulse of the waltz is matched, in a pas de deux, by the way the woman forever eludes the man. The ballerina and a group of attendant girls are now in pointe shoes, and the succeeding Scherzo develops this lightening of the mood and acceleration of the dance tempo as a boy and girl dart amid the corps de ballet. With the Tema con variazioni, moonlight and long dresses are gone. Set for a principal pair, with four supporting couples and a corps de ballet of sixteen, it celebrates the rigours and the beauties of the classical academic style. The progress of the musical variations marks a development in the elaboration of the choreography which fully extends the capabilities of both ballerina and *premier danseur*. For those of us fortunate enough to have seen him, the image of Igor Youskevitch crossing the stage in a diagonal of prodigious *ronds de jambe sautés* is one of the ballet's lasting memories. The writing for the ballerina is no less demanding, and after the final Polonaise—a grandly Balanchinian device—she is held high and triumphant upon her partner's shoulder while the full corps de ballet honours her.

# The Three-Cornered Hat

*Ballet in one act. Music by Manuel de Falla. Choreography by Leonide Massine. Scenery and costumes by Pablo Picasso. First performed by Diaghilev's Ballets Russes at the Alhambra Theatre, London, on July 22, 1919, with Massine as the Miller and Tamara Karsavina as his Wife.*

The Three-Cornered Hat (*Le Tricorne*) was the result of a summer's trip through Spain which Diaghilev and Massine took with Manuel de Falla at a time when the main body of the Ballets Russes was on tour in America. With a remarkable gypsy dancer, Felix, as guide, they studied the dances of southern Spain while de Falla noted down popular music as source material for the score which Diaghilev had asked him to write. At the same time Massine was being coached in all the nuances of Spanish dance by Felix. Massine's quick intelligence and his lively theatre sense, allied to the marvellous score that de Falla created, and Picasso's quintessentially Spanish designs, produced a masterpiece. It is a unique work in that it succeeded in translating Spanish dance to the ballet stage. As the Miller, Massine made his greatest role for himself, in which his dancing—notably of the *Farucca*—and his magnetic stage presence were unforgettable.

SYNOPSIS

*Opposite: In 1947 Massine staged The Three-Cornered Hat for the Sadler's Wells Ballet at the Royal Opera House, Covent Garden. He danced his original role of the Miller, Margot Fonteyn as the Miller's Wife, and John Hart was the Corregidor.*

*Below: The Corregidor gets his first sight of the Miller's Wife: John Hart and Margot Fonteyn.*

Based on a play by the Spanish poet Alarcón, *The Three-Cornered Hat* presents us with a Miller in a Spanish village and his beautiful wife. The Miller is standing in front of his house and he is joined by his wife; their love is evident. But as they go to a well to draw water a dandy passes by on the bridge and the wife flirts with him. The governor of the province, the Corregidor, the wearer of the three-cornered hat, passes by with an escort, tottering beside the sedan chair in which his wife is seated. He too tries to flirt with the Miller's Wife, but she mocks the old dodderer. Subsequently the Miller flirts with one of the village women and then leaves.

The Corregidor returns and tries to dance with the Miller's Wife, but collapses. The Miller returns and joins his wife in making fun of the old man, who then departs. A general dance is interrupted by the governor's guards, who arrive to arrest the Miller. His wife watches, distraught, as he is led away, and at once the Corregidor returns to force his attentions upon this beautiful young woman. She pushes him into the river and after threatening him with a musket she leaves, and the Corregidor, drenched to the skin, seeks warm clothing in the Miller's house. The Miller now returns, having escaped from the guards, and they in turn arrive and mistake the figure of the Corregidor, who is wearing the Miller's thick-hooded coat, for the Miller himself. They drag him away while the Miller and his wife celebrate this outcome in a final *jota* with neighbours.

# Le Tombeau de Couperin

*Ballet in one act. Music by Maurice Ravel. Choreography by George Balanchine. First performed by the New York City Ballet at the State Theater, Lincoln Center, on May 29, 1974.*

Maurice Ravel loved beautiful little machines, exquisite clocks, finely made automata. He would surely have rejoiced in Balanchine's realisation of four movements from his *Le Tombeau de Couperin* (the idea of a *tombeau* is a homage to the manner of an earlier master and also, in the case of Ravel's music, a memorial to friends who were killed in the First World War). Ravel was writing music on the dance rhythms of the eighteenth century; after a Prélude come a Forlane, a Rigaudon, and a Menuet. Balanchine conceived the work for two quadrilles of young dancers, each comprising four boys and four girls. They work in parallel for the most part, so that, studying one half of the stage, one is aware, without too close inspection, of action going on in the other half—though, in fact, the reflection and interaction of the dance patterns is part of the delight of this fascinating and beautiful ballet. Balanchine's choreography mirrors Ravel's homage to the forms of eighteenth-century social dance. The eighteenth-century dance insisted upon the pre-eminence of floor patterns, and so does Balanchine: *Tombeau* is to be ideally viewed from above. Shapes form and break, as in a kaleidoscope, and re-form in constantly fresh lines, curves, squares. In the closing section we are shown the clear links that lead from the country dances of the past to the square dances of today.

*Members of the New York City Ballet in* Le Tombeau de Couperin.

# Twilight

*Ballet in one scene. Music by John Cage (*Perilous Night *for prepared piano). Choreography by Hans van Manen. Scenery by Jean-Paul Vroom. First performed by the Dutch National Ballet at the Stadsschouwburg, Amsterdamn, June 20, 1972 with Alexandra Radius and Han Ebbelaar. Restaged for the Sadler's Wells Royal Ballet on March 2, 1973, with Patricia Ruanne and Paul Clarke.*

*Patricia Ruanne and Paul Clarke in the Sadler's Wells Royal Ballet production of van Manen's* Twilight.

The setting for this ballet is a meticulously painted view of an industrial complex. The pianist is seated on the right-hand side of the stage. The characters are a boy and a girl, the girl in a short pink dress and spike-heeled shoes. The atmosphere is tense, urban, aggressive, as the young couple stalk and taunt each other, involved in a courtship that is harsh and unforgiving. Towards the end of the ballet the girl removes her shoes—an act which seems to acquire strong erotic significance—and launches herself at the boy. By its extreme economy of means, and through van Manen's brilliant reaction to the curious sonorities of the prepared piano, *Twilight* seems an entirely modern depiction of the traditional balletic pas de deux.

# The Two Pigeons

*Ballet in two acts and three scenes. Music by André Messager, arranged by John Lanchbery. Choreography by Frederick Ashton. Scenery and costumes by Jacques Dupont. First performed by The Royal Ballet Touring Company at the Royal Opera House, Covent Garden, on February 14, 1961, with Lynn Seymour as the Young Girl, Christopher Gable as the Young Man, Elizabeth Anderton as a Gypsy Girl, and Richard Farley as the Gypsy Leader.*

*The Two Pigeons* was originally produced at the Paris Opéra on October 18, 1886, with choreography by Louis Mérante. Its story had been adapted from a fable by La Fontaine and the work was memorable for the delightful performance by Rosita Mauri as the heroine. The ballet stayed intermittently in the repertory of the Paris Opéra Ballet and was revived in 1952 by Albert Aveline for that company. (Latterly it has been revived again for the students of the Paris Opéra Ballet school.) But it was the discovery of the score in the archives of Covent Garden, where it had remained since the piece was mounted at the Royal Opera House in 1906, which inspired Ashton to make his own version for the beautiful and talented Seymour, Gable, and Anderton. A work full of sentiment, *The Two Pigeons* seems a gentler reflection of the young love which Ashton had so joyously celebrated in *La Fille Mal Gardée* the previous year.

## SYNOPSIS

### Act I
*A studio in Paris*

A young artist is endeavouring to paint a portrait of his girlfriend but she is a fidget and drives him to distraction. Despite all her winning ways he becomes more and more exasperated with her inability to sit still. Her friends enter the studio and suddenly their attention is caught by the sound of a troupe of gypsies in the street. They invite them into the studio and soon the painter has fallen head-over-heels for the wiles of a beautiful gypsy girl. The young girl and the gypsy vie determinedly in dance for the young man's affections. When the gypsies leave, the painter is seized with wanderlust and goes after them. The girl is left sorrowing, and outside the window of the studio a pigeon flies away.

### Act II, Scene 1
*The gypsy camp*

The gypsies dash and flaunt themselves through their dances and the young painter becomes more and more enraptured with the gypsy girl. Her protector provokes a quarrel with the painter and eventually the boy is beaten up and abandoned by the troupe of gypsies.

### Scene 2
*The studio*

After a frontcloth scene in which the disillusioned young painter is seen making his way home (a white pigeon has recalled his true love to him), the action moves back to the studio, where the young girl is waiting dejectedly. The door opens and her errant, repentant lover returns to her arms. They are united in a pas de deux of reconciliation and at the end a second white pigeon flies in to join the one who had led the young man home.

*Opposite: Lynn Seymour and Christopher Gable at the end of Ashton's* The Two Pigeons. *In this dress rehearsal picture, for unfathomable reasons, a third pigeon was on hand to perch on the chair.*

# Union Jack

*Ballet in three scenes. Music by Hershy Kay, adapted from traditional British sources. Choreography by George Balanchine. Scenery and costumes by Rouben Ter-Arutunian. First performed by the New York City Ballet at the State Theater, Lincoln Center, on May 12, 1976.*

Union Jack is a huge, affectionate, and amused look at Britain, very much from the other side of the Atlantic—which seems to disconcert some British viewers. But on the expanse of the State Theater stage in New York it can be an exhilarating display, reminding us of Balanchine's grand skill as a showman who has known great success on Broadway: it must not be forgotten that Balanchine choreographed a notable list of hit shows in New York, among them *On Your Toes*, *Babes in Arms*, *The Boys from Syracuse*, *Cabin in the Sky*, and *Song of Norway*.

SYNOPSIS

It was an amusing comment upon the American Bicentennial Year that George Balanchine and the New York City Ballet should have made a tribute to Britain as their contribution to the celebrations. (Balanchine's 1958 *Stars and Stripes*, with its roaring Sousa score, would seem the choreographer's tribute to his adopted land.) *Union Jack* divides into three sections, each commenting balletically upon rituals that are part of Britain's heritage.

The first section is an evocation of the Edinburgh Tattoo, with the massed forces of the City Ballet drawn up on stage in full Highland military dress of tartans and plaids—the men in costumes entirely authentic, the women deliciously on pointe. The various clans march and counter-march to a selection of piper's tunes and reels. The second section is a costermonger pas de deux for a pearly king and queen, complete with donkey cart and two small children. The final section salutes the Royal Navy, with the men in authentic rig, and the girls looking like Eleanor Powell in *Born to Dance*. It is hornpipe time. The finale has the entire company semaphoring "Rule Britannia" while the backcloth turns into the Union Jack.

*New York City Ballet dancers signal "Rule Britannia" in the final moments of* Union Jack.

# La Valse

*Ballet in one act. Music by Maurice Ravel. Choreography by George Balanchine. Costumes by Karinska. First performed by the New York City Ballet at the City Center, New York, on February 20, 1951, with Tanaquil LeClercq, Nicholas Magallanes, and Francisco Moncion.*

Overleaf: *Patricia McBride and Nicholas Magallanes in Balanchine's* La Valse *with the New York City Ballet.*

*La Valse* was commissioned by Diaghilev, who, to Ravel's extreme annoyance, then rejected it as being untheatrical. Thus it fell to Bronislava Nijinska to choreograph a first version for Ida Rubinstein's company during a season at the Paris Opéra in 1929, with designs by Alexandre Benois set in a splendid Second Empire ballroom. Cyril Beaumont described it in his *Complete Book of Ballets* as "a lovely conception," but it did not survive.

The most important version other than Balanchine's is that by Frederick Ashton, staged originally for the ballet of La Scala, Milan, on January 3, 1958, and revived for The Royal Ballet at Covent Garden on March 10, 1959, with designs by André Levasseur. Set for twenty-one couples, the ballet is a plotless realisation of the Ravel score.

Ashton has twice choreographed ballets to Ravel's *Valses Nobles et Sentimentales*: first in 1935 for the Ballet Rambert as *Valentine's Eve*, and then in 1947 for the Sadler's Wells Theatre Ballet, under the music's title —this last being a work of extraordinary sensitivity and charm. Its claret-coloured costumes and designs of screens were by Sophie Fedorovitch, Ashton's long-time collaborator. Inexplicably dropped from the repertory, it is still treasured in the memories of those who saw it.

SYNOPSIS

Balanchine prefaces his staging of *La Valse* with a realisation of Ravel's *Valses Nobles et Sentimentales*. These are set as delightful, light interludes between boys and girls who meet and part at a ball. With the beginning of Ravel's apotheosis of the waltz the mood changes. There have been hints of unease in the preceding *Valses Nobles et Sentimentales*, but with the dark orchestral introduction to *La Valse* we enter a more disturbed and disturbing world. Ravel said of this score that it suggested "dancing on the edge of a volcano." For Balanchine it becomes an exercise in romantic doom—which is, in essence, the feeling that Ravel expresses in his describing the music as "a fantastic and fatal whirling."

As *La Valse* begins the men dart in quest of their partners; then the rhythms of the waltz seem to emerge from chaos into order and light, and gradually couples pass and swirl and revolve. A girl in white appears, dancing with her partner in a graceful first encounter. But the score seems to lose momentum, and it sounds at one moment as if on the point of disintegrating: as this occurs the black-clad figure of Death enters the ballroom followed by a page carrying a ball dress and a looking glass. The girl is attracted by the figure of Death. She approaches him and he offers her a jet necklace which she puts on, and then gazes at herself in the glass, which she discovers is horrifyingly cracked. As the waltz regains its momentum the girl is offered long black gloves into which she plunges her arms; then a black overdress which covers her white ballgown. She puts these on in a kind of ecstatic acceptance of ill-omened gifts. She dances with the sombre figure; he whirls her about the room and as the waltz reaches a pitch of energy the girl rises in the embrace of Death and then falls lifeless. Death leaves and the girl's lover returns to take up her body. He bears her away, but as the aghast guests join in the dance the young man appears again with the girl, and her body is held on high by the male dancers as the whirlwind of the waltz circles frantically around them.

# La Ventana

*Ballet in two scenes. Music by Hans Christian Lumbye and Wilhelm Christian Holm. Choreography by August Bournonville. First performed at the Casino Theatre, Copenhagen, on June 19, 1854; revised October 6, 1856, for the Royal Danish Ballet at the Royal Theatre, Copenhagen.*

*nnemarie Dybdal and*
*rne Villumsen in the*
*:ond scene of* La
*entana, as staged by the*
*yal Danish Ballet.*

Bournonville created this Spanish divertissement for his favourite ballerina, Juliette Price, and he made the work in order to capitalise upon the popularity of Spanish dancing in the middle of the nineteenth century. Typically, Bournonville sought to avoid the sensuality which he abhorred in much theatrical dance of his time. The mirror dance in the first scene is skillfully staged by having another dancer appear as the mirror image of the señorita, and the pas de trois and Seguidilla in the second scene are brilliant examples of Bournonville's craft.

The pas de trois from *La Ventana* was staged by Erik Bruhn for American Ballet Theatre in 1975, and by Stanley Williams—another former Royal Danish Ballet soloist and since 1964 a teacher at the School of American Ballet—for the New York City Ballet in 1977, as the third section of its *Bournonville Divertissements*.

## SYNOPSIS

*Scene 1*
*A room overlooking a square in Spain*

A señorita enters her room and thinks of the young man she met at the alameda. She dances with her image in the mirror, then hears the sound of guitars outside her window. It is the young man serenading her and she replies by playing her castanets and then tossing him the bow from her hair.

*Scene 2*
*Outside the house*

The young man and his friends are dancing, and they are joined by a young woman who hides her face behind her mantilla. Eventually she is revealed as the señorita; she and the young man dance happily together.

303

# Vienna Waltzes

*Ballet in five scenes. Music by Johann Strauss, Jr., Franz Lehár, and Richard Strauss. Choreography by George Balanchine. Scenery by Rouben Ter-Arutunian. Costumes by Karinska. First performed by the New York City Ballet at the State Theater, Lincoln Center, on June 23, 1977, with Karin von Aroldingen and Jacques d'Amboise, Patricia McBride and Helgi Tomasson, Sara Leland and Bart Cook, Kay Mazzo and Peter Martins, and Suzanne Farrell and Jean-Pierre Bonnefous.*

*Vienna Waltzes* at its first performance gave the New York City Ballet a gigantic box-office success. It offered the kind of luscious spectacle which Balanchine can so skillfully contrive. *Vienna Waltzes* reflects also Balanchine's continuing fascination with the waltz as a dance form for the theatre. *Le Cotillon* in 1932, *La Valse* in 1951, and, supremely, *Liebeslieder Walzer* in 1960 suggest what riches he finds in triple time.

SYNOPSIS

Opposite: *Suzanne Farrell in the final* Rosenkavalier *section of* Vienna Waltzes.

Below: *The last waltz in* Vienna Waltzes, *with the entire cast swirling to the sound of the* Rosen-kavalier *waltzes.*

The ballet falls into five scenes. *Tales from the Vienna Woods* seems an exact realisation of the title of the Strauss waltz. A group of girls in long pink ball dresses meet and flirt gently with young officers in a forest setting. Charm is all. As they waltz away into the night their place is taken by more balletic figures, a leading couple with a corps de ballet of eight girls, who sparkle merrily amid the trees to *Voices of Spring*. The Johann Strauss section ends with the ebullience of the *Explosion Polka*, which is choreographed for a group of *incroyables* led by a virtuoso couple. The scene then changes to an art nouveau ballroom. We are in the world of *The Merry Widow* and Maxim's, although the Lehár score is the *Gold and Silver* waltz. A black-clothed, enigmatic beauty—who could be Hanna—has a rendezvous with the dashing, red-uniformed figure of a Hussar (who should be Prince Danilo) and here, romance is all.

Finally comes the apotheosis of the waltz itself as the back of the stage turns into a huge reflecting glass. Into the ballroom comes a young girl in a long white satin dress. She drifts along on the beginnings of Richard Strauss's *Rosenkavalier* waltzes, her presence occasionally haunted by a mysterious partner. Gradually the stage fills with other couples—a mass of swirling black and white reflected in the mirrored setting. The ending of the ballet is irresistibly heart-lifting, as twenty-five couples sweep over the stage, the girls in white silk dresses whose skirts, sweeping with the beat of the dance, are as much a part of the choreography as their bodies.

# Viva Vivaldi!

*Ballet in one act. Music by Antonio Vivaldi. Choreography by Gerald Arpino. Costumes by Quintana and Anthony. First performed by the Joffrey Ballet at the Delacorte Theatre, Central Park, New York, on September 10, 1965.*

The exclamation point in the title of this ballet gives some hint of its exuberance. In its general flamboyance and the sultry romanticism of its adagio movement, *Viva Vivaldi!* reflects the Spanish flavour of Vivaldi's Violin Concerto in D major, arranged for guitar for the ballet. So do the women's handsome costumes of white lace and black velvet. Although each of its four sections is led by soloists, *Viva Vivaldi!* has come to exemplify the Joffrey Ballet's "all-star, no-star" policy. Everybody dances like crazy. It is the oldest extant work by Arpino, the Joffrey company's resident choreographer.

*Cameron Basden of the Joffrey Ballet in Gerald Arpino's* Viva Vivaldi!

# Voluntaries

*Ballet in one act. Music by Francis Poulenc. Choreography by Glen Tetley. Scenery and costumes by Rouben Ter-Arutunian. First performed by the Stuttgart Ballet at the Württembergische Staatstheater, Stuttgart, on December 22, 1973, with Marcia Haydée and Richard Cragun.*

"Voluntaries—by musical definition—are free-ranging organ or trumpet improvisations often played before, during or after religious services. The Latin root of the word can also connote flight or desire, and the ballet is conceived as a linked series of voluntaries." Glen Tetley's programme note indicates a starting point for his ballet; characteristically, his choreography shows how, from this basic idea, a super-structure of movement and emotional relationship is created. When first seen, *Voluntaries* seemed inevitably to relate to the fact of Tetley's assumption in Stuttgart of the mantle of John Cranko, who died tragically young earlier that year. The central couple, who are shown in the ballet's opening pose, were Marcia Haydée and Richard Cragun, and it is not unlikely to see in their presence that feeling of grief and desolation which the Stuttgart Ballet knew following the loss of their greatly loved director. The ensemble in *Voluntaries* comprises six couples, and they and a secondary trio are presented in huge sweeps of activity which race and eddy round the principal couple. There are moments when the choreography seems to indicate extremes of grief; at other moments there seems some resolution of this unhappiness, and images of consolation and love as well as of loneliness are expressed.

The choreography is extremely demanding in its response to the music. *Voluntaries* evokes a similarly powerful emotional response not only from its audience but also from its dancers. It is now in the repertory of The Royal Ballet and American Ballet Theatre.

*Mark Silver, Vergie Derman, and Wayne Eagling of The Royal Ballet in Glen Tetley's* Voluntaries.

# A Wedding Bouquet

*Ballet in one act. Music by Lord Berners. Words by Gertrude Stein. Choreography by Frederick Ashton. Scenery and costumes by Berners. Libretto by Berners, Ashton, and Constant Lambert. First performed by the Vic-Wells Ballet at Sadler's Wells Theatre, London, on April 27, 1937, with Ninette de Valois as Webster, Robert Helpmann as the Bridegroom, Mary Honer as the Bride, Margot Fonteyn as Julia, June Brae as Josephine, Michael Somes as Guy, Leslie Edwards as Arthur, Pamela May as Violet, and Julia Farron as Pépé.*

*"Josephine may not attend a wedding." Deanne Bergsma is seen in these "before" (opposite) and "after" (below) "champagne" pictures in* A Wedding Bouquet *as danced by The Royal Ballet.*

A Wedding Bouquet is a very special ballet. It is not often performed, but to its devotees it remains one of the most beguiling of works. All its components seem exactly matched. The sly wit and remarkable sophistication that marked everything that Lord Berners produced—novels, music, or painting; the inconsequentialities of Gertrude Stein's text; the elegance of Ashton's humour expressed through the choreography; all combine in perfect proportion. The Stein text has become part of an international balletic *lingua franca*; such phrases as "I am older than a boat" or "This is now Scene One" will serve as passwords among devotees. The roles are exceptionally demanding stylistically and we must record with gratitude that Leslie Edwards was irreplaceably Arthur ("Everything is going on nicely, nicely") for nearly forty years. No one has ever approached Constant Lambert's performance as the narrator.

**SYNOPSIS** *A Wedding Bouquet* is a picture of the comic disasters attendant upon a French provincial wedding at the turn of the century. At the side of the stage, seated at a table, is a narrator in morning dress, with a bottle of champagne, and it is he who declaims the Gertrude Stein commentary which fixes the flavour of each character and each situation. At curtain rise Webster, the officious maid, is inspecting the staff who are preparing for the wedding. The guests arrive: Josephine and her two friends Paul and John; Violet, who is in pursuit of the timid Ernest; the fey Julia ("known as Forlorn") and her Mexican dog Pépé. Now the bride appears ("charming, charming, charming") and her thoroughly shifty groom ("they all speak as if they expected him not to be charming"). Part of the groom's problem stems from the fact that most of the ladies have known him rather too well, and Julia in particular has an embarrassing habit of clinging onto his leg as he greets the guests. Josephine imbibes too much champagne ("Josephine may not attend a wedding") and is asked to leave. There is a final glorious tango and everyone leaves, with Julia abandoned by everyone except her little dog.

# Who Cares?

*Ballet in one act. Music by George Gershwin, orchestrated by Hershy Kay. Choreography by George Balanchine. Scenery by Jo Mielziner. Costumes by Karinska. First performed by the New York City Ballet at the State Theater, New York, on February 5, 1970, with Karin von Aroldingen, Patricia McBride, Marnee Morris, and Jacques d'Amboise.*

Gershwin brought Balanchine to Hollywood in the 1930s. With *Who Cares?*, Balanchine brought Gershwin to New York's hall of classicism. *Who Cares?* is a suite of dances that amalgamates the innate elegance of ballet with the equally innate elegance of the hoofer. That these two elegances *are* equal is the ballet's thesis, and its source of delight. Each dance is a kind of transformation scene, in which common ballet gestures and dynamics look sometimes softer, sometimes more piquant, simply because of a particular accent which one calls "showbiz": a hand on hip here, a touch of rubato there, a casualness juxtaposed with intense syncopation.

   *Who Cares?* is a long ballet, and it takes a while to percolate. The first few numbers are clearly introductory. The piece begins to gather force with a series of duets for demi-soloists. It reaches full power as soon as the hoofer-hero and his three girls are introduced. From there on in it's onward and upward — a pyramid of moods and personalities built upon Gershwin's suggestions. The dominant figure is the male; possibly Balanchine meant *Who Cares?* to be as much a tribute to the special American charm of Jacques d'Amboise as it is to the songs. It was certainly d'Amboise's greatest role.

SYNOPSIS

The set is of a starry Manhattan skyline. An ensemble of girls perform the first three dances, followed by a soft-shoe for five boys. They invite five girls to dance, in five pas de deux spanning four songs. While each couple dances, the back-up team provides a continuous hum of small gestures, much like a crooning chorus line. Now the stage clears and the cavalier enters for the first time, leading the first of the ballerinas. Solo variations alternate with duets, until each of the ladies has danced by herself and with the man. He then dances a solo, and is joined by all three women for another dance. (This quartet is often deleted.) The finale is for the entire cast.

Opposite: *Patricia McBride in the "Fascinating Rhythm" solo from Balanchine's* Who Cares?

# THE DANCE STEPS

*Natalia Makarova and*
*Anthony Dowell rehearsing*
Giselle.

# Barre Work

Every dancer's day begins with a class. The classical dancer's practice begins with work warming and tuning the body at the barre. The barre is a horizontal rail fixed to the wall of the studio and the dancer uses it to assist in achieving balance and correct posture before moving into the centre of the room for the continuation of the class.

Barre work usually lasts about half an hour and follows a set pattern. First come *pliés* in different positions. *Pliés* are fundamental to classical technique, as, without the elasticity they provide, movement would be shallow and brittle, and, indeed, dangerous. After this first set of exercises come others designed to elongate and strengthen the muscles of the legs and torso.

All exercises are performed to both the left and right so that each leg is equally worked. The great Italian pedagogue Carlo Blasis remarked that "a dancer who can only dance with one leg may be compared with a pianist who can only play with one hand."

Dancers must accept the rigours and disciplines of the barre work, as until these have been mastered, they will not have the strength or technique to progress through the rest of the class.

*Mikhail Baryshnikov of American Ballet Theatre and Zhandra Rodriguez of the Hamburg Ballet relaxing in the classroom. Baryshnikov is leaning against the barre.*

## Positions of the Feet

There are five basic positions of the feet in classical ballet. All steps begin and end in these positions. There are complementary positions for the arms, known as *ports de bras*. In all the positions of the feet the legs are turned out from the pelvis so that the toes point out to the sides. Turning out enables dancers to be more flexible and have a greater range of movement as well as greater beauty of line.

The photograph below left (**1**) shows the girl standing in the first position; the heels are together and the weight is evenly distributed between both feet. The arms are raised in front and curved, with a small space between the fingertips. The boy is standing in second position; his feet are separated by approximately one and a half times the length of his own foot.

The arms have been opened from first position, retaining the same curved and moulded shape.

Opposite top left (**2**), the girl is in third position; the heel of the front foot is crossed halfway over the other. This position is used only for training younger dancers who have not yet acquired the strength and turn-out necssary to achieve fifth. The boy demonstrates fourth position; the feet are separated and parallel.

Right (**3**), the girl stands with both arms and feet in fifth position. The front heel is against the big toe of the back foot.

The two photographs below right show the boy in fifth position on half-pointe (**4**) and the girl in the same position on pointe (**5**).

1

*Stance*   The most immediately noticeable characteristic of classically trained dancers is their carriage and posture.

From the beginning of their training these dancers learn to use the centre of the body to support the upper back and shoulders. This "inner strength" makes possible all the feats of virtuosity they will eventually acquire.

It is essential that the classical dancer appear totally at ease; the limbs should move freely from the centre of the body and not seem just appendages.

*Pliés*   As we have said, *pliés* are the first formal exercises of barre work. "*Plier*" means to bend, and in these exercises

the knees and ankles are warmed up by the gradual easing. There are both *grand* (full) and *demi-* (half) *pliés*. In *demi-plié* the heels remain on the floor and the foot should not move at all. In *grand plié* the heels are allowed to lift, except in second position, in which the heels remain on the floor. In rising from the lowest point of the *grand plié* the heels should return to the floor at the earliest possible moment.

Unless a dancer understands the use and values of *demi-plié* it will be impossible to achieve elevation. *Plié* is both the springboard and then the cushion to all movement.

*In the photograph above the boy demonstrates* demi-plié *in first position while the girl goes into a* grand plié *in first.*
Right: *The boy stands in* demi-plié *in fifth position and the girl has descended into* grand plié *in fifth.*

## Battement Tendu

"*Tendu*" means stretched and in *battement tendu* the leg is extended from the fifth or first position to the front (*devant*), side (*à la seconde*), or back (*derrière*), and then returned to its starting position. All the weight should be on the supporting leg and never on the extended one. *Battement tendu* can also be done with *demi-plié*.

**1** Battement tendu devant
**2** Battement tendu à la seconde
**3** Battement tendu derrière

3

## Grand Battement

*Grande battement* is a free and high throw of the leg, departing and returning through *pointe tendue* with as little movement as possible in the pelvis. Apart from their obvious value in loosening the hip joints they are essential to the steps of *grand élévation*.

The outward sweep of the leg should be done with speed and determination; the recovery should be slightly more sustained in order to assist in the eventual control of and landing from big jumps.

1

3

**1** Grand battement devant
**2** Grand battement à la seconde
**3** Grand battement derrière

2

## Retiré

*Retiré* is the basic position for pirouettes. In *retiré*, the toe of the raised foot is held firmly just below the knee of the supporting leg.

*Retiré* is used as an intermediary position in adagio to stabilise and reassert correct balance. In this position the dancer should always be conscious of the perpendicular line running through the body from the head to the toes. Obviously, without this centre of balance, good pirouettes are impossible.

## Fondu

The exercise of *fondu* is as essential to the control of movement as is breathing. Both legs bend and extend in the same rhythm. The working leg has the same amount of resistance against the air as the supporting leg has against the ground. The quality should be that of the literal translation of the French word, which means "to melt." The three photographs below show the coordination of both the legs and the arm as the dancer opens to the front.

## Echappé Relevé

*Echappé relevé* is a basic exercise for pointe work until their feet, ankles, and backs work. "*Echappé*" means "to escape," are sufficiently strong to cope with the and "*relevé*" means "to rise." rigours that this aspect of classical

It is essential that the body be well ballet imposes.
"pulled up" and the legs and ankles
fully stretched when on pointe. Girls
should never be introduced to pointe

**1** Demi-plié *in fifth position.*
**2** *The legs "escape" from each other with a slight spring onto the toes to second position, with the weight evenly distributed between the legs.*
**3** *The completion of the echappé movement, with the foot that started in front now in back (echappé changé).*

1

2

3

*Stretches*  Many dancers complete their work at the *barre* by performing stretching exercises. These exercises can be set by a teacher, but professional dancers who understand their own bodies' needs limber up in the manner they find most beneficial.

# Centre Work

*Dancers of The Royal Ballet performing an* adagio *during centre work in the classroom. In the front line are Margot Fonteyn, Annette Page, and Svetlana Beriosova.*

After the initial warming up at the barre, dancers move into the centre of the studio. Here, without the help of the barre, they repeat many of the movements in order to re-establish their balance. The first exercise may be a *port de bras*. This gives the dancers a chance to use their arms in a more free and expressive manner than has hitherto been possible. There follow the repetitions of *battements tendus, grands battements, fondus*, etc.

Pirouettes are usually introduced at this stage. Anybody who is new to ballet always marvels at multiple pirouettes. These series of rapid turns

are possible for classical dancers because they have been trained to "spot." This means that the eyes are the last to leave the front and the first to return, always focusing on a fixed spot.

Then comes that part of the class designed specifically for control of balance. This is known as adagio and is essential preparation for sustaining line, both on the ground and in the air. As the term implies, all the movements are done slowly and should be phrased so that one position flows into another.

Now the dancers will have tuned up their bodies sufficiently to embark on

leaving the floor. They begin with very small, low jumps with much emphasis on replacing their feet on the ground with precision in the required position. Any attempt to jump very high without this preparation can result in injury.

The dancer's vocabulary of steps of elevation is enormous. It ranges from intricate footwork just off the ground to the most thrilling and space-devouring leaps. Generally, during the class there will be an exercise given for each of the different levels and qualities of elevation.

Professional dancers generally will do the entire class in pointe shoes. In less advanced classes the girls will change into pointe shoes and, at the end of class, will practise general pointe work as well as their own steps of virtuosity, the most famous of which are *fouettés*. The boys, meanwhile, will concentrate on their own *tours de force*.

As a final gesture of respect and thanks to the teacher, the dancers will make a *révérence* (curtsey by females, bow by males). If a class has been particularly enjoyable, there will be a spontaneous burst of applause.

## Epaulement

*Epaulement* can be used in barre work but it is only in the centre that the dancer is really free to use it to its full extent. Without *épaulement* ballet would lose much of its beauty and variety in the balance and distribution of the limbs.

Croisé devant

Effacé devant

Croisé derrière

Effacé derrière

Ecarté devant

## Attitude

*Attitude* is a position derived from the famous statue of Mercury by Giovanni da Bologna. The dancer stands on one leg with the other leg raised either behind or in front with the knee bent. The arms can vary but they should always be in harmony with the dancer's raised leg.

*The boy is in* attitude derrière *and the girl in* attitude devant.

*Merrill Ashley of the New York City Ballet in* attitude croisé.

## Arabesque

*Arabesque* is surely the most famous and most easily recognised of all ballet positions. There are many *arabesques* but the basic rule is that the raised leg is always directly behind the body.

Top: *Second* arabesque. *There is a continuous line from the finger tips of the front arm through the body to the toes of the raised leg.*

Bottom: Arabesque penchée. *Keeping the leg raised, the dancer pivots forward from the hip.*

### Allegro

Allegro is the general terms that covers all fast movements (again, as in music), including all jumps. The pointed foot plays an essential part in steps of elevation. Any movement through the air without stretched legs and pointed feet will look ugly and clumsy. When a dancer leaves the floor for a jump, the very action of stretching the legs and pointing the feet gives the final thrust.

*Flemming Ryberg of the Royal Danish Ballet in* Etudes.

### Batterie

*Batterie* is the beating of the legs against each other with speed, accuracy, and attack, to give added brilliance to a jump. *Petite batterie* is performed only high enough off the floor to allow the beat to take place. *Grande batterie* can be performed at the maximum height of elevation of which the dancer is capable.

*Both dancers are in the air with feet and legs stretched. This is the position in which a beat would be done.*

## Pas de chat

*Pas de chat* (cat's step) is one of the first jumps ever taught in the dancing class. It does, however, require co-ordination, elevation, and a sense of balance. The dancer starts in fifth position, jumps from one leg, raises both underneath him, and alights on the first leg, immediately closing the second to it in fifth position.

*Pas de chat* is performed in the dance of the four Cygnets in *Swan Lake* and by the White Cat in the last act of *The Sleeping Beauty*.

**1** *Preparation for the rise into the air.*
**2** *Both legs raised beneath the body in the air.*
**3** *The landing.*

## Brisé Volé

*Brisé volé* is a very famous step of *batterie* used in the Blue Bird's solo in *The Sleeping Beauty*. It gives the illusion of flight. It should have a very aerial and light quality, although it requires much strength and stamina to perform. To be effective it must look effortless. *Brisés volés* are often performed in pairs. In the first *brisé volé* the beat takes place in front of the body (**1**) and the dancer lands inclined over the supporting leg (**2**). In the second *brisé volé* the beat takes place in back (large picture).

Opposite: *Michael Coleman of The Royal Ballet dancing the Blue Bird's solo in* The Sleeping Beauty.

**1**

## Grand Allegro

*Grand allegro* includes the steps of high elevation, both leaping and travelling across the stage. The amount of force used to gain height should be disguised, and when alighting there should be no jarring throughout the body.

Apart from certain roles for girls, such as the Queen of the Wilis, or the ballerina role in the third movement of MacMillan's *Concerto*, steps of *grand allegro* are the forte of the male dancer.

It is almost impossible for a man to have a career in classical ballet unless he has mastered the full range of steps of *grand allegro*. The Russian school was for long the supreme exponent of this type of virtuosity. Today dancers throughout the world emulate its achievements but favourite virtuoso pieces for male dancers are still chosen from the old Russian repertory, for example, the *Corsaire* and *Don Quixote* pas de deux.

*Ann Kristin Hauge and Ib Andersen of the Royal Danish Ballet leaping joyously in the first act of Erik Bruhn's staging of Giselle.*

## Jetés

The word "*jeter*" means "to throw" and in these jumps the dancer throws one leg up, embarking upon a jump in which the weight of the body is thrown from one foot to the other. *Jetés* can vary from very small ones, barely skimming the floor, to the huge leaps of the *grand jeté*, in which the dancer soars to maximum height and lands with a minimum of noise on one foot.

Top: *Philip Broomhead in a* grand jeté *in a classroom at the Royal Ballet School.*

Bottom: *Colleen Neary, formerly of the New York City Ballet, in a* grand jeté *in Balanchine's* Serenade.

# Double Work

Double work (pas de deux) is not part of a ballet class but a separate course of study which should be embarked upon only when the boy and the girl have attained sufficient strength and understanding of their own physiques and technique.

During double work in classical ballets there should be dignity and assurance, and complete harmony of the bodies and minds of the two executants so that they seem to dance as one. No effort or strain should be shown and the interpreters of the choreography should be in sympathy with each other. This is only possible through many hours of rehearsal. Pas de deux is generally taught by male teachers who, during their dancing careers, have acquired the abilities to support and lift and understand the problems that must be overcome so that the male dancer can present the ballerina to the greatest effect.

*Sean Lavery and Merrill Ashley of the New York City Ballet in Balanchine's* The Four Temperaments.

Above left: *Raissa Struchkova in an exultant leap in the Bolshoi Ballet's spectacular* Moskowsky Waltz, *choreographed by Vasili Vainonen. Struchkova's feats of virtuosity in this pas de deux were made possible by the strength and security of the partnering by her husband Alexander Lapauri. At one moment in the dance she used to fly at him horizontally to be caught nonchalantly with one hand.*

Above right: *Philip Broomhead and Victoria Dyer practising together at the Royal Ballet School.*

Right: *Nadia Nerina and Erik Bruhn in the* Don Quixote *pas de deux.*

Above: *Philip Broomhead
and Victoria Dyer in a pose
from* Triad *by Kenneth
MacMillan.*

Right: *Antoinette Sibley
dances* Triad *with Anthony
Dowell.*

Students practice many of the lifts and poses they may later dance. Philip and Victoria are shown in positions from La Fille Mal Gardée *(opposite, top left) and* Swan Lake *(opposite, top right, and right)*.

Below: *Lesley Collier and David Wall in The Royal Ballet's production of MacMillan's* Manon.

One of the most effective theatrical feats of partnering is the "fish dive" in which the ballerina is supported by her partner with her weight on his knee.
**1** *Philip and Victoria show the fish dive in which Aurora concludes three of her pirouettes in the final pas de deux in* The Sleeping Beauty.
**2** *Merle Park and David Wall in the final pose of this pas de deux.*
**3** *Veronica Tennant and Raymond Smith in* Swan Lake.
**4** *Patricia McBride and Helgi Tomasson in* Le Baiser de la Fée.
**5** *Thérèse Thoreux and Cyril Atanasoff in* Concerto.
**6** *Nina Sorokina and Mikhail Lavrovsky in* Spartacus.

**1**

**4**

**6**

# THE
# CHOREOGRAPHERS
# AND THE STARS

*George Balanchine rehearses Mikhail Baryshnikov for* The Prodigal Son.

# The Choreographers

## Frederick Ashton
b. 1904
Cinderella;
The Dream; Enigma
Variations; Façade;
La Fille Mal Gardée;
Monotones I and II;
A Month in the
Country; Ondine;
Les Patineurs;
Les Rendezvous;
Rhapsody; Romeo and
Juliet; Scènes de Ballet;
Symphonic Variations;
The Two Pigeons;
A Wedding
Bouquet

It was Anna Pavlova who "injected the poison," as he puts it, in the veins of the little English boy who saw her in Lima, Peru, where she was touring and where he was then living. Ashton determined at that moment to become a great dancer. A conventional English schooling did not dissuade him and Ashton became a pupil of Massine and then of Marie Rambert.

By 1926 Rambert had—characteristically—goaded the young Frederick Ashton into making his first choreography. For her occasional Sunday performances, Ashton went on to stage more and more ballets. For a year, in 1928–29, he worked in the Ida Rubinstein Ballet, observing Nijinska as a choreographer and learning his craft from her. He returned to London and made his early ballets: *Façade, Capriol Suite, Les Rendezvous*. In 1935 he joined Ninette de Valois at the Sadler's Wells Theatre as choreographer and dancer: thereafter his ballets were vital in the forming of an English style of classical dancing.

His early muse had been Markova; in 1935 he found the young Margot Fonteyn and her career and his ballets became mutually inspiring. After war service he returned to his parent company, and with the installation at Covent Garden of the Sadler's Wells Ballet in 1946 he made *Symphonic Variations* and in 1948 *Cinderella*, the first three-act classical ballet by an English choreographer. His creativity, manifested in both his full-length ballets and his many one-act pieces, is intimately linked with The Royal Ballet's emergence as a great company.

## George Balanchine
b. 1904
Agon; Apollo; Ballo della
Regina; Chaconne;
Concerto Barocco; Duo
Concertant; Episodes; The
Four Temperaments;
Harlequinade; Jewels;
Kammermusik No. 2;
Liebeslieder Waltzer;
A Midsummer Night's
Dream; Mozartiana; The
Nutcracker; Orpheus;
Piano Concerto No. 2; The
Prodigal Son; Robert
Schumann's Davids-
bündlertänze; Serenade;
Stars and Stripes; The
Sleeping Beauty;
Stravinsky Violin Concerto;
Symphony in C; Symphony
in Three Movements;
Swan Lake; Tarantella;
Tchaikovsky Pas de Deux;
Tchaikovsky Suite No. 3;
Le Tombeau de Couperin;
Union Jack; La Valse;
Vienna Waltzes; Who Cares?

Born into a family of musicians—his father and brother were both composers—Balanchine's own musical studies continued when, after seven years at ballet school in Petrograd (the one-time Imperial Ballet School), he graduated into the State Ballet in 1921. This musical inheritance and education are central to Balanchine's achievement—he is the most musical of choreographers. A gifted dancer, he started choreographing while only eighteen. Two years later, in 1924, he quit Russia and joined Diaghilev as ballet master and dancer (though his dancing career was soon curtailed by injury). For Diaghilev he produced a series of ballets culminating in *Apollo* in 1928, in which he discovered his future as a creator, and *The Prodigal Son*. After Diaghilev's death, he worked in Paris and Copenhagen, in music hall, and then with the first season of the René Blum Ballet Russe de Monte Carlo.

In 1933 he was ballet master of the short-lived Les Ballets 1933. In that year he was invited by Lincoln Kirstein to start a school and a company in the United States: this represents the successful implanting of classical academic dance in the New World. For the first appearance of the American Ballet in 1934, he created *Serenade*. During the next decade he worked for the American Ballet and its successor companies, and also staged ballets for the Ballet Russe de Monte Carlo and worked successfully on Broadway and in Hollywood. In 1946 he and Lincoln Kirstein formed Ballet Society, the direct forerunner of the New York City Ballet, which was installed in 1948 at the New York City Center. In 1964 the company moved to the State Theater at Lincoln Center.

George Balanchine is the greatest choreographer of this century: a master of the neoclassic ballet, which he has developed for America from his own Imperial Ballet traditions. In the New York City Ballet we see the precise instrument, in training and temperament, which he has forged for his work. His ballets are danced by many companies—he is generous in allowing others to stage his work—but the New York City Ballet remains the only authentic exponent of them.

## Maurice Béjart
b. 1927
Bolero; The Firebird;

Intimately linked with the Ballet du XXième Siècle, a company based at the Théâtre Royal de la Monnaie in Brussels, Maurice Béjart was its director from 1960 to 1980. His years in Brussels have shown him as a choreographer with a vast appeal for a young, and often rebellious,

341

*Les Noces; Petrushka; The Rite of Spring*

public—one much concerned with the discovery of some form of spiritual renewal. Béjart has guided the fortunes of his troupe—which is exceptional for its dedication to his choreography—and brought it to vast international success, playing in huge sports halls and stadiums, in tents and circuses, and in other unconventional surroundings.

Béjart's ballets are concerned with a highly personal ideology, often mystical and flavoured with Hindu ideology. Such ballets as *Nijinsky, Clown of God* (about Nijinsky's madness), *Golestan* (a Persian extravaganza), *Trionfi* (a version of

Petrarch's poetic "triumphs"), and *Notre Faust* (an updating of the German legend); his versions of scores by Boulez, Mahler, and Wagner, and his highly individual realisations of such scores as Stravinsky's *Les Noces, Petrushka,* and *Firebird*; his versions of *Bolero* (Ravel) and *Gaîté Parisienne* (Offenbach), show him as a forceful theatrical character whose work inevitably invites mixed reception: critically admired in Europe, adored by the general public in Europe and almost wherever he plays, he is still much disliked by many professional observers. But he and his ballets and his dancers cannot be ignored.

## August Bournonville

*1805–1879*
*Far from Denmark; Flower Festival in Genzano; A Folk Tale; Kermesse in Bruges; Konservatoriet; Lifeguards of Amager; Napoli; La Sylphide; La Ventana*

Through his father, a distinguished French dancer, August Bournonville was linked to the traditions of the French eighteenth-century dance. This link was confirmed by a crucial period of study with Auguste Vestris between 1824 and 1829 in Paris, which shaped Bournonville for life. The Vestris school—which is the elegant French eighteenth-century school—remains the bedrock of Bournonville training and of Bournonville's attitudes to dance. In 1830 he was engaged as teacher, dancer, choreographer, and ballet master to the moribund Royal Danish Ballet. His career for the next forty-seven years was dedicated to the raising of this company and its dancers to a position of eminence and respectability.

The list of his ballets is long and represents many creations, from heroic studies of Nordic myths to historical works and the enchanting genre ballets which resulted from his extensive travelling. The comparative isolation of the ballet in Copenhagen meant that the Bournonville repertory and style were relatively unchanged across the years, and unlike the works of Perrot, Bournonville's ballets are still to be savoured in Copenhagen in something like authentic condition. Bournonville retired from active work in 1877 and died two years later, but not before he had witnessed the début of Hans Beck (1861–1952), who did much to edit and preserve the Bournonville inheritance.

## Lew Christensen

*b. 1909*
*Con Amore*

Lew Christensen was one of three brothers who eventually formed a dance dynasty in the American West. Before settling there, however, Christensen joined the Balanchine enterprise in New York. As a charter member of the American Ballet, he was, in 1937, the first American to perform Balanchine's *Apollo* and is commonly regarded as America's first native *premier danseur*. When Balanchine's associate Lincoln Kirstein formed Ballet Caravan in 1936, Christensen joined the new company and began choreographing. *Filling Station* (1938), one of several works he made for Ballet Caravan, became a classic Americana ballet. In the 1940s Christensen was a director of a small company called Dance Players, and he was a ballet master of the New York City Ballet in its early years.

The second chapter of Christensen's career began when he became artistic director of the San Francisco Ballet in 1952, replacing his brother Willam, who was to found Ballet West in Utah. (The third brother, Harold, was in charge of the San Francisco Ballet school.) For his company Christensen choreographed the comic *Con Amore* in 1953, and he has been making ballets for it ever since. His work reveals a sure flair for comedy and a refined sense of craftsmanship. In 1973, in an effort to bring new blood into the company, Christensen invited Michael Smuin to share the directorship of the San Francisco Ballet with him. Christensen still provides the company with some of its strongest works, however. A few of his most recent are *Don Juan, Scarlatti Portfolio*, and *Stravinsky Pas de Deux*.

## John Cranko

*1927–1973*
*Carmen; Onegin;*
*Pineapple Poll; Romeo and*
*Juliet; Swan Lake; The*
*Taming of the Shrew*

Early recognised as an exceptionally gifted and fluent creator, John Cranko made his first ballet while still a student in South Africa. With the end of the Second World War he, like many other Commonwealth dancers, came to London to study at the Sadler's Wells (now Royal) Ballet School. He joined the newly formed Sadler's Wells Theatre Ballet in 1946 and soon started choreographing. His early successes for this company, *Pineapple Poll* of 1951 among them, led to work with the main company at Covent Garden, and at the Sadler's Wells Theatre. In 1957 he made his first full-length work, *The Prince of the Pagodas*—a ballet distinguished by the fact that it was the first score created by a British composer (Benjamin Britten) for a full-length ballet.

Cranko created ballets for the New York City Ballet; the ballet of La Scala, Milan; Ballet Rambert; and the Paris Opéra Ballet, and produced revues

and dances for West End shows. His bubbling energies needed greater outlets than The Royal Ballet could offer and in 1961 he accepted the invitation to become director of the Stuttgart Ballet. That company he swiftly turned into the most creative and interesting in Germany, and under his leadership, and with such artists as Marcia Haydée, Ray Barra, Egon Madsen, Richard Cragun, and Birgit Keil, he guided it to huge international triumphs. He produced a series of full-length ballets—*Romeo and Juliet, Onegin, Carmen, The Taming of the Shrew*—as well as many shorter works, and he led his company with untiring zeal, inspiring intense love and devotion from his dancers. He died on the way back from a New York season. Cranko had an amazing gift for theatrically effective dance: his style could encompass plotless, dramatic, and avant-garde works, and he had an outstanding gift for comedy.

## Agnes de Mille

*b. 1909*
*Fall River Legend;*
*Rodeo*

A niece of the celebrated film director Cecil B. de Mille, Agnes de Mille came to London and studied with Marie Rambert (her descriptions of her first years in London are brilliantly evoked in her fine book of memoirs, *Dance to the Piper*). She became a close friend of Antony Tudor and Hugh Laing and participated in Tudor's ballets while making her own first choreographic essays as solos for herself. On her return to the United States in 1940 she joined the newly formed Ballet Theatre. Her great success came in

1942 when she staged *Rodeo* for the Ballet Russe de Monte Carlo. This led to further triumph for her dances in the musical *Oklahoma!* Thereafter she worked both with ballet companies and on Broadway. For American Ballet Theatre she has made many works over the years, among them *Fall River Legend*. On Broadway, she choreographed *Carousel, Brigadoon,* and *Paint Your Wagon,* and she has also worked for television and the cinema. Her choreography stresses the popular and folk elements in American art.

## Ninette de Valois

*b. 1898*
*Checkmate;*
*The Rake's Progress*

Her career as a child dancer began in 1914, and her wide range of dance experience culminated for Ninette de Valois in two years spent as a soloist with the Diaghilev ballet from 1923 to 1925. Thereafter she dedicated her energies to the preparing of the ground for the formation of a British national ballet. This she achieved, and in 1931 the opening of the Sadler's Wells Theatre as a home for de Valois' school and dancers marked the inception of today's Royal Ballet. De Valois was, among other things, its

choreographer. Her taste for vivid dramatic themes and her belief in the British dramatic and artistic traditions meant that many of her ballets are essentially English in feel, especially those surviving in today's repertory, *The Rake's Progress, Checkmate,* and *Job*. Though her greatest attainment must inevitably be The Royal Ballet organisation, the value and continuing theatrical life of her creations indicate the sound structure and the continuing vitality of her choreographic imagination.

## Eliot Feld

*b. 1943*
*Intermezzo*

Eliot Feld studied at the School of American Ballet, the academy of the New York City Ballet. He was one of the first little princes in Balanchine's *Nutcracker* and as a teenager appeared

in *West Side Story* and the Earl Robinson musical *Sandhog*. The dramatic talent he showed as a child was evident when he joined American Ballet Theatre in 1963, where he performed a superb *Billy the Kid* and *Fancy Free*.

Feld's career as a choreographer began as an overnight success story. Within the same year, 1967, he made two highly acclaimed ballets, *Harbinger* and *At Midnight*. In 1969 he left Ballet Theatre to from his own American Ballet Company. Two years later the company had to disband for financial reasons, and Feld went free-lance. In 1976 the Eliot Feld Ballet made its début, and it is still in operation. The troupe's repertory is devoted almost exclusively to Feld's ballets. His works range from the lyric (*Intermezzo*) to the comic (*Half Time*) to the melancholy (*At Midnight*). Most of his ballets have moods rather than stories, and are obviously inspired by music, which is usually of high caliber.

## Mikhail Fokine
### 1880–1942
*Cinderella; The Dying Swan; The Firebird; Petrushka; Prince Igor; Schéhérazade; Le Spectre de la Rose; Les Sylphides*

His gifts destined Mikhail Fokine for an illustrious career as a *premier danseur* with the Imperial Ballet at the Maryinsky Theatre, which he entered in 1898, but he soon became disillusioned by its hidebound attitudes of performance and choreography. A man of exceptional gifts, a musician and painter, and of great intelligence, Fokine was dismayed by the sterile and stereotyped manner of the ballet in the closing years of Petipa's long reign. He sought to initiate change in ballet making, first by presenting appeals for reform to the directorate of the Imperial Ballet. More practically, he initiated these reforms in his first choreographic attempts, and with *Le Pavillon d'Armide*, in 1907, and the version of *Chopiniana* which he made for his students at the Imperial Ballet School, he suggested new developments in choreographic manner.

But it was the first Diaghilev ballet seasons with which his name will forever be associated. In Fokine's choreography Diaghilev was to find the innovations in ballet making that were needed for his danced assault upon Paris in 1909. Fokine provided the choreography. The innovations in design and music which were to follow—in the work of Benois, Bakst, Stravinsky—were fired by the same concern for greater truth, greater expressiveness, greater poetic force which marked Fokine's work. With *Schéhérazade* and *Firebird* in 1910 (his first two creations for Diaghilev after the *Prince Igor* Polovtsian Dances of the 1909 season), Fokine showed the power of the new ballet. Thereafter he was to create *Petrushka*, *Le Spectre de la Rose*, *Daphnis and Chloe*, *Narcisse*, and other works which were the choreographic backbone of the first and glorious Diaghilev seasons.

The rupture with Diaghilev came when Fokine discovered that Nijinsky was being promoted and fostered as a choreographer. On Nijinsky's dismissal, in 1913, he returned temporarily to the Ballets Russes but this was a mere stopgap and the declaration of war in 1914 ended his association with the company. He continued to work in Petrograd but, disappointed in his hopes for a further career in Russia, he left in 1918. Between that date and his death he worked extensively in the United States, dancing, staging spectacles, and teaching. He revived many of his great successes from the Diaghilev era but, with a few exceptions, his later choreographic career was less than satisfying. For the Ballet Russe companies of the 1930s and for Ballet Theatre he revised and revived ballets and also created such pieces as *Paganini*, *Les Elfes*, *Don Juan*, and *L'Épreuve d'Amour*. His last ballet was *Bluebeard*. *Helen of Troy*, unfinished at the time of his death, was completed (for Ballet Theatre) by David Lichine.

## Yuri Grigorovich
### b. 1927
*Ivan the Terrible; The Nutcracker; Romeo and Juliet; Spartacus; The Stone Flower; Swan Lake*

A product of the Leningrad Kirov school and company—in which he danced character roles—Grigorovich made his earliest choreographic success in 1957 with a production for the Kirov Ballet of Prokofiev's *The Stone Flower*. He next produced choreography for *Legend of Love*: in both these works his ability to extend the manner of the full-length ballet, in the context of the Soviet ballet, was much admired. Named a ballet master in Leningrad in 1962, he was transferred to Moscow (where his *Stone Flower* had already been produced) as chief choreographer and ballet master to the Bolshoi Ballet in succession to Leonid Lavrovsky. For that company he has restaged the classical repertory—*Swan Lake*, *Nutcracker*, *The Sleeping*

*Beauty*—and produced a sequence of blockbuster balletic spectaculars initiated by his vastly successful *Spartacus* in 1968. *Ivan the Terrible*, *Angara*, and *Romeo and Juliet* are among his ballets of the 1970s. *Ivan* and *Romeo* have been staged at the Paris Opéra.

His choreographic manner, contrasting hugely energetic work for the corps de ballet with more intimate and introspective writing for his heroes (Ivan, Spartacus), is a formula which has earned him great acclaim in Russia and in some Western countries. He is married to the ballerina Natalia Bessmertnova.

## Robert Joffrey
*b. 1930*
*Pas des Déesses*

Born Abdulla Jaffa Anver Bey Khan, Robert Joffrey grew up in Seattle and studied dance there with the well-known teacher Mary Ann Wells before coming to New York. From early childhood he had always wanted to direct his own ballet company, and in 1954 he did so: the Robert Joffrey Ballet Concert. Since then Joffrey's company has changed its name several times and has undergone financial upheavals, but several important factors have remained constant. The dancers have always been drawn from Joffrey's school, the American Ballet Center; Gerald Arpino has always been a close associate, first as dancer and then as resident choreographer; and Joffrey has always been in charge of artistic policy. The responsibilities of this position have taken increasing precedence over choreography, but the quality of his work makes up for the scarcity of his output. His most famous ballet is *Astarte* (1967), because it coincided with and encapsulated the mania for psychedelic, mixed-media theatre. Other of his earlier works, such as *Gamelan*, *Pierrot Lunaire*, and *Persephone*, are remembered for their musicality and originality. His most recent work for the Joffrey Ballet was *Postcards* (1980), to the boulevard music of Erik Satie.

Joffrey is primarily known now as the talent scout *par excellence*. He is active in the regional ballet movement, always on the lookout for talented students. And he has a passion for reconstructing lost or rarely seen classics of the twentieth century by such choreographers as Massine, Jooss, and Ashton.

## Jiří Kylián
*b. 1947*
*Soldier's Mass;*
*Symphony of Psalms*

After studies in his native Prague, Jiří Kylián came to work at the Royal Ballet School in London and joined the Stuttgart Ballet in 1968, where he began to choreograph. He was invited to become artistic director of the Nederlands Dans Theater in 1976 and for that company has produced a considerable body of work, many of his ballets marked by the highly demanding and energetic choreographic style which he has developed in recent years.

## Harald Lander
*1905–1971*
*Etudes*

A pupil of the Royal Danish Ballet School, and of Hans Beck, Harald Lander was a distinguished character dancer who studied in Russia, the United States, and Mexico and worked with Fokine before returning, in 1930, to Copenhagen. That year he was appointed ballet master at the Royal Theatre, and in 1932 head of the Royal Danish Ballet School. His works were part of a renaissance of the Danish ballet. Under him, too, the Bournonville repertory was much revised and revitalised. In 1952 he left Denmark and worked in Paris, where he directed the Opéra Ballet School. He also staged his ballets for companies in Europe and America. He returned to Copenhagen in 1962 to reinstate some of his ballets to the repertory. His best-known work is *Etudes*.

## Leonid Lavrovsky
*1905–1967*
*Romeo and Juliet*

A product of the school in Petrograd (the former Imperial Ballet School), Leonid Lavrovsky joined the company and began teaching and choreographing early in his career. His earliest full-length ballets were *Fadetta* (1934) and *Caterina* (1935). He became director of the Maly Theatre in Leningrad in 1935, then proceeded to the Kirov (the former Maryinsky) Theatre as director in 1938, where he remained until invited to Moscow to direct the Bolshoi Ballet (1945–56, 1960–64). In Leningrad he created some of the most influential Soviet ballets: *Prisoner of the Caucasus* (1938) and *Romeo and Juliet* (1940). His stagings of the classics in Moscow—notably his *Giselle* (1944)—set standards for sensitive dramatic production; he also produced short ballets, notably

*Paganini* in 1960. He was appointed director of the Bolshoi Ballet School in 1964 and died in Paris while on tour with his Moscow students. His son, Mikhail, is a leading dancer with the Bolshoi Ballet.

## David Lichine
### 1910–1972
### Graduation Ball

Lichine made his début as a dancer in Paris with Ida Rubinstein's company and worked briefly with Pavlova's company. But it was the formation of The Blum–de Basil Ballet Russe de Monte Carlo which brought David Lichine to fame. In this company, noted for the strength of its male dancing, he created many important roles and by 1933 had started to make ballets. For the Ballet Russe he created many works—notably *Francesca da Rimini* and *Graduation Ball*. With his wife, Tatiana Riabouchinska (one of the three "baby ballerinas" of the

1930s), he joined Ballet Theatre and later worked in South America. He returned to Europe in 1948, when he created two important works for the Ballets des Champs-Elysées: *La Création* (a ballet performed in silence) and *La Rencontre*, a retelling of the myth of Oedipus' encounter with the Sphinx. He worked with several companies thereafter, staging *Graduation Ball* and a production of *The Nutcracker* for London Festival Ballet. He taught with his wife in Los Angeles until his death.

## Serge Lifar
### b. 1905
### The Firebird;
### Suite en Blanc

A pupil of Nijinska in Kiev (where he was born), Serge Lifar took his fate in his own hands when he decided to accompany a group of three other young dancers who were invited from Kiev to join Nijinska with Diaghilev's Ballets Russes. Hardly trained, Lifar attracted attention by his physical beauty and his enthusiasm. Placed by Diaghilev under the tutelage of Enrico Cecchetti, the young man became an outstanding dancer and Diaghilev's last protégé. For Lifar, roles were made in ten ballets during the last four years of the company's existence, when he was named a *premier danseur* of the troupe. He was the first Apollo and Balanchine's first Prodigal Son.

In 1929, Lifar made his first ballet, producing a version of *Renard* for the Diaghilev enterprise. With Diaghilev's death and the disbanding of the company, Lifar was invited to the Paris Opéra, as *premier danseur étoile* and ballet master. He remained there from 1929 until 1945, returning in 1947 for another ten years' service as ballet master. He revitalised the Paris Opéra Ballet, creating a great number of works, some of them full-length: *Joan de Zarisse, Alexandre le Grand, David*

*Triomphant, Le Chevalier et la Demoiselle*. He rehabilitated the male dancer through his own exultantly glamorous example, invited many distinguished ballerinas to work with him in Paris (Semyonova, Spessivtseva, Vyroubova), and encouraged generations of French ballerinas, including Darsonval, Chauviré, and many more. A tireless publicist for dance, he has also written many books and polemical works, as well as historical surveys. His choreography at its finest has a neoclassic dignity and a rhetorical energy.

In 1944, after his wartime efforts to preserve the work of the Opéra Ballet, he left, accused of collaboration. Reinstated in 1947, he worked for another ten years at the Opéra. After his departure, the Opéra sadly lacked any positive or consistent and continuous identity. Lifar was an outstanding dancer—a great (if overdominant) Albrecht, a superb figure in his own ballets, which were much more than vehicles for his own gifts. For thirty years Lifar was synonymous with ballet in France: without him, French ballet seems still to lack focus.

## Eugene Loring
### b. 1914
### Billy the Kid

A product of the School of American Ballet, Eugene Loring danced with Mikhail Fokine's company during its seasons in New York and then joined the Kirstein-Balanchine American

Ballet when it was first formed in 1935. For Kirstein's Ballet in Caravan, Loring made several ballets, notably *Yankee Clipper* and *Billy the Kid*. When, in 1940, he joined the newly formed

Ballet Theatre, he staged *Billy the Kid* for that company, which still dances it today. He worked on Broadway and with his own ensemble and then moved to California and worked in Hollywood, where he staged dances for films. He taught at, and later became chairman of, the Dance Department at the University of California, Irvine.

## Kenneth MacMillan
b. 1929
*Anastasia; Concerto; Elite Syncopations; La Fin du Jour; Las Hermanas; The Invitation; Isadora; Manon; Mayerling; Requiem; The Rite of Spring; Romeo and Juliet; Song of the Earth*

A product of the Sadler's Wells School, Kenneth MacMillan joined the Sadler's Wells Theatre Ballet as one of its first members in 1946. After some workshop successes, he made his first professional choreography for that company in 1955 with *Danses Concertantes*. He followed this with several other successful works staged both for the Theatre Ballet and the Sadler's Wells Ballet at Covent Garden. With *The Burrow* in 1958 and *Le Baiser de la Fée* in 1960 he started an association with Lynn Seymour, who became his muse. Thereafter he remained chiefly associated with the Covent Garden troupe, producing such works as *The Invitation* (1961) and *The Rite of Spring* (1962), and culminating in his *Romeo and Juliet* in 1965, written for Seymour and Christopher Gable.

In 1966 he went to Berlin as director of the Deutsche Oper Ballet, returning in 1970 to become director of The Royal Ballet, a post he held for seven years. During this time he continued to produce a great many ballets, including *Anastasia* and *Manon*. In 1978, following his resignation as director of The Royal Ballet, he staged *Mayerling*, and he continues as principal choreographer to the company. He has worked also for the Stuttgart Ballet, for whom he made *Song of the Earth, Requiem*, and *My Brother, My Sisters*. His ballets are noted for their concern with the psychology of character, as well as with extending the possibilities of the classical academic style.

## Leonide Massine
1895–1979
*La Boutique Fantasque; Mam'zelle Angot; Parade; The Rite of Spring; The Three-Cornered Hat*

Born into a theatrical family in Moscow, Leonide Massine studied at the Theatre School there and performed in both plays and ballets. He was seen by Diaghilev in 1913 at the time when the great impresario was in search of a young dancer to take the role of Joseph in the projected Strauss-Fokine *Legend of Joseph*—as a replacement for Nijinsky, whom Diaghilev had just dismissed. Massine joined Diaghilev and embarked upon a career that was to significantly influence Western ballet. When war broke out in 1914, Diaghilev and various collaborators remained in Western Europe. The Ballets Russes was dispersed, but Diaghilev started afresh with Massine as dancer and choreographer: he found in this young artist a brilliant intelligence and great theatrical skill, which he was to guide. With *Parade* and *The Good-Humoured Ladies* in 1917, Massine made two of his early successes. He followed them with *La Boutique Fantasque* and *The Three-Cornered Hat* in 1919, which received their premières in London after the Ballets Russes, having managed to survive the war, had come to the city to initiate a new era of the Diaghilev ballet. In Massine's work could be seen the vivid theatricality that was so much his, both as dancer and choreographer. He split from Diaghilev in 1921 following his marriage to Vera Savina. He was to return intermittently thereafter to create other ballets, but his great years came in the 1930s when, after the death of Diaghilev and the dissolution of the Ballets Russes, the revival of the expatriate Russian ballet under René Blum and Colonel de Basil brought Massine to a position of unrivalled supremacy as choreographer and dancer (mainly in his own works). He choreographed the series of "symphonic" ballets—to such scores as Tchaikovsky's Fifth Symphony, Brahms's Fourth Symphony, Berlioz's Symphonie Fantastique, and Beethoven's Seventh Symphony—which were the sensations of their time.

During the Second World War Massine worked in the United States, first with the Ballet Russe de Monte Carlo, then with Ballet Theatre (for whom he staged *Mam'zelle Angot*). In 1946 he returned to Europe. His later career was spent in creating new ballets and reviving his earlier triumphs, notably for The Royal Ballet and London Festival Ballet, whose repertories include *Le Beau Danube, Parade, Gaîté Parisienne, La Boutique Fantasque, The Three-Cornered Hat*, and *Mam'zelle Angot*.

## John Neumeier
### b. 1942

Trained in America and Britain, John Neumeier worked with Cranko's Stuttgart Ballet as a dancer and made his first ballets there in the late 1960s. He became director of the Frankfurt Ballet in 1969 for four very successful years, moving from there in 1973 to Hamburg, where he has directed the ballet with success, producing many works for his own company and also staging them for American Ballet Theatre, the Royal Danish Ballet, and the National Ballet of Canada. His versions of established classics and older repertory works are marked by considerable intellectual interest, notably his *Nutcracker, Swan Lake, The Sleeping Beauty, The Legend of Joseph*, and *Romeo and Juliet*.

## Bronislava Nijinska
### 1891–1972
### Les Biches; Les Noces

Sister of Vaslav Nijinsky, Bronislava Nijinska entered the Imperial Ballet School in St. Petersburg in 1900 and graduated into the ballet company of the Maryinsky Theatre. She joined the first Diaghilev Russian season in 1909 and participated in the later seasons until her brother was dismissed by Diaghilev. She then returned to Russia in 1914 and opened a school in Kiev the following year. She returned to Diaghilev in 1921 to dance in his celebrated *Sleeping Princess* and also provided some choreography for that staging, notably the dance of the Three Ivans.

Without a choreographer following Massine's departure, Diaghilev invited Nijinska to prepare the choreography for Stravinsky's *Renard* in 1922. Satisfied that he had discovered another creative talent, Diaghilev entrusted her with *Les Noces* in 1923. In the following years she created *Les Biches, Les Fâcheux*, and *Le Train Bleu*. After this she left Diaghilev and her later career found her working in South America, in Paris for Ida Rubinstein (whose chief choreographer she was for some seasons) and for de Basil's Ballet Russe de Monte Carlo (*Les Cent Baisers*), and in England for the Markova-Dolin Ballet. She spent the war years in the United States; thereafter she was ballet mistress for the de Cuevas company for a time, restaging some of her ballets. Her importance as a choreographer was reaffirmed when, in 1964 and 1966, she revived *Les Biches* and *Les Noces* for The Royal Ballet. Ashton has constantly paid tribute to her influence upon his career as a choreographer.

## Vaslav Nijinsky
### 1888 (or 1889)–1950
### L'Après-midi d'un Faune; The Rite of Spring

Born in Kiev, when his dancer parents were on tour, Nijinsky entered the Imperial Ballet School in St. Petersburg in 1898 and graduated in 1907. His exceptional gifts as a technician—notably his extraordinary elevation—earned him early success and fame. But it was his participation in the first Diaghilev Russian season in Paris in 1909 which decided his fate. He was shown off in this and the subsequent seasons as a dancer of genius. The Favourite Slave in *Le Pavillon d'Armide*, the Poet in *Les Sylphides*, the Golden Slave in *Schéhérazade*, Harlequin in *Carnaval*, and the title roles in *Le Spectre de la Rose* and *Petrushka* all revealed his genius—exotic, often otherworldly, thrillingly perceptive in dramatic intensity, and technically amazing. But Diaghilev, who loved him, also intended him to be a choreographer of ballets as "new" and forward-looking as his dancing. Hence he choreographed *L'Après-midi d'un Faune*; then *Jeux*; then *The Rite of Spring* for the Diaghilev company. These are the first truly innovative ballets of the twentieth century—more so than Fokine's. The walking steps of *Faune*; the mystery of *Jeux*, in its contemporary setting; the primitivism and total rejection of classical dance in *Rite*, all suggest the new dance to go with the "new" music. Nijinsky's break with Diaghilev, following his marriage, was never mended.

Nijinsky was freed from wartime internment through high-powered intervention, and he went to join the Diaghilev company on its two ill-managed visits to the United States in 1916–17. Here he choreographed his last ballet, *Tyl Eulenspiegel*. But the varied and oppressive tensions imposed by his need to work away from Diaghilev, his marriage, and the strain of mental instability in his family brought about the onset of madness, which ended his career as a choreographer and dancer in 1917. He died in London in 1950.

## Jules Perrot

*1810–1892*
*La Corsaire;*
*Giselle; Ondine*

Born into a theatrical family—Perrot's father was chief machinist at the theatre in Lyon—the young Jules started his theatrical career as a comic and "grotesque" dancer. In his teens he abandoned a successful career in the boulevard theatres of Paris to work with the greatest teacher of the period, Auguste Vestris. It was Vestris who shaped him as an amazing virtuoso dancer of excellent style, urging upon his pupil a manner of the greatest aerial brillance (in part because Perrot was no beauty, and Vestris urged him to "jump about, turn, move around, but never give the public time to look at you closely").

Perrot appeared with Marie Taglioni and won a public acclaim which slightly annoyed that divinity. In 1835 he quit the Paris Opéra, where he had danced for five years, and set out on a tour of Europe, appearing in his own ballets. In Naples he met a very young dancer, Carlotta Grisi. She became his pupil and his mistress and he developed her talent to such effect that in 1840 they appeared together in Paris and had a great success. The following year, Carlotta made her début at the Opéra. *Giselle* was soon afterward staged for her, with Perrot responsible for most of Carlotta's choreography.

Disappointed in hopes of returning to the Opéra himself, Perrot went to London, and between 1842 and 1848 he staged many important ballets at Her Majesty's Theatre. These included *Alma, Ondine, Le Délire d'un Peintre, La Esmeralda, Eoline, Catarina, Lalla Rookh*, and the celebrated divertissements which showed off the great Romantic ballerinas: *Pas de Quatre, The Judgement of Paris, The Elements*, and *The Four Seasons*.

Perrot's ballets are some of the most significant works of the Romantic era, through their dramatic and expressive qualities. In 1848 Perrot was invited to St. Petersburg, where he remained for a decade, reviving some of his London triumphs and staging new works. What little choreography by Perrot now remains is thanks to this Russian sojourn, for some fragments have been preserved there. In 1859 he returned to Western Europe, but the decline of public interest in ballet meant that he was no longer in demand as a choreographer, though he continued to teach—and he can be seen as an old gentleman in Degas' paintings of the ballet classes at the Paris Opéra. He retired to the country and died in Brittany.

## Marius Petipa

*1818–1910*
*La Bayadère;*
*Cinderella; Coppélia;*
*Don Quixote; Giselle;*
*Paquita; Raymonda;*
*The Sleeping Beauty;*
*Swan Lake*

Born into a family of dancers—his father, Jean, was a choreographer; his elder brother Lucien a favourite *premier danseur* (and later a choreographer) of the Romantic period, the first Albrecht in *Giselle*—Marius Petipa travelled and worked throughout Europe and visited the United States, dancing and making his first choreographic essays. In 1847 he went to St. Petersburg, as a *premier danseur*. Here he worked with Jules Perrot and then with Saint-Léon. His ambition was to become a choreographer and ballet master to the Imperial Ballet, and with the success of his first full-length ballet (*Pharaoh's Daughter*, 1862) this was achieved. Until 1869 he worked as second ballet master, and on Saint-Léon's departure Marius Petipa became responsible for the choreography of the Imperial Ballet, both in Petersburg and Moscow.

His achievement from 1869 until 1903, when he was forced to retire, was the creation of a tradition of grand, spectacular ballets, plus the revising of previous productions and the staging of shorter ballets for special occasions. His ballets were built to a formula of splendid complexity, redeemed and illumined by his skill as a creator of dramatic scenes and his power to produce formally brilliant and thrilling dances. *La Bayadère, The Sleeping Beauty*, the two court acts of *Swan Lake*, the grand pas in *Paquita, Raymonda*, and his revision of *Giselle* all stand today as his permanent memorial. His creations were complex, using all the forces of a company whose greatness he fostered.

In 1903, after the failure of his ballet *The Magic Mirror*, he was retired. He died in the Crimea in 1910. Petipa is the supreme exponent of the classical ballet of the nineteenth century. The style of dancing which he encouraged in Russia was a combination of French elegance and Italianate virtuosity, both developed and extended by Russian taste and temperament.

## Roland Petit
b. 1924
Carmen; Coppélia;
Le Loup

A product of the Paris Opéra Ballet School, Roland Petit was a leading member of that generation of French dancers who seceded from the Opéra at the time of the Liberation of Paris in 1944. Petit was the key figure in the activities which led in 1945 to the birth of Les Ballets des Champs-Elysées, with Cocteau, Bérard, and Kochno as godfathers. For three years Petit and the company amazed and delighted Europe with Petit's choreography—Les Forains, Le Jeune Homme et la Mort, and many more—and the superb dancers, headed by Nina Vyroubova and Jean Babilée. Petit left in 1948 to form the Ballets de Paris; from this time dates his artistic association (and marriage) with Zizi Jeanmaire, which produced Carmen as its most famous choreographic achievement.

Petit maintained his troupe across the years, always staging ballets for it, but his interest also took him into music hall, cinema, and Broadway, besides his work for other companies, such as The Royal Ballet and the ballets of the Paris Opéra and La

Scala. His work is always infused by his lively sense of theatre and embellished by his constantly admirable visual taste. The designers who have worked for him are the most distinguished of the age; his ballets have also launched great designers and set examples for other companies to copy, in the work of Antoni Clavé, Tom Keogh, and Paul Delvaux.

Since 1972 Petit has been head of the Ballet de Marseille—a company which he has made second in importance only to the Opéra in France, and which has toured with his ballets worldwide. He has created full-length works—Notre Dame de Paris, Cyrano de Bergerac, Le Fantôme de l'Opéra, Les Intermittences du Coeur—as well as a great number of short ballets. He has produced interesting revisions of established classics, such as The Nutcracker and Coppélia; made choreography for films; staged shows starring Jeanmaire at the Casino de Paris; and created ballets to show off such stars as Plisetskaya and Baryshnikov. He is a wonderfully gifted entertainer.

## Jerome Robbins
b. 1918
Afternoon of a Faun;
The Cage; The Concert;
Dances at a Gathering;
Fancy Free; The Goldberg
Variations; Les Noces;
Other Dances

After his first dance experiences in Broadway musicals, Jerome Robbins joined American Ballet Theatre at its inception in 1940, in which company he soon began to dance leading character roles. In 1944, with Leonard Bernstein, he created his first ballet, Fancy Free, whose immense success launched a career which has encompassed choreography both for ballet companies and for Broadway shows. He became director and/or choreographer of such smash hits as On the Town, The King and I, Gypsy, Funny Girl, and Fiddler on the Roof. His West Side Story of 1957, in which he again collaborated with Bernstein, opened new vistas for the musical as a form of dance drama. His earliest successes as a ballet choreographer included works made during 1950–59 when he was associate director of the New York City Ballet: The Cage, The Pied Piper, Age of Anxiety, Afternoon of a Faun, The Concert.

He formed his own company, Ballets: U.S.A., in 1958 for a series of tours which were more successful in Europe than in the United States. For this company he staged Moves (danced in silence), and New York Export: Opus Jazz. In these as in much of his other work he showed how the "popular" forms of dance and behaviour could be incorporated into the formal language of theatre dance. After a period in which he devoted much of his time to research into a multimedia theatrical form, he returned to classical ballet and to the New York City Ballet with Dances at a Gathering in 1969. Since then, his ballets have been an important part of the repertory of this company, of which he is a ballet master. He has shown himself able to create both in the bright and energetic language of the popular theatre and for the classically exact forms of the academic dance.

## Glen Tetley
b. 1926

A late-comer to dancing, Tetley's choreographic style seems dictated by the fact that he studied both classical and contemporary dance as a mature student, and there resulted from this a

willingness to use both forms and to amalgamate them in his work. He danced with various companies, including the Martha Graham company and Ballet Theatre, during

*Pierrot Lunaire; The Rite of Spring; Voluntaries*

the 1950s. His earliest success as a choreographer was in 1962 with *Pierrot Lunaire*. That same year he came to Europe, joining the Nederlands Dans Theater as a dancer and choreographer. For that company he made many ballets, including *The Anatomy Lesson, Sargasso,* and *Circles*. At the same time he was influential in helping to reshape the identity of Ballet Rambert, providing that company with several new works to strengthen its new image as a contemporary troupe—*Ziggurat, Free Fall, Embrace Tiger and Return to Mountain,* and *Rag Dances*—as well as reviving *Pierrot* and *Ricercare*. He staged ballets elsewhere in Europe and the United States and in 1974 was invited to direct the Stuttgart Ballet. He remained there for three years, creating *Voluntaries, Daphnis and Chloe,* and *Greening,* among other works. For The Royal Ballet he has created *Field Figures, Laborintus,* and *Dances of Albion,* and he made *Contredances* for Natalia Makarova and Anthony Dowell at American Ballet Theatre.

## Twyla Tharp
### b. 1942
### As Time Goes By; Push Comes to Shove

Twyla Tharp grew up in California, where she spent much time riding in cars and listening to the radio. She also took lessons in everything. Coming to New York to attend Barnard College, she studied dance with everybody. She was with the Paul Taylor company from 1963 to 1965 and then left to make dances of her own. Her first works were conceptual, experimental, and on the small-audience circuit. The Tharp style as one knows it today began in 1971 with *Eight Jelly Rolls*. Set to piano rags by Jelly Roll Morton, it was the first of her many dances to use popular American music as a way to analyse social mores and gesture in a rhythmically interesting way. Tharp invented a more or less new way of dancing, incorporating and then distorting elements of social dance with the speed and precision of ballet technique.

Tharp's popularity began to grow, and she became a celebrity of sorts when she made *Deuce Coupe* for the Joffrey Ballet in 1973. Her own company then expanded and has had tremendous popular as well as critical success. In 1980 the Twyla Tharp Dance Company was on Broadway for three weeks.

While maintaining a repertory for her own group, Tharp has continued to work in as varied a context as possible. She has made two other dances for the Joffrey, *Push Comes to Shove* for American Ballet Theatre, some solos for the ice skater John Curry, a dance for a football player, and choreography for the movie version of *Hair*. She is quite a marvellous dancer too.

## Antony Tudor
### b. 1908
### Dark Elegies; Echoing of Trumpets; Jardin aux Lilas; Pillar of Fire; Romeo and Juliet

Another of the exceptional generation of dancer-choreographers shaped by Marie Rambert in her Ballet Club in London during the early 1930s, Antony Tudor was a student, then assistant, in the Rambert School. He staged his first ballets in 1931. Five years later he made one of his early masterpieces, *Jardin aux Lilas*, following this in 1937 with *Dark Elegies*.

He formed his own, short-lived small company, the London Ballet, in 1938, but in 1940 accepted an invitation to go to the United States to work with the newly formed American Ballet Theatre. For them he created *Pillar of Fire, Romeo and Juliet,* and several other major works. By 1948 he was working with the Royal Swedish Ballet; from 1951–52 he was with the New York City Ballet; and thereafter he spent much time as a teacher in New York, at the Metropolitan Opera and the Juilliard School. He choreographed *Echoing of Trumpets* for the Royal Swedish Ballet in 1963 and returned to his native land in 1967–68 to stage *Shadowplay* for The Royal Ballet and *Knight Errant* for its touring company.

He returned to American Ballet Theatre as an associate director in 1974 and created for that company *The Leaves Are Fading* and *Tiller in the Fields*. His ballets are staged by many companies. His choreography at its finest provides a profoundly moving depiction of human suffering, mental and physical, and his dance language has been most skilled in the revealing of the innermost feelings and torments of the human psyche.

# The Stars

This list of some of the world's principal dancers inevitably is not comprehensive. Many fine artists have of necessity been excluded, and the biographies are brief. Promotions and retirements will necessarily make any list impermanent. Our hope has been to give some slight indication of the wealth of today's dance talent.

### Ib Andersen
*Born Copenhagen, 1954*

Ib Andersen trained at the Royal Danish School and entered the Royal Danish Ballet in 1973. An ebullient and brilliant soloist with that company; he joined the New York City Ballet in 1979, rapidly assuming many roles in the Balanchine repertory as well as creating roles in ballets by Balanchine and Peter Martins.

### Merrill Ashley
*Born St. Paul, Minnesota, 1950*

Merrill Ashley studied at the School of American Ballet and joined the New York City Ballet in 1967. A gradual development of a now prodigious technique brought her to principal dancer status in 1978. In Ashley's dancing we see a dazzling display of speed, musicality, darting energy, and attack. In two recent but contrasting works, *Ballo della Regina* and *Ballade*, Balanchine has shown a further extension of Ashley's gifts both in dizzying precision and in lyricism.

### Frank Augustyn
*Born Hamilton, Ontario, 1953*

Frank Augustyn studied at the school of the National Ballet of Canada and joined the company in 1970. Three years later his developing partnership with Karen Kain received the accolade of the gold medal for the best couple at the Moscow International Ballet Competition. With Kain, he has danced leading roles in the classical and modern repertories. In 1980 he took a leave of absence to dance in Berlin.

### Patrice Bart
*Born Paris, 1945*

Patrice Bart studied at the Paris Opéra Ballet School and entered the company in 1959. Winner of the gold medal at the first Moscow International Ballet Competition in 1969, Bart was nominated *étoile* at the Opéra in 1972. A dancer of bright technique, Bart has danced frequently with London Festival Ballet. His repertory encompasses both traditional roles and modern works.

### Mikhail Baryshnikov
*Born Riga, Latvia, 1948*

Mikhail Baryshnikov began his dance studies in his native city and then went to the Kirov School in Leningrad, where the great formative influence upon him was Alexander Pushkin.

He entered the Kirov Ballet in 1967 and at once attracted great public attention by the beauty and effortless brilliance of his classic style. He made his first Western appearance in London in 1970 and four years later, while on tour in Canada, chose to remain in the West. He became a principal dancer with American Ballet Theatre and spent almost a year working with the New York City Ballet, and in 1980 assumed the directorship of American Ballet Theatre.

### Natalia Bessmertnova
*Born Moscow, 1941*

Natalia Bessmertnova studied at the Bolshoi School and entered the Ballet Company in 1961. She leapt to fame as the Autumn Fairy in *Cinderella*, and thereafter danced all the classical and modern heroines of the Bolshoi repertory. A dancer of exquisite line with a gazelle-like jump, she has been a guest artist in many countries.

## Patrick Bissell
*Born Corpus Christi, Texas, 1958*

Patrick Bissell studied at the North Carolina School of the Arts and at the School of American Ballet. After appearances with the Boston Ballet, Bissell joined American Ballet Theatre in 1977, where he was promoted to soloist in 1978 and to principal in 1979. He has appeared as a guest artist with the National Ballet of Canada and has made numerous guest appearances throughout the United States and abroad.

## Paolo Bortoluzzi
*Born Genoa, 1938*

After private studies with such teachers as Nora Kiss and Asaf Messerer, Bortoluzzi made his début in 1957 at the Nervi Festival. For a decade thereafter he was a star of the Béjart company, creating many roles. Since 1972 he has made an international career with such companies as American Ballet Theatre and the Vienna State Opera Ballet.

## Fernando Bujones
*Born Miami, 1955*

Fernando Bujones was a product of the School of American Ballet, but he joined American Ballet Theatre in 1972. He was made a principal two years later and has remained with that company ever since, dancing all the classical repertory, which he illuminates with an exemplary technical prowess.

## Olga Chenchikova
*Born Moscow, 1956*

Olga Chenchikova studied in Perm and joined the ballet company there in 1974. In December 1977, Chenchikova was invited to join the Kirov Ballet, where she has been revealed as a ballerina of radiant youthful assurance and impeccable schooling.

## Lesley Collier
*Born London, 1947*

Lesley Collier studied at the Royal Ballet School and graduated into the company in 1965. A dancer of sparkling technique and speed, she has a wide range, from the traditional classics to a large contemporary repertory of works by Ashton, MacMillan, and Tetley.

## Bart Cook
*Born Ogden, Utah, 1949*

Bart Cook studied with Willam Christensen in Salt Lake City and won a scholarship to the School of American Ballet. He joined the New York City Ballet in 1971 and was soon entrusted with important roles. A dancer of great musicality, he excels in *demi-caractère* work, as in *Vienna Waltzes* and as a sailor in *Fancy Free*. In *The Four Temperaments* he gives a superlative performance in the Melancholic section.

## Richard Cragun
*Born Sacramento, California, 1944*

Richard Cragun studied at the Royal Ballet School and joined the Stuttgart Ballet in 1962. His virtuosity swiftly won him principal rank in the company and many roles were created for him by Cranko, notably *Opus 1*, Petruchio in *The Taming of the Shrew* (in which he is one of the few dancers to perform triple *tours en l'air*), and *Initials R.B.M.E.* He and Marcia Haydée have enjoyed a famous and successful dance partnership.

## Jacques d'Amboise
*Born Dedham, Massachussetts, 1934*

Jacques d'Amboise studied at the School of American Ballet and joined the New York City Ballet in 1950. His career has seen him recognised as one of the most outstanding American dancers of his time, a magnificent Apollo as well as an ideal exponent of such very American roles as the leads in *Who Cares?* and *Stars and Stripes*. He has also appeared in films (he was one of the brothers in *Seven Brides for Seven Brothers*) and has recently been doing valuable work as a propagandist for dance in education.

## Michael Denard
*Born Dresden, 1944*

Michael Denard studied in Paris and danced with various companies before joining the company of the Paris Opéra. He was nominated *étoile* in 1971, and his noble, romantic style has seen him as the leading figure in many ballets staged in Paris, from Béjart's *Firebird* to Lacotte's *La Sylphide*, and from Albrecht in *Giselle* to Tetley's *Tristan*. He has made guest appearances with many companies, including American Ballet Theatre.

## Jorge Donn
Born Buenos Aires, 1947

Jorge Donn studied at the Teatro Colón and then came to Europe and joined Béjart's company in 1963. From that time he remained one of the central figures of the Ballet du XXième siècle, creating roles in many Béjart ballets, notably *Nijinsky, Clown of God, Romeo and Juliet, Notre Faust,* and *Trionfi.* In 1980 he succeeded Maurice Béjart as artistic director of the company.

## Anthony Dowell
Born London, 1943

Anthony Dowell is a product of the Royal Ballet School and entered the company by way of the Opera Ballet in 1961. His elegant classical manner and an easy virtuosity swiftly earned him principal dancer status. His partnership with Antoinette Sibley, initiated in 1964 in Ashton's *The Dream,* was for a decade one of the glories of The Royal Ballet. In 1978 he went to New York to work with American Ballet Theatre and continued his partnership there with Natalia Makarova. Among the roles he created are Ashton's *A Month in the Country, Jazz Calendar,* and *Enigma Variations*; Tudor's *Shadowplay*; and MacMillan's *Manon* and *Triad.*

## Patrick Dupond
Born Paris, 1959

Patrick Dupond was a pupil at the school of the Paris Opéra and entered the company in 1976. He achieved instantaneous fame in the summer of that year when he won the gold medal in the junior section of the Varna International Ballet Competition. A dancer of supple and brilliant technique, Dupond has already made international guest appearances, but it is at the Paris Opéra that he has been best displayed—notably as the Messenger in *Song of the Earth.* John Neumeier created *Vaslav,* a Nijinsky tribute, for Dupond in 1979.

## Wayne Eagling
Born Montreal, 1950

Wayne Eagling studied at the Royal Ballet School and joined The Royal Ballet in 1969. A dancer of very individual style marked by unusual suppleness and speed, Eagling has had many roles created for him in the MacMillan repertory and has had notable success in *Manon* and *Mayerling.* He has also danced the traditional repertory.

## Eva Evdokimova
Born Geneva, 1948

Eva Evdokimova studied in Munich, London, Copenhagen, and Leningrad. Her first appearances were in 1966 with the Royal Danish Ballet. Since that time she has made an international career and is now a ballerina of both London Festival Ballet and the Berlin Deutsche Oper Ballet. Naturally endowed for the Romantic repertory, she also dances the traditional classics and works by Glen Tetley and Valery Panov.

## Suzanne Farrell
Born Cincinnati, 1945

Suzanne Farrell studied at the School of American Ballet and entered the New York City Ballet in 1961. For eight years she developed in that company as an outstanding Balanchine dancer but in 1970 she left to work with Maurice Béjart's company in Brussels. She returned to the New York City Ballet in 1975. She is recognised as one of the greatest dancers of our time. An artist of rare musicality and exceptional technical finesse, she is the ideal interpreter of the Balanchine repertory, in which she has created many important roles.

## Carla Fracci
Born Milan, 1936

Carla Fracci studied at the Ballet School of La Scala and entered the company in 1954. She was made ballerina in 1958 and commenced an international career thereafter which reached its apogee in the years during the 1960s and 1970s when she danced with Erik Bruhn for American Ballet Theatre. With her exceptional affinity for the style of the Romantic ballet, she has become the best-known Italian ballerina of this century.

**Denys Ganio**
*Born Villeneuve,*
*France, 1950*

Denys Ganio studied at the Paris Opéra Ballet School and joined the Opéra company in 1965. He moved to Roland Petit's Ballet de Marseille and was soon revealed as an outstanding dance actor in such works as Petit's versions of *Coppélia* and *The Nutcracker* and also in his *Notre Dame de Paris* and many other Petit ballets. In all his work a clear, strong technique is allied to unforced charm and dramatic sensitivity.

**Alexander Godunov**
*Born Riga, Latvia, 1949*

Alexander Godunov studied in Riga and then Moscow at the Bolshoi Ballet School, entering the company in 1967. A dancer of heroic physique and exultant style, he excelled in such roles as Karenin in Plisetkaya's *Anna Karenina*. In August 1979, during a Bolshoi tour of the United States, Godunov opted to stay in the West and was granted asylum. Since then he has danced with American Ballet Theatre and appeared as a guest artist with companies around the world.

**Vyacheslav Gordeyev**
*Born Moscow, 1948*

Vyacheslav Gordeyev studied at the Bolshoi Ballet School and joined the company in 1968. A versatile and gifted artist, he has won golden opinions for the distinction and quiet elegance of his classical dancing.

**Cynthia Gregory**
*Born Los Angeles, 1946*

Cynthia Gregory joined the San Francisco Ballet in 1961 and then transferred to American Ballet Theatre four years later. She has remained associated with that company ever since as a principal dancer of strong technique. Her roles include the traditional classics as well as many contemporary works.

**Marcia Haydée**
*Born Niteroi, Brazil, 1939*

Marcia Haydée studied with Tatiana Leskova in Brazil before coming to Europe to work at the Royal Ballet School. She studied in Paris and then joined the Grand Ballet du Marquis de Cuevas. In 1961 she was invited by John Cranko to join the Stuttgart Ballet. Cranko made many works for her, among them *Romeo and Juliet*, *Onegin*, and *The Taming of the Shrew*, and her gifts have also been celebrated by Kenneth MacMillan in *Las Hermanas*, *Song of the Earth*, and *Requiem*. Haydée became director of the Stuttgart Ballet in 1976.

**Mette Hønningen**
*Born Copenhagen, 1944*

Mette Hønningen studied at the Royal Danish Ballet School where she profited from the teaching of Vera Volkova. A performer of very wide range, she has danced the Bournonville and modern repertories with great distinction.

**Zizi (Renée) Jeanmaire**
*Born Paris, 1924*

Zizi Jeanmaire studied at the Paris Opéra Ballet School and joined the Opéra company in 1939. She came to fame as a member of the Nouveau Ballet de Monte Carlo, and then joined Roland Petit's Ballets de Paris. Petit has created many of the roles which have brought her international stardom—*Carmen* in 1949 being the vital revelation of her stage personality. Her career has encompassed music hall, musical comedy, and cinema.

**Stephen Jefferies**
*Born Reintelm, West Germany, 1951*

Stephen Jefferies studied at the Royal Ballet School and joined The Royal Ballet Touring Company in 1969. He joined the National Ballet of Canada for a year and on his return to London became a member of The Royal Ballet. His roles included Rudolf in *Mayerling* and Petruchio in *The Taming of the Shrew*, as well as the traditional classical repertory.

**Lis Jeppesen**
*Born Copenhagen, 1956*

Lis Jeppesen stole all hearts during the 1979 Bournonville Centenary Festival when she appeared as the heroine in *A Folk Tale*, as the Sylphide in *La Sylphide*, and as a cadet in *Far from Denmark*. She has lightness, beautiful line, and a dramatic sensitivity ideally suited to making real the Victorian grace of Bournonville's heroines.

## Karen Kain
Born Hamilton, Ontario, 1951

Karen Kain is a product of the School of the National Ballet of Canada and of the National Ballet itself, where she has established a reputation as the company's leading ballerina. She has made guest appearances with Roland Petit's Ballet de Marseille, and has also danced at the Paris Opéra, where Petit created *Nana* for her. Her partnership with Frank Augustyn has done much to help the developing image of the National Ballet of Canada.

## Niels Kehlet
Born Copenhagen, 1938

Niels Kehlet trained at the Royal Danish Ballet School and soon became a leading dancer with the company. An outstanding virtuoso, and a brilliant mime and comedian, he has appeared as a guest artist all over the world but remains true to the Royal Danish Ballet.

## Birgit Keil
Born Kowarschen, West Germany, 1944

Birgit Keil was a product of the Stuttgart Ballet School and entered the company in 1961. Under Cranko's guidance she became a ballerina of the company and created several roles, notably in *Initials R.B.M.E.* Now one of the leading ballerinas in Germany, she has also created roles in works by MacMillan, notably in *My Brother, My Sisters* and in Tetley's *Voluntaries* and *Greening*.

## Allegra Kent
Born Los Angeles, 1938

Allegra Kent studied with Nijinska and then at the School of American Ballet. She joined the New York City Ballet at the age of fifteen, became a principal in 1957, and has since created important roles in many works for Balanchine and Robbins. The wonderfully seamless quality of her dancing has been admired in such works as *Bugaku*, *Episodes*, and *Dances at a Gathering*, all of which contain roles created for her.

## Gelsey Kirkland
Born Bethlehem, Pennsylvania, 1953

Gelsey Kirkland studied at the School of American Ballet and entered the New York City Ballet in 1968, where her exquisite technique made her a principal dancer almost immediately. In 1974 she left to join American Ballet Theatre, where she performed the traditional repertory to considerable acclaim. Recently she has made guest appearances with The Royal Ballet at Covent Garden.

## Irina Kolpakova
Born Leningrad, 1933

Irina Kolpakova studied at the Kirov School and entered the company in 1951. The last pupil of A. Y. Vaganova, Kolpakova epitomises the Leningrad style at its purest and best. Her exquisite presence, as well as her exquisite style, fitted her for the greatest demands of the classical repertory, and her Aurora represents for many people the most beautiful interpretation of our time.

## Henning Kronstam
Born Copenhagen, 1934

Henning Kronstam was given his first great opportunity in 1955, when he created the role of Romeo in Ashton's version of the Prokofiev score for the Royal Danish Ballet. He danced all the leading roles in the Danish repertory and toured extensively throughout the United States with Kirsten Simone in Ruth Page's Chicago Ballet. In 1978 he became director of the Royal Danish Ballet, and he continues to perform impeccably in character roles, both comic and serious.

## Sean Lavery
Born Harrisburg, Pennsylvania, 1956

Sean Lavery studied in New York with Richard Thomas and Barbara Fallis and in 1972 joined the San Francisco Ballet. Two years later he joined the Frankfurt Opera Ballet. On his return to the United States he attended the School of American Ballet and in 1977 joined the New York City Ballet. He was quickly named a principal and was cast in a considerable number of Balanchine ballets. A dancer of great promise, Lavery has brought a positive and clear classical style to all his roles.

### Mikhail Lavrovsky
Born Tiflis, USSR, 1941

Mikhail Lavrovsky trained at the Bolshoi Ballet School in Moscow and entered the company in 1961. His partnership with Natalia Bessmertnova has made them the leading couple in most of the Bolshoi repertory. Lavrovsky brings a fine technique and handsome presence to all his roles, which range from the Prince in *Cinderella* to Spartacus. He is the son of choreographer Leonid Lavrovsky.

### Adam Lüders
Born Copenhagen, 1950

Adam Lüders studied at the school of the Royal Danish Ballet and entered the company in 1968. In 1972 he joined the London Festival Ballet, and in 1975 he was invited to join the New York City Ballet as a principal dancer. In 1980, Balanchine created for him the central role in *Robert Schumann's Davidsbündlertänze*.

### Patricia McBride
Born Teaneck, New Jersey, 1942

Patricia McBride studied at the School of American Ballet and joined the New York City Ballet in 1959. Two years later she became a principal of that company. For twenty years McBride has been one of the brightest stars in the City Ballet constellation, an artist adored by her public, and admired for her exceptional technical brilliance.

### Natalia Makarova
Born Leningrad, 1940

Natalia Makarova entered the Kirov School and graduated into the company in 1959. She was soon acknowledged as an outstanding ballerina in the classical repertory. In 1970 during a Kirov season in London she chose to remain in the West. Since then she has danced all over the world but has retained a base with American Ballet Theatre. In 1980 she mounted the first production in the West of the full-length *La Bayadère* for American Ballet Theatre.

### Peter Martins
Born Copenhagen, 1946

Peter Martins studied at the Royal Danish Ballet School and joined the company in 1965. He was soon promoted to principal rank, but in 1969 he joined the New York City Ballet. Martins has been recognised as an outstandingly noble interpreter of the Balanchine repertory—though he makes occasional guest appearances in the traditional repertory with other companies and has never severed his link with the Royal Danish Ballet. A dancer of grand and magnificently easy technique, Martins has also choreographed a number of ballets for the New York City Ballet, including *Calcium Light Night* (1977), *Lille Suite* (1980), and a suite from *Histoire du Soldat* (1981).

### Monica Mason
Born Johannesburg, 1941

Monica Mason had her early training in Johannesburg before entering the Royal Ballet School. She joined The Royal Ballet in 1958 and ten years later was named a principal. Her appearance in MacMillan's *Rite of Spring* in 1962 indicated the special qualities of stage presence and technical power which have marked all her interpretations in the traditional and modern repertories.

### Ekaterina Maximova
Born Moscow, 1939

Ekaterina Maximova studied at the Bolshoi Ballet School and graduated into the company in 1958. She was early recognised as an exceptional artist with her adorable Kitri in *Don Quixote*. She was coached by Galina Ulanova for her début in *Giselle*, and with Vladimir Vasiliev she established a partnership which has been central to a great many of the Bolshoi ballet performances. She is a dancer of effortless and enchanting technique and winning stage personality.

### Magali Messac
Born Toulon, France

Magali Messac began her dance training with Olga and Henry Taneef in Toulon. In 1969 she became a member of the Hamburg State Opera Ballet, where she was made a principal dancer in 1972. In 1978 she joined the Pennsylvania Ballet, and in 1980 she joined American Ballet Theatre as a principal dancer.

*Kyra Nichols*
*Born Berkeley,*
*California, 1957*

Kyra Nichols began her dance training with her mother, former New York City Ballet dancer Sally Streets. She attended summer courses at the School of American Ballet and appeared with the New York City Ballet as an apprentice in the spring of 1974, joining the company later that year. She was soon promoted to soloist, and became a principal dancer in 1979. Nichols is married to fellow NYCB principal dancer Daniel Duell.

*Rudolf Nureyev*
*Born on a train,*
*USSR, 1938*

Rudolf Nureyev entered the Kirov School in Leningrad, as a late starter, in 1955 and benefitted from three years' teaching by Alexander Pushkin. He joined the Kirov Ballet in 1958, where his gifts soon won him leading roles. In 1961, at the end of a Paris season by the Kirov Ballet, he opted to stay in the West. An indefatigable performer, he is one of the greatest star dancers of the century. An early and important partnership with Margot Fonteyn gave Nureyev a vital base in The Royal Ballet. Since 1961, it must seem that he has danced everywhere and with everyone. His productions for many companies include revivals of the nineteenth-century repertory as well as such creations as *Romeo and Juliet* for London Festival Ballet and *Manfred* for the Paris Opéra.

*Galina and Valery Panov*
*Born Archangel, USSR, 1949;*
*Vitebsk, USSR, 1938*

Valery Panov studied in Leningrad and entered the Maly Ballet in 1957. A *demi-caractère* dancer of great vivacity, Panov had several roles created for him in Leningrad, where he worked also with the Kirov Ballet. He married the Varna gold medallist Galina Ragozina and in 1972 both artists applied to emigrate to Israel. After two years, and worldwide agitation, the Panovs were allowed to leave Russia. Since then they have appeared with various Western companies and Panov has produced choreography—*The Idiot, The Rite of Spring, Cinderella*—for the Berlin Deutsche Oper Ballet.

*Merle Park*
*Born Salisbury,*
*Rhodesia, 1937*

Merle Park was trained at Elmhurst Ballet School, Surrey, and joined the Sadler's Wells Ballet in 1954, becoming a principal in 1959. A dancer of bright technique and exceptional musicality, she has created roles in Tudor's *Shadowplay*, Ashton's *Jazz Calendar*, and MacMillan's *Mayerling*. She has danced the entire classical repertory.

*Nadezhda Pavlova*
*Born Tsheboksari,*
*USSR, 1956*

Nadezhda Pavlova studied in Perm and won high acclaim at international ballet competitions. She danced in New York in 1973 and entered the Bolshoi Ballet in 1975. A dancer of brilliant technique and unforced charm, Pavlova is one of the brightest hopes of the Bolshoi Ballet.

*Jennifer Penney*
*Born Vancouver,*
*British Columbia, 1946*

Jennifer Penney had her early training with Gweneth Lloyd and Betty Farrally before entering the Royal Ballet School. She joined The Royal Ballet in 1963 and became a principal in 1970. A dancer of beautifully easy style and physique, Penney has danced all the traditional classical roles and has made a particular impression in the MacMillan repertory, as Manon and in *La Fin du Jour* and *Gloria*.

*Noëlla Pontois*
*Born Vendôme,*
*France, 1943*

Noëlla Pontois studied at the Paris Opéra Ballet School and joined the company in 1960. She was nominated *étoile* in 1968. A dancer of brilliant technique and clarity, Pontois is an exemplar of the French classical style at its best today. She dances most of the leading roles in the Opéra repertory.

*Marguerite Porter*
*Born Doncaster,*
*Yorkshire, 1948*

Marguerite Porter studied with Louise Browne before joining the Royal Ballet School. She entered The Royal Ballet in 1966, was made a principal dancer in 1978, and has danced the traditional repertory and a wide range of modern works. Her delicate charm has been particularly appreciated in such roles as Juliet, and in *A Month in the Country* she brings dramatic conviction to the role of Natalia Petrovna.

## Patricia Ruanne
### Born Leeds, 1945

Patricia Ruanne had her early training in Yorkshire, partly with Louise Browne, and then attended the Royal Ballet School. In 1962 she graduated into the Touring Company, where she danced for eleven years. In 1973 she joined the London Festival Ballet, with which she has danced the classical repertory and created such leading roles as Juliet in Nureyev's *Romeo and Juliet* and the Siren in Barry Moreland's *Prodigal Son in Ragtime*.

## Galina Samsova
### Born Stalingrad, 1937

Galina Samsova trained in the ballet school in Kiev and joined the company there in 1956. In 1961 she joined the National Ballet of Canada. In 1963 she came to Europe, dancing in the last productions of the de Cuevas ballet, and in 1964 she joined London Festival Ballet. For ten years she and André Prokovsky led the company, dancing all the classics. She and Prokovsky toured with their own company for some years. More recently Samsova has found a base with the Sadler's Wells Royal Ballet. She also makes guest appearances throughout the world.

## Christine Sarry
### Born Long Beach, California, 1946

Christine Sarry studied in California with Carmelita Maracci and in New York with Barbara Fallis and Richard Thomas. She joined the Joffrey Ballet in 1963, and American Ballet Theatre the following year. In 1969 she left ABT to join Eliot Feld's newly formed American Ballet Company; when this company disbanded two years later, Sarry rejoined ABT as a soloist, and was made a principal dancer in 1973. The following year she left to rejoin Feld in his new company, the Eliot Feld Ballet.

## Peter Schaufuss
### Born Copenhagen, 1949

Peter Schaufuss, the son of the celebrated Danish dancers Mona Vangsaae and Frank Schaufuss, studied at the Royal Danish Ballet School and graduated into the company in 1965. He soon began to make international guest appearances and for two years was a member of the New York City Ballet. Although he now maintains a schedule of appearances with the National Ballet of Canada and London Festival Ballet, as well as preserving his link with Denmark, Schaufuss dances internationally as a virtuoso of exceptional brilliance and verve.

## Ludmila Semenyaka
### Born Leningrad, 1952

Ludmila Semenyaka studied at the Kirov School and entered the company in 1970, transferring to the Bolshoi Ballet two years later. Her Kirov training has given her an exquisite classical style. She is a magnificent Aurora and brings to the role of Masha in *The Nutcracker* a lovely distinction.

## Alla Sizova
### Born Moscow, 1939

Alla Sizova studied at the Kirov Ballet School and joined the company in 1958. Her youthful talent was acknowledged in the West when she made her début as Aurora in London in 1961. In 1964 she won a gold medal at Varna. Her career was interrupted by ill health, but she returned to dancing, and retains great public affection.

## Marianna Tcherkassky
### Born Glen Cove, New York, 1955

Marianna Tcherkassky received her early dance training from her mother and then studied at the Washington School of Ballet and in New York at the School of American Ballet. Her first professional appearances were with the Eglevsky Ballet. In 1970 she joined American Ballet Theatre, was promoted to soloist two years later, and became a principal dancer in 1976. She is married to ABT ballet master Terry Orr.

## Elisabetta Terabust

Elisabetta Terabust studied at the Rome Opera Ballet School and joined the company in 1964. She was swiftly promoted to ballerina rank and has danced extensively throughout Europe and the United States. Since

*Born Varese, Italy, 1946*

1973 she has appeared frequently with London Festival Ballet and has also made guest appearances with Roland Petit's Ballet de Marseille.

### Ghislaine Thesmar
*Born Peking, 1943*

Ghislaine Thesmar studied at the Paris Opéra School and made her début with the Grand Ballet du Marquis de Cuevas in 1961. She danced with the Ballet National des Jeunesses Musicales de France, founded by Pierre Lacotte, whom she married in 1968. Since 1972 she has been an *étoile* at the Paris Opéra Ballet, and has made guest appearances with the New York City Ballet.

### Nina Timofeyeva
*Born Leningrad, 1935*

Nina Timofeyeva trained at the Kirov Ballet school and entered the company in 1953. Three years later she joined the Bolshoi Ballet, of which she has been a respected principal dancer for two decades. She dances the classic repertory, and is best known in the West for such roles as Aegina in *Spartacus* and the Queen in *Legend of Love*.

### Helgi Tomasson
*Born Reykjavik, Iceland, 1942*

Helgi Tomasson studied with Vera Volkova in Copenhagen before going to the School of American Ballet. He danced with the Joffrey Ballet and the Harkness Ballet and in 1970 joined the New York City Ballet as a principal dancer. For that company he has danced many leading roles.

### Martine van Hamel
*Born Brussels, 1945*

Martine van Hamel trained for several years in Toronto at the school of the National Ballet of Canada and joined that company in 1963. In 1965 she won the gold medal at Varna. She moved to New York in 1970 and for a short time was a member of the Joffrey Ballet, then joined American Ballet Theatre, with whom she has been a principal since 1973. An artist possessing the grand manner, van Hamel shines in both the classical and the contemporary repertories.

### Vladimir Vasiliev
*Born Moscow, 1940*

Vladimir Vasiliev studied at the Bolshoi Ballet School and joined the company in 1958. A dancer who typifies the Soviet ideal of heroic and gallant youth, Vasiliev was first admired as the Ivan of Radunsky's *Humpbacked Horse*, a role in which his essentially *demi-caractère* abilities were displayed. He has danced the entire classical repertory with distinction, but it is as Spartacus that he will be forever remembered.

### Karin von Aroldingen
*Born Berlin, 1941*

Karin von Aroldingen studied first in Germany and joined the Frankfurt Opera Ballet in 1959. She appeared with Lotte Lenya in *The Seven Deadly Sins*, and Lenya was so impressed that she arranged for Balanchine to see von Aroldingen dance when he came to Germany in 1962. She was at once invited to join the New York City Ballet, where she has been a principal since 1972. She has remained one of the most musically responsive of Balanchine's dancers.

### David Wall
*Born London, 1946*

David Wall studied at the Royal Ballet School and entered The Royal Ballet Touring Company in 1963. He early displayed exceptional ability and presence in the traditional princely roles of the repertory. Wall joined The Royal Ballet in 1972 and created roles in *Manon* and, supremely, in *Mayerling* in which MacMillan gave him a character as demanding physically as it was dramatically, and one in which Wall was revealed as a great artist.

### Heather Watts
*Born Los Angeles, 1953*

Heather Watts studied at the School of American Ballet and joined the New York City Ballet in 1970. She was promoted to soloist in 1978, and was made a principal dancer the following year.

# Index

*Numbers in italic refer to illustrations.*

# *Picture Credits*

Clarke-Crisp Collection 8, 9, 10, 11, 15(L), 16(R), 22(R), 23, 25, 26(L), 42, 43(C&B), 44, 45, 48, 49, 50, 51, 52–3, 54, 55, 58, 59, 66, 81, 83, 84, 103, 110, 118, 121, 122, 128, 129, 130, 137, 146, 147, 186(T), 188, 191, 192, 194, 209, 213, 221, 222, 223, 225, 237, 239, 243, 249, 254, 263, 278, 280, 283, 295, 299. Martha Swope 65, 67, 75, 76, 79, 86, 88, 94, 106, 135, 140, 142, 148, 150, 159, 161, 166, 182, 183, 193, 198, 204, 219, 220, 234, 251, 256, 260, 264, 269, 275, 276, 277, 293, 296, 300, 302, 304, 305, 334. Zoë Dominic 34–5, 36, 37, 39, 40–1, 57, 64, 72, 108, 179, 202, 208(B), 216, 224, 244, 253, 272, 322. Anthony Crickmay 93, 103, 111, 124, 149, 153, 154, 172, 180, 181, 189, 201, 207, 229, 241, 282, 288, 289, 297, 308, 326, 335(B). John R. Johnsen 4–5, 95, 116, 144, 162, 164, 165, 185, 203, 250, 281, 285, 303, 328, 339(TR). Costas 2–3, 60–1, 62–3, 97, 107, 158, 160, 211(T), 218, 333, 340. Leslie Spatt 69, 134, 176, 177, 227, 331, 336, 337, 338. Houston Rogers 80, 126, 127, 157, 339(BR). Serge Lido 101, 131, 156, 186, 261, 279. Paul Kolnik 98, 143, 266, 267, 311. Rigmor Mydtskov 123, 132, 133, 145, 212, 332. Fritz Peyer 1, 230, 313. Roger Wood 91, 211(B), 248. Mike Humphrey 96, 112, 174. Baron 139, 284, 294. Reg Wilson 33, 56, 236. Fred Fehl 22(L), 178. J. W. Debenham 117, 206. Edward Mandinian 170, 171. Herbert Migdol 205, 306. Jorg Fatauros 257, 287. Hannes Kilian 196. Bill Mosley 197. Denis de Marney 214. National Ballet of Canada 113. Donald Southern 92. Frank Sharman 89. Steven Caras 71. Musée National d'Art Moderne, Paris 46. Mike Davis 43(T). Anthony 26(R). ET Archives 16(L). City of London Museum 15(R). Roy Round 232. Daniel Cande 246. Lipnitzki 270. Royal Opera House, Covent Garden 274. Mira 291. Peggy Leder 307. G.B.L. Wilson 309. Edward Griffiths 312. Jas. D. O'Callaghan 335(T). Andrew Oxenham 339(TL). Jean Petitjean 339(BL). Dance Collection New York Public Library at Lincoln Center, Astor, Tilden, Lennox Foundations 265.